The Renaissance and the Wider World

The Renaissance and the Wider World

Joanne M. Ferraro

BLOOMSBURY ACADEMIC
LONDON • NEW YORK • OXFORD • NEW DELHI • SYDNEY

BLOOMSBURY ACADEMIC
Bloomsbury Publishing Plc
50 Bedford Square, London, WC1B 3DP, UK
1385 Broadway, New York, NY 10018, USA
29 Earlsfort Terrace, Dublin 2, Ireland

BLOOMSBURY, BLOOMSBURY ACADEMIC and the Diana logo are trademarks of
Bloomsbury Publishing Plc

First published in Great Britain 2024

Copyright © Joanne M. Ferraro 2024

Joanne M. Ferraro has asserted her right under the Copyright, Designs and Patents Act, 1988, to be identified as author of this work.

For legal purposes the Acknowledgments on p. xiii constitute an extension of this copyright page.

Cover image: St. Mark Preaching in Alexandria by Gentile and Giovanni Bellini © Leemage/Getty

Bloomsbury Publishing Plc does not have any control over, or responsibility for, any third-party websites referred to or in this book. All internet addresses given in this book were correct at the time of going to press. The author and publisher regret any inconvenience caused if addresses have changed or sites have ceased to exist, but can accept no responsibility for any such changes.

Every effort has been made to trace the copyright holders and obtain permission to reproduce the copyright material. Please do get in touch with any enquiries or any information relating to such material or the rights holder. We would be pleased to rectify any omissions in subsequent editions of this publication should they be drawn to our attention.

A catalogue record for this book is available from the British Library.

A catalog record for this book is available from the Library of Congress.

ISBN: HB: 978-1-3501-5896-2
PB: 978-1-3501-5895-5
ePDF: 978-1-3501-5897-9
eBook: 978-1-3501-5898-6

Typeset by Newgen KnowledgeWorks Pvt. Ltd., Chennai, India
Printed and bound in Great Britain

To find out more about our authors and books visit www.bloomsbury.com and sign up for our newsletters.

CONTENTS

List of Figures vi
List of Maps xi
List of Boxes xii
Acknowledgments xiii

Introduction: The Invention of the Renaissance 1
  1 Foundations: Ancient and Medieval Legacies 17
  2 Urban Revitalization: 1000–1350 37
  3 Spheres of Culture: 1000–1375 71
  4 Daily Life and Modes of Socialization 97
  5 Fifteenth-Century Politics 129
  6 Humanism and the Circulation of Knowledge 155
  7 Fifteenth-Century Art and Its Patrons 181
  8 A Shifting World: Sixteenth-Century Italy 223
  9 Sixteenth-Century Culture 255
10 Worldly Connections: The Renaissance Exchange 291

Glossary 309
Index 309

FIGURES

1.1 Arena (30 CE). Verona, Italy. Photo by Sb616, 2008, via Wikimedia Commons 17
1.2 Church of St. Apollinare in Classe. Apse Mosaic. Ravenna, Italy. Photo by Berthold Werner, 2009, via Wikimedia Commons 23
1.3 Church of San Vitale (546–547 CE). Mosaic of Empress Theodora. Ravenna, Italy. © Petar Milošević, 2015, via Wikimedia Commons 24
1.4 Benedictine Monastery. Monte Cassino, Italy. © Pietro Scerrato, 2010, via Wikimedia Commons. Reproduced under a Creative Commons Attribution 3.0 Unported license (CC BY 3.0) 26
1.5 Cathedral of Santa Maria Assunta. Pisa, Italy. © Vyacheslav Argenberg, via Wikimedia Commons. Reproduced under the Creative Commons Attribution 4.0 International 30
2.1 Ambrogio Lorenzetti (1290–1348). *Effects of Good Government* (1338–1339). Fresco panel. Public Palace, Siena, Italy. Photos.com via Getty Images 40
2.2 *Ruralia Commoda*. Agricultural calendar from a manuscript written by Pietro de' Crescenzi between 1304 and 1309, *c.* 1470–1475. Collection of Musée Condé, Chantilly. Fine Art Images/Heritage Images via Getty Images 42
2.3 Nanni di Banco (*c.* 1385–1421). *Stonemasons at Work*. Relief under the tabernacle of the Guild of Stone and Wood Masters. Fourteenth century. Chiesa di Orsanmichele, Florence, Italy. Photo courtesy of DEA/ATLANTIDE via Getty Images 43
2.4 Medieval Towers, Bologna, Italy. Photo by Bouncey2k, 2006, via Wikimedia Commons 57
2.5 Fondaco of Ca' Farsetti, Venice, Italy. Photo by Joanne M. Ferraro 61
3.1 Palazzo Pubblico, Siena, Italy. © Jimmy Harris, 1995, via Wikimedia Commons. Reproduced under the Creative Commons Attribution 2.0 Generic 72
3.2 *Trota of Salerno*. Illustration from *Miscellanea medica* XVIII (early fourteenth century, France), Manuscript 544, f. 65. Wellcome Library, London, UK, via Wikimedia Creative Commons. Reproduced under the Creative Commons CC0 1.0 Universal Public Domain Dedication 78

3.3 *Saint Clare*, 1318. Detail from the frescoes by Simone Martini (*c.* 1284–1344). Chapel of St. Martin, Lower Church, Papal Basilica of St. Francis of Assisi, Assisi, Italy. Photo by De Agostini via Getty Images 81
3.4 Baptistery on Campo dei Miracoli, Pisa, Italy. © Lunna Campos, 2015, via Wikimedia Commons. Reproduced under the Creative Commons Attribution 2.0 Generic 84
3.5 Doge's Palace (on right), Venice, Italy. Photo by Joanne M. Ferraro 86
3.6 Giotto di Bondone (1267–1337). *The Arrest of Christ*, or *Kiss of Judas* (*c.* 1303–1305). Fresco. Scrovegni Chapel. Padua, Italy. Photo by De Agostini via Getty Images 89
4.1 *Victims of the Black Death Being Buried at Tournai*, then part of the Netherlands, 1349. From the *Chronique et Annales de Gilles le Muisit* (1272–1352). Photo by Hulton Archive/Stringer via Getty Images 98
4.2 Filippo Brunelleschi (1377–1446). *Ospedale degli Innocenti* (1419–1445). Florence, Italy. Warburg/Warburgs Gallery, via Wikimedia Commons. Reproduced under the Creative Commons Attribution-Share Alike 3.0 Unported 103
4.3 Masaccio (1401–1428). *Desco da Parto* (Tray Celebrating Birth), 1420. Gemäldegalerie der Staatlichen Museen zu Berlin, Germany. The Yorck Project (2002) *10.000 Meisterwerke der Malerei* (DVD-ROM), distributed by DIRECTMEDIA Publishing GmbH. ISBN: 3936122202, via Wikimedia Commons 104
4.4 Jan Van Eyck (*c.* 1390–1441). *The Arnolfini Portrait* (1434). Oil on panel. The National Gallery, London, UK. Photo12/Universal Images Group via Getty Images 109
5.1 Ducal Palace, Urbino, Italy. Mid-fifteenth Century. Photo by Hans Borg, 2007, via Wikimedia Commons 130
5.2 Andrea del Verrocchio (1435–1488). *Monument to Bartolomeo Colleoni* (*c.* 1481–1488). Campo SS. Giovanni e Paolo, Venice, Italy. © Didier Descouens, 2016, via Wikimedia Commons. Published under the Creative Commons Attribution-Share Alike 4.0 International 135
5.3 Andrea Mantegna (1465–1474). *Decoration of the Camera degli Sposi*. Fresco and dry tempera. Detail. Northern wall or wall of the fireplace. Ducal Palace, Mantua, Italy. Hulton Fine Art Collection. Mondadori Portfolio/Contributor via Getty Images 142
6.1 Vittore Carpaccio (1465–1526). *The Vision of St. Augustine* (1502–1504). Oil on canvas. Scuola di San Giorgio degli Schiavoni, Venice, Italy. Hulton Fine Art Collection. Mondadori Portfolio/Contributor via Getty Images 155
7.1 Benozzo Gozzoli (1421–1497). *Journey of the Magi* (1459–1461). Fresco. Palazzo Medici Riccardi, Florence, Italy. Photo by Saiko,

2014, via Wikimedia Commons. Reproduced under the Creative Commons Attribution 3.0 Unported 183

7.2 Duccio di Buoninsegna (*c.* 1255–1319). *Madonna and Child* (1285–1286). Detail. Tempura on wood. Siena, Museo Dell' Opera Metropolitana (Cathedral Museum). De Agostini Editorial. DEA/G. DAGLI ORTI/Contributor via Getty Images 184

7.3 Leonardo Da Vinci (1452–1519). *Mona Lisa* (1503–1506). Oil on panel. Louvre Museum, Paris, France. Photo by Dcoetzee, 2011, via Wikimedia Commons 185

7.4 Donatello (1386?–1466). *Saint Mark* (1411–1413). Marble sculpture. Orsanmichele Church, Florence, Italy. Photo by Zvonimir Atletić, 2019, via Alamy stock photo 187

7.5 Lorenzo Ghiberti (1378–1455). *Joseph and the Gates of Paradise*. Gilt bronze. Baptistery, Florence, Italy. © Jebulon, 2011, via Wikimedia Commons. Published under the Creative Commons CC0 1.0 Universal Public Domain Dedication 188

7.6 Masaccio (1401–1428). *Tribute Money* (*c.* 1425–1427). Fresco. Brancacci Chapel in the Basilica of Santa Maria del Carmine, Florence, Italy. Antonio Quattrone/Archivio Quattrone/MONDADORI PORTFOLIO via Getty Images 188

7.7 Piero della Francesca (?–1492). *The Flagellation of Christ* (1455–1460). Oil and tempera on panel. Galleria Nazionale delle Marche, Urbino, Italy. © Arte & Immagini srl/CORBIS/Corbis via Getty Images 189

7.8 Antonello da Messina (1430–1479). *Virgin Annunciate* (1476). Oil on wood. Galleria Nazionale della Sicilia, Palermo, Sicily. The Yorck Project (2002)/Zenodot Verlagsgesellschaft mbH, via Wikimedia Commons. Published under the GNU Free Documentation License 190

7.9 Donatello (1386?–1466). *Equestrian Statue of Gattemelata* (*c.* 1443–1453). Bronze. Piazza del Santo, Padua, Italy. © Saiko, 2005, via Wikimedia Commons. Published under the Creative Commons Attribution-Share Alike 3.0 Unported 191

7.10 Masaccio (1401–1428). *Trinity* (1426–1428). Fresco. Church of Santa Maria Novella, Florence, Italy. The Yorck Project (2002) *10.000 Meisterwerke der Malerei* (DVD-ROM), distributed by DIRECTMEDIA Publishing GmbH. ISBN: 3936122202, via Wikimedia Commons. Published under *the GNU Free Documentation License* 193

7.11 Sandro Botticelli (1445–1510). *Birth of Venus* (1486). Detail. Tempera on canvas. Uffizi Gallery, Florence, Italy. Photo by Franco Origlia via Getty Images 194

7.12 Filippo Brunelleschi (1377–1446). Duomo (1420–1436) of the Church of Santa Maria del Fiore, Florence, Italy. © Clément Bardot,

2016, via Wikimedia Commons. Published under the Creative Commons Attribution-Share Alike 4.0 International 195

7.13 Michelangelo Buonarotti (1475–1564). *David* (1501–1504). Marble sculpture. Galleria dell' Academia, Florence, Italy. © Jörg Bittner Unna, 2008, via Wikimedia Commons. Published under the Creative Commons Attribution 3.0 Unported 196

7.14 Giovanni and Bartolomeo Bon. *Porta della Carta* (begun 1438). Doge's Palace, Venice, Italy. Photo by Joanne M. Ferraro. 198

7.15 Piero della Francesca (?–1492). *Federigo da Montefeltro and Battista Sforza, the Duke and Duchess of Urbino* (1473–1475). Tempera on wood. Uffizi Gallery, Florence, Italy. © Livioandronico 2013, 2015, via Wikimedia Commons. Published under the Creative Commons Attribution-Share Alike 4.0 International 201

7.16 Pietro Perugino (*c.* 1446/52–1523). *Christ Delivers the Keys to St. Peter* (1481–1482). Fresco. Sistine Chapel, Vatican Museums, Rome, Italy. Photo by Fine Art Images/Heritage Images via Getty Images 202

7.17 Gentile Bellini (1429–1507). *Sultan Mehmed II The Conqueror* (1480). Oil on canvas. National Gallery, London, UK. Photo by Fine Art Images/Heritage Images/Getty Images 203

7.18 Palace of Ca' D' Oro, Venice, Italy. Photo by Joanne M. Ferraro 205

7.19 Marco del Buono (1402–1489). *The Story of Esther* (1422–1489). Tempura and gold on wood. Roger's Fund, 1918, Metropolitan Museum of Art, New York, via Wikimedia Commons. Published under the Creative Commons CC0 1.0 Universal Public Domain Dedication 207

7.20 Vittore Carpaccio (1465–1526?). *Birth of the Virgin* (1502–1504). Oil on canvas. Guglielmo Lochis Collection, 1866, Accademia Carrara, Bergamo, Italy. The Yorck Project (2002) *10.000 Meisterwerke der Malerei* (DVD-ROM), distributed by DIRECTMEDIA Publishing GmbH. ISBN: 3936122202, via Wikimedia Commons. PD-US. Published under *the GNU Free Documentation License* 208

7.21 Gentile Bellini (1429–1507). *Procession of the True Cross in St. Mark's Square* (1496). Tempura and oil on canvas. Galleria dell' Accademia. Venice, Italy. Photo by Fine Art Images/Heritage Images via Getty Images 212

7.22 Gentile (1429–1507) and Giovanni Bellini (*c.* 1430–1516). *Saint Mark Preaching in Alexandria* (1504–1507). Oil on panel. Pinacoteca di Brera, Milan, Italy. © Getty Images via Leemage/Corbis 216

7.23 Gentile da Fabriano (1370–?). Detail from *The Adoration of the Magi* (1423). Painting/Polyptych. Tempera on panel. Uffizi Gallery, Florence, Italy. The Yorck Project (2002) *10.000 Meisterwerke der*

Malerei (DVD-ROM), distributed by DIRECTMEDIA Publishing GmbH. ISBN: 3936122202, via Wikimedia Commons. PD-US 218
8.1 Martin Waldseemüller (1470–1520). *Map of the World*, 1507, via Wikimedia Commons 226
8.2 Andrea Palladio (1508–1580). *Villa Barbaro* (1554–1560). Maser (Treviso), Italy. Photo by Oursana, 2007, via Wikimedia Commons. Published under the Creative Commons Attribution-Share Alike 3.0 Unported 234
8.3 Michelangelo Buonarotti (1475–1564). *The Last Judgment* (1536–1541). Fresco. Sistine Chapel, Vatican Museums, Rome, Italy. Photo by Fine Art Images/Heritage Images via Getty Images 241
8.4 Paolo Veronese (1528–1588). *Feast in the House of Levi* (1573). Oil on canvas. Galleria dell' Accademia, Venice, Italy. Photo by: Universal History Archive/Universal Images Group via Getty Images 242
8.5 School of Tintoretto (*c.* 1575). *Veronica Franco*. Oil on canvas. Worchester Art Museum, Massachusetts, USA. The Picture Art Collection via Alamy Stock Photo 245
9.1 Raphael (1483–1520). *The School of Athens* (1511). Fresco. Vatican Museums, Rome, Italy. Photo by Universal History Archive via Getty Images 255
9.2 Raphael Sanzio (1483–1520). *Portrait of Baldassare Castiglione* (1514–1515). Oil on canvas. Louvre Museum, Paris, France. Photo by VCG Wilson/Corbis via Getty Images 259
9.3 Sebastiano del Piombo (1485–1547). *Portrait of Vittoria Colonna* (1520–1525). Oil on wood. Museu Nacional d' Art de Catalunya, Barcelona, Spain. Photo by Photo 12/Universal Images Group via Getty Images 263
9.4 Leonardo da Vinci (1452–1519). *The Last Supper* (1495–1498). Mural painting. Church of Santa Maria delle Grazie, Milan, Italy. Photo by Art Images via Getty Images 271
9.5 Sofonisba Anguissola (1532–1625). *Self Portrait*. Oil on canvas. Łańcut Castle, Łańcut, Poland. Photo by Ali Meyer/Corbis/VCG via Getty Images 276
9.6 St. Peter's Basilica, Rome, Italy, via Wikimedia Commons 278
9.7 Süleymaniye Mosque, Istanbul, Turkey. Photo by A. Savin, 2020, via Wikimedia Commons 279
9.8 Giorgione (?–1510). *The Tempest* (1505). Oil on canvas. Galleria della Accademia, Venice, Italy. Mondadori Portfolio/Contributor, Hulton Fine Art Collection via Getty Images 282
9.9 Jacobo Tintoretto (1519–1594). *The Birth of St. John the Baptist* (1554). Oil on canvas. Hermitage Museum, St. Petersburg, Russia. Photo by Zuri Swimmer via Alamy Stock Photo 286

MAPS

1.1 The Roman Conquest of Italy 21
1.2 Byzantine and Lombard Italy 25
1.3 Italy in the Year 1000 31
2.1 The Major Italian Communes (*c.* 1200) 44
2.2 Genoese and Venetian Trade Routes 47
2.3 The Silk Routes 53
5.1 Italy in 1494 146
8.1 European Sea Routes and Colonial Claims of Spain and Portugal (Fifteenth and Sixteenth Centuries) 227
8.2 Europe in 1500 230
8.3 Political Divisions in 1600 231

BOXES

1.1 The Western Roman Catholic Church and the Eastern Greek Orthodox Church 27
2.1 The Venetian Arsenal 46
2.2 Marco Polo and the Polo Brothers 49
2.3 The Florentine Woolen Industry 51
3.1 Clare of Assisi (1194–1253) 80
4.1 The Marriage Dispute of Giovanni and Lusanna 107
4.2 The Misericordia of Florence 113
4.3 The Control of Plague and State-Building in Fifteenth-Century Milan 116
4.4 The Wars of the Fists 122
5.1 Cola di Rienzo (1313–1354) 140
8.1 The Religious Repudiation of Art 240
8.2 Domenico Scandella (1532–1559): A Sixteenth-Century Miller Tried and Burned for Heresy 243
8.3 Veronica Franco (1546–1591): A Sixteenth-Century Poet and Courtesan 246
9.1 Sofonisba Anguissola (1532–1625) 275
9.2 Michelangelo Buonarroti (1475–1564) and Mimar Sinan (*c.* 1490–1588) 277
9.3 Andrea Palladio (1508–1580) 280
9.4 Renaissance Music 286

ACKNOWLEDGMENTS

It is always a pleasure to acknowledge those who have helped in bringing a long-term project to fruition. My first debt of gratitude is to all the scholars, listed in suggested readings, whose work informs my own and without whom this synthetic work would not be possible. A word of thanks is also due to colleagues who generously took the time to read portions of this manuscript. Among them Elyse Katz Flier, whose expertise in the history of Renaissance art was incredibly helpful; my colleagues at San Diego State in world history, Paula De Vos, Kate Edgerton, and Ranin Kazemi; and political scientist Ron King. Of course all errors remain my own. I am thankful as well for the funding the History Department at San Diego State provided for the purchase of books consulted for this project. Over the years many colleagues and friends have accompanied me on my scholarly journey, all too many to list here, but I am especially grateful for the insights of Guido Ruggiero and Laura Giannetti, whose own work I greatly admire. Further, the insights, vision, and support of Rhodri Mogford, Senior Publisher at Bloomsbury Academic, is what has made this textbook possible. Lastly, many thanks to my sister, Ann Maimone, for listening tirelessly and offering me her affection and years of wisdom.

Introduction: The Invention of the Renaissance

Millions of people each year stand in line, sometimes for hours, to enter the doors of St. Peter's Basilica, the Vatican Museums, and the Sistine Chapel in Rome; St. Mark's Basilica in Venice; the Prado in Madrid; the National Gallery in London; and the Louvre Museum in Paris. Tourists are advised to buy tickets in advance for world-renowned museums like the Uffizi Galleries in Florence. Students throng to study programs abroad in Italy, France, England, and Spain. What are they going to see? The works of great artists and architects like Michelangelo and Leonardo da Vinci, whose aesthetic sensibilities and forward-looking engineering still hold great meaning for twenty-first-century individuals. For millions of people worldwide the legacy of the Renaissance still holds deep resonance as evidenced in mass tourism, Renaissance fairs, theater, a neo-Renaissance art market, and historical period pieces in cinema. But what was the Renaissance, when did it take place, and where did it unfold? Apart from a general recognition that the cultural works it left to humanity in art, architecture, classical languages, literature, and science are foundational and still worth our attention, there is no consensus, at least among scholars, on how to answer these questions.

From as far back as the fourteenth century, writers in Tuscany such as Petrarch (1304–1374), with a focus on Italy, celebrated antique Greek and Latin letters, setting the foundations for an initial Renaissance paradigm whose contours and attributes would continue to change over the next 700 years with the ideals and aspirations of each subsequent generation of intellectuals. The self-congratulatory humanist-minded thinkers of the fourteenth to sixteenth centuries were eager to distinguish themselves from the intellectuals in Western Europe that had preceded them, asserting they were the harbingers of a new modern age that was implicitly superior to the church-dominated medieval culture that came before and that still prevailed in some circles. They divided history into two parts, with the ancient world coming to a close around 400 CE with the disintegration of the western Roman Empire and then followed by the Middle Ages. They were critical of the church-dominated scholastic teaching of literature, philosophy, science, and theology that had begun in Europe's medieval universities, looking instead to create more objective methods of knowing about the world through observation and deduction. They reassessed the learned knowledge in ancient manuscripts, experimented with and applied new theories, and drew from the world of experience derived from the artisan's workshop to arrive at new understandings of nature. They circled in private academies that initially emphasized the humanities, namely, poetry, grammar, rhetoric, ethics, and history, an educational program fitting for the male elites governing the republics and courts of Italy and other European cultural centers and for learned females who communicated their concerns via letters, poetry, and discussion in aristocratic venues and sometimes by serving as ruling regents for their husbands or sons. They began to write in the vernacular, the language of the people, in addition to erudite classical Latin rather than medieval Latin, to develop political theories that served their material rather than spiritual aims, and to search for ancient wisdom that would teach them about the workings of the universe. In all this by the late fifteenth and sixteenth centuries intellectuals were assisted by movable type and the printing press, a revolutionary German invention with Chinese roots that afforded the wide dissemination of knowledge.

But contemporary thinkers did not use the term "Renaissance." In 1550 the sixteenth-century painter and biographer of famous artists, Giorgio Vasari, who was organizing artistic achievements in historical ways, introduced an Italian term, *rinascita*, signifying a rebirth of antique forms that was anglicized and popularized much later as "Renaissance." Greco-Roman artifacts were ubiquitously present in Italy and throughout the Mediterranean world for that matter, fostering a natural interest in researching the ancient origins of things in legal and religious thought, epigraphy, numismatics, sculpture, and architecture, a curiosity with foundations in the fourteenth century that flowered as a multifaceted cultural movement in the fifteenth and sixteenth centuries. As artists developed linear perspective with the tools of ancient geometry, physics, and optics, they represented the three-dimensional world that surrounded them on plastered walls, wood panels, canvas, and stone. As practicing mathematicians, they captured the essence of a more material world that was often grounded in Greco-Roman and Christian forms. Vasari's periodization of Renaissance art focused on the central Italian region of Tuscany, beginning with the painters Cimabue (*c*. 1240–1302) and Giotto (1226–1337) and culminating with the death of Michelangelo Buonarotti in 1564. Many art historians today still subscribe to a periodization of the Renaissance that is similar to Vasari's, roughly corresponding with the early fourteenth to late sixteenth centuries. Historians, however, have moved the chronological, conceptual, and spatial parameters of Renaissance studies in many directions. A vast historical literature has produced "Renaissances" with different chronologies and attributes in Italy as well as multiple parts of Europe.

Three centuries after Vasari, the first real use of the term "Renaissance" in a historical context was introduced by the French art critic Jules Michelet (1798–1874), who in 1855 referred to the classicizing styles of the fifteenth and sixteenth centuries on the Italian Peninsula in his monumental history of France. It is unlikely that fifteenth- or sixteenth-century Italian contemporaries would have embraced a French descriptive, yet they would have shared Michelet's point of view: he defined the period as a drastic break from the medieval past, interpreting the fine arts and writings of the fifteenth and sixteenth centuries as a "rebirth" of the ancient forms of Greece and Rome. The Swiss historian Jacob Burckhardt (1818–1897) reinforced Michelet's vision of the Renaissance as a critical era in European history just a few years later, with the publication of *The Civilization of the Renaissance in Italy* (1860). A topical work set in the years between 1300 and 1530, Burckhardt recounted the story of a discovery of the self, a revival of the artistic forms of antiquity, a change in aesthetics and innovation in politics and the arts, and a story about the birth of the modern age. Focusing on the biographies of despotic rulers, autobiographical writings, individual portraits, and the letters of merchants and humanists, Burckhardt, representative of his generation of intellectuals, was searching for the origins of individualism, of republican government, of secularism, and of capitalism, important ideals for nineteenth-century intellectuals. Like the fifteenth-century scholars before him, Burckhardt told of the birth of the modern age, the transition from the church-dominated culture of the Middle Ages to one of lay secular control, a narrative that later scholars cited and continued to assess well into the first decades of the twentieth century.

Both Michelet, Burckhardt, and their followers generated much reaction among twentieth-century historians, who questioned in particular such concepts as "secularism," "individualism," "Great Men," "modernity," and even the use of the term "Renaissance" to delineate a historical period. While its application to arts and letters and some areas of early scientific inquiry in natural philosophy resonated, in that we can see the tangible emulation of ancient models in sculpture and architecture and a reverence for Greek medicine and science, it seemed irrelevant to economic and social developments, to advances in technology, to the ubiquity of religious life, and to the masses of people toiling the land and steeped in their own popular cultures. Moreover, the evidence from the two earlier writers was fundamentally elitist, referring to only a handful of individuals from the past. Other debates centered around whether the Renaissance period was truly innovative or a nostalgic return to ancient Greece and Rome. Some scholars, such as Charles Homer Haskins during the 1920s, asserted that the qualities attributed to the Renaissance, such as humanism, were already present during the Middle Ages, particularly in the church-sponsored culture of the twelfth century in France; that the fourteenth and fifteenth centuries in Italy were a late phase of the medieval period, an argument that holds some weight, as we shall see in the early chapters of this text.

During the mid-twentieth century, central and northern Italy between 1300 and 1530, particularly their political, artistic, and intellectual history, became a serious subject of study in North America and Great Britain. After the Second World War, scholars devoted attention to the transition in parts of Western Europe from a politically fragmented, largely agrarian feudal society to that of politically independent city-states ruled by capitalist-minded elites. Five large Italian city-states (Florence, Venice, Milan, the Papal States, and to a lesser degree the Kingdom of Naples in the south) stood at the forefront of these new studies, especially in the United States. Why did Americans begin to study the Renaissance? Historian Edward Muir explains in a 1995 historiographical essay that "the experience of the educated-in-the-classics, civic-minded, self-governing citizens of Renaissance Italy spoke a message that Americans can best understand, a message about the ideological and institutional underpinnings of republics."[1] Indeed, Renaissance studies blossomed on the heels of the Second World War, a war against the tyranny of Fascism and the oppression of Jewish intellectuals. In the 1930s several academics fled the horrors of totalitarian Germany to the United States, Great Britain, and Canada. Among them were political historians Felix Gilbert and Hans Baron, the art historian Erwin Panofksy, and the premier scholar of humanism, Paul Oskar Kristeller. These scholars were keenly interested in the history of independent Italian city-republics in central and northern Italy and the new political, intellectual, and cultural forms that were emerging. They were pathbreakers in their respective fields. Panofksy, for example, introduced iconographical analysis to the discipline of Renaissance art history, that is, reading art works as documents that were a product of their historical environment and then formulating interpretations connected to contemporary literary, religious, and philosophical currents. He posited that there were artistic revivals prior to the fourteenth century, during the Carolingian Renaissance of the eighth and ninth centuries and the Renaissance of the twelfth century, but that developments in the history of art during the fourteenth and fifteenth centuries were unique and blossomed into a wider cultural movement. In the area of intellectual history, Kristeller redefined Renaissance studies after the Second World War with his writings on humanism as an academic and scholarly movement based in rhetoric and distinct from philosophy. He accepted the critique of medievalists that Renaissance humanism did not represent a dramatic break with the past. However, in education it did reform the medieval subdivision of the liberal arts. Moreover, there was a greater emphasis on close study of classical texts. This postwar generation thus did not entirely abandon Burckhardt's account of changing intellectual life and aesthetics in Renaissance Italy, but rather explored it more deeply and in the process inspired future generations of students and scholars to create broader fields of inquiry. Some concentrated on the revival of classical forms and ideas in

Italy; others focused on how texts were read and understood throughout Europe. Still others combined iconographical analyses with close textual readings to understand the connections between visual and literary material. The variations and examples are innumerable.

Turning away from Burckhardt, a group of scholars during the 1960s and 1970s moved beyond using humanist scholarship and the biographies of famous individuals as organizing principles for the age, devoting attention to the growth of commerce and banking, urbanization, labor history, and family history. They employed new methodologies and embraced new subjects such as the social history of art and architecture, artistic patronage, the relationship between family behavior and politics, science and technology, and economic development. Of note, the term "Renaissance" persisted, even though the descriptive as it pertains to an emphasis on Greco-Roman models and Judeo-Christian values fit better with the fine arts and the humanities rather than with developments in social or economic history or the experiential and experimental research in the natural sciences (called natural philosophy). "Renaissance" is a more suitable descriptive for an intellectual and cultural movement rather than a historical period. Yet it is also used as a convenient adjective to refer to a broad range of developments over a period of time, with very fluid margins and boundaries that have earned little agreement among scholars. The Renaissance as a period of time in Italy between 1350 and 1600 appealed especially to Anglophone audiences rather than the European academy, where the tendency was to view 1500 as the beginning of the modern age and 1800 as the start of contemporary history. But some scholars in both Europe and North America began to devote more attention to explaining the social and economic underpinnings of cultural development in Italy that took place prior to 1350 and to underlining the connections between urbanization, court society, and the flowering of the imagination. Among them was Lauro Martines, whose history of the Italian city-states covered the years between 1000 and 1600 and demonstrated that the resources and values of the eleventh and twelfth centuries laid the foundations for developments in high culture between 1300 and 1600.[2] Martines's foundational study remains an influential voice in my own account here of the early Italian Renaissance period, especially in showing connections between the classes in power and developments in arts and letters. My own account of the Renaissance in Italy also stresses a continued interest in Greco-Roman culture and Judeo-Christian values throughout the medieval and Renaissance periods rather than an abrupt break during the fourteenth century.

For much of the mid- to late-twentieth century, the master narrative of the Renaissance placed its origins in the cities of fourteenth-century Tuscany, where merchants and early capitalists sponsored new artistic and literary styles alongside those that continued from earlier centuries, and who secularized ethical and political thought to fit urban life. The multifaceted artistic and intellectual movements then spread to Italian cities like Venice and Rome and to the courts of Urbino, Ferrara, Mantua, and Milan. By the late fifteenth century they had reached the courts of Matthias Corvinus in Bohemia and Ivan III in Russia, and during the sixteenth century that of Bona Sforza in Poland, Francis I in France, Charles V in Spain, Mary of Austria in the Netherlands, and Elizabeth I in England, among others. While in the fifteenth century scholars from around Europe came to study the humanist curriculum in Italy before taking it home, by the sixteenth century a sojourn in Italy was no longer necessary. Guido Ruggiero's most recent analysis of a *rinascita* or *rinascimento* (rebirth) in Italy, *The Renaissance in Italy*, published in 2015, falls in line with this chronological thread, offering a conceptual paradigm that has also greatly influenced the writing of this textbook. Ruggiero envisions two different urban civilizations on the Italian Peninsula. The first, spanning the period between 1250 and 1450, witnessed a revival of classical forms and ideas and the celebration of Latin culture in the Italian cities of the center and the north, developed by the denizens of a non-noble, nonclerical business elite. The second, spanning from 1450 to 1575, witnessed a shift to aristocratic culture, influenced by European courts outside Italy, in the peninsula's center and north and also included the south. These two civilizations unfolded against the background of new inventions, religious transformations, and globalization, developments that were of European and not just Italian origins.

A subset of Renaissance historiography of the late twentieth and early twenty-first centuries, including a number of Ruggiero's other works besides *The Renaissance in Italy*, moved in sync with developments in the academy, ushering in what might be termed collectively as a second important turn after the Second World War. It was influenced by the 1960s civil rights and labor movements in the United States and Great Britain, respectively, and the women's movement in the 1970s. Together these transformations in politics and social life brought new questions about what was important to study. Moreover, they broadened membership in the academy, bringing in scholars of both genders from working-class origins. Academics then wanted to know more about ordinary people, about farmers and laborers, about domestic space, and about women's work and their contributions to the historical period. As a result, the boundaries of Renaissance studies once again expanded, and that expansion inevitably revived unsolved questions about definitions. First, Renaissance for whom? Not everyone in this historical period was painting or writing or perhaps conscious of a "rebirth" of classical culture. Many were producing that culture as artisans, but they had not been credited with authorship of the Renaissance. The vast majority, however, those toiling in the fields or in unskilled labor, might have viewed the artistic works of the period but they did not participate in the production of high culture. It is difficult to know whether they were even aware of humanism, for example. Their stories, however, belong to the genre of popular culture, with its oral traditions, rituals, and folklore, an influential legacy in its own right.

Second, was there a Renaissance for women, since they could not obtain formal membership in the councils of the Italian republics, nor teach, nor preach? In fact, despite these limitations, new research has shown that women writers tutored in the humanities were engaging with their male counterparts and contributing great works of poetry and letters. Some, in princely aristocratic circles, were governing in place of husbands or sons away from home, both in Italy and in the courts of Europe. Others were producing art, literature, and dramas in convents, the institutionalized shelters for unmarried women. Still others worked in the crafts, though they did not go through formal training. They must now be worked into the master narrative. Third, was it legitimate to confine developments between 1350 and 1600 to central and northern Italy, when in fact southern Italy, the rest of Europe, and the Islamic world for that matter could be credited with important technological and cultural innovations? Contributions from outside of Italy need to be addressed as well in the story of the Renaissance. Finally, why stop the narrative with 1494, the date the Italian city-states were invaded by the great Atlantic monarchies and struggling for their independence? Should such a political transition define the end of the period? The answer to each of these questions was no, but each generated lively debates among scholars of history, literature, the arts, and sciences that are well beyond the scope of this textbook.

Yet another subset of scholars, including art historians, economic historians, and cultural historians, began in the 1970s to pursue studies in Renaissance materialism. That is, the preoccupation on the part of elites with collectible objects—fragments from monuments, coins, statues, relics, and other curiosities—fit for Renaissance palaces and museums. The collections, like humanist writings, provide an important window into what prosperous consumers valued and desired as part of their cultural patrimony. At the same time, like humanist texts, they document another dimension of how contemporaries created their own historical memory of an age. The libraries of ancient and medieval manuscripts and newly printed books and the palaces and museums filled with Greco-Roman, Etruscan, and Egyptian antiquities all formed part of an enduring legacy that continues to attract scholars and tourists alike to visit these heritage sites and gives them contact with the cultural Renaissance.

Cultural historians are also finding other ways, besides the collection of antiquities, that contemporaries created their own historical memory of their age. Studies of the activities in Renaissance academies now reveal that the story of the Renaissance did not just belong to Michelet or Burckhardt but also to sixteenth-century contemporaries, along the lines of Vasari, who used the methods of humanist study to examine the artistic and literary achievements of their own world and in the process created their own histories. They began to see their accomplishments in the context of the Italian Peninsula and Europe as a whole, crafting their own vision of the historical period.

The twenty-first century has brought still other transformations in the way scholars conceive of the Renaissance period, as a result of something historians have named "the global turn." It signifies a greater consciousness of the importance of non-Western contributions to the Western experience. In the case of this textbook it applies to developments beyond the Italian Peninsula that contributed to the Italian experience. Led by its port cities, the Italian Peninsula was in fact part of an ancient and medieval global network that stretched from the Mediterranean Sea across Greater Asia and included North Africa. The Iberian Peninsula, southern Italy, and the medieval Islamic world were part of this network, which disseminated a variety of cultural traditions and values, religious and scientific ideas, and material artifacts. The Italian Peninsula's geographical position gave it an initial edge over the northwestern territories of Europe, which were largely feudal and agrarian as opposed to urban and commercial. Travelers along the Afro-Eurasian trading networks bought the traditions and material cultures of Byzantium and medieval Islam to the peninsula, importing ideas and material objects that helped shape culture on the Italian Peninsula. Parts of medieval southern Spain and France were part of that Mediterranean network. However, it was not until the late fifteenth century that the monarchies of Western Europe began to catch up with Italian commerce and state building and to embrace some of the classical forms developed in Italy for their own intellectual and cultural needs. At that point the Portuguese opened new markets along the west African coast, the continent's sub-Saharan interior, and southeast Asia, and Spain reached the Americas. New contacts set the stage for further transcontinental encounters and intellectual exchange, while moving the economic axis of development from the Mediterranean to the Atlantic. They virtually shook the foundations of Renaissance knowledge, for the new worlds that explorers conquered and settled introduced new peoples and ways of life, flora, and fauna that were unknown to the ancients they had so arduously studied.

The late fifteenth and sixteenth centuries were also the time when the humanist study of classical languages and literature and humanist methods of scholarly inquiry penetrated northwestern Europe, both through traveling scholars and through individuals who had studied in Italian intellectual centers and then used their learning to reform educational and religious programs at home. At that point humanism, which had originated in Italy, became the central intellectual movement of Europe as a whole. It intersected with the religious reformation movements, offering vernacular translations of the Bible and Church Fathers based on readings in their original languages, and it was fueled by the new and burgeoning printing industry. Along with the humanist movement, classical art and architecture also attracted European-wide patronage.

The ongoing scholarly investigation of global material and intellectual encounters, of the lives of the subaltern classes, of the experiences of women, and of the application of gender in addition to social class as a category of analysis propels us to broaden our vision of the Renaissance as a phase developing first in the various regions, cities, and courts of the Italian Peninsula and then in their European counterparts across the Alps. Thus this textbook combines the political, cultural, economic, and social narratives of earlier scholars with current findings of the twenty-first century. To do so, however, means to confront certain challenges. One is the term "Italy," which this textbook often uses as a convenient descriptive. In fact the various regions of the Italian Peninsula only coalesced politically and began to use the name "Italy" in 1861. Prior to that time the peninsula's history was divided into regional states. A second challenge is how to use the term "Renaissance," since it is rife with controversy but still used widely. Here every effort will be made to avoid using the term as a monolithic descriptive of an "age." Instead it will be employed as a convenient chronological reference for the time period on the Italian Peninsula roughly between 1350 and 1600, while the preceding periods will be referred to as ancient (to 500 CE) and medieval (500–1350 CE), respectively. One could easily argue about these chronological boundaries, especially that the period between 1350 and 1500 in Italy was a late phase of the Middle Ages in the west. In fact there is no precise moment in time when the Middle Ages, which were also a period of important intellectual and artistic creativity in their own right, ended. But because the Renaissance is concerned foremost with the culture of cities, and many aspects of that culture flowered first in the highly urbanized regions of the Italian Peninsula, this textbook remains more in line with scholars who have now for more than a century focused on this geographical area. In the Italian regions there was an increasing emphasis on the humanities and on human potential; a vigorous interest in the Greco-Roman world in arts and antiquities, letters, and science; and the introduction of new artistic styles and techniques. These were important cultural shifts, albeit for the middle and upper levels of society. An initial recovery of classical texts and experiments in art took place between 1350 and 1400, and in the following century the humanistic values and literary and artistic styles that defined Renaissance culture gained momentum and became more firmly established. Thereafter, during the sixteenth century, the penchant for more European, aristocratic lifestyles and courtly society following a dramatic period of foreign invasion transformed art and ideas. Various Italian innovations spread to the courts of Europe, where they took on their own individual forms, but the peninsula also absorbed cultures from abroad, including that of the Ottomans, whose capital, Istanbul, stood at the crossroads between Europe and Greater Asia.

There is also some additional justification for setting developments in the cities of the Italian Peninsula apart from the rest of continental Europe: they were characterized by greater urban density and an urban culture sustained by international finance, commerce, luxury production, and consumption. They were also nodal points of local trade between city and countryside. While population also surged in southern Germany and the southern

Netherlands, in Italy it was more intense and it was under the patronage of new secular energies beyond the church, the landed nobility, and the encroaching power of monarchs. Much of the demographic and economic groundwork for this urbanization, treated in Chapter 2, took place between the eleventh and early fourteenth centuries. By 1500 five of the six largest European centers were on the Italian Peninsula: Venice, Milan, Florence, Rome, and Naples. Paris was the only European city on a par with them, although Istanbul surpassed them and was experiencing its own Renaissance of sorts. Over the "long sixteenth century," between 1470 and 1600, the larger Italian city-states developed coherent forms of governance and social organization that also shaped arts, science, and letters. They were major cultural diffusers as well as consumers of goods and ideas, whether in Italy's ports, marketplaces, palaces, or places of worship.

But what of the title of this textbook—*The Renaissance and the Wider World*? The developments that unfolded on the Italian Peninsula will constitute the centerpiece of this text, but every effort will be made to give credit where due to innovations and influence coming from the greater Mediterranean world, continental Europe, Greater Asia, North Africa, and the Americas. This is a somewhat daunting challenge, but demonstrates a commitment to the critical importance of the global turn in historical inquiry. A case in point is my exposition of the Italian Peninsula's ancient and medieval legacies at the outset of this textbook. It draws attention to the medieval intellectual contributions that reached the developing cities from the wider Mediterranean world, where Greek natural philosophy continued to thrive and Islamic medicine excelled in its own right. Those bodies of knowledge came to Italy and Western Europe for that matter, via medieval Islam, with the translations into Latin from the Arabic language emanating from southern Spain, southern Italy, and Sicily. Moreover, the Muslim presence in southern Italy and Sicily during the tenth century, as well as the ongoing commercial exchange among entrepôts in the eastern and western Mediterranean during the eleventh to thirteenth centuries, were conduits for the transmission of technical knowledge leavened in Greater Asia. Thus, while early Italian letters, sculpture, and architecture harkened back more directly to Greco-Roman forms, science, technology, and medicine were mediated by medieval Islamic scholarship. Italian cultural and technological developments in the late fifteenth and sixteenth centuries were further mediated by outside influences from various parts of Europe, the Mediterranean, and the Americas, even as Italian art and humanism became models to others.

Equally important is to recognize that a variety of peoples moved in and out of the Italian Peninsula, whether as migrants, slaves, merchants, artisans, pilgrims, wet nurses, sex workers, laundresses, or domestic servants. Stated differently, a more global picture complicates the Renaissance, underlining that the societies of the Italian Peninsula were not insular and that global interaction afforded people a degree of agency. For this reason the text is not confined to famous people and events, but rather recognizes the material and cultural contributions of laboring women and men. Even the great artists and inventors of the Renaissance were tied to crafts and trades in some fashion. Artists, for example, were alchemists of color who made paints from plants and minerals and goldsmiths skilled in forming metal. Some came from humble origins. Renaissance material culture and the arts were produced by skilled laborers who supervised work in the handicrafts and traded in those commodities. Their work, produced in workshops, usually took place in domestic settings.

Workshop and home raise a further subject of analysis: the role of the domestic setting in the Renaissance era. In the world of male and female artisans, workplace and home often converged, making the domestic setting an essential site of production as well as reproduction. In the world of elites, the home took on even more complex significance. It often served as a center of public life, where societal, diplomatic, and political actors interacted. Further, it reflected the status of its residents and represented the continuity of the family. Still more, it was a central location for social, cultural, and religious life. Finally, it was a receptacle for and transmitter of the cultural patrimony and material culture of the age. The domestic setting thus deserves a place alongside city, court, and church in the history of Renaissance culture. It also helps us to gender the Renaissance experience, blurring the lines between public and private and between masculine and feminine space.

Recent research also demands a reevaluation of the place of women in historical narratives about Renaissance culture. For example, we now know more about how aristocratic women participated in political life and diplomacy as regents and served as powerful marriage brokers for their children. Furthermore, scholars have demonstrated how, through their letter writing, women were trained in humanism and engaged in important intellectual discussions. As patrons they influenced the development of the arts and music. A very few were recognized painters and musicians in their own right. Aristocratic women also held substantial properties and oversaw innovative land projects, while ordinary women constituted an important component of the world of work, which often unfolded in the domestic sphere or in convents. This text will attempt to bring their achievements to the forefront, alongside those of men.

How This Textbook Is Organized

All historical writing inevitably brings in the perspectives of its authors, and this vision of the period is no different. It is an effort to offer another way of looking at Renaissance culture, politics, and society, with wide parameters, deep origins, and broad diversity and inclusivity. However, it must be emphasized that the Renaissance, whether conceived of as a historical period or as a cultural movement, has generated an enormous body of scholarship in multiple fields. It is not possible for a textbook of this size to cover all the important work that has and continues to emerge. This is, then, a selection of topics in what is now a vast and growing field, and readers are encouraged to consult the "Further Reading" section at the end of each chapter to explore in greater detail the wide array of scholarship that informs this textbook. The "Further Exploration" section in each chapter, on the other hand, encourages readers to conduct independent research beyond this textbook on a number of specific historical questions.

This text situates Renaissance beginnings on the Italian Peninsula, grounding its political structures and cultural foundations in the ancient and medieval Mediterranean world. Chapter 1 traces the peninsula's Greco-Roman past; the fall of the Roman Empire in the West; the fragmentation into Germanic, Byzantine, Muslim, and Latin components; and the new Christian and Islamic societies that preceded the revitalization of Italian cities from the eleventh century. Chapter 2 begins by setting out the economic underpinnings of urban revitalization during the eleventh to thirteenth centuries, including improved agricultural production, the rise of manufacture and construction, and the opening of new markets in the southeastern Mediterranean and Levant (Southwest Asia) during the Crusader period. It then traces the rise of communal government in central and northern Italy, beginning with its eleventh- and twelfth-century communal forms and ending during the thirteenth and fourteenth centuries with more narrowly based oligarchies and despotisms. The south of Italy, on the other hand, follows a different political trajectory and source of cultural patronage: it is ruled by a succession of royal dynasties beginning with the Normans in the eleventh century and followed by the Swabians, Angevins, and Aragonese. Chapter 3 remains in the eleventh to fourteenth centuries, outlining some of the major cultural developments in Italian urban civilization. They include the revival of knowledge neglected by the West since antiquity; new learning with the establishment of universities; the rise of vernacular poetry and writing; and new experiments in painting and architecture. Chapter 4 explores daily life on the Italian Peninsula, including the various stages of the human life cycle and the overall standard of living, with broad chronological boundaries loosely applied to the second half of the fourteenth through the sixteenth centuries. The chapter also attempts to define the ways in which people were socially categorized and interacted, complicating broad definitions of class and gender by examining the vertical and horizontal ties embedded in modes of socialization. Chapter 5 traces the consolidation of power on the Italian Peninsula during the fifteenth century into five principal states (the Republics of Florence and Venice, the Duchy of Milan, the Papal States, and the Kingdom of Naples.) In the course of this process the Italian regional states develop more efficient methods of warfare, administration, and diplomacy, phenomena that some historians have argued to be the first template for a modern state. The chapter also underlines the important relationship between political consolidation, public life, and kinship, for it was essentially family dynasties that stood at the helm of Italy's republics, principalities, and kingdoms. Astute marriage alliances and estate planning among the families of Italy's ruling elites helped them accumulate and retain power. Alongside male rulers, aristocratic wives, mothers, and daughters played key roles in this process by using their wealth and governing talents to influence the peninsula's power dynamics. Chapter 6 is situated in both the fifteenth and sixteenth centuries and explores the self-conscious cultural movement in letters and education called humanism, when Italian intellectuals intensely studied the Greek and Latin classics and the ancient Church Fathers in hopes of fostering worthy ideals and values. Primarily a literary and rhetorical current grounded in ancient texts, humanism harkened back to the development of the medieval Italian commune. It was also part of a shared Greco-Roman and, to a lesser degree, Arabic classical tradition that informed all parts of the Mediterranean intellectual world. Scholars advocated the *studia humanitatis*, the liberal arts study of grammar, rhetoric, poetry, history, politics, and philosophy, to celebrate the dignity and capacity of humankind and to prepare for a life of virtue, a complex concept that implied exercising skill and achieving success. These goals first developed in the courts and republics of Italy during the late fifteenth century and, with the advent of the printing press, spread rapidly to the rest of Europe. By the sixteenth century they were not just an Italian phenomenon but a European one that evolved in response to the changing political, educational, and religious developments of the age. The chapter ends with a brief survey of the impact of humanistic studies on European intellectual and religious life. Chapter 7 centers on fifteenth-century achievements in art, architecture, and material culture, the elements for which the Renaissance in Italy has been immortalized. The preponderance of the chapter aligns artistic achievements with the motivations of contemporary patrons, for in its various forms, from canvas to stone and textiles to precious objects, art held propagandistic, civic, devotional, charitable, and familial messages. It is a window into identity, status, honor, opulence, erudition, faith, and piety. The peninsula's artistic traditions not only included sculpture, painting, and architecture but also the decorative arts, such as weaving, embroidery, carpentry, masonry, smithing, ceramics, and glassmaking, that is, the work of female and male artisans who drew both from classical models but also from medieval, artisanal techniques and from cross-cultural assimilation and adaptation. There was also an important antiquarian tradition that included not only ancient artifacts but also contemporary works of art that patrons collected for their historical legacies. Chapter 8 reviews the dramatic developments that brought the fifteenth century to a close and ushered in the last phase of Italian Renaissance culture over the sixteenth century. Hapsburg–Valois rivalries to conquer Italian territories ended, after more than a half century of warfare, with most of the peninsula losing its political independence to Spain. The leadership in most of the cities abandoned its corporate and commercial foundations for a more aristocratic and courtly ethos. For them, landed investments took central stage, ushering in a villa culture that stood in juxtaposition to that of the city, while the center of economic gravity gradually moved from the Mediterranean to the Atlantic. During the sixteenth century the Renaissance church gained significant ground in political and international affairs, and with the advent of Protestantism church leaders were constrained to play a greater role in both the social welfare and moral discipline of their constituencies. Chapter 9 examines the variety of cultural and intellectual responses to the dramatic changes of the sixteenth century. Foreign incursions and oscillating Italian regimes sparked debate about the fate of the city-states, including an assessment of the strengths and weaknesses of principalities and republics. At the same time, the body of knowledge that had been accepted since ancient times was coming under fire. New oceanic trade routes were enlarging the known world and exposing Europeans to unfamiliar flora, fauna, and peoples with different ways of life. In astronomy, new methods of scholarly inquiry were challenging traditional explanations of the cosmos. In other branches of science, the conclusions of the ancients, particularly Aristotle, were no longer satisfactory, prompting scholars to rely more on observation and practical experience than readings of ancient texts. In religious study, on the other hand, new translations of ancient texts brought new versions of the Bible and with it new religious ideas and calls for reform. Taken together, these European-wide changes challenged more than a thousand years of church authority. Paradoxically, the world of uncertainty and turbulence that inaugurated the sixteenth century also ushered in the High Renaissance in Italian art, with its new vision of human grandeur and heroism, and its various genres gradually became the arm of a reforming church grappling with the winds of change. Chapter 10 sums up the major arguments of this textbook. It also traces the worldly connections and innovations both in and outside of Italy that afforded the exchange of ideas and technology and fostered a more European Renaissance. Finally, it assesses what that culture meant not only to the Italian Peninsula but also to other parts of Europe and why its legacy still attracts widespread interest today.

Notes

1 Edward Muir, "The Italian Renaissance in America," *American Historical Review*, 100:4 (October 1995), 1096.
2 Lauro Martines, *Power and the Imagination: City-States in Renaissance Italy* (New York: Vintage Books Edition, 1980), ix.

Further Reading

Brotton, Jerry. *The Renaissance Bazaar. From the Silk Road to Michelangelo.* Oxford: Oxford University Press, 2003. An interpretation of the Renaissance that examines some of its Islamic underpinnings.

Findlen, Paula, and Kenneth Gouwens. "Introduction. The Persistence of the Renaissance." *American Historical Review*, 103:1 (February 1998): 51–4. A thoughtful introduction to an *American Historical Review* forum discussing the persistence of the Renaissance as a field of study.

Goody, Jack. *Renaissances. The One or the Many?* Cambridge, UK: Cambridge University Press, 2010. The renowned anthropologist compares European developments to those unfolding in India and China.

Grendler, Paul. *The Renaissance in American Life.* Westport, CT: Praeger Publishers, 2006. An examination of the popularity of the Renaissance as a field of study in North America.

Martin, John J., ed. *The Renaissance World.* New York: Routledge, 2007. A collection of insightful essays that cover the Renaissance in Europe in both its elite and popular dimensions from the thirteenth to the seventeenth centuries.

Martines, Lauro. *Power and the Imagination. City States in Renaissance Italy.* Baltimore, MD: Johns Hopkins University Press, 1988. A magisterial survey of medieval and Renaissance Italian developments that draws connections between cultural patrons and power.

Moyer, Ann E. *The Intellectual World of Sixteenth Century Florence. Humanists and Culture in the Age of Cosimo I.* New York: Cambridge University Press, 2020. An important study of the ways in which Florentine intellectuals examined their own achievements and created their own history.

Muir, Edward. "The Italian Renaissance in America." *American Historical Review*, 100:4 (October 1995): 1095–1118. An analysis of the Renaissance as a period of study in North America.

Rowland, Ingrid, and Noah Charney. *The Collector of Lives: Giorgio Vasari and the Invention of Art.* New York: W. W. Norton, 2017. A lively biography of the author of the classic *Lives of the Artists*, a book that invented the genre of artistic biography and established the canon of Italian Renaissance art.

Ruggiero, Guido, ed. *A Companion to the Worlds of the Renaissance.* Hoboken, NJ: Wiley-Blackwell, 2002. An important collection of essays that together view the Renaissance from both world and European perspectives.

Ruggiero, Guido. *The Renaissance in Italy.* New York: Cambridge University Press, 2015. An important new conceptualization and periodization of the rebirth of antique forms in Italy between 1250 and 1575.

Web Resources (As of June 27, 2022)

Iter, Gateway to the Middle Ages and Renaissance. https://www.itergateway.org/.

Oxford Bibliographies. https://www.oxfordbibliographies.com/browse?module_0=obo-9780195399301.

1

Foundations: Ancient and Medieval Legacies

FIGURE 1.1 Arena (30 CE). Verona, Italy. One of the best-preserved Roman arenas, used for oration and spectacle, of its time. It is also an example of the many uses of the revolutionary Roman arch, wedge-shaped blocks locked by a keystone spanning large spaces by directing weight to the ground.

Timeline

c. 700s BCE	Greeks found Magna Graecia in southern Italy and Sicily
509 BCE	End of Etruscan rule in Rome
509 BCE	Founding of the Roman Republic
330 BCE	Foundation of Constantinople as second capital of Roman Empire
27 BCE	Augustus (formerly Octavian) becomes first Roman Emperor
410 CE	Goths invade Italy; imperial court withdraws from Milan to Ravenna
452	Huns destroy cities of northeast Italy
476	Germanic Odoacer (476–493) replaces the last western Roman Emperor
493–526	Ostrogoth king Theodoric rules Italians in name of the emperor
523	Boethius (c. 475–525) composes *The Consolation of Philosophy*
529	Benedict establishes *The Rule*; with the foundation of Monte Cassino monastery
535–554	Byzantine Emperor Justinian conquers the Italian Peninsula
c. 540	Cassiodorus (490–583) promotes classical and religious learning
568	Lombards invade the Italian Peninsula
	Founding of Venice in the wake of Lombard invasions
590–604	Reign of Pope Gregory I the Great
632–750	The Muslims establish an empire stretching from Iberia through North Africa and Arabia to India
750–1258	Muslim Abbasid Dynasty intensified spread of Islamic culture
751	The Lombards capture Ravenna; collapse of Byzantine power in north Italy
756	Pepin the Frank defeats the Lombards; confers Ravenna to Pope Stephen III
768	Charlemagne becomes king of the Franks
774	Charlemagne conquers the Lombard kingdom
800	Pope Leo III crowns Charlemagne emperor of the Romans
831	The Muslims capture Palermo
841–871	The Muslims hold Bari
875–962	The Kingdom of Italy declines; local bishops and nobles assume power
876–c. 1025	Byzantine political hegemony over southern Italy

900	Sicily absorbed by the Muslims; Palermo becomes a center of scholarship in science and the arts
962–1002	Otto I of Saxony emperor in Rome
992	Golden Bull granting trading privileges to Venetians in Byzantine Empire
999–1139	Normans in southern Italy and Sicily
1076	Pope Gregory VII claims the right to invest bishops; outbreak of the Investiture Conflict
c. 1080	Central and northern Italian communes form under magnate rule
1082	Venetians granted trade privileges in Constantinople in return for naval support against the Normans
1085	Toledo becomes contact point between Islamic and Christian culture
1095	Pope Urban II calls First Crusade to liberate Jerusalem from the Seljuq Turks
c. 1097–9	Genoese and Pisan fleets support the crusaders in the Levant
1122	Concordat of Worms temporarily settles the Investiture Conflict
1127	Norman King Roger II unites southern Italy and Sicily
1138	Florence initiates communal government
1143	Commune of Rome formed
1145–9	Second Crusade
1155	Frederick I (Hohenstaufen) crowned Holy Roman emperor
1154; 1158	Diet of Roncaglia
1160–260	Tower Societies in Italy. Magnate rule
1167	Formation of First Lombard League against Frederick Barbarossa
1176	The Lombard League of Italian communes defeats Emperor Frederick Barbarossa at Legnano
1183	Peace of Constance; Frederick concedes jurisdiction of Lombard League cities
1189–92	Third Crusade
1190	Death of Frederick Barbarossa on Crusade; succession of Henry VI (1191), who conquered Naples and Sicily (1194) by inheritance right of his wife Constance
1197	Death of Henry VI; Frederick II king of Sicily, Germany, and Italy; contested by Swabian dynasty to 1208
1198	Innocent III Pope rules Papal State in central Italy to 1216
1202–4	Fourth Crusade. Venice raids Constantinople
1220	Frederick II takes the throne in southern Italy and Sicily

1226	Second Lombard League in northern Italy challenges Emperor Frederick II
1250	Death of Emperor Frederick II. End of Hohenstaufen ambitions in Italy
1252	Gold genovins and florins first coined
1268	Angevins replace the Hohenstaufen dynasty in Sicily (to 1282) and Naples (to 1442); capital of the kingdom transferred from Palermo to Naples
1277–8	First Genoese galleys sent to Flanders and England
1282	Sicilian Vespers; Angevins lose Sicily to Aragonese
1293	Ordinances of Justice in Florence
1309	Pope Clement VII transfers from Rome to Avignon France, where popes reigned until 1376

The artists, artisans, thinkers, and patrons of Renaissance Italy's towns and cities hailed from a rich, multicultural legacy, for the long and narrow boot that protrudes from the southern edge of the European continent spilling into the Mediterranean Sea was populated from its earliest times by an assortment of indigenous tribes, migrating peoples, and invaders. It did not exist as a single political unit, named Italy, until the nineteenth century but instead witnessed a series of incursions that produced a myriad of shifting political forms and a confusion of authorities. These incursions, however, also created conditions for the exchange of diverse cultures which gradually blended together in various local venues over time. They were reinforced by the peninsula's geographical position as a gateway between the eastern and western Mediterranean and a stepping stone to northern Europe. Trade with Byzantium, the Levant (Southwest Asia), and the Silk Road to the east; North Africa to the south; the Iberian Peninsula to the west; and the European regions to the north fueled a vibrant multiculturalism.

Antiquity

Renaissance culture is primarily the culture of cities, whose ancient foundations on the Italian Peninsula itself drew from Greek, Etruscan, and Roman legacies. Migrants to Italy from Greece founded flourishing cities in the mainland South and Sicily around the eighth century BCE, bringing their art, architecture, theater, and education, termed "Hellenic civilization," to the indigenous tribes. Shortly thereafter, the Etruscans, a people with a non-Indo European language whose origins in Asia Minor are uncertain, urbanized a strip of land in what is now Tuscany, western Umbria, northern Lazio, and parts of the north bringing their ideas of city life, their military technology, their religion and burial rites, and their metalwork, pottery,

FOUNDATIONS: ANCIENT AND MEDIEVAL LEGACIES

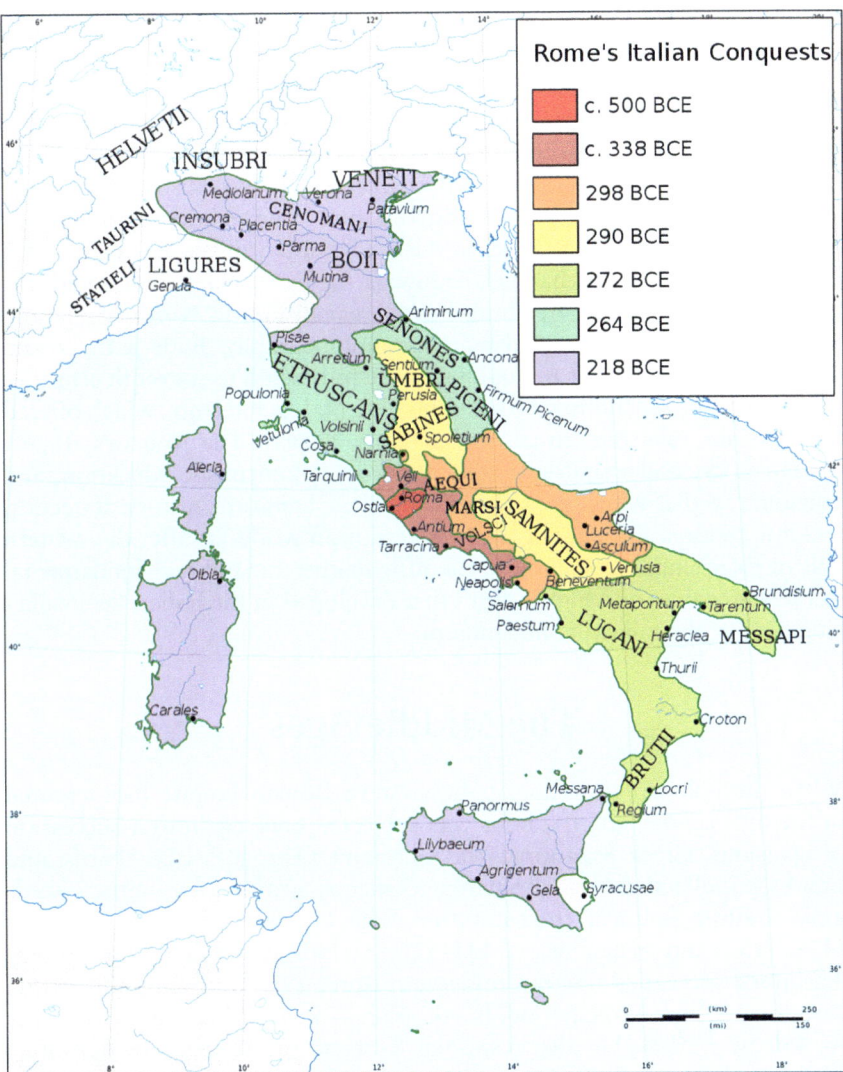

MAP 1.1 The Roman Conquest of Italy.

jewelry, and textile handicrafts. To their southeast, indigenous tribes of Oscans, Volsci, and Samnites had settled in Umbria, while the Latins occupied the hilltops of Rome. The Etruscan kings managed to subdue the Latins and rule Rome from 650 to 509 BCE, when an independent Roman Republic was established. A century later the Celts, who had made their home in the Po Valley in the north, drove the Etruscans out of the peninsula.

It was the Romans who by 265 BCE managed to bring together the panoply of ancient peoples inhabiting the peninsula (see Map 1.1). Led by a senatorial aristocracy beginning in 509 BCE, they set up a system of clientage with the city's plebeian class and constructed a military strong and efficient enough to enable them to systematically conquer the tribes throughout the peninsula and establish a consolidated position. The Romans offered their conquered subjects citizenship and connected their settlements through a series of all-weather roads. As brilliant civil engineers they established a unifying architectural lexicon of grid-iron streets and towns, bridges, aqueducts, temples, forums, and arenas (such as the one in the city of Verona in Figure 1.1 at the beginning of this chapter), endowing the peninsula, together with the greater Roman Empire stretching from Great Britain to North Africa and Southwest Asia, with an enduring urban topography. Both patrons and artists of the Renaissance period during the fourteenth to sixteenth centuries CE admired the functions of Roman monumental architecture, which offered insights into rulership, ritual, and military display. The Roman's respect for Greek art and visual language, philosophy, humanistic education, and religion, together with their Latinate language, literature, history, statecraft, and law endured throughout the Mediterranean world far after the western half of their empire collapsed in the fifth century CE and was fundamental to the elite values and high culture that developed in the Italian Peninsula's cities during the following millennium.

The Middle Ages

When the political structure of the western Roman Empire disintegrated in the fifth century CE, the boot was subjected once again to a succession of invasions. Greek Byzantines and Germanic Ostrogoths, Lombards, and Franks populated the old Roman settlements, sowing new cultural seeds amid shifting political fragmentation. The Ostrogothic rulers, Odoacer (476–493) and Theodoric (495–526), continued Roman traditions. Theodoric sponsored the transmission of Roman civilization by supporting two great writers of the period, Boethius (*c.* 475 to *c.* 524) and Cassiodorus (*c.* 490 to *c.* 583). He also respected Roman law. Theodoric's Byzantine successor, Justinian, who captured North Africa and Spain as well as parts of eastern Italy, established a fundamental body of civil law, the *corpus juris civilis*, that would be used throughout the Renaissance period. It was the vehicle through which Roman law challenged customary Germanic law in the twelfth century CE, and it was critical to the development of subsequent legal systems, including the canon law of the Latin Church. In the religious sphere, Odoacer and Theodoric embraced both Arian (Jesus is not cocternal with God the Father, but subordinate to him) and Latin Christianity, using them as a means to buttress patriotism. Justinian, however, created a seat of Byzantine power in the west with the Exarchate of Ravenna in 535 and replaced Arianism with Greek Orthodoxy. Each one of these rulers imported artisans from Constantinople to adorn their capital, Ravenna,

FIGURE 1.2 Church of St. Apollinare in Classe. Apse Mosaic. Ravenna, Italy. The early Christian churches took the Roman basilica form: a large oblong hall or building with double colonnades and a semicircular apse, used in ancient Rome as a court of law or for public assemblies. The mosaics, an art form borrowed from the Christian east, related the story of Christianity to early converts.

with magnificent Byzantine mosaics, a Latin-Greco technique that narrated the story of Christianity with cubes of glass set amid shimmering gold backgrounds (Figure 1.2).

Justinian, together with his wife Theodora, inaugurated a golden age of Byzantine art that was highly influential in the centuries that followed (Figure 1.3). The church of San Vitale (*c.* 526–547) in Ravenna became a model for Byzantine ecclesiastical architecture, and its exalted form of sacred adornment spread, for example, to the churches of seventh-century Venice and the twelfth-century Sicilian cities of Cefalù, Monreale, and Palermo. The gold-leaf decoration was also prominently manifested much later in the panel paintings of thirteenth- and fourteenth-century central Italy, which referred to the style as *maniera greca*. Byzantine art and learning continued to influence the culture of the Italian Peninsula through the Middle Ages and Renaissance periods. It advanced through the maritime trade of Venice, Genoa, and Pisa during the eleventh to thirteenth centuries, and then with the immigration of artists, artisans, and intellectuals from Constantinople (which was renamed Istanbul in 1453) to Italy after the fall of the eastern capital of the Roman Empire to the Ottomans in 1453. Intellectuals and artists in the Italian cities would draw on this rich classical heritage, which included Greek philosophy, science, and literature, and the

FIGURE 1.3 Church of San Vitale (546–547 CE). Mosaic of Empress Theodora. Ravenna, Italy. The mosaic of Empress Theodora and her retinue exhibits the carryover of imperial rule from the ancient to the early medieval period. With the royal halo around her head, the mosaic recognizes her as co-regent with her husband Justinian, who was not only the head of the Byzantine Empire but was also the leader of the Greek Orthodox Church, a term called *caesaropapism*. Theodora is surrounded by court dignitaries and her maidservants.

decorative mosaics, enamels, textiles, precious stones, painting, and gold work of Mediterranean crafts people.

The Lombards, who were also Germanic peoples, replaced the Ostrogoths and Byzantines on the peninsula's east coast in 568. They also proceeded to occupy most of the Po Plain and central and southern Italy as far south as Benevento. However, the inhabitants of the northeast mainland—elite lines from the ancient Roman imperial administration and military hierarchy that had peopled Treviso, Oderzo, Altino, Padua, and Aquileia—escaped the Lombard grip, constructing island settlements on raised, wet salt flats on the Adriatic. They were joined by clerics, carpenters, ironworkers, and glassmakers to populate a loose conglomeration of islands that became the famous city of Venice. The Byzantines walled themselves off from the Lombards, keeping much of the south, including Sicily and Sardinia, as well as a strip of Italy between Ravenna and Rome, but they did not have the resources to rule Venice. Through much of the eighth century, then, the peninsula was divided between the Byzantine Empire in the south and the Lombard kingdom and duchies in the north (see Map 1.2), while Venice established its political independence from Byzantium but retained both economic and cultural ties with Constantinople.

FOUNDATIONS: ANCIENT AND MEDIEVAL LEGACIES 25

Key:

■ a) territories that are Byzantine

■ b) territories that are Lombard

▨ c) territories that are in the Kingdom of the Franks

MAP 1.2 Byzantine and Lombard Italy.

Despite the political fragmentation that had followed the disintegration of Roman rule in the West, several universalist connections emerged during this time that would shape medieval and Renaissance culture in enduring ways. First, amid the chaotic migrations, Benedict of Nursia (*c.* 480 to *c.* 547 CE) established a system for monastic living called *The Rule* in the sixth century that was modeled on ascetic practices in Egypt and Gaul. His Benedictine *Rule* spread from Monte Cassino, just 80 miles south of Rome, to the rest of the European continent (Figure 1.4).

Living in relative isolation, the monks devoted much of their day to agricultural labor and prayer, and, importantly, to copying ancient literary

FIGURE 1.4 Benedictine Monastery. Monte Cassino, Italy.

works onto parchment that they stored in libraries. Female nunneries were also established during this time, with the support of donations of land, houses, and money from wealthy benefactors. Some nuns adopted the *Rule of Benedict*, devoting their time to prayer, religious studies, copying manuscripts, and helping the needy. Over the following 200 years the Benedictines preserved the ideas and literature of the ancient world, playing a significant role in establishing the critical foundations for subsequent intellectual developments. Secondly, also in the sixth century, Rome became the home of the Papacy, an institution that over the next 600 years would constitute the core of the Latin (now known as the Roman Catholic) Church, a major force in shaping society and culture in the western half of the old Roman Empire. In contrast, the Greek Orthodox Church in the eastern half of the Roman Empire, as well as parts of southern Italy, the Balkans, Eastern Europe, and Russia would be dominated by the eastern Emperor. However, in the west Emperor Theodosius (r. 379–395) had given the Latin Church privileged status during his reign. Bishops, considered the successors of the twelve apostles, provided an infrastructure for the religion. Initially the popes of Rome in an Italy dominated by Germanic peoples were confirmed by the Byzantine emperors and remained attached to the eastern half of the Roman Empire. Gradually, however, they began to build their own power base and launch the ideal of a universalist spiritual kingdom. Pope Gregory I (r. 590–604) laid the groundwork for a papacy in Rome that would claim unique spiritual authority inherited from Christ's apostle Peter and separate from Byzantium. From the seventh century Gregory's successors, however, were forced to rely on the military support of Carolingian Frankish kings from the north, who furnished them with protection from the raiding Lombards during the eighth century. In exchange for military safeguarding, however, the popes inadvertently helped create another rival institution with universalist claims of ruling the western half of the old Roman Empire, the Holy Roman Emperor, beginning with the crowning of Charlemagne in 800.

BOX 1.1 THE WESTERN ROMAN CATHOLIC CHURCH AND THE EASTERN GREEK ORTHODOX CHURCH

Christianity was legalized in the Roman Empire by the emperor Constantine the Great in 313. In 380 the emperor Theodosius made it the state religion. Gradually, Christianity split into its Latin, or Roman Catholic, and Greek Orthodox forms. Both sides contended that their origins harkened back to Jesus and the Apostles, with the Greek Orthodox prelates insisting they were the successors of the original Christians. In the east, the emperor was considered the head of both church and state, an arrangement called caesaropapism, while in the west commencing in the sixth century the pope became the head of Latin Christianity, but secular powers remained separate from the church. Each side appointed bishops to organize their churches. In the east the bishops were called patriarchs; of the five, four were Greek orthodox, while the patriarchy of Venice adapted Latin Christianity even though its services adhered to the eastern liturgy. In the west, bishops organized the dioceses of the church. Among the major differences between the Latin and the Greek Orthodox Churches were the designated spiritual leader, the endorsement of worshiping religious icons in the east, and the claims of the latter that people and not just priests and saints have the Holy Spirit within them. In 1054 the church split, an event known as the Great Schism. Both sides continued to claim that they were the successors of the original Christians. The Latin Church continued under papal leadership in Rome, claiming supremacy, an idea that the East resisted. The Greek Orthodox Church, which had spread to the Bulgarians, Serbians, and Russians, remained independent. With the fall of Constantinople in 1453, the Orthodox Church came under the rule of the Ottomans.

While Charlemagne and his successors were not centered in Italy, they claimed sovereignty over the lands they had conquered in Tuscany, the Romagna, Lombardy, and—temporarily—Venice, and superiority over church authority. It was a somewhat fictional sovereignty that still permitted the ascendency of local aristocracies with feudal loyalties but nonetheless contributed to further political fragmentation. The counts that Charlemagne installed were eventually replaced by dependents of the Germanic royal dynasties; thus there was no political continuity in the north with the Franks. Weak sovereignty, both Frankish and Germanic, also permitted the hegemony of bishops. Bishops, and their counterparts, the abbots, who led the great monastic estates, were the social and economic equals of the lay aristocracy. Together they formed the landowning elite of the post-Roman west. The church had furnished infrastructure on the peninsula during the period of invasions, with powerful archbishops and bishops providing government in the cities that had endured the transition from Roman rule. The bishops followed canon, or church law in their dioceses, a Roman term meaning the subdivision of a province. They organized communities, trained priests to bring the word of Christ, and provided for the needy. They also commissioned the building of walls, fortified towers, and cathedrals, and fostered Christian education with the elevation of martyrs and saints that could bring comfort to people in times of trouble. Bishops collected tolls and public revenues and administered courts of justice. The church thus brought spiritual and cultural continuity as well as administrative organization to what was a chaotic world of competing sovereignties. It availed of considerable powers until the early fourteenth century.

The arrival of the Muslims in the ninth-century mainland south and Sicily created an additional and important cultural zone on the Italian Peninsula. During the previous two centuries Muslim peoples, following the Abrahamic religion espoused in the Qur'an, had managed to shatter the Christian dominance of the Mediterranean. They prevailed through much of the south and eastern basin, seizing many rich Byzantine areas. By 750 CE the Muslims[1]) had established an empire that stretched from Portugal and Spain through North Africa and Arabia to India. They became the cultural heirs of the great civilizations of Greece and Rome, Persia, India, and China, assimilating the older traditions in addition to developing their own. They adapted Greco-Roman architecture to their own styles; absorbed Averroës' (Ibn Rusud) commentaries on Plato and Aristotle; expanded on the ancient medical doctrines of Galen and other Greek natural philosophers as well as those of the Persian physician al-Razi; learned from Indian and Chinese sources; and strove to perfect the conclusions of the second-century Egyptian astronomer Ptolemy. Muslim mathematicians borrowed geometry and trigonometry from Greece and Algebra from the Hindus. They adopted "Arabic" numerals, nine numbers plus zero, from Indian mathematicians. Islamic civilization, which owed a large debt to Greek, Indian, and Chinese traditions, was far more advanced than Western Europe. Its thinkers availed of rich libraries in Baghdad, Aleppo, Shiraz, Cairo, Alexandria, and Cordoba that far exceeded the collections in European monasteries. They established academies of Greek philosophy, medicine, mathematics, history, and poetry and built hospitals well before the Europeans. Thus the arrival of the Muslims in southern Italy and Sicily, and the southern regions of Spain and France for that matter, enriched the knowledge of the peoples of the western Mediterranean. Their achievements, particularly in science and medicine, would eventually feed into Italian Renaissance culture.

Much of Sicily was absorbed by the Muslims by 900, while other mainland cities in the Italian south witnessed periodic raids. The Muslims brought in skilled Jewish crafts people, including Berbers from Morocco, who became acclaimed weavers in Syracuse, and goldsmiths known for the gold wire they produced for filigree jewelry. Artisans became primary agents of cultural transfer, particularly in the exportation of Islamic models in textiles. Silk weaving, for example, was exported from Palermo to Lucca. The Muslims also transformed the agricultural landscape and diet of Sicily, cultivating rice, cotton, pistachios, sugarcane, apricots, and peaches. They established a perfume industry using jasmine and roses and planted groves of mulberry to feed the silkworms that were the basis of the silk industry. Tenth-century Palermo became a center of scholarship in science and the arts, one that rivaled Cordoba and Cairo. It is important to add that the Muslims were tolerant of the Jews, who by this time had populated several cities in Sicily, the mainland south of Italy, as well as Rome and Milan. Their intellectual contributions, particularly in translating manuscripts from the Arabic into Latin, as well as their services in medicine and finance were of critical importance.

Importantly, the arrival of these advanced peoples to Sicily encouraged cross-cultural fertilization throughout the peninsula, leaving a permanent imprint on the intellectual and artistic development of Italy. The great commercial towns that were emerging in the ninth and tenth centuries— Venice, Bari, Amalfi, Salerno, Naples, Gaeta, Pisa, and Genoa—traded profitably with the Muslims, as well as with Byzantines, Lombards, and Germans, and the merchants of Barcelona. Islamic influence is still notable in the Cathedral of San Matteo in Salerno (1076–84), the Cloister of Paradise in Amalfi (1266–8), and the Duomo of Pisa (thirteenth century) (Figure 1.5). It is also evident in some of the decorative arts, such as the eleventh-century tin-glazed painted bowls set into church façades and towers and the fourteenth-century luxury cloths produced in Venice, Lucca, and Genoa, textiles that also found their way into early Renaissance paintings.

The founding in the late ninth and tenth centuries of the medical school in Salerno benefitted highly from Muslim traditions. During the tenth century it availed of the surgical work of Abu al-Qasim (Abulcasis), a physician who conducted the earliest dissections of human beings. In the following century Constantinus Africanus (d. 1099?), a Muslim physician from North Africa, came to work in the Salerno medical school. Toward

FIGURE 1.5 Cathedral of Santa Maria Assunta. Pisa, Italy. The church (begun 1063), an example of the Pisan Romanesque, is a combination of eclectic styles reflecting Byzantine, Islamic, and Lombard influences that draw upon the international merchant experience.

the end of his life he converted to Christianity, became a Benedictine monk, and joined the abbey of Monte Cassino. There he translated the works of great Muslim physicians, including Razes, Ibn Imran, Ibn Suleiman, and Ibn al-Jazzar. Constantinus's compilations sparked the revival of medical inquiry in Europe. They became the continent's textbooks of medicine until the seventeenth century. Salerno also received these eleventh-century texts, and its physicians developed a culture of prevention that drew upon the translations of the Hippocratic core of writings, Galen, and Dioscorides as well as Muslim medical practices that were known throughout Sicily and North Africa. Salerno thus housed an important synthesis of both Greek and Muslim medical traditions, which were taught to both male and female physicians, and by the eleventh century were attracting students from all over Europe, Asia, and Africa (see Chapter 3).

While the tenth century began with Byzantines and Muslims in the south and Lombard Italians in the north, as well as a plethora of independent aristocracies, toward the end of the century, the kings of Germany, beginning with the Ottonians in 962, occupied the entire northern plain, with the exception of Venice, as well as both coasts in central Italy. (Map 1.3 shows the political complexity of the Italian peninsula by the year 1000.) Their sway on the mainland stopped with the papal territories around Rome, nor would they net the independent territories of Salerno and Benevento in the south. The

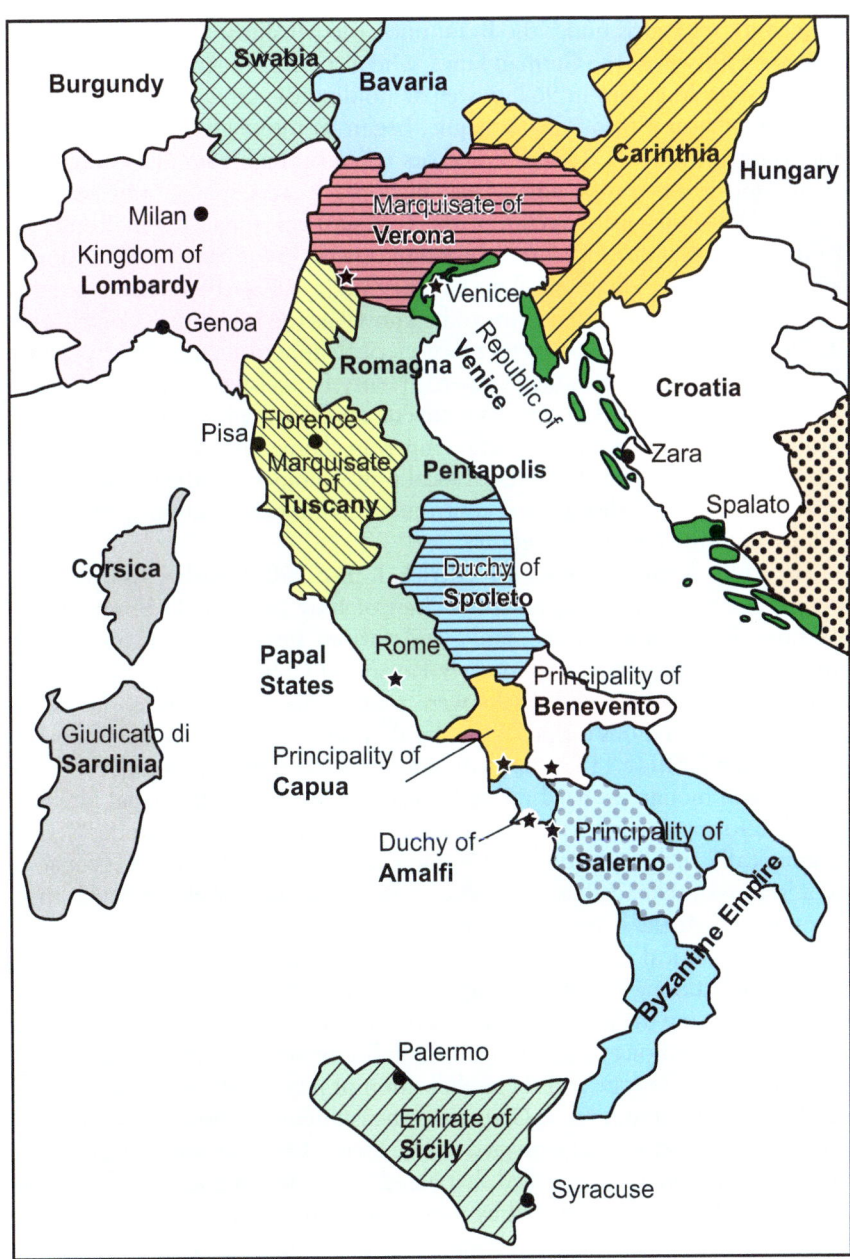

MAP 1.3 Italy in the Year 1000.

deep south remained under the Byzantines, the Muslims, and from 1070 the Normans. However, the German kings, who also proclaimed themselves kings of the Italian kingdom in 962 as well as holding the crown of Holy Roman emperor inherited from Charlemagne, began to intervene in papal politics. Importantly, the Holy Roman Emperors relied on highly literate churchmen to administer their domains. Thus bishops, legates, papal ambassadors, and tax collectors were agents of the ecclesiastical apparatus in Rome, an arrangement that produced a confusion of powers in the center and the north, from Benevento to Piedmont. Pope Gregory VII (r. 1073–1085) challenged this arrangement, a conflict that came to be known as the Investiture Controversy (1076–1122), by attempting to place clerical appointments entirely under the papacy. The Hohenstaufen emperor Henry IV resisted the pope's designs, making his own claims to universal sovereignty. Throughout the twelfth and thirteenth centuries both popes and emperors claimed university sovereignty. The conflict divided the loyalties of local power holders on the peninsula and created a crisis of authority that contributed to the permanent fragmentation of Italy until the nineteenth century.

The Holy Roman Emperor Frederick I, also called Barbarossa, made a second bid to conquer the northern cities of Italy between 1154 and 1158, claiming their customs, tolls, mints, and various jurisdictions at the Diet of Roncaglia. While some areas, namely Pavia and Cremona, were disposed to Frederick, and Bolognese lawyers were touting his absolute rule, the urban communal associations formed a Lombard League in 1167 with the support of Pope Alexander III (r. 1159–1181) in order to hold on to their autonomy. Thus the German monarchs faced multiple obstacles, including pro-papal factions, church reformers, recalcitrant landowning elites (termed "feudatories"), and economically energized cities. Italy's major centers resisted German incursions in a series of exhausting wars that concluded with their winning their autonomy with the Treaty of Constance in 1183. Although the communes won their political and financial independence, the treaty did not end the factionalism among Guelf (pro-papal) and Ghibelline (pro-imperial) forces. Moreover, during the first half of the thirteenth century Frederick I's successor, Frederick II, tried once again to claim Lombardy, sparking the reconstitution of the Lombard League and the mobilization of papal resistance. Fredrick II's death in 1250 put an end to German Hohenstaufen ambitions. The rich and powerful Italian cities had managed to free themselves from sovereign control, an important political watershed that aided in the development of new urban societies and cultures sponsored by non-noble, commercial elites.

During the last half of the eleventh century, while the cities in the north were gaining their independence, the Normans arrived in southern Italy and Sicily, welding into a Catholic kingdom a diverse people of Muslims, Italians, Greeks, Jews, and Lombards who followed different laws and spoke different languages. Their campaign was an important aspect of the extension of Latin Christendom that was gradually unfolding in al-Andalus (the Muslim portion of Iberia) with the Catholic conquest of Muslim territories and with the

European establishment of Crusader states in the Balkans and the Levant. At this point western Europeans were less culturally advanced than the peoples of the Byzantine and Islamic worlds, and thus these religious, intellectual, and cultural encounters were extremely important to their development. When King Alfonso VI took Toledo in 1085, for example, the city became a crucial contact point between Islamic and Christian culture through the collaboration of Christian and Jewish scholars who translated scientific and philosophical treatises from Arabic into Latin. Like Toledo, Palermo also became a significant source of translations from Arabic and Greek into Latin. As an important center of cultural exchange among Latin, Byzantine, and Muslims traditions, it helped establish the cornerstones of subsequent intellectual achievements, including university curriculum in the thirteenth century.

In southern Italy the Normans respected the Islamic laws of Muslims, the customs of the numerous Jewish communities, and Greek orthodox religious rites. They combined their own feudal law with Byzantine, Muslim, and Lombard forms of government, establishing a multicultural meritocratic bureaucracy. The Norman Kingdom of Sicily became perhaps the strongest state in Italy. Its economy by no means matched those of the burgeoning northern Italian cities but it sponsored significant artistic and intellectual activities based upon Greco-Roman, Byzantine, and Arabic literature. The Greek texts of Plato, Aristotle, and Ptolemy were translated. At Monreale and Palermo magnificent edifices adorned with Byzantine mosaics akin to those of the Basilica San Marco in Venice sprung up. The Normans also introduced the architectural language of the French Romanesque, a style also characteristic of Pisa. Norman rule astonished the great medieval poet Dante (c. 1265–1321) enough to put the conquering warrior Robert Guiscard in his *Paradiso*, the first book of the celebrated *Divine Comedy*.

The Hoenstaufen dynasty in southern Italy that succeeded the Normans in 1194 continued to foster multiculturalism, and in the chapters to come we shall see that in the following centuries the south continued to have a place in Italian Renaissance history, politically, economically, and culturally. Albeit under royal dynasties, princes, and barons, important cultural patronage took place in southern Italy, with the commission of manuscripts, with classical education, with the study of civil law and medicine, and with humanistic culture. The artist Giotto (c. 1266/76?–1337) and the pre-humanist writers Petrarch (1304–1374) and Boccaccio (1313–1375) all spent some time there, in Naples, the region's largest city.

Conclusion

This chapter has laid out the dramatically complex political history of a peninsula whose constant subjection to invasion as well as migration produced a civilization with multicultural roots. In the ancient period the

Romans managed to subjugate Italy's indigenous tribes and various new settlers, including a large Jewish population in Rome, into an overarching political structure and to establish a common, Greco-Roman cultural lexicon. The disintegration of Roman rule in the west in the fifth century CE brought in a variety of Germanic tribes, Byzantine rulers tied to Constantinople, and Muslim settlers over the next 600 years. The Italian boot then devolved into multiple sovereignties, divided among Lombard and Frankish magnates, German kings, and various Christian bishops who ruled over cathedral towns with episcopal courts. As a result, the foundations of Renaissance culture became more complex.

While the central and northern Italian cities featured in the traditional master narrative about the Renaissance adhered primarily to a Latinate culture, with a self-conscious examination of Greco-Roman monuments and sculpture, they also paid attention to Byzantine and Islamic styles in southern Italy and the eastern Mediterranean and to the Romanesque and Gothic styles that adorned European buildings to their north. Moreover, their intellectuals benefitted from Greek, Hebrew, and Muslim traditions and innovations as well as from the legal traditions of the Roman and post-Roman world. Likewise, artisans absorbed styles and techniques in the decorative arts from a wide, geographical area that stretched from the Iberian Peninsula across the Mediterranean to North Africa and from southwest Asia along the Silk Road to China. These included textile designs deriving from Islamic models or from fourteenth-century Tatar production in Asia, Persia, and Syria; ceramic designs drawn from Islamic Spain; and the importation of Chinese porcelain. Thus, while this history of the Renaissance will remain grounded in Italian developments in the following chapters, it is important at the same time to keep in mind that the cultural foundations of the peninsula were fundamentally connected to the wider European and Mediterranean world.

Think Critically

1. How did ancient Greco-Roman cultural foundations leave enduring marks in the visual arts, education, and political ideology during the Middle Ages and Renaissance?
2. What aspects of Roman culture did the Germanic tribes preserve? Christian culture?
3. How did the arrival of the Muslims in southern Italy impact Italian intellectual and cultural development?
4. Why was monastic life an important unit of social and cultural organization?
5. What was the role of the Latin Church in medieval Italy's social, political, and economic development?

Further Exploration

1. What visual remains of Roman town planning can you identify in cities such as Ostia Antica or Verona? Nimes and Orange in France? Ephesus in Turkey?
2. What were the ways in which Justinian's reign was both Roman and Christian?
3. Why was the *Rule of St. Benedict*, and joining a monastic order, attractive to some men and women?
4. What aspects of the Cathedral of Santa Maria Assunta of Pisa (Figure 1.5) exhibit Islamic influence? Byzantine? Romanesque? Gothic?
5. What were the most important translations from Arabic into Latin emanating from Toledo and Palermo?

Note

1 These were not just Arabs, but also included other ethnic groups such as Berbers, Turkic peoples, and Persians of the Muslim faith.

Further Reading

Abulafia, David. *Frederick II: A Medieval Emperor*. London: Penguin Press, 1988. A revisionist biography of Frederick II that assesses the monarch's cultural, religious, and politics ambitions.
Astarita, Tommaso. *Between Salt Water and Holy Water: A History of Southern Italy*. New York: Norton, 2005. A history of southern Italy from the Normans and Angevins, through Spanish and Bourbon rule, to the unification of Italy in 1860.
Duggan, Christopher. *A Concise History of Italy*. Cambridge, UK: Cambridge University Press, 1994. A brief history of the peninsula from the collapse of the Roman Empire to the twentieth century.
Holmes, George. *The Oxford Illustrated History of Italy*. Oxford, UK: Oxford University Press, 1997. A collection of essays covering the history of the peninsula from the Roman Empire to the twentieth century.
Mack, Rosamond. *Bazaar to Piazza. Islamic Trade and Italian Art, 1300–1600*. Berkeley: University of California Press, 2002. A study of the impact of Mediterranean trade in luxury goods on Italian aesthetics and production.
O'Connell, Monique, and Eric R. Dursteler. *The Mediterranean World. From the Fall of Rome to the Rise of Napoleon*. Baltimore, MD: Johns Hopkins University Press, 2016. A superb study of the Mediterranean's economic, cultural, and political interactions from 500 CE to 1798.

2

Urban Revitalization: 1000–1350

Timeline

900s	End of invasions from Asia, northern Europe, and North Africa
999–1039	Normans in southern Italy and Sicily
1061	Norman conquest of Sicily under Robert and Roger Hauteville begins
1072	Palermo made capital of the Norman Kingdom of Sicily
1076	Pope Gregory claims right to invest bishops; outbreak of Investiture Conflict
c. 1080–140	Communes form in central and northern Italy
1082	Venice obtains trade privileges with Constantinople in return for naval support against the Normans
1095	Pope Urban II calls the First Crusade to liberate Jerusalem from the Seljuq Turks
c. 1097–9	Genoese and Pisan fleets support the crusaders in the Levant
1122	Concordat of Worms temporarily settles the Investiture Conflict
1127	Norman King Roger II unites southern Italy and Sicily
1138	Florence initiates communal government
1143	Commune of Rome formed
1145–9	Second Crusade
1155	Frederick I (Hohenstaufen) crowned Holy Roman Emperor
1154; 1158	Diet of Roncaglia
1160–260	Tower Societies in Italy. Magnate rule
1167	Formation of First Lombard League against Frederick Barbarossa

1176	The Lombard League of Italian communes defeats Emperor Frederick Barbarossa at Legnano
1183	Peace of Constance; Frederick I concedes jurisdiction of Lombard League cities
1189–92	Third Crusade
1190	Death of Frederick Barbarossa on Crusade; succession of Henry VI (1191), who conquers Naples and Sicily (1194) by inheritance right of his wife Constance
1197	Death of Henry VI; Frederick II king of Sicily, Germany, and Italy; contested by Swabian dynasty to 1208
1198	Innocent III Pope rules papal state in central Italy to 1216
1202–4	Fourth Crusade. Venice raids Constantinople
1220	Frederick II takes the throne in southern Italy and Sicily
1226	Second Lombard League in northern Italy challenges Emperor Frederick II
1237	Frederick II defeats the Second Lombard League at Battle of Cortenuova
1250	Death of Emperor Frederick II. End of Hohenstaufen ambitions in Italy
1250	Conrad IV (Hohenstaufen) succeeds Frederick II as king of Sicily
1250	Guilds take control of Florence. Pro-papal government
1252	Gold genovins and florins coined
1254	Conradin (Hohenstaufen) succeeds Conrad IV as king of Sicily
1258	Manfred (Hohenstaufen) succeeds Conradin as king of Sicily
1259	Mastino I della Scala is governor of Verona; lord in 1262
1260	Popular government in Florence falls to pro-imperial factions
1262	Ottone Visconti is archbishop of Milan
1264	Obizzo d'Este II rules Ferrara
1265	Birth of Dante Alighieri in Florence
1266	Pope Clement IV (r. 1265–1268) invites Charles of Anjou to replace Hohenstaufen dynasty in southern Italy and Sicily
1268	Angevins replace the Hohenstaufen dynasty in Sicily (to 1282) and Naples (to 1442); capital of the kingdom transferred from Palermo to Naples
1268	Popular rule restored in Florence
1277–8	First Genoese galleys sent to Flanders and England

1277	Archbishop Ottone Visconti becomes Milan's ruler
1282	Sicilian Vespers. The Angevins expelled from Sicily and replaced by Aragonese Pedro III
1286	Charles II of Anjou succeeds Charles I as king of Naples
1293	Ordinances of Justice regulate magnates under popular rule in Florence
1296	Florence cathedral (Santa Maria del Fiore) begun
1297	Venice makes its Grand Council hereditary; further restrictions are implemented in 1323
1302	Exile of Dante
1304	Petrarch born
c. 1305	Giotto completes frescoes in Arena Chapel in Padua
c. 1308–21	Dante writes the *Divine Comedy*
1309	Robert the Wise (of Anjou) becomes king of Naples
1309	Pope Clement VII transfers from Rome to Avignon France, where popes reigned until 1376
1310	Council of Ten in Venice is formed
1313	Boccaccio is born
1318	Padua ruled by Jacopo I da Carrara (to 1405)
1324	Marsilius of Padua writes *Defensor pacis* advocating subordination of church to state
1328	Venice establishes Book of Gold, listing the ruling family dynasties
1328	Ludovico Gonzaga rules Mantua; found dynasty that lasts 300 years
1341	Petrarch crowned poet laureate in Rome
c. 1342–5	Collapse of Bardi and Peruzzi banks
1342	French Walter of Brienne usurps Florence; ousted in 1343
1343	Joanna I of Naples succeeds Robert the Wise as queen of Naples
1348	Bubonic plague strikes Italy
c. 1350	Boccaccio writes *The Decameron*

FIGURE 2.1 Ambrogio Lorenzetti (1290–1348). *Effects of Good Government* (1338–1339). Fresco panel. Public Palace, Siena, Italy. Lorenzetti's vibrant depiction of urban life was a reminder to magistrates to govern with wisdom in order to ensure the peace and wealth of the city, in this case Siena. The artist also painted in fresco form an allegory of bad government. See also the discussion of this painting in Chapter 3.

Demographic Growth and Agrarian Change in Central and Northern Italy

The revival of cities, townspeople, merchants, and crafts was the result of a confluence of demographic and economic developments that ensued after the ninth and tenth-century Germanic, Muslim, and Byzantine invasions ended. A period of stabilization followed, and with it three centuries of demographic expansion that increased the availability of labor, contributed in some areas to the breakup of feudal land tenure, stimulated economic growth in the countryside, and created the basis for a money economy. Improved climate and agrarian technology helped fuel the demographic growth by increasing the food supply and raising the standard of living. A surplus of agricultural products permitted economic diversification, including the expansion of textile manufactures and the construction industry. The abundance of land in proportion to the relatively sparse population was key to this expansion, for the basis of the economy was fundamentally agrarian, depending on the local and regional exchange of grain, oil, wine, salt, foodstuffs, and textiles. Town inhabitants were committed to agrarian production, both as landowners and because their urban centers made massive demands on the rural economy to supply the commodities they consumed and marketed.

Among the developments outlined earlier, perhaps the two most important factors contributing to urbanization were the rise in population, which doubled on the Italian Peninsula between the tenth and the fourteenth centuries, and improvements in agricultural technology. The total population of the Italian Peninsula rose to between seven and nine million people. Largely because of rural emigration, smaller towns and cities became larger. Towns rose from 5,000 or 6,000 people to 30,000. Bologna and Palermo reached approximately 50,000 souls, Florence to around 90,000, and Venice, Milan, and Genoa to as many as 100,000.[1]

The abatement of foreign incursions no doubt also assisted in accelerating the birth rate, but the demographic expansion was also the result of higher fertility, owing at least in part to an improved diet, better nutrition, and an increased food supply. The introduction of the heavy moldboard plow sometime in the seventh century, credited to the Slavs, improved labor efficiency, for this apparatus, which harnessed two oxen or horses, could do the work of several humans. The more effective means of turning the soil increased yields and permitted the cultivation of lands that had until then been uncultivable with simple scratch plows or wooden hoes. Laborers in the peninsula's valleys and northern plain began extensive land irrigation, building canals and dikes, and applying new agricultural technology that included the three-field system of crop rotation. One field was allowed to rest, another was planted with grain, and a third grew pulses, peas, or beans, putting nitrogen back into the soil. Crop rotation prevented soil exhaustion and gave peasants a better diet. Pulses, lentils, peas, beans, and chickpeas,

FIGURE 2.2 *Ruralia Commoda*. Agricultural calendar from a manuscript written by Pietro de' Crescenzi between 1304 and 1309, *c.* 1470–1475. Found in the Collection of Musée Condé, Chantilly. Crescenzi's *Ruralia commoda* was one of the most widely read works on agriculture, animal husbandry, and horticulture during the fourteenth to sixteenth centuries. It was first put into print in 1471 and went through several editions.

importantly, were all sources of inexpensive protein that improved what was otherwise a poor person's diet of bread and gruel or, in times of famine, bulbs and roots. Agricultural laborers also assimilated ways of harnessing power. This included the water mill, which was not only used for agriculture but also to full cloth, produce iron, and saw wood; nailed horseshoes, known to the Celts prior to the Roman conquests, which provided an effective means of increasing horse power; and the tandem harness, which originated in China and diffused into Europe during the ninth century. New breeds of horses were imported from the Islamic world and began to substitute for the ox. Thus animals significantly replaced human labor, increasing energy for cultivation.

Population growth during the eleventh century changed both property relations and the division of labor. Not as many agricultural laborers were

FIGURE 2.3 Nanni di Banco (c. 1385–1421). *Stonemasons at Work*. Relief under the tabernacle of the Guild of Stone and Wood Masters. Fourteenth century. Chiesa di Orsanmichele, Florence, Italy.

needed in the fields, permitting some to specialize in crafts (Figure 2.3). Landlords allowed those who were willing to undertake the arduous work of cutting down forests, draining marshland, and irrigating arid land to leave their manors to establish new settlements, which they controlled and taxed through charters. Serfs in much of Tuscany and Lombardy bought off compulsory labor and services for more flexible tenancies. Gradually throughout the peninsula's valleys and northern plain the manorial system wore away, money payments were substituted for services and rent in land, and funds were invested in agriculture. Importantly for our understanding of urban revitalization, the surplus of labor repopulated the long-dormant Roman towns and encouraged the integration of the countryside with new settlements along the seacoasts, fords, mountain passes, rivers, and old Roman roads. The most urbanized areas lay beneath the Alps on the northern plain with its abundance of rivers and tributaries and along the Apennines in north-central Italy. The former was home to Torino, Pavia, Milan, Piacenza, Crema, Brescia, and Mantua as well as the Veneto cities of Verona, Vicenza, Treviso, and Padua. The latter included the multiple towns in the regions of Emilia, Tuscany, and Umbria (Map 2.1).

The economies of town and countryside were vitally linked, for the investment in land improvement was an essential feature of urban life.

MAP 2.1 The Major Italian Communes (*c.* 1200).

Many landowners lived in towns. Typically they had moved from the countryside to exercise their activities as notaries, merchants, or some other profession, and while they achieved prominence in their towns and cities, rising in status, they remained devoted to agrarian enterprise. Their urban centers depended on their rural hinterlands for food, fuel, labor, building materials, investment outlets, and markets. Their textile industries depended on rural, labor, primarily from women, in what later came to be termed the domestic system of manufacture. Cities and towns also banked heavily on taxing rural inhabitants, relying on them for seasonal labor, and at times to staff their armies and/or fleets. Thus the rise in population was beneficial to growing urban centers.

Urban Economies

The urban economies of the Italian Peninsula varied enormously. At one end of the scale were small, agrarian-based economies whose profits depended on marketing grains, meat, and fish. In the Romagna, for example, townspeople labored in the countryside, returning to their walled urban nuclei at night. Medium-sized towns throughout the Po Valley, ruled by urbanized landowners and business people, also depended on their local hinterlands for agricultural labor and products. Landowners reinvested some of the gains they made in agriculture and trade into moneylending. Larger centers like Milan, in contrast to the small and medium towns, were able to market foodstuffs and handicrafts in a much larger sphere, stretching across the Po plain and northward over the Alps. The Lombard capital also commanded profitable metallurgical and woolen industries. At the top of the scale of economic power were the great maritime cities of Venice, Genoa, and Pisa, and the industrial and financial city of Florence, the former benefitting from international networks of colonies and international trade; the latter enjoying both regional commercial networks, healthy textile industries, trade in the countryside, and a banking system that extended from Italy to all of northern Europe. Even among the large economies, however, there were variations. Pisa, able to take advantage of both the rich countryside and the islands of Sardinia and Elba for the supply of agriculture and raw materials, retreated from maritime competition in the thirteenth century to concentrate more on industrial development. Genoa, in contrast, compressed between the Apennines and the Mediterranean harbor, was unable to develop a strong hinterland and thus focused on maritime ventures. Venice exploited her natural resources of salt and fish, but like Genoa was mostly oriented toward the sea in order to insure adequate food supplies, raw materials, western metals, and manufactures.

BOX 2.1 THE VENETIAN ARSENAL

Venetian watercraft were owned by the state, which founded one of medieval Europe's earliest industrial enterprises, the arsenal (from the Arabic word signifying "house of manufacture") in 1104. Teams of carpenters, sawyers, caulkers, cordage, and sailmakers worked quickly to produce a variety of vessels. Among them was the galley, a boat propelled by oarsmen whose short-distant travels down the Adriatic generated great wealth for the city. Another type of watercraft was the round ship, called a cog, which sailed in groups of eight to eleven. By the fourteenth century the arsenal was also producing war galleys, a naval enterprise that grew over the following four centuries in tandem with the state's expanding seaborne empire. What began as a dockyard in the twelfth century grew to be a large industrial complex that employed a massive number of people.

While the occupation of oarsman was well-regarded during the thirteenth century, later it became more difficult for the state to recruit men from Venice. Greeks and Dalmatians began to fill the ranks of these associations of seamen, but by the sixteenth century Venice was also condemning criminals to obligatory service. Among the thousands of workers who brought in wood for Venice's privately owned forests on the mainland, those who built wooden frames, manufactured rope, caulked wood, made oars, smithed, made casks and barrels, and manufactured rigging and nautical supplies were women who cut, sewed, and repaired canvas. Venice also had its own foundry for the manufacture of arms. The arsenal workers, called *arsenalotti*, were highly regarded by the state. They lived on site at the arsenal and enjoyed special recognition among the city's various crafts.

Further reading: Davis, Robert C. *Shipbuilders of the Venetian Arsenal: Workers and Workplace in the Preindustrial City*. Baltimore: Johns Hopkins University Press, 1991.

The seacoast towns began developing economic strength as early as the mid-tenth century, benefitting from their central place in the Mediterranean between East and West. They had managed to maintain vibrant urban cultures even during the chaotic period of invasions through their trade with Constantinople and the port cities of Palestine, Syria, and Egypt. Throughout the ninth to eleventh centuries Jewish merchants had linked western Christendom with the civilizations of Islam and Byzantium. The port towns also helped introduce Islamic accounting techniques, commercial contracts, and business methods. In the south of Italy, Bari and Amalfi were among the first ports to thrive, availing themselves of contacts with Byzantium, the Levant, Egypt, Spain, and the Barbary Coast, but their merchant ventures

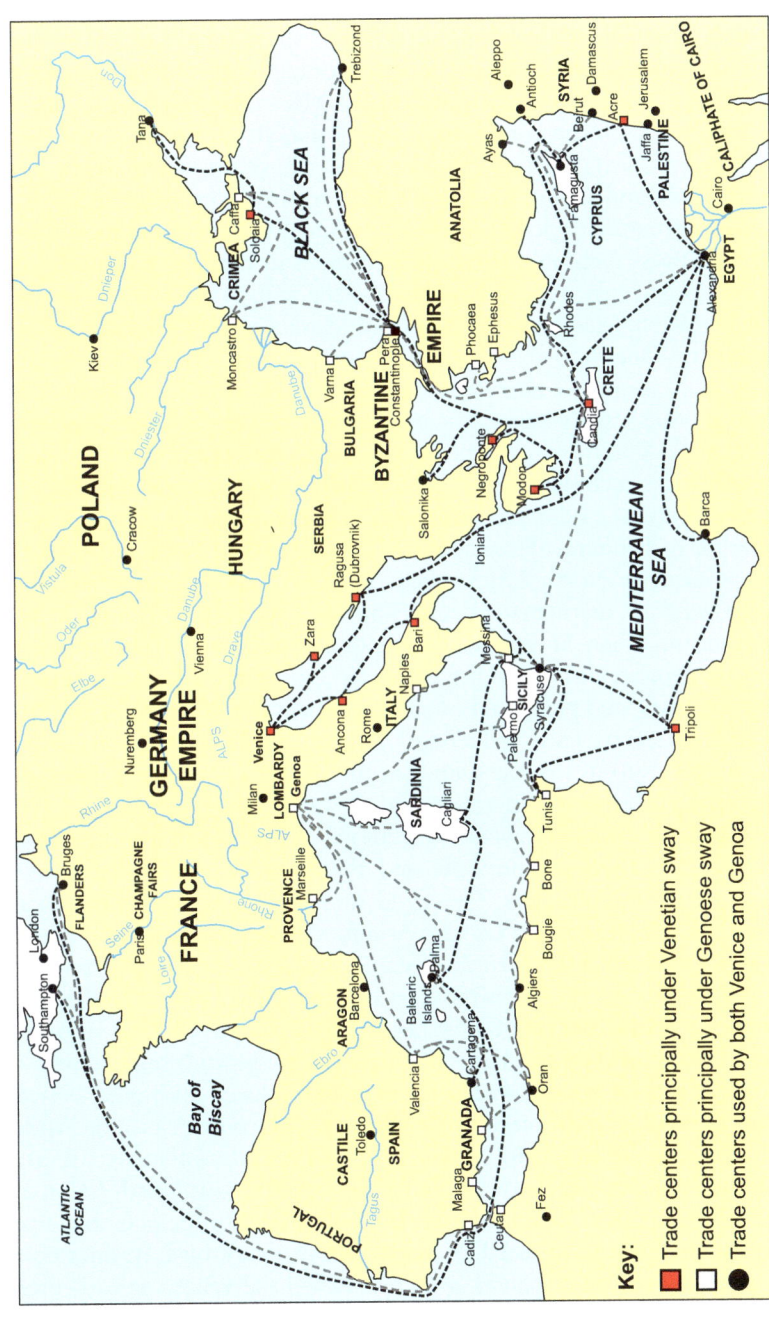

MAP 2.2 Genoese and Venetian Trade Routes.

were short-lived compared to Venice, Genoa, and Pisa. The latter three began to drive the fragmented Muslim world from the western Mediterranean, and by the time of the First Crusade in 1095 their ships could sail safely all the way to Palestine (see Map 2.2). The Norman conquest of Sicily completed the work of giving Christians control of the Mediterranean. Genoa, Venice, and Pisa, along with the Kingdom of Catalonia, also traded heavily on the North African coast, taking wool, leatherwork, grain, dried fruits, ivory, slaves, and gold and selling wool and cotton textiles, wine, spices, and arms.

The Italian mariners' long-distance travel to Muslim entrepôts in North Africa, Southwest Asia, and Persia helped them to develop a sophistication in navigation by replacing the bowl-and-needle with the nautical compass, a Chinese invention. Merchants learned from Muslim institutional and business arrangements. One was the eleventh-century *commenda*, a type of stock exchange that permitted anyone with liquid funds to invest in commercial ventures; another was the thirteenth-century joint partnership, where investors pooled capital. A number of important business techniques were developed during this time, including fairs, manuals of commerce, new techniques of accounting, bills of exchange, insurance, and monetization. Of note is the contribution of Leonardo Fibonacci (1170–c. 1240/50), a scholar who grew up in a port city in North Africa where his father was a commercial consul. Fibonacci studied mathematics, traveling the wider Greek and Muslim Mediterranean. When he returned to Italy, he authored several important treatises on geometry and number theory. In one of the most important, he explained the base-ten positional numerical system that Muslims had learned in India. Fibonacci was also influential in the shift in European practice from Roman numerals to Arabic ones, and for the system invented earlier in India that incorporated positional notation and the "zero."

Normans, Genoese, and Venetians colonized the Mediterranean world, reaching as far as Constantinople and the Black Sea region, important points of access to Jaffa, Tana, Trebizond, and the routes to both Russia and the Danube to the north and Greater Asia to the east. Their crusades during the eleventh to thirteenth centuries became an important stimulus to Italian economic growth, for the maritime powers were called upon to be the agents and carriers for the armies of European Christians traveling to reconquer the Holy Land and establish Crusader states in the Levant. Importantly, the Venetians and the Genoese would forge broad links of exchange, between northwest Europe and the preexisting Islamic trading networks in the Middle East that spread westward to North Africa, Morocco, Marseille, Gibraltar, and southern Spain and eastward to Persia, Afghanistan, North India, and Western China. Following Pope Urban's summons to European Christians to reconquer the Holy Land in 1095, Venice began to establish trading points on the Aegean and in Jaffa and Haifa. By 1123–4 the Venetians had entered the Muslim territories of Ascalon, Acre, and Tyre, where they loaded their galleys with gold, silver, and spices. They were able to secure major trade routes between Europe and Greater Asia, accumulating great wealth in antiquities, relics, and slaves. Like Venice, Genoa also linked the economy of Europe with Asia until at least 1261. Both cities depended on the Mongolian unification of central Asia and Mongol conquests in China to profit from their bases in Constantinople, where they collected Asian wares to market in Europe. Venice and Genoa also joined the central caravan routes from Palestine and Baghdad to the Persian Gulf and the Indian Ocean. From the East they imported spices, sugar, silk, cotton, textiles, dyewoods, wine, and art, exporting iron, wood, hides, furs, linen, cloth, and slaves in exchange. Both cities also established bases in Acre, an international community of Muslim merchants, Christian Arabs, Armenians, Jews, and Greeks. There they met the caravans coming from Mecca and Damascus with bales of eastern drugs and spices. They also profited from trade in Alexandria, Cairo, and Mamluk Egypt via the Red Sea to the Indian Ocean. Their travels east exposed them to a variety of cultures: that of the Persians and Muslims around the western side of the Indian Ocean on one hand and that of the Hindus and Buddhists farther east, between Java and China. Genoa also held important connections in Western Europe. The city obtained commercial privileges and residential quarters in Seville in 1251, which became a springboard into the Atlantic Ocean. From there the Genoese competed with Catalonia, Castile, and Portugal for Northern African markets in textiles, gold, iron, and other commodities. In the fifteenth century they would enter the slave and sugar markets in Madeira and the Canaries and help finance the voyages to the Americas.

BOX 2.2 MARCO POLO AND THE POLO BROTHERS

Venetians, as well as Europeans in general, learned a great deal about the cultures and ways of life of the peoples of Greater Asia from the travels of the Polo brothers. Niccolò and Matteo Polo began their business activities in Constantinople in 1261, where they traded a variety of products coming from Anatolia (now Turkey) and the Black Sea. They lived with the Mongols for a period of time and then moved across the Silk Road to China. In 1269 they returned to Venice and Niccolò's son, Marco, joined them on their subsequent journeys to China, via Syria and Tabriz. The three merchant travelers reached the Great Khan in China in 1275. Marco then lived among the Chinese for the next seventeen years. His return journey to Venice between 1292 and 1295 brought him to the west coast of India and the Persian Gulf. A few years later he chronicled his observations about Chinese production, taxation, and administration as well as the economic potential of the Spice islands, which included sugar, silk, and cotton, for Venice. Marco Polo's life story remains among the great travel literature of all times.

Further reading: Polo, Marco. *The Travels of Marco Polo*. Ronald Latham, translator. London: Penguin Classics, 1958.

The revival of Italian international trade enlarged the scope of economic, material, and cultural exchange both in Europe and afar. Besides north-central Italy, the southern region of the Low Countries, Castile, the Rhineland, and the towns of the Northern Hansa were also leading areas of economic and urban growth during the eleventh to thirteenth centuries. A number of trading channels developed in these areas, including the Champagne Fairs in northern France and the textile industries in Flanders, which were both linked to one another and to north-central Italy through subsystems. New products were sold in the Rialto market in Venice as well as at the Champagne fairs in the north of France. A number of Italian cities—Genoa, Milan, Piacenza, Bologna, and later Florence and Venice—established trading connections with the Low Countries and England, centers of the cloth trade. On the Italian mainland, the availability of eastern goods to market throughout the peninsula as well as across the Alps to Germany and France created the necessity to build new roads and revive ancient towns, thus stimulating urbanization as well as the growth of a new merchant class. Cities like Milan, which benefitted from its proximity to the Alpine passes between northern and southern Europe, and Pavia, Cremona, and Mantua, were infused with new vitality, together with the smaller towns of Piacenza, Verona, Crema, and Padua on the rich northern plain.

Florence maximized its geographical position as a crossroads between northern and southern Italy, developing important textile and banking industries. The city on the Arno River held accounts in all the principal European currencies and maintained banking branches throughout Europe, including Paris, Bruges, and London. Tuscan bankers serviced merchants by transferring money for them for a commission. Merchants could also purchase insurance for their enterprises, making it possible by the late thirteenth century to remain at home rather than accompany their goods abroad. Tuscan bankers also began to lend large sums to Europe's royalty and the popes, a profitable but also risky business. When King Edward III of England repudiated his enormous debt to the Peruzzi and Bardi families of Florence in the 1340s, for example, they went bankrupt.

The mercantile and banking activities of Tuscans and Lombards also drew them into the textile industry during the thirteenth and fourteenth centuries. They secured raw wool from England, Scotland, France, Spain, and North Africa and manufactured the material at home, through shops and the domestic system, which was based largely on female labor. Florentines elaborated on the coarse wool from Flanders by dyeing, dressing, and finishing it. By the fourteenth century the woolen industry had become an important capitalistic enterprise, giving employment to thousands of people. Venice and Milan developed textile industries as well. The Lombard capital was also able to take advantage of the rich iron ore in the Valtrompia to profit from metallurgical production.

BOX 2.3 THE FLORENTINE WOOLEN INDUSTRY

The wool industry was among the most important economic enterprises in Florence by the thirteenth century, giving employment to thousands of workers. Its steady expansion to the sixteenth century contributed substantially to the demographic growth of the city, drawing in laborers from the surrounding countryside. The wool industry is a prime example of how the economies of city and countryside were intricately linked.

Cloth manufacture, from the inception of raw material to the finished product, involved a complex and hierarchical array of workers and their subcontracted collaborators. The process was regulated at every step of the way, at first by the Arte di Calimala, a corporation of importers involved in the processes of dyeing and finishing cloth that also included merchants, manufacturers, shipwrights, and bankers, and from the second half of the fourteenth century by the Arte della Lana or wool guild. Both corporations were among Florence's seven major guilds, associations that enjoyed full political rights in city government. Overseeing the enterprise were capitalist investors, merchants, bankers, managers, and directors. The skilled workers in the production process included weavers, fullers, and dyers, with spinners at the bottom of the scale. An array of unskilled workers were tasked with the preparation of the raw material for spinning. To begin, the Arte di Calimala, the guild of cloth finishers and merchants in foreign cloth, imported the raw material from Flanders, England, Champagne, and Spain. It was distributed to the various shops and domestic domiciles scattered across the city that prepared the wool for spinning. That work was done by unskilled labor, including washers, beaters, carders, and combers who worked for bare subsistence wages. The wool guild and the city fed them in times of famine, and they were forbidden to organize. There were also a number of subcontractors involved in this early process, such as the rural suppliers of goats' horns to manufacture combs. The next step in the process was spinning the thread, a task primarily undertaken by women in city and countryside. Brokers delivered the raw material to them and then collected the spun yarn, paying them miserly wages on a piece-rate basis. The yarn was then distributed to weavers, whose looms were constructed by a specialized subset of craftsmen. The finished cloth was sent to fullers who cleansed it at their water mills. Finally, master craftsmen in the Florentine shops dyed, sheared, and mended the fabrics. The cloth was then sold in both European and Levantine markets.

While Florence attracted an international clientele, it also wrestled with competition from markets to its east, in China, the Mongol Empire, Persia, and the greater Islamic world. Early on the Tuscan manufacturers responded to this by imitating the products of their eastern competitors and adapting naturalistic and botanical motifs.

Further reading: Brucker, Gene. *Renaissance Florence*. Berkeley: University of California Press, 1969, pp. 56–68.

Although the internal markets of these urban conglomerations were somewhat interconnected, the cities were by no means cooperative with one another. They competed for resources and access to roads and seas. Venice, Genoa, and Pisa, for example, all vied for access on the transit roads to Rome. The landlocked Tuscan towns like Florence also competed for access to Rome and the seacoasts, while the Lombards struggled to control the Po River and its tributaries. Each city developed its own alliances and enmities, which continually shifted.

New Foods and Textiles

How did urbanization and the revival of international trade affect daily life? Most people did not travel afar, remaining in villages or at most moving from the countryside to cities and towns. Urban centers consistently drew in people from the countryside to work in producing goods or performing various services. Food, clothing, and shelter were core demands; for this, cities and towns depended on rural labor and raw materials, which they finished and reexported. Hence it is important not to lose sight of the importance of the agrarian sector of the economy. With respect to international exchange, however, that sector of the economy brought in enormous wealth for the entrepreneurial classes (Map 2.3 illustrates the wide circulation of trade on land and sea between the Mediterranean world and Asia associated with the so-called Silk Routes or Silk Road.), but the consumption of luxury products was limited to the rich. Social class and financial means attenuated the degree to which the treasures of foreign exchange could be consumed by ordinary people, even though they might be exposed to them through their travels or as vendors in markets and fairs or as domestic servants. Most

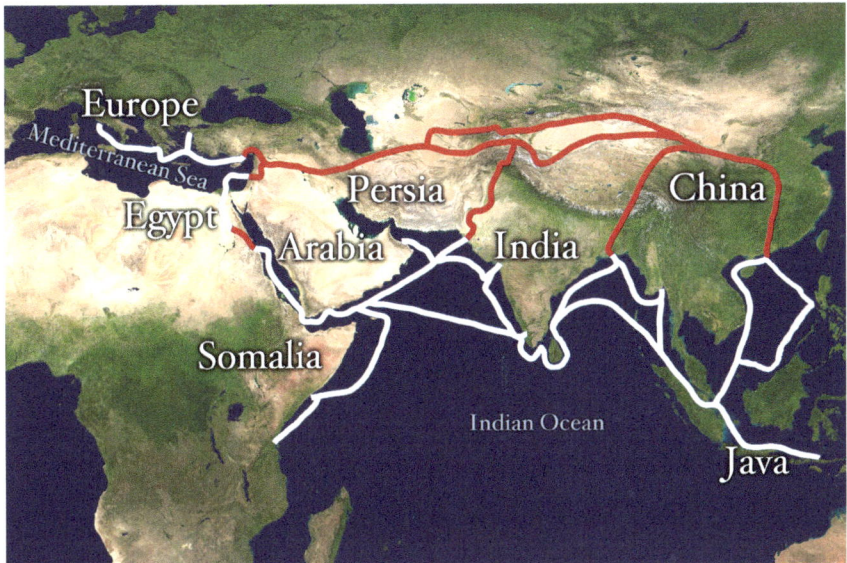

MAP 2.3 The Silk Routes.

people were agricultural laborers that survived on a simple diet of bread (on the Po plain often made from millet), soups, and gruel, and even that repast was not assured, for bad weather, poor harvests, price speculation, and unfair methods of distribution regularly brought on famine and dearth. Local economies also provided legumes, fruits, cereals, and wine for mass consumption. However, trade with the peoples of the southern Italian mainland and Sicily, Dalmatia, the Aegean, Byzantium, the Jewish nations, and the Islamic world did help supplement the European diet for those with some purchasing power. In Italy a supply of pulses for ordinary people's soups and gruels came from Alexandria. Genoa imported grain from the Black Sea, Venice from the Apulia region in southern Italy, and Tuscany from Sicily, where the financial houses of Florence were connected with the great grain estates. The rich, however, benefitted the most from international commerce. Among the most important foodstuffs for aristocratic tables was the Levantine import of wheat from the Black Sea. Rice, common in al-Andalus after Muslim colonization in the eighth century, also reappeared in Europe as a luxury item. Venice imported it from the Islamic world of the Levant and sold it in spice shops. Olive oil, also from the Levant, began to replace the consumption of animal fat. Further, new fruits and vegetables arrived during the Crusades, including eggplant from southeast Asia and Baghdad, spinach from Persia, chickpeas from Salonica, apricots from Damascus, bananas from Egypt, asparagus from Armenia, and dates from Maghreb. Finally, spices entered the aristocratic diet as well as a collection of medicinal drugs. From the Levant came black pepper, cinnamon, cloves, cumin, nutmeg, ginger, and saffron. These spices were too costly for ordinary people, who relied on the thyme, marjoram, bay leaves, savory, aniseed, coriander, garlic, sage, mustard, and parsley they grew in their gardens. Sugar was also a new luxury commodity, borrowed from the Islamic world but then grown by Venetians on the island of Cyprus. Distillation was also reintroduced. The world alcohol derived from the Arabic *al-kuhl*.

The aesthetics of luxury textiles had already been inspired by the Greek east as early as the sixth century, well before the Crusades. Venice took its inspiration from the iconography of Byzantine Church mosaics. However, the Crusades of the eleventh to thirteenth centuries introduced a new cultural lexicon from Greater Asia into the cloth industries of the Italian cities. Among the new weaves was calico cotton from Calcutta, Damaschin silk from Syria, Levantine silk (*tabino*, a heavy silk from Baghdad), Ormesin silk from Ormuz, an island on the Persian Gulf, and taffeta from Asia. Silk production became an important industry on various parts of the peninsula, both north and south. Raw silk was cultivated for luxury consumption. The technique had gradually spread from China, to the Islamic world, to Sicily, and then to the rest of the Italian Peninsula. Farmers planted mulberry, home to the silkworm, and mainly women unwound the silk from the cocoons, combing and spinning it to sell to dyers and weavers of both sexes, who in turn supplied the cloth to the markets and fairs. Many names for clothing came from the Levant: giubba for jacket, caffettano for caftan, and tabarro for cloak.

Most of these products were for the very rich. The poor, in contrast, wore homespun, more coarser blends of wool, cotton, and linen, some of them acquired from the trade fairs of Champagne and the Low countries. In Venice, which by the twelfth century was a multiethnic city, the various immigrant groups preserved their own dress from their places of origin. Armenian monks, Greek prelates, and Turkish and Armenian merchants all wore their own dress. Jews wore black. However, from 1425 they were obliged to wear yellow cords, and after 1515 yellow berets.

The Rise of Communal Government: Eleventh and Twelfth Centuries

As the peninsula's demography and economy evolved during the eleventh and twelfth centuries, all over central and northern Italy, with some exceptions around the Friuli, Piedmont, Tyrol, parts of Lombardy, and Venice, landless people gained their freedom from serfdom and left the great secular and ecclesiastical estates to live in new towns or older urban agglomerations and start handicraft manufacture, especially in the cloth-making and construction industries. Originally these skilled laborers were expected to manufacture goods for their lords, both lay or ecclesiastical, but eventually they formed protective associations and challenged their overseers in financial matters such as tolls and tariffs. The newly urbanized zones held a complex mix of social energies with great economic differentiation and occupational diversity. They included priests and nuns; bishops and secular magnates (landowning elites from the feudal class); vassals who served the landed elites, often in armed retinues; various imperial and episcopal officials; citizens in commerce, land investment, and the professions whose families were among the earliest and most prominent inhabitants of the town; merchants; and an assortment of humbler folk engaged in crafts, domestic service, shopkeeping, farming, and seasonal unskilled labor. They were joined by peddlers, thieves, and sex workers. People formed associations through neighborhoods and parishes and around markets, wells, and ovens. Importantly, the new urban dwellers did not replicate the feudal world that they had left, a vertical, hierarchical world of secular and ecclesiastical lords, vassals, and serfs that prioritized the birthright of a nobility that demanded service. Instead, they began by forming more horizontal associations, based on mutual interests. The failure of the Holy Roman Empire (to which they belonged) to coalesce assisted this process.

The formation of communes, or sworn associations, which appeared in central and northern Italy between 1080 and 1140, was a result of the breakdown of imperial and feudal government. The contest for power in which both popes and emperors claimed universal authority during the eleventh to thirteenth centuries created political anarchy, encouraging initiatives that were both anti-monarchical and anti-theocratic (see Chapter 1). This contest played out in several phases. The first, termed the "Investiture Controversy," was a battle over who had the right to invest bishops with office, the pope, or the Holy Roman Emperor. During the ninth and tenth centuries the Holy Roman Emperor had acquired this important right. Bishops during this period held great secular power in politics and administration, collecting taxes and serving as judges. A reformed papacy and clergy from 1050 wished to control this, setting up a competition that eventually ended with an inconclusive compromise in 1122. In the midst of this international power struggle, some northern Italian cities were troubled with contending bishops jockeying for local power, splitting both the clergy and the laity into warring factions. This drama played out in an environment already filled with violence and encouraged the formation of associations for mutual protection, particularly because both humble and prosperous folk lived side by side with a landowning nobility that built fortified palaces and towers and formed sworn leagues that engaged in factionalism, personal feuds, and vendetta. Some of the nobles, descendants of medieval counts, viscounts, marquises, and captains that had derived their titles and status from the Holy Roman Emperor, still held fiefs and considerable lands in the countryside; others mainly resided in their country castles, claiming power and tolls from the cities. Bishops, who had administered over the main urban centers since the disintegration of Roman rule, also retained vast landed estates and power, some serving as agents of the Holy Roman Emperor. Some of these families had little interest in civic government, guarding their special jurisdictions in the countryside. Nonetheless, whether they still held rein over fiefs, monasteries, comital (referring to a count, a rank of the nobility), or episcopal courts, they had embraced the city as an additional sphere of influence. Towers of 164–295 feet (50–90 meters) sprang up in the newly revitalized urban centers between 1160 and 1260, the work of violent clans that attached to specific streets and parishes, their rivalries connected both to pro-papal (Guelf) or pro-imperial (Ghibelline) interests and to their own independent interests (Figure 2.4).

Between 1035 and 1180, at the same time that papal and imperial factions were enacting their violent dramas in the urban areas of central and northern Italy, financially prosperous men from among the oldest citizenry were forming communal organizations and demanding social status from the rural nobility and clergy as well as freedom and self-government. Headed by consuls in sworn associations, the citizenry, or *cives* as they were called, together with some of the more urbanized nobles, were intent upon ousting the unruly nobility from their cities—a revolutionary idea after centuries in which power had been conceived as radiating from a hierarchy of officials under pope and emperor. The pressure came from those with great wealth—merchants, bankers, moneylenders, and entrepreneurs—not the artisans or small tradespeople with whom they remained divided in values and aspirations. They formed general assemblies and ad hoc councils, led at first by chief consuls and later by judges and advisors. By 1160 the general assemblies began to wane, replaced by prominent families that had moved to the forefront and established the makings of a defined oligarchy. As they accumulated wealth, and in some areas military or naval force, these elites—*cives* and urbanized nobles—were able to subdue the landed nobility and high clergy, whose privileges they resented and, in northern Italy, shun the investiture of bishops and gradually break with the Holy Roman Emperor.

A second bid by a Holy Roman Emperor, in this case Frederick I Barbarossa (red beard), to gain financial and military control of northern Italy further encouraged the coalescence of urban forces to thwart imperial ambitions. When at the Diet of Roncaglia (1154–8) the emperor reaffirmed his right to tax the Italian cities and appoint court magistrates, sixteen cities, including Milan, Brescia, Lodi, Mantua, Padua, and Venice rose up in rebellion. In 1167 they formed the Lombard League and carried out a long, drawn-out war that received the backing of Pope Alexander III (r. 1159–1181). Such papal interference in imperial ambitions may be considered the second round in the struggle between two political forces for universal power, following the Investiture Controversy. In the end, Frederick I was forced to admit loss at Legnano in 1176 and recognize the pope's authority. The two leaders concluded a truce, which was finally settled in 1183 with the Peace of Constance. At that point the Italian communes won the right to self-government. Though in theory they promised allegiance to the emperor, in practice they did not

FIGURE 2.4 Medieval Towers, Bologna, Italy.

respect their pledge, nor did the Peace of Constance quell the violence of the nobility, which continued to scramble for power and resources. Still further, the Peace of Constance did not put an end to the rivalries between popes and emperors, who continued to play an important role in the political life of the peninsula. Frederick I's successor, Frederick II, with a secure base in southern

Italy and Sicily, attempted in 1226 to restore imperial authority in northern Italy. Once again the pope allied with the northern Italian cities, employing foreign armies, to thwart Hohenstaufen ambitions, and once again the Guelfs and Ghibellines split into their respective factions. Papal–imperial rivalries would continue well into the thirteenth century, ending with the replacement of the Hohenstaufen dynasty in southern Italy with the Angevin dynasty in 1268, at the invitation of Pope Clement IV (r. 1265–1268), and the Italian cities retaining their autonomy.

From the late twelfth century both old citizens and some urban nobles in several of the Tuscan, Lombard, and Veneto cities aimed to crush noble violence. Guilds of powerful bankers, notaries, lawyers, and judges sprang up, their unions guarding their interests with exclusive membership requirements and standards. In some instances they were paramilitary organizations, neighborhood militias that aimed to offset the tower societies. In an effort to repress the factionalism among the nobility, podestral government replaced the consul. The podestà (a commander in chief) was charged with guarding the law, running the bureaucracy, chairing councils, and keeping internal peace, while councils retained legislative and fiscal competencies as well as taking charge of foreign policy. Podestral government was designed in theory to protect the commune from the violence and factionalism of the great magnates. It was a step in the transition from noble to more popular government, where the more prosperous among the middle class would curb noble privilege and have a voice in public policies such as taxation. However, this movement was not democratic; the leaders in this merchant-landowning milieu felt much more in common with the upper classes than with commoners.

Social change also helped bring about a more peaceful commune. The old citizens gradually intermarried with the more urbanized noble dynasties, ones that had invested in city life and capitalist enterprise. They formed fundamentally elitist citizen bodies that were neither socially homogeneous nor egalitarian. Merchants, for example, ran big businesses but at the same time reinvested their earnings in country estates and emulated noble behavior, while some old noble families turned to banking, commerce, and law. In Florence's case the guilds were able to seize power by 1250 and by the end of the century they had exiled unruly magnates, banning them from government and destroying their towers. The new urban oligarchies were set on conquering the countryside surrounding their cities, which they deemed vital to their economic and military survival. Thus, they increasingly encroached upon the feudal world that still held sway beyond their city walls, some with more success than others. The Guelfs (pro-papal factions) of Tuscany also forged strong commercial and diplomatic ties with the Angevin kings in Naples. The new hybrid citizen class that emerged in the thirteenth century developed elective magistrates with the right to vote, discuss, and legislate. These were not democratic institutions; they did not include women, artisans, seasonal laborers, the young, or the poor. Rather, they were oligarchies of prosperous individuals that had ousted counts and bishops from power in order to advance their interests as long-distance traders, bankers, notaries, and judges.

The general outline of developments described earlier did not apply everywhere. There was no universal model for the social and political evolution of the Italian cities; each developed uniquely, in part because their economies varied widely. Some like Venice, Florence, Milan, and Pisa had strong commercial and industrial bases; the wealth of others, on the other hand, was more agrarian. But even those with strong commercial and industrial bases varied widely. Florence fits the narrative of communal development described earlier the best. The settlement on the Arno River became a commune in 1138, freeing itself from the throws of lords and bishops and establishing its own administrative and tax system. In 1183 the city achieved independence from the Holy Roman Empire in the Peace of Constance and proceeded to oust the old imperial aristocracy. It became one of the richest cities in Italy because of its manufacture and trade of wool and its banking industry, with merchants operating throughout Europe and the Middle East and bankers dominating the credit market. Florence became a center of international trade, with operations in Valencia, Hamburg, London, and Tunis. Florentine markets plied carpets from Persia, spices from India, furs from Russia, leather from north Africa, and silks from China. Prosperous merchants and bankers allied with the pope (Guelfs) and began to challenge the feudal authority of nobles who supported the Holy Roman Emperor (Ghibellines). In 1282 elected officials, the priors, replaced the old municipal council and eliminated aristocratic factions. Every two months eight priors were elected from among the guilds; aristocrats were excluded from office. In 1293 the Ordinances of Justice banned noble disorders and excluded aristocrats from government, making mercantile wealth necessary for political office. The major guilds took control of civic renewal and with it civic pride, controlling secular and sacred building. Riddled with the brawls and burnings of factionalism, in 1299 the business people built a great new city hall, the Palazzo della Signoria (Vecchio), with big stone walls and fortified turrets to endure the violent politics. Also during this time the wool merchants sponsored the building of the great cathedral Santa Maria del Fiore (begun 1296); the cloth merchants funded the baptistery as well as the Palazzo della Signoria mentioned earlier, and the churches at Santa Croce and San Miniato; and the silk merchants sponsored the granary (and church) at Orsanmichele.

Unlike Florence, in Milan and many of the Lombard cities such as Brescia, the rural, feudal nobility continued to play a dominant role in the city. Lombardy did not expel the noble families from their cities and replace them with mercantile aristocracies. Large landholding dynasties like the Pallavicini, Rossi, and Malaspina around Milan and the Martinengo and Gambara around Brescia held considerable dominion in both the agrarian plains and mountain districts. The professional groups of lawyers, judges, physicians, and notaries held important places in civic government, but they were flanked by a feudal nobility that continued to play out their rural factionalism in the urban arena.

In contrast to Florence and Milan, Venice was not involved in the conflicts between popes and emperors on the mainland, nor it did pay homage to them, but it did join the Lombard League to defend communal independence against the Holy Roman Emperor. From the outset the city's major challenge was to subjugate its aquatic environment, that is, to control the tides and dry the soil for construction. The early inhabitants exchanged fish and salt for raw materials. They grew some produce, raised pigs, and hunted fowl but for the most part boated in supplies. Their economy was oriented toward the sea, and thus their ruling class was entirely urban and mercantile, with few roots in the countryside. In the beginning the noble families dominated island parishes, sharing noble governance. Gradually over the twelfth and thirteenth centuries the business denizens gained preeminence. The climbing birth rate, immigration, and a growing building trade encouraged great land reclamation and construction, sponsored by the major families as well as the religious orders of Dominicans, Franciscans, and Augustinians between 1280 and 1340. Rather than island parishes, Venice was then divided into six districts, three oriented toward the land and three toward the sea. While the city did suffer from factionalism, it did not have urban walls or violent tower societies. In contrast to the towers of central Italy the nobility had arcaded, waterfront palaces, and trading posts and docks (*fondaci* from the Arabic *fondouk*) to load and unload products from the storerooms beneath their dwellings, as exemplified in Figure 2.5. As merchants returned from ventures in the Levant and North Africa, they constructed a town plan that borrowed from the Islamic typologies they encountered in Damascus, Aleppo, Cairo, and Jerusalem. By the thirteenth century the dominant families had consolidated their wealth in trade, glassmaking, shipbuilding, banking, forced loans, and state convoys. They minted the gold ducat in 1284, which they named the *zecchino*, after the Arabic *sikka* meaning mint, and towards the end of the thirteenth century they began to close their political ranks to newcomers.

Political Consolidation: Thirteenth and Fourteenth Centuries

Between 1280 and 1350 the communes faced serious internal and external challenges that ultimately altered their constitutions. This was due in part to economic difficulties. The downturn was not just affecting the Italian Peninsula but rather was part of a cyclic phenomenon affecting most of Europe, China, and Inner Asia. In the agricultural sector yields were declining, and war exacerbated the food shortages. Landowners, ignoring their obligations to maintain cereal prices, resorted to speculation and fiscal corruption, depriving the general population of adequate supplies. At

FIGURE 2.5 Fondaco of Ca' Farsetti, Venice, Italy.

the same time rents increased, real wages fell, and taxation became more oppressive due to the expenses of warfare. The financial sector also faced a temporary downturn. In Florence the Peruzzi and Bardi banks failed in the 1340s when their royal borrowers in Europe failed to repay their loans. Textile production slumped, and consumers experienced a decline in purchasing power. Abroad, the land routes to Asia were also closing due to the weakening of the Mongol Empire, which affected Venetian and Genoese commerce; the declining economies of the Turkic Mamluk Empire in Egypt and Syria; and the Muslim sultanates of Northern Africa. Finally, when the bubonic plague, a trans-hemispheric pandemic spreading through the exchange networks between Europe and Asia, struck Italy in 1348–50 (see Chapter 4), governments came to a halt. Further, the population declined anywhere from a third to a half, causing extreme disruption and destructuralization of previous labor arrangements.

The political response to the economic downturn was conservative. Now free from imperial and papal powers, the various cities in central and northern Italy struggled with one another in order to ensure their food supplies and secure major trade routes. The strain on their finances, caused by constant war, made efficiency in government increasingly important. Thus the era of social experimentation ended, and political participation markedly narrowed to either a few prominent families or one lordly prince (termed a *signore* whose regime was a *signoria* or principality). The transfer of public power took place as a result of a variety of conditions, including endemic civic strife and factionalism, periodic fiscal crises, and the vicissitudes of war. Some principalities were temporary, but a great many more became permanent dynasties. The oligarchies also became fixed and ossified over time. For all the triumphant rhetoric about the rise of the *popolo* and the demise of imperial and ecclesiastical hierarchies, the governments of central and northern Italy became fundamentally elitist institutions whose entrepreneurial classes developed noble aspirations that in many ways were no different than the royal dynasties and feudal lords of Italy's southern regions or those of northern Europe. Enriched oligarchies felt more in common with nobles than with small retailers or craftspeople who worked with their hands. Landed princes also cultivated a noble ethos. Many were non-aristocrats that usurped power and then manufactured a noble aura; others came from the peninsula's great feudatories, representing the victory of the landed classes. In the end, the rise of the eleventh- and twelfth-century communes did not result in the absolute triumph of the city over the countryside's great landowners but rather in some hybrid combination of both the landed and commercial-industrial classes.

Among the various explanations historians have provided for why communes evolved into either oligarchies or despotisms, the economic explanation historian Lauro Martines has offered is persuasive.[2] In those cities with strong commercial and industrial bases—Venice, Florence, Siena, and Lucca—the entrepreneurial classes resisted despotism. Milan was the major exception. There the nobility opted *en mass* by the mid-thirteenth century to rely on the support of the powerful archbishop Ottone Visconti (r. 1277–c. 1287). Elsewhere, cities with weak industrial bases, such as Ferrara and Verona, were inclined toward despotic rule, which in essence represented the victory of landed power and the merging of municipalism with feudalism.

Despotisms

Principalities were more common in the Veneto, Lombardy, and the Romagna than in Tuscany, where corporate republican rule continued, save for a few brief intervals. Some cities sought leadership from imperial or papal factions or from the great feudatories of Piedmont, Lombardy, the Veneto, and the Romagna, men who were able to raise great armies from among their dependents and offer protection and resources. One of the earliest examples of despotism was in Verona, where Ezzelino III da Romano (1194–1259), a feudal lord of German descent with strong support from the Holy Roman Emperor Frederick II, intervened in the factional quarrels of the city. In 1226 he established hegemony over Verona, and later the Veneto cities of Vicenza in 1237 and Padua and Treviso in 1237. Upon da Romano's death another family rose to power, the della Scala (Scaligeri), this time not from landed interests but from the leadership of the merchant guilds. This was another route to establishing a *signoria*, that is, by controlling communal offices or guilds. The transfer of power might seem voluntary, but it was more often usurped by the *signore* and his allies. The Scaligeri survived for a century and a half before the Veneto cities were incorporated into the Venetian territorial state. Likewise Padua was ruled by a powerful dynasty, the Carrara (1328), before Venetian incorporation. Jacopo I da Carrara was named captain of the city in 1318, a post that was transformed into a signory that lasted until Venetian annexation in 1405.

Great families ruled over much of Lombardy. The Bonacolsi governed Mantua until 1328; they were followed by the Gonzaga, imperial vicars who aimed to quell the city's repeated factionalism. Elsewhere, Cremona, Piacenza, Pavia, and Vercelli were part of the Pallavicini domains during the thirteenth century. The most hegemonic of the Lombard cities, of course, was Milan, a great Metropolitan See from the early Middle Ages whose geographical position between the base of the Alps and the fertile Po Plain made it an important center for supplying goods and services throughout the region. When the Visconti became lords in 1277 it followed that they would have considerable political sway over most of the other Lombard cities as well, some of which they governed through deputies. These included Cremona, Piacenza, Pavia, Lodi, Como, and Bergamo. The thirteenth-century nobility vied for control of Milan. A group of lesser urban nobles allied with the commercial and business families ultimately won out over the nobles who had curried the support of both artisans and shopkeepers. Archbishop Ottone Visconti (1207–1295), a bishop-seigneur who fused civic lordship with ecclesiastical authority, emerged the victor. He possessed vast landed estates that he distributed in fiefs to many noble families in exchange for their support. Ottone's son Matteo I (1250–1322) established an enduring signory that gradually extended into the Lombard plain. The emperor installed his successor, Giangaleazzo (1351–1402), as Duke of Milan (1395). The duke quickly set his sights on Tuscany. He was followed by Filippo Maria (1392–1447). Even with a communal council in Milan, the Visconti held the authority to make law, impose taxation, declare war, and conclude peace.

In the Romagna region serious external threats—from aggressive neighboring cities, from imperial overlords, from a papacy seeking to consolidate its territorial powers—led to one-man rule in many towns. For reasons of efficiency and for protection, the threatened communes turned to men with military resources. This was more expedient for making rapid decisions that rely on councils or governments where offices were periodically rotated. The Romagna towns came to be dominated by country landlords who were interested in using urban administration to market their produce independent of communal restrictions. The Este family, marquises that descended from an old clan of imperial feudatories with branches in Tuscany, Liguria, and the Po Valley, established an enduring signory in Ferrara, a town that had failed to develop a strong guild system or popular institutions and where feudal landed interests prevailed. Owners of vast landed estates in the hinterland, the Este were able to triumph over their rivals in Ferrara with the help of the Venetians, who were interested in promoting their own commercial interests. They eventually took Modena and Reggio under their wing, holding much of the eastern Po Valley. Landed power was the foundation of princely dynasties like that of the Este, for it rendered them food, natural resources, and military strength. Landed possessions also equated with social prestige, even among family dynasties that did not vaunt aristocratic antecedents.

In contrast to the more enduring dynasties, some cities witnessed short-term lordships, conferred in moments of military and financial crisis. The Angevin king Robert of Naples was overlord of Genoa between 1318 and 1335. Experiencing military defeat with Lucca in 1325, the Florentines accepted Charles, Duke of Calabria and son of Robert of Anjou for a brief tenure, which lasted only three years. When the Florentine banks failed in the 1340s the oligarchy again conferred temporary power, this time to Walter of Brienne (1304–1356; r. 1342), but refused to make his stay permanent. He was ousted in 1343.

Oligarchies

In contrast to the principalities, Venice, Florence, Siena, and Lucca formed oligarchies. Genoa, on the other hand, oscillated between oligarchy and lordship until 1528, when it settled on the former. The seaport elite had made its living from shipping and trade but also had a strong feudal nobility given to the profession of arms that drew considerable income from rural estates. A wealthy middle class also collaborated with the shipping, trading, and magnate classes and entered the oligarchy.

Venice's ruling class had ossified by 1320. With the closing of the Great Council in 1297 few new families could enter the government's ranks, and the popular elements in the floating city were too weak to penetrate the constitutional elite. The oligarchy was made up of merchants and investors who, unlike the other Italian republics, defined themselves legally as the dominant political and social class. The wealthiest families engineered to control the government's most important offices. An attempt to overthrow the government in 1310, led by two important family clans, the Querini and the Tiepolo, failed and from thenceforward the oligarchy strived to keep tight control over the government. Despite the exclusive membership of the political class, however, over time the government developed mechanisms that gave voice to the concerns of the people (see Chapter 5).

The inland republics of Florence, Lucca, and Siena in Tuscany, Perugia in Umbria, and Bologna in the Romagna were more successful in imposing their authority on the feudal magnates of their rural hinterlands. As we have seen earlier in the case of Florence, the entrepreneurial classes and more urbanized nobility either defeated the violent nobility in their cities or transformed them. Thus city councils were able to thwart the pretensions of any one family. In thirteenth-century Florence, merchants and major manufacturers were prominent in government. Seven major guilds (foreign cloth merchants, finishers, and dyers; wool merchants and manufacturers; silk merchants and weavers; bankers and money changers; judges and notaries; apothecaries and physicians; and furriers and skinners), five middle guilds (butchers; shoemakers; blacksmiths; stone masons and woodcarvers; and retail cloth- dealers and linen manufacturers), and nine minor guilds held some voice in urban affairs. The major guilds dominated political power until 1378, the date that the Ciompi woolworkers revolted and temporarily held the reins of power. The revolt was a turning point, after which the government became more conservative. Gradually the Medici family came to dominate Florentine politics, putting an end to political experimentation. Their method of rule was subtle, permitting the rotation of offices and the establishment of small fiscal, judicial, military, and executive councils to avoid the appearance of a lordship. However, the family dynasty held tremendous power, sustained by its wealth in banking and industry and its capacity to offer employment to thousands of individuals. Overall Florence enjoyed an economy of regional as well as international importance. It was wealthy enough to develop a territorial state that endowed the city with labor and resources and that cushioned it from conquest by a larger city state.

The oligarchies of Italy eventually became fixed, with aspirations to be aristocratic. Once again birth and family became more important than merit. Wealth, occupation, family antiquity, marriage connections, behavior patterns, and attitudes sorted out the elite classes from the majority of the population. A restricted group of enfranchised citizens, perhaps no more than 2 percent, dominated the major offices of their cities. Small, powerful councils rotated memberships. Family dynasties fortunate enough to enjoy longevity through the reproduction of male heirs with astute marriage alliances and vast wealth sat at the acme of urban power, designing tax strategies and public finance, directing the military and diplomatic affairs, and meting out justice. Like the lords of Italy they too were fascinated with noble ideals.

The Kingdoms of Southern Italy

The political development of southern Italy moved in a different direction than that of the cities of the center and the north. Since the eleventh century it had been ruled by successive royal dynasties from outside Italy, first Norman (1030), then the Germanic Hohenstaufens (1197), and then the French Angevins (1266). Frederick II, crowned Holy Roman Emperor in 1220, had held the Kingdoms of Sicily and Naples-Apulia since 1197. His ambitions as well as those of his successors to claim northern Italy into his orbit, however, met the formidable resistance not only of the independent and civic-minded cities of that region but also of successive popes, and ultimately led to the fall of the Hohenstaufen's in the mainland south and Sicily to the French Angevin dynasty by 1268. As allies of the papacy, who had actually gifted the realm to Charles I of Anjou (r. 1262–1285) as a papal fief in 1266, the Angevins ruled the mainland south for almost two centuries, until they were supplanted by the Aragonese in 1442. However, they quickly lost Sicily due to the excessive taxation and unpopular policies of the French nobles installed to rule the island's inhabitants. In the uprising known as the Sicilian Vespers in 1282, the Sicilians ousted the French and accepted Pedro III of Aragon as their king. Sicily thenceforward came under the orbit of the Iberian Peninsula. Charles kept control, however, of Naples and the mainland south, which in essence became the administrative capital of a French kingdom. It was dominated by a cosmopolitan nobility of diverse origins that reflected centuries of royal dynastic rule, with descendants of Lombards, Normans, and Germans in addition to the French shaping cultural and political life and gradually acquiring great tracts of land at the expense of the royal crown. Under the rule of the French Angevin kings, the south also became involved in the dynastic politics of Europe. Charles's son, Charles II, for example, married into a Hungarian dynastic line, while his grandson Robert the Wise married into an Aragonese noble family. Robert's granddaughter, Joanna, queen of Naples and the county of Provence (r. 1343–1382), married her cousin Andrew, the younger brother of King Louis of Hungary. Thus French, Hungarian, and Aragonese families were interlocked in a complex web of alliances. The Angevin kings, as well as the nobility, were great cultural patrons, attracting a broad swath of artists, writers, and other intellectuals from northern Italy and Europe. They employed Florentine bankers and patronized Florentine intellectuals like Boccaccio. Yet royal rule in the south of Italy, together with its strong, landowning baronage, shaped its political culture in ways that were different from that of the cities to its north. The prevalent form of government was legitimate dynastic rule and not the product of newly prosperous business denizens or mercenary captains lacking noble lineages. In this sense its hierarchical structure and dynastic ambitions were more in line with the feudal monarchies of England and

France than the more civic-minded governments of Italy's center and north. Further, because the kings of Naples were vassals of the papacy, dating back to the Norman period, they were consistently subject to the latter's political interests and maneuvers.

Conclusion

This chapter began by reviewing the demographic and economic underpinnings of urbanization in central and northern Italy from the eleventh to the early fourteenth centuries, a period characterized by overall growth and the development of a broad, urban middle class that shunned imperial and papal authorities and established its own forms of communal self-government. Political organization among the various Italian cities, however, was far from uniform. By the thirteenth century rule by exclusionary councils or one-man despots replaced communal forms of government. This lack of political uniformity in some ways mirrored Transalpine Europe. The royal courts of England, France, and Spain were also loosely organized, albeit under the hierarchical structures of feudal society, with early but premature attempts to strengthen royal authority over the church and the nobility. Great noble and ecclesiastical holdings, however, impeded the process of political centralization until well into the fifteenth century. The Holy Roman Empire, on the other hand, failed to coalesce altogether, a process encouraged in the eleventh to thirteenth centuries by papal interference, and remained instead with largely decentralized centers of power, including the Italian cities of the north until the twelfth century. The Italian south went through a succession of royal dynasties, first Norman, then Hohenstaufen, then Angevin, and eventually Aragonese, with dynasts competing for jurisdictions with the great landed families of the region. The papacy was also divided. It underwent a serious crisis between 1309 and 1377. The office of the pope was moved from Rome to the southern French town of Avignon, where seven French popes were successively under the tutelage of the French kings. The institution thus was unable to provide any unifying influence in Italy. The Italian Peninsula and Europe as a whole remained politically divided.

Think Critically

1. Why was the agrarian sector the most fundamental aspect of the economy?
2. What demographic and economic factors contributed to the revitalization of towns and cities during the eleventh and twelfth centuries?

3. How did the rivalries between popes and emperors help shape the development of urban politics in the Italian cities?
4. What was the nature of early forms of government in the revitalized cities?
5. What role did the Crusades play in Italian urbanization? The economy? Cultural exchange?
6. How did international networks of exchange shape food consumption and material culture in Italy?

Further Exploration

1. What are the visual signs of good government in Ambrogio Lorenzetti's *Effects of Good Government* in Figure 2.1?

Notes

1 Philip Jones, "Italy," *The Cambridge Economic History of Europe, Volume I, The Agrarian Life of the Middle Ages*, edited by M. Moissey Postan (Cambridge, UK: Cambridge University Press, 1966), 344–5.
2 Lauro Martines, *Power and the Imagination: City-States in Renaissance Italy* (New York: Vintage Books Edition, 1980), 130–61.

Further Reading

Abu-Lughod, Janet L. *Before European Hegemony: The World System AD 1250–1360*. New York: Oxford University Press, 1989. The author finds the roots of the modern world economy in the exchanges stretching from northwest Europe to China.
Cipolla, Carlo M. *Before the Industrial Revolution: European Society and Economy 1000–1700*. New York: Norton, 1994. Explores the economic and cultural processes that led to the European transformation from an agrarian to an industrial society.
Epstein, Steven A. *Genoa and the Genoese 958–1528*. Chapel Hill: University of North Carolina Press, 1996. Traces Genoa's evolution over six centuries from a minor city to a vibrant republic with an extensive overseas empire.
Ferraro, Joanne M. *Venice: History of the Floating City*. Cambridge, UK: Cambridge University Press, 2012. Traces the history of Venice from its sixth-century beginnings to the twenty-first century.
Hyde, J. Kenneth. *Society and Politics in Medieval Italy*. New York: St. Martin's Press, 1973. A solid history of late medieval Italy.

Larner, John. *Italy in the Age of Dante and Petrarch, 1216–1380*.
London: Longman, 1980. A survey of Italian history during the thirteenth and fourteenth centuries.

Marino, John. "Economic Encounters and the First Stages of a World Economy." In *A Companion to the Worlds of the Renaissance*. Edited by Guido Ruggiero, 277–95. Oxford, UK: Blackwell, 2002. Situates the Italian and Iberian economies on the world stage as the fifteenth- and sixteenth-century voyages of discovery open new markets and create new systems of global exchange.

Martines, Lauro. *Power and the Imagination: City-States in Renaissance Italy*. New York: Baltimore, MD: Johns Hopkins University Press, 1988. A magisterial survey of medieval and Renaissance Italian developments that draws connections between cultural patrons and power.

Waley, Donald, and Trevor Dean. *The Italian City Republics*, 4th ed. London: Routledge, 2014. Surveys the social, political, and religious world of the Italian towns beginning in the eleventh century.

3

Spheres of Culture: 1000–1375

Timeline

Eleventh to fourteenth century	Foundation of universities
Eleventh century	Notarial arts begun in Bologna
Eleventh century	Romanesque architecture
Eleventh to thirteenth century	Roman and Canon law developed in Bologna
1170	Fibonacci born (to *c.* 1240/50?)
c. 1181	Francis of Assisi born (to 1226)
1194	Clare of Assisi born (to 1253)
Twelfth century	Trota of Salerno
Thirteenth century	University of Padua offers Muslim pharmacy
Thirteenth century	Mendicant building programs
Thirteenth century	Civic palaces constructed
c. 1220/25	Nicola Pisano born (to *c.* 1284)
c. 1250	Giovanni Pisano born (to *c.* 1315)
c. 1265	Dante Alighieri born (to *c.* 1321)
c. 1267	Giotto born (to 1337)
c. 1280	Pietro Lorenzetti born (to 1348)
c. 1285	Ambrosio Lorenzetti born (to 1348)
1296	Florence cathedral Santa Maria del Fiore begun
1300	Dante's *Vita Nuova*
1302	Dante exiled from Florence

FIGURE 3.1 Palazzo Pubblico, Siena, Italy. The town hall, a symbol of communal pride, was typical of those in Tuscany, constructed in fortified brick with defensive features.

1304	Petrarch born (to 1374)
c. 1305	Giotto completes frescoes in Arena Chapel in Padua
c. 1308–21	Dante writes the *Divine Comedy*
1313	Boccaccio is born (to 1375)
1324	Marsilius of Padua writes *Defensor pacis* advocating subordination of church to state
c. 1350–8	Boccaccio writes *The Decameron*

The Culture of Cities

The urban cultures of the various Italian regions evolved in close tandem with their social and economic evolution. What made their intellectual and artistic output different from other areas of Western Europe were the urban societal forces that sponsored and shaped them. Importantly, the northern third of the Italian Peninsula was highly urbanized, and thus many aspects of the culture of its cities stood out from the rest of Western Europe. By the thirteenth century the entrepreneurial classes had managed to dominate Europe's international trade and finance and to establish centers of manufacture, drawing enormous profits that allowed them to match the power of the landed nobility, who were either thrown out or absorbed, and become a sponsor of new art and ideas. Wealth gave the various Italian cities and their major families the means to produce and sustain a culture that did not fit in with the three recognized classes during the Middle Ages of nobles, clergy, and peasants. They lived in and ruled in cities and towns and were oriented toward worldly success and with it a sense of the practical. Urban nobles, large manufacturers, international merchants and bankers, lawyers, and notaries absorbed regional and more worldly cultural legacies and shaped them to accommodate their contemporary needs in business and government, with the help of male and female artisans who executed the more worldly aesthetic.

The culture the Italian cities inherited was part of the greater Mediterranean world. Along with Greek and Roman literature, myths, language, architecture, and sculpture, their legacy included Byzantine and Islamic decorative arts, and scientific and philosophical texts that were brought to the peninsula via translators from al-Andalus, Sicily, and the Crusader kingdoms in the Levant. Merchants, together with their entourages of helpers, returned from their travels in North Africa or along the Silk Road from Constantinople to China with new elements of material culture, including decorative work in textiles, Islamic pottery, metalwork, art objects, and food as well as the Chinese inventions of gunpowder and paper. Christians exchanged with Muslims, Muslims with Hindus, Hindus with Buddhists or Confucians, and vice versa or some other combination of peoples via the sea and caravan routes of Afro-Eurasia. Memories of the Italians' sojourns abroad can also be found in sculpture, architecture, and early Renaissance painting. The evolving cultures of the various urban centers were not uniform in style, instead reflecting wide geographical differences as well as aesthetic preferences.

It is important to underline that in addition to this broad, worldly aesthetic deriving from international interaction, the Latin Christian church was also an omnipresent spatial, societal, and cultural force, not just on the Italian Peninsula but throughout Europe as a whole. Celtic missionaries had been instrumental in the spread of Christianity throughout Europe in the centuries following the disintegration of Roman government in the west, and between the sixth and tenth centuries it was in monasteries and cathedrals that the manuscripts of antiquity were preserved and reproduced. From the early Middle Ages, thus, Latin Christianity was the dominant religion and cultural force. It is evident in the spread of religious movements ranging from male and female monasticism to the new mendicant orders; the cults of saints; the long-distance travel of pilgrims and missionaries; monastic and cathedral schools; the international circulation of university teachers; the ecclesiastical courts of canon law; church-sponsored diffusions of style in art and architecture; and the everyday life of people who followed a calendar of holy days and experienced the rituals of baptism, marriage, and death. Women in particular fostered greater spirituality and sanctity through the cults of living saints, sacred rituals, and cloistered and non-cloistered religious orders. Cities were organized into parish districts with streets and squares taking the names of saints and walls adorned with shrines. Churches, with their sacred relics, also marked out the city's spiritual space, while their bells and chimes helped people to keep time, along with the religious calendar and its commemoration of saints, feast days, and holy rituals. Members of guilds and civic government took Christian oaths, and laypeople founded Christian confraternities for charitable purposes. Art, whether in a church, a guild hall, a civic space, or a domestic setting, was ubiquitously religious. Finally, the rites associated with the stages of the human life cycle—birth, marriage, and death—were all enveloped in religious doctrine and ritual. The cities were filled with strong, religious feeling, which thrived in tandem with new, more material secular values, and also created among the wealthy deep moral and ethical conflicts over achieving the spiritual goal of salvation encouraged by the church in the midst of their worldly success and material consumption.

The majority of people were not directly occupied with the patronage of high culture, but artists, stonecutters, masons, and builders, who were considered crafts people during this period, were directly engaged in its production whether as supervisors or workers. Moreover, ordinary people were spectators of the new art—paintings, frescos, altarpieces, and stone statues—and architecture that adorned the urban environment, especially that which was didactic in nature and held a moral message, inviting viewer interaction. Still further, both women and men were also able to leave a lasting presence through the artistic patronage of their guild associations, religious communities, and confraternities, which honored their activities as well as their patron saints. Some could also afford to purchase or trade artistic commodities.

Education

Although there was no one model of government, Italy's evolving urban agglomerations shared several common needs, including a working bureaucracy; law codes; a mint; a judicial system, tax and revenue strategies; and a system of defense. Citizens demanded more literacy for themselves, both in communal affairs like speechmaking and in commercial affairs, where they needed arithmetic and bookkeeping. They relied on a more utilitarian Latin for their contracts and businesses but also expressed new interest in the vernacular. They prized literary and rhetorical skills—writing, reading, and figuring—over military skills. The new hybrid ruling classes thus proposed an alternative state, culture, economy, and set of values that developed alongside the traditional rituals, literature, art, and architecture of the Latin Church.

The need for trained professionals to run government and merchant firms, especially civil servants with law degrees, motivated the founding of universities in the eleventh to thirteenth centuries, initially in Italy and then in England, France, and Spain. Prior to the late eleventh century, northern Italy had dual Latin cultures, one that took place in ecclesiastical schools and the other under the supervision of the laity, especially notaries and judges. The rest of Europe had no equivalent for this second tier of Latin education. In northern Italy cathedral and monastic schools still taught theology and basic education, but the preparation of notaries and judges, that is, legal professionals who were very important for recordkeeping and business transactions, developed separately. It grew in the late eleventh and twelfth centuries, primarily in Bologna, to include the *ars dictandi*, or notarial arts, the study of Roman law, and eventually canon law. By the thirteenth century students began to learn rules of composition, civic rhetoric, and letter-writing to assist the new men in government. Scribes may also have been influenced by the earlier Arabic books on humanism in the chancery schools of medieval Sicily. These books also came to the monastery at Monte Cassino. They were the technical foundations of the humanist movement that would develop during the fifteenth century.

Women were generally excluded from all of these schools and especially from universities. However, nuns who took religious vows often had skills in reading and writing, and they produced manuscripts about mysticism, their own personal devotion, compendiums of prayers, and musical chant. Among the most famous was the German Benedictine abbess Hildegard of Bingen (*c.* 1098–1179), a composer, philosopher, Christian mystic, visionary, and polymath who was subsequently sainted. The majority of people, in contrast, did not achieve basic literacy, but they were often skilled in farming and crafts, the former contributing to the peninsula's economic development, the latter important to the experiential and practical knowledge necessary in science and technology.

Alongside the ecclesiastical and lay-supervised schools, universities began at first as centers for the study of academic jurisprudence and medicine. The Investiture Controversy of the eleventh to thirteenth centuries between emperors and popes competing for political hegemony stimulated the development of both Roman law and canon law in the northern Italian city of Bologna, as each side attempted to legally justify its claims. Further, the new communal rulers that had benefitted from the conflict used Roman law, and the model of the Roman Republic, to defend their claims to rule themselves. Students studied Justinian's *Corpus Juris Civilis*, the foundation of secular legal studies, or canon law, which was based on the biblical writings of the late Roman churchmen, the canons of church councils, and the decrees of popes. Gratian, a twelfth-century Camaldolese monk and lawyer in Bologna, developed a central body of canon law in 1140 with his *Decretum*. Students in Bologna, who came from all of Europe, would hire professors, set their pay, and negotiate their lecture topics. From 1316 the institution also offered rhetoric, logic, philosophy, grammar, dialectic, astronomy, and the notarial arts. Logic and natural philosophy were considered preparations for a degree in medicine. Grammar, dialectic, and the notarial arts prepared men for careers in government. In 1420 the university added Greek to its curriculum, and in 1460 Hebrew, language training that enabled scholars to read ancient texts with a critical eye in their original languages. Bologna's university attracted some one to two thousand students at a time, becoming a magnet for new wealth in the city because it stimulated the demand for lodging, food, servants, and tutors.

Other cities in Italy and the rest of Europe quickly followed Bologna in establishing universities, usually as a result of the migration of students and teachers from one institution to another. Among the long list was Paris (1160), Oxford (1167), Cambridge (1209), Salamanca (1218), Montpellier (1220), Padua (1222), Naples (1224), Siena (1240), and Rome (1240s). Ferrara followed in 1391 and Turin in 1411. Others were founded in Portugal, Bohemia, and parts of the Holy Roman Empire. Padua, like Bologna, offered courses in canon and civil law as well as natural philosophy, but its greatest attraction was the study of medicine. The university granted doctorates to prospective physicians who then served at courts, in cities, and for private hire. Padua became a conduit for Muslim pharmacy in the Latin West, along with the University of Bologna, with the introduction of the pseudonymic author John Mesua's (*c.* 777–857) *Grabadin* during the late thirteenth century. The institution was first supported by the commune, later by the Carrara lords (1318–1405), and ultimately by the Venetian state, which made it the only university in its dominions when the city came under its aegis in 1405.

Padua was not the first place to specialize in medicine in Italy or to produce important translations and commentaries on Arabic works. As discussed in Chapter 1, Salerno's medical school began sometime during the ninth century and grew between the eleventh and thirteenth centuries to become one of Western Europe's most important sources, along with Montpellier in France, for medical knowledge and pharmacy. The Salerno curriculum drew from such ancient authors as the Hippocratic corpus (Greece, fifth to fourth century BCE), Dioscorides (Asia Minor, first century CE), and Galen (Pergamon, second century CE) as well as Muslim medical practices known throughout Sicily and North Africa. Sources first came from the translations from the Arabic compiled by Constantinus Africanus (d. 1099?) at Monte Cassino. By the thirteenth century Arabic sources on how to formulate the best medicines arrived by sea from al-Andalus and the Levant, including the books of Avicenna (Ibn Sīnā, *c.* 980–1037), a Persian polymath and physician, and Averroës (Ibn Rusud, 1126–1198), a philosopher from Andalucia in southern Spain. Salerno's scholars produced writings about natural substances that were derived from plants, animals, and minerals and used as healing remedies. The school also specialized in women's medicine, producing the well-known *Trotula*, three texts that circulated in all of Europe, from the Iberian Peninsula to Poland and from Sicily to Ireland from the twelfth through the fifteenth centuries. The *Trotula*, put together in the twelfth century from oral traditions as well as the writings of the ancient natural philosopher Galen, included *Conditions of Women*, *Treatments of Women*, and *Women's Cosmetics*. Trota of Salerno (Figure 3.2), a twelfth-century medical practitioner, authored the text on treatments. The Salerno medical school later fell under the shadow of the University of Naples, which the Hohenstaufen emperor Frederick II founded in 1224 to train bureaucrats in royal law and administration. However, the emperor decreed that physicians were obliged to pass an examination in the medical school of Salerno in order to legally practice medicine in his kingdom.

During the twelfth century Jewish, Christian, and Muslim scholars in Toledo, the capital of the Muslim al-Andalus kingdom, and Palermo, which was part of Norman and then Hohenstaufen Sicily, preserved and translated into Latin several core texts that would circulate throughout Europe, including Euclid, Ptolemy, and the Greek physicians. Some of the texts went from the original Greek through successive translations into Arabic, Hebrew, Ladino, and finally Latin. In the thirteenth century the Holy Roman Emperor Frederick II (king of Sicily from 1198, king of Germany from 1212, king of Italy and Holy Roman Emperor from 1220 and king of Jerusalem from 1225), based in southern Italy, sponsored Fibonacci, a mathematician from Pisa who popularized the Hindo-Arabic numeral system. Frederick II arguably made the south the center of European life in terms of culture

FIGURE 3.2 *Trota of Salerno*. Illustration from *Miscellanea Medica* XVIII (early fourteenth century, France), Manuscript 544, f. 65. Wellcome Library, London. A copy of the intermediate Trotula ensemble. Pen and wash drawing meant to depict "Trotula," clothed in red and green with a white headdress, holding an orb.

during the thirteenth century. His court attempted to reconcile ancient Jewish and Islamic culture with the world and ideas of western Christianity.

Many of the translated texts became part of the universities' curricula. Every student was given a foundation in the liberal arts prior to advanced study in either sciences, medicine, theology, or law. That foundation included Latin grammar, rhetoric, and logic (termed the *trivium*) and arithmetic, geometry, astronomy, and music (termed the *quadrivium*). Thanks to the translators, the first three sciences of the quadrivium—arithmetic, geometry, and astronomy—progressed from studies on the elementary level to be foundations for the mathematics that were necessary for advanced scientific inquiry. In astronomy, for example, the curriculum was significantly expanded through the translation in Sicily of Ptolemy's *Almagest* (second century CE). There were also translations on the subjects of physics, optics, mechanics, biology, and meteorology, and in mathematics, on algebra, geometry, and trigonometry. In Paris, the study of philosophy flowered by the second half of the twelfth century, with great thinkers like Anselm and Abelard. Thanks to the translations of Aristotle either from the Greek or from the Arabic, they founded a new logic that would constitute the basis for intellectual ideas in theology and philosophy well into the thirteenth century.

Latin was the common language in all universities, for lectures, disputations, and examinations, whether in Italy, England, France, or Spain. There was also a common core of texts. In natural philosophy, Aristotle was the primary source. His *libri naturales* were the foundation of thirteenth-century natural philosophy. The arts curriculum included his expositions on logic, metaphysics, and moral and natural philosophy, understood through Latin commentaries and the translations of Averroes. In medicine, students read Avicenna's *Canon of Medicine*, which synthesized Aristotelian natural philosophy with Galenic medicine. This was an essential part of the western European university medical curriculum to at least the mid-seventeenth century. Students also became familiar with Ptolemy's geocentric, mathematical astronomy and Pliny the Elder's natural history. In law the bases of the curriculum were the *corpus juris civilis* and the *corpus juris canonici*, and in theology, Peter Lombard's *Sentences* and the Bible. It was generally assumed that such knowledge had already been established, and that the task of students was to read the core texts, organize them, and comment on them, a method known as scholasticism. The result was a consolidation of the learning of the past, organized into fields of systematic study.

Among the leading teachers of the thirteenth-century universities were Franciscan and Dominican friars, also known as mendicants, that is, orders that served the poor. Mendicants traveled from city to city to preach against heresy to the masses. Many had sprung up from among the rich, like Francis of Assisi (1181–1226), who turned away from the materialism of the thirteenth century. Besides preaching to the poor, the friars set up study centers and produced texts of scholastic theology. Among the great thinkers known for their attempts to integrate Christian faith with rational philosophy were the Dominican Thomas Aquinas (1225–1274) and the Franciscan Bonaventure (1221–1274), both of whom studied at the University of Paris. The male mendicant orders also took up the task of channeling female orders, directing their temporal and spiritual activities both in cloistered and in non-cloistered venues. Excluded from universities and the priesthood, women still took up the vocation of serving the poor, with members of the aristocratic houses, like their male counterparts, also establishing mendicant communities, and women's writings became more evident in thirteenth-century urban centers. Among the most well-known founders of female mendicants was Clare of Assisi (1194–1253), who was inspired by her compatriot Francis of Assisi. Reputedly from a rich family, she and other aristocratic followers renounced their material wealth for a life of poverty. The Order of the Clares, founded in 1212, quickly spread throughout Italy and Europe and was formally recognized by Pope Innocent IV in 1253.

BOX 3.1 CLARE OF ASSISI (1194–1253)

Chiara Offreduccio of Assisi, a small Umbrian town not far from Rome, was the daughter of a wealthy nobleman who came from an old Roman family. Her mother too was of noble lineage and very devout. Chiara (Figure 3.3), known as Clare in English, was unwilling to follow the track to marriage commonly assigned to young women of her social class. It may be assumed that her father planned to arrange a union that was socially beneficial to the family. Clare, however, discovered another path to self-fulfillment, that of becoming a nun, married only to Jesus.

Living in Assisi, the town of St. Francis, Clare had the opportunity to hear this popular religious preacher and founder of the Franciscan Order. She was so inspired that she sought him out and asked him to help her live in the manner of the Gospel. Francis himself, the son of a wealthy merchant, had renounced a life of material prosperity in favor of one lived in poverty. His was a rejection of the rising prosperity of the peninsula's business denizens. At the age of eighteen Clare managed to escape her father's grip and, with the help of Francis, enter a convent of Benedictine nuns. After her father made several attempts to have her return home, Francis moved Clare to a monastery at a more reclusive site. Her sister Catarina joined her. Eventually another sister and Clare's mother entered the order she founded—the Order of St. Clares, or Poor Clares. Clare and the other women who joined her eventually settled in a building near the Church of San Damiano in Assisi. They were referred to as the Poor Ladies

FIGURE 3.3 *Saint Clare*, 1318. Detail from the frescoes by Simone Martini (*c.* 1284–1344). Chapel of St. Martin, Lower Church, Papal Basilica of St. Francis of Assisi, Assisi, Italy.

of San Damiano. They lived in enclosure, unlike the Franciscan male friars that traveled the towns and countryside to preach. Clare became the abbess of the congregation in 1216 and was the first woman to write a rule for female monastic living. It was set apart from the concurrent Benedictine rule, with stricter guidelines and an insistence on the vow of poverty. Clare's writings went from Italy to other places abroad. She sent letters to other abbesses of convents in Europe promoting her order. She was also in contact with the popes of her age, whose directives she often resisted. Clare was determined that her order, unlike many others of the time, would not benefit from endowments or gifts, but rather would live in poverty and remain devoted to a life of spirituality. At the same time, the Poor Clares would help the poor. Pope Alexander IV canonized Clare two years after her death, in 1255. In 1260 the Basilica of St. Clare was constructed in Assisi, and the saint's remains were interred there. Pope Urban IV changed the name of the congregation to the Order of St. Clare in 1263.

Clare's life, and that of her fellow nuns, is important for several reasons. To begin, it represents another current that flowed alongside the growing wealth of the nobility and the more commercial classes of medieval Italy, a current that rejected materialism as well as secularism. Second, it highlights a group of women, who like St. Francis, were attuned to the needs of the poor, both materially and spiritually. Holy women and men were an inspiration to the masses, and sainthood fulfilled a certain need to believe in the rewards of leading a spiritual life, despite the hardships of the material world. This religious current would thrive throughout the Renaissance and into the modern period, alongside developments in secular culture. In 1872 Clare's relics were transferred to the crypt of the Basilica, where they are still venerated today. Moreover, she has a feast day in the Roman calendar, August 11, which is still celebrated. Finally, Clare's rule and the letters she wrote to other abbesses are testimony to the literacy and influence of upper-class women. They circulated in less public spheres than the male mendicants, but they too were actively engaged in the religious culture of their times.

Religious Architecture

For most of the European Middle Ages it was the Latin Church that sponsored innovations in architecture, such as the Romanesque churches of the eleventh and twelfth centuries and the Gothic edifices of the thirteenth and fourteenth centuries, found throughout Western Europe. The Byzantine style in Italy still lingered as well, as exemplified in the ceiling of the Florence Baptistery, decorated between 1225 and 1330. In architecture, new cultural trends spread from the monasteries to the towns. The eleventh-century Romanesque, with classical roots that took its name from the use of rounded arches found in Roman construction, was an international style that flourished in Italy with regional variations, such as the Lombard style produced by the master masons of the Comaco and exemplified in Milan's Basilica di Sant'Ambrogio; the central Italian style in Pisa, Lucca, and Pistoia that combined both Lombard and classical lines with decorative art borrowed from Greater Asia; and the southern and Sicilian styles that mingled Islamic, Byzantine, and Norman styles, again with the decorative arts of the East. The buildings were predominantly made of stone, with little external ornamentation, but the interiors might be richly illustrated, in either painting, mosaics, or sculpture, with didactic, religious scenes aimed at the illiterate masses. Among the most common themes were the life of Christ, the salvation of the blessed, and the damnation of the wicked. The Normans brought the architectural language of the Romanesque, found in their French and English dominions, to Palermo, Monreale, and Cefalù, in Sicily. The Gothic style, which originated in France, also found its way into Italy in a much less flamboyant fashion. Gothic engineering resolved the most important problem of linking walls together by means of vaulting with ribs and panels. Its signal characteristic was the pointed arch. The decorative elements, on both the exterior and interior, continued to be didactic, ranging from stories and figures from the Bible and scenes of daily life.

Several great churches sprung up in Italy during the eleventh to thirteenth centuries, particularly those of the great maritime powers intent on displaying their commercial and naval ascendency. Among them was the cathedral complex in the powerful maritime Republic of Pisa, built with the spoils of the Pisans' expeditions to the Levant, which fostered a Pisan-Romanesque style. The cathedral's exterior was decorated with colored marbles that created geometric patterns (see Figure 1.5). The *intarsia* (inlayed mosaics) on the façade evidenced the strong influence of both the Islamic and Byzantine worlds where Pisan merchants had circulated. The style of the Romanesque leaning tower (c. 1173–372) was similar to those found in Byzantium. The baptistery's (Figure 3.4) lower segment is in the Pisan Romanesque, with rounded arches, while the upper segment is Gothic, with its pointed arches. Pisa was also an important center of Gothic sculpture during the thirteenth century, with the pulpit of Nicola Pisano (c. 1220/1225–80) in the baptistery and that of his son Giovanni (1250–1315) in the cathedral. Nicola also carved the pulpit in Siena's black and white marble cathedral between 1266 and 1268, while his son worked on the edifice's façade. The father's style was modeled on the sculptural reliefs of Roman sarcophagi as well as Byzantine art. One can find references to Assyrians, Romans, and Bacchic pagans as well as Christians. His son, on the other hand, displayed a penchant for the French Gothic, with pointed arches. Both craftsmen achieved a vigorously expressive realism that inspired later artists whose interest in displaying the human body continued.

FIGURE 3.4 Baptistery on Campo dei Miracoli, Pisa, Italy. The lower section of the Baptistery is in the Pisan Romanesque style, with rounded arches, while the upper sections are in the Gothic style, with pointed arches.

The other great maritime Republic, Venice, also built a great church, the Basilica San Marco, which was designated the chapel of the Doge, the titular head of state. It was modeled after the sixth-century Church of the Holy Apostles in Constantinople. The original church, begun in 829, burned down in 976. Reconstruction, begun in 1063, was carried out to the end of the eleventh century; the building was consecrated in 1094. This great monument mirrored a number of styles from Byzantium, the Levant, and North Africa. The exterior recalled the architectural and mosaic art of the Great Umayyad Mosque in Damascus and the Dome of the Rock in Jerusalem, while the interior mosaics displayed the kind of iconography that was familiar in Constantinople and Alexandria. The colored stones on a background of gold, with camels and pyramids, recreated an Egyptian home for the bones of St. Mark, which had been pirated from Alexandria in 828 and laid to rest in the church crypt. The vaults, domes, and upper walls depicted eastern saints, stories from the Bible, and the life of Saint Mark. The atrium of the church also recalled Egyptian scenes of merchant travel and trade, and after the Fourth Crusade in 1204 there were references to the classical tradition in the basilica as well.

Mendicant friars throughout Italy from Venice to Naples also influenced religious architecture during the thirteenth and fourteenth centuries, introducing Gothic styles in large complexes, churches, and monasteries.

The various orders—Franciscans, Dominicans, Humiliati, Servites, Augustinians, and Carmelites—undertook conspicuous building programs after 1250 on the periphery of urban centers. This building boom created a large space for outsiders on the fringes of society who were often struggling with subsistence. The Franciscans and Dominicans arrived in Venice during the thirteenth century, where they adapted a Gothic building style for large churches, noble palaces, and confraternities. These edifices were a departure from the older parish churches that had been built in the Veneto-Byzantine style. The great families donated to the building program, using Gothic ornamentation similar to northern Europe but with wooden ceilings because Venice's amphibious environment could not sustain the weight of heavy stone structures. Venice's merchants and craftsmen also erected confraternities, or secular brotherhoods, as places to meet, to assist the needy, to stage rituals and pageants, and to represent all parts of the city. The minor brotherhoods accommodated the growing communities of Albanians, Greeks, and Slavs as well as minor craftsmen and traders. This construction reached its acme in 1348, when the bubonic plague epidemic brought activity to a temporary halt.

Secular Architecture: Civic Palaces

In the urban centers of central and northern Italy, in line with the participatory government that was evolving, a new form of architecture sprang up at the end of the thirteenth century, the civic palace. Among the earliest were the Palazzo Pubblico in Siena (1297) (see Figure 3.1) and the Palazzo Vecchio in Florence (1299). Sponsored by the commune rather than the church, the civic palace, or town hall, served new urban governments as meeting places. Further, they were symbols of civic pride and major features of urban skylines. The names of these new buildings were normally taken from the city's form of government: Palazzo Pubblico (Public) in Siena and Verona; Palazzo della Ragione (Justice) in Verona; Palazzo Ducale (Ducal) in Venice; Palazzo del Podestà (Governor), now the Bargello in Florence; Palazzo dei Priori (Priors) in Perugia and Volterra; and in the Lombard towns of Bergamo, Brescia, Como, and Monza, Broletto (little orchard). Their architectural style was of two types: the more open loggias of cities with more political stability, such as Venice (as seen in Figure 3.5 on the right side), and the closed, fortified brick building with defensive features, characteristic of towns riddled with urban violence and external threats in Tuscany (as seen in Figure 3.1). Commonly made of brick, together with local materials, the tall towers of the central Italian municipalities vaunted the power of communal government, while their walls, bells, and small windows offered protection from invading neighbors.

In contrast to the tall towers of central Italy, Venice's visual appearance reflected merchant contact with the Byzantine and Islamic world and

FIGURE 3.5 Doge's Palace (on right), Venice, Italy. The various styles of the palace reflect merchant contact with the Byzantine and Islamic world as well as the Gothic of northern Europe.

the Gothic styles of northern Europe (Figure 3.5, on right). The town plan borrowed from Islamic typologies in Damascus, Aleppo, Cairo, and Jerusalem, and its aquatic environment made the city stand apart from its Italian neighbors. The Palazzo Ducale originated as a fortress-like stronghold for the head of state (the Doge), with Byzantine features, but when it was rebuilt in 1340 and 1424 it incorporated Islamic and Gothic elements that derived from the travels of its merchants. Unlike the town halls of its neighbors, either in Lombardy or in central Italy, the Palazzo Ducale borrowed heavily from monumental Mongol (east Asian) and Mamluk (Egyptian) architectures. Cushioned by the sea, it boasted an open loggia facing the waterfront, with light and air permeating the decorative lace of a façade that recalled the monuments of Mongol rulers. One could also find elements of the Mosque of St. Athanasius in Alexandria or the fourteenth-century hall of justice in Cairo. Further, the pinnacled roofline was characteristic of Egyptian architecture, with mosque crenellations. The Palazzo Ducale could have been the palace of Mamluk sultans, important trading associates of the Venetians. It brought back visions of the trade route to Alexandria and of the Silk Road to Persia. When the state rebuilt the Palazzo Ducale in the mid-fourteenth century, it added Gothic ornamentation to the Veneto-Byzantine and Islamic elements.

Secular Architecture: Domestic Palaces

New architecture also arose from the sponsorship of great families in the Italian cities. However, distinct architectural forms did not develop everywhere. In Florence prior to 1350, for example, the residences of the urban rich were made of indiscreet rustic stone, without much decoration save a coat of arms. It was not until the fifteenth century that domestic architecture entered the vanguard of new styles. The rich in Venice, on the other hand, were innovative much earlier. Venetian merchants used their homes as headquarters for their commercial ventures, choosing prime locations that gave them access to the port, the commercial marketplace at Rialto, and the Grand Canal, the conduit for transport. Unlike the massive stone structures of Tuscany, Venetian palaces on the waterfront were more open. The earliest architectural example of aristocratic housing was the Veneto-Byzantine palaces of the twelfth century, the Palazzi Loredan and Farsetti (see Figure 2.5) and the Fondaco dei Turchi. Each had a two-story arcade facing the waterfront, where merchandise was loaded and unloaded. The ground floor housed storerooms and offices; the great noble families lived on the floor above. Behind the palace was a courtyard with a well. This type of building could also be found in the Levant. Most likely the Venetian merchants adapted their model from the Arabic *fondouk*, or trading post. They also named their warehouses *fondaci*. Venetian exteriors were highly decorated, a luxury that elites on the mainland could not afford because their palaces were designed as fortifications to protect them. Many of the Venetian decorations were brought back from the Crusades, and the palaces along the Grand Canal commemorated Venice's trading conquests as well as each family dynasty's status within the ruling class. During the thirteenth century family palaces also favored Gothic ornamentation for their facades.

Trends in Painting and Sculpture

New Renaissance styles in painting did not begin to flower until the fifteenth century, but the artists of the late thirteenth and fourteenth centuries paved the way, working for the commercial denizens of central Italy, in Florence, Pisa, and Siena, as well as the urban conglomerations in the north, stretching from the Apennines to the Alps and from the French border to the Adriatic. Thirteenth-century painting was also often tied to the Franciscans, the first of several mendicant orders that transformed cities including Assisi,

Florence, and Venice with their large churches and convents. The life of the Franciscans' founder, Francis of Assisi, whose life the Dominican friar Bonaventure wrote about, was an important subject of painting in Assisi, Florence, and Padua.

The thirteenth and fourteenth centuries witnessed an increasing interest in portraying the human body in a realistic manner, through calculated, albeit imperfect, ratio and proportion, and setting it in a realistic space that mirrored the urban environment. Rich families began to spend lavishly for private chapels, frescoes, religious panels, and their own tombs in commemoration of their success, but also to send a message to urban laborers attending mass. In Florence, for example, at the Church of Santa Croce, which was begun at the end of the thirteenth century, a number of prominent families—the Bardi, Peruzzi, and Baroncelli—decorated their chapels and furnished them with liturgical accessories. Giotto di Bondone's (c. 1267–1337) frescoes in the Bardi chapel conveyed the moral messages of the cult of St. Francis, a humanistic and empathic ethos spreading throughout Italy that appealed to the poor and humble. In the northern city of Padua, Enrico Scrovegno of Padua, a wealthy merchant intent on displaying his piety and distancing himself from the sins of his usurious father, commissioned Giotto, who was the son of a peasant, to fresco between 1302 and 1305 the classical Arena Chapel with the lives of the Virgin Mary and Christ (Figure 3.6).

With Giotto's decoration of the Arena Chapel, painting in Italy turned a corner, introducing a new view of reality that reflected the rise of the urban classes, city life, and deep religious feeling. The painter had not mastered the mathematical rules of perspective—that would come in the fifteenth century. However, one can see that he was trying to portray three-dimensional objects and figures on a two-dimensional wall mural. Giotto's figures were more natural than a lot of art that had come before, with weight, mass, and psychological depth. He was greatly influenced by the painter Cimabue (1240–1302), whose frescos in the upper Basilica of Assisi had evoked a new sense of pathos. Giotto's art depicted a range of human emotions, including anger, love, astonishment, grief, and despair, with such intensity that they brought religious narrative to life, offering spectators of all social classes the sensation of witnessing dramatic scenes from a play. He filled the Scrovegni Chapel with paintings that told the life story of Mary and her son Jesus. His artistic style, following Cimabue, was a marked departure from the more conventional, static madonnas staring into space with ornate gold halos on flat, two-dimensional planes, a style called *maniera greca* that had derived from the devotional art of the Byzantines. The sixteenth-century art historian, Giorgio Vasari, conceptualizing the development of Renaissance art, saw its birth with Giotto. Art historians since then, however, have pointed out that Vasari did not give enough credit to the Byzantine east, where the life forms of artists from Constantinople were not all static and one can find fresco paintings that give weight, mass, and emotion to human figures.

FIGURE 3.6 Giotto di Bondone (1267–1337). *The Arrest of Christ*, or *Kiss of Judas* (*c.* 1303–1305). Fresco. Scrovegni Chapel, Padua, Italy. The faces of Christ and his apostles express intense, human emotion and psychological depth, which was more natural than a lot of art that had come before.

Giotto's painting is also significant because he created scenes that celebrated the city and urban life in the late thirteenth- and early fourteenth-century commune, with subject matter that was religious, and didactic, making available to people Christ's lessons and everyday life. One may imagine that such scenes, while filled with religious symbolism, would be appealing to urban dwellers whose lives were situated in mundane rather than mystical circumstances. And it was these very mundane urban inhabitants, the victors of power in the commune, organized into guilds, family blocks, religious corporations, and communal councils that sponsored a new art that celebrated both urban space and the riches of the countryside. Following Giotto, two brothers, Pietro (1280–1348) and Ambrosio (1285–1348) Lorenzetti, also explored architectural and landscape settings in their paintings. Lorenzetti's allegorical painting *The Effects of Good Government on City Life* (see Figure 2.1), commissioned by the Sienese government and situated in a chamber of the Palazzo Pubblico, portrayed the positive effects of a strong civil order both in city and countryside. It was filled with streets and squares, houses and palaces, and prosperous city dwellers. Happy citizens danced in the streets. The artist also depicted a healthy countryside, filled with farms and orchards, villas and castles, and peasants at work. On the opposite wall the painter depicted the negative outcomes of poor government, the worst of which was tyranny, a strong message sent from the denizens of the new government.

Both Byzantine and French Gothic traditions continued into the fourteenth century, along with the new realism. Duccio di Buoninsegna (active 1278–1318), for example, remained one of the strongest proponents of the Byzantine style. With his *Madonna in Majesty* (*Maestà*), painted for the Cathedral of Siena beginning in 1308, mosaic was translated into paint. The commemoration of the Virgin was part of the special devotion to the mother of Christ that was spreading throughout Europe during this time. Duccio was also influenced by the Gothic techniques of Giovanni Pisano (*c*. 1250–1315), but his landscapes and urban backgrounds also show the new interest to set subjects in the real world. The larger altarpiece, of which the *Maestà* was a part, also displayed an interest in textiles, which Siena had imported from the far east, Persia, and North Africa, especially in the passion story (the suffering and death of Christ). Other painters, including Giotto, also brought in Islamic motifs in their work: Pseudo-Arabic (Kufic) scripts were used as decorations in religious halos. Another painter, Simone Martini (1284–1344) breaking with the Byzantine style after working for King Robert of Anjou at Naples, imported the French Gothic style of the early fourteenth century to Siena.

Literature

The narrative continuum, found in the sculptures of the Pisani and the paintings of Giotto, also found expression in the adaption of the vernacular language, which was another dimension of the consciousness of humanity and the culture of realism that unfolded during the thirteenth century and was a forerunner of the Renaissance. It was the century in which modern Italian came to be written and spoken and came to be an art form. The use of the vernacular began in Sicily, where Emperor Frederick II sponsored the Sicilian Poetic School, a cultural group of intellectuals writing in the Italian vernacular. The Sicilian school of poets adapted Provencal literary models and produced the earliest formal literature into Italian. It was from here that Dante Alighieri (c. 1265–1321) adopted his *dolce stil nuovo*, a "new, sweet style," together with the writers Guido Cavalcanti, Lapo Gianni, Cino da Pistoia, and Brunetto Latini. The *dolce stil novo*, steeped in the communal experience, was a vernacular poetry that discussed the morals of the citizenry, attacking the vices of the parvenue and new money while celebrating the civilizing effects of love. Together these authors made Italian a literary language during a time when most poetry was written in Latin, a language only accessible to learned readers. Realizing the need for a unified literary language in a time when writers expressed themselves in a variety of Italian dialects, Dante wrote a defense of the vernacular and advanced the use of the Tuscan dialect. Petrarch and Boccaccio would follow.

A white Guelf (supporter of the papacy) from Florence, embroiled in local and imperialist politics, Dante found himself aligned with the losing political party and was exiled in 1302. After his expulsion he wrote *The Divine Comedy*, a description of his journey through Hell, Purgatory, and Paradise guided by the poet Virgil and his idealized beloved Beatrice that was actually a commentary on friends and enemies, historical figures, and people he thought had betrayed humanity and deserved damnation. Dante intended to reach a wide readership that included the laity, the clergy, and other writers as he described the concerns of his day, which included the urban violence of families and factions as well as the conflicting claims of popes and emperors. The *Divine Comedy* came to be considered one of the most important poems of the Middle Ages and one of the greatest literary works in the Italian language.

Petrarch (1304–1374)

A poet and scholar, Francesco Petrarca, known as Petrarch, was born in Arezzo, Italy. He was the son of a Florentine notary who had been exiled to this small, Tuscan town. Petrarch spent his childhood in Avignon, France, where his father worked in the court of Pope Clement V during the period of papal exile (1309–76). There he was exposed to the French Provençal poets who wrote about courtly love. Later Petrarch would write his own sonnets, a body of literature that would have a lasting influence on Europe over the following three centuries. Petrarch began his training in law in France at the University of Montpellier. Later he continued his legal studies in Bologna (Italy). In his adult years he worked in Italy with princely, republican, and clerical patrons. During that time he became familiar with the Italian lyrical tradition. Although Petrarch's sonnets exhibit some similarities with the rhyming couplets of the medieval Persian poets composing Arabic verse (*ghazal*) about love and loss, the writer took his models from the Latin Classics as well as the Church Fathers.

Petrarch was interested in antiquity, in reviving such classical genres as epic poems, famous lives, and famous events. He resuscitated these genres with a new sense of historical distance that humanist writers in the fifteenth century would recall in their movement to separate themselves from the medieval past. Perhaps what stands out the most about Petrarch, however, is his interest in the self, that is, in his own interests, outlook, and personality. In one of his most important letters, the *Ascent of Mont Ventoux*, a recollection of a mountain-climbing experience, he questions his own life choices. It is an essay inspired by the *Confessions* of the early Christian writer Augustine. The work is autobiographical, and with it Petrarch shows himself to posterity. He preferred sacred to secular literature, antiquity to contemporary life, and country living over that of the city. Another of Petrarch's essays, "To Posterity," is a reflection on what he had accomplished in life. With these essays we see a change in autobiography, as the author creates his own historical persona. This becomes a model for later poets who focus on personal discourse.

Over his lifetime Petrarch produced many prose works, both in Latin and in the vernacular. He traveled throughout northern Europe, searching for the manuscripts of classical authors and the early Christian writers. He wrote biographies of the ancients. He considered religious life, the notion of fame, and above all the power of love, based on his own deep feelings for a woman named Laura. She became the object of his imagination and many of his love poems. In 1341 Petrarch was crowned poet laureate in Rome, a honor that brought him fame. Afterwards he settled in Verona during the Black Death of 1347–8. Many of his friends and his beloved Laura died. Once the epidemic subsided he continued his career in Milan, and then in Padua and the small Veneto town of Arquà. His fame rests on both his poetry and his letters, both of which would influence Italian, French, Spanish, and English writers for centuries to come.

Giovanni Boccaccio (1313–1375)

The celebrated prehumanist writer Giovanni Boccaccio did not break away entirely from the medieval tradition. His humorous stories in *The Decameron*, set against the background of a raging plague in the Tuscan countryside, are not new, but rather borrowed from the larger Mediterranean world as well as Persia and India. The stories tell of Jewish and Muslim merchants, sultans and kings from Anatolia and Egypt, and the bazaars of Cairo, Alexandria, and Acre, reflecting the cosmopolitan, mercantile world of the Crusades as well as the medieval, chivalric tradition of courtly love and knightly deeds. Class difference is everywhere in the stories, and the writer assumes his readers know that nobles do not mix with commoners and that rank matters. Yet at the same time, Boccaccio offers some new perspectives that we might ground in the more secular city-state milieu: the heroes and heroines of his stories are those who know how to take care of themselves in this world. Naiveté and stupidity are the unforgiveable sins of the losers, while intelligence, wit, and adroit manipulation reward the victors, including brazen liars and cheats. Might this be the ethos of the new entrepreneurial classes that dominated the Italian cities, whose business acumen has brought them success; the merchants, moneylenders, and skilled artisans driven by earthly goals rather than spiritual transcendence? Or was the author's cynicism colored by the famines, plague, financial reverses, and wars of the early fourteenth century? Either way, bearing in mind that literature was written to entertain, the author paints a broad picture of humanity's strengths and weaknesses with the same quality of naturalism that we see on the walls decorated by Giotto's brush. Bocaccio holds the clergy in contempt, attacking its hypocrisy, love of money, and lust with apparent ill-regard for the preparation of the world to come. Women, surprisingly, demonstrate strength, rationalism, and sensuality, even though an examination of the laws of the period, in sync with the misogynistic perspectives of clerics and natural philosophers, shows them at a legal disadvantage should they show an appetite for passion. Boccaccio's women appear to be emancipated from societal constraints, guided by chance rather than divine providence to attain human enjoyment. Boccaccio influenced another great writer across the English Channel, Geoffrey Chaucer (1340–1400), who like his Italian counterparts did a great deal to elevate the vernacular dialects of England. In his *Canterbury Tales*, a collection of stories about pilgrims journeying to the shrine of St. Thomas à Becket, Chaucer, like Boccaccio, paints lively portraits of the various types of human character.

Conclusion

The revival of cities on the Italian Peninsula during the eleventh to early fourteenth centuries brought with it new forms of culture. Cities and towns established systems of law to organize civil, criminal, and commercial affairs, while the church used canon law to regulate family, religious, and monastic life. Universities were established with curricula that drew both on the ancient past and on medieval Christian and Islamic culture. Law and medicine became important subjects of study. The rise of a middle class warranted improved mathematical skills and writings in the vernacular in addition to the more erudite Latin language. Boccaccio's writings celebrated intelligence and guile, emphasizing the secular ambitions of the new merchant class. Urban prosperity brought new building initiatives in the Romanesque and Gothic styles, largely undertaken by the religious orders. In art the human form in an urban setting took on new life, as Giotto and the

Pisano brothers brought human emotion to fresco and stone, respectively. All of these developments were important underpinnings of a cultural and intellectual revival that blossomed during the fifteenth century.

Think Critically

1. How did universities change education? What other venues offered men and women places to learn? What were the practical applications of higher learning?
2. What forms of secular and ecclesiastical architecture filled the needs of the revived Italian cities?
3. What was the importance of the vernacular language for Italy's medieval cities?

Further Exploration

1. What human emotions can you see in the painter Giotto's depiction of the betrayal of Christ and his consequent arrest (Figure 3.6)?
2. Compare the Palazzo Pubblico in Siena with the Doge's Palace in Venice (Figures 3.1 and 3.5). What role did geography and environment play in the stylistic features of these two buildings?

Further Reading

De Vos, Paula S. *Compound Remedies: Galenic Pharmacy from the Ancient Mediterranean to New Spain*. Pittsburgh, PA: University of Pittsburgh Press, 2020. Traces the evolution of the Galenic pharmaceutical tradition from its foundations in ancient Greece to the physician-philosophers of medieval Islamic empires and the Latin West and eventually through the Spanish Empire to Mexico.

Goldthwaite, Richard A. *The Building of Renaissance Florence. An Economic and Social History*. Baltimore, MD: Johns Hopkins University Press, 1980. Reconstructs the labor and costs of building this major Renaissance city as well as the cultural climate in which conspicuous consumption developed.

Graham-Dixon, Andrew. *Renaissance*. Berkeley, CA: University of California Press, 2000. Surveys the art and architecture of the Renaissance in the context of the politics, morality, and philosophy that advanced their development.

Howard, Deborah. *Venice and the East. The Impact of the Islamic World on Venetian Architecture, 1100–1500*. New Haven, CT: Yale University Press, 2000. A deep exploration of the influence of merchant trade in the east on Venetian architecture.

Makdisi, George. "Scholasticism and Humanism in Classical Islam and the Christian West." *Journal of the American Oriental Society*, 109:2 (April to June 1989): 175–82. Explores the debt of scholasticism and humanism to Islam.

Martines, Lauro. *Power and the Imagination. City-States in Renaissance Italy*. Baltimore, MD: Johns Hopkins University Press, 1988. A magisterial survey of medieval and Renaissance Italian developments that draws connections between cultural patrons and power.

Matter, E. Ann, and John Coakley, eds. *Creative Women in Medieval and Early Modern Italy*. Philadelphia: University of Pennsylvania Press, 1994. A collection of essays on women's participation in the religious and artistic life of the Italian Peninsula from the thirteenth to the seventeenth centuries.

Witt, Ronald G. *The Two Latin Cultures and the Foundation of Renaissance Humanism in Medieval Italy*. New York: Cambridge University Press, 2012. Introducing the concept of dual Latin cultures in medieval Italy, one ecclesiastical and the other lay, the author traces the antecedents of humanist learning.

4

Daily Life and Modes of Socialization

At the beginning of the fourteenth century the Italian Peninsula, and Europe itself, faced a series of economic crises, its stability undermined by a series of famines, followed by the bubonic plague epidemic called the Black Death (1347–50), which killed at least a third of the overall population or more (see Figure 4.1). The disruption and catastrophic levels of mortality impacted every level of society, including politics, literature, and the arts. While the great epidemic eventually came to an end, this infectious disease did not totally disappear. Instead it visited the population regularly well into the eighteenth century. Following the mid-fourteenth-century debacle, demographic numbers steadily shrank, bringing changes to the state of the labor market as well as to secular and ecclesiastical institutions. They leveled out once again during the fifteenth century and then grew dramatically after 1500.

One underlying problem triggering economic instability during the fourteenth century was an agrarian crisis, which began around 1300. Steady demographic growth over the previous 300 years began to outstrip landed resources. Persistent exploitation of farmland, coupled with limited agrarian technology, produced a series of low yields. Heavy rains and global cooling also contributed to crop failure, resulting in a series of famines. The years between 1315 and 1317 were particularly difficult. Peasants, resorting to gruels and sops and bread cooked with inferior flours, suffered from malnutrition. Vitamin deficiencies lowered their resistance to certain diseases, like scurvy, rickets, and pellagra. Many flocked to urban centers, which fared somewhat better than the countryside because urban officials kept grain reserves, but overall the laboring classes suffered a decline in their standard of living.

The periodic agrarian crises also impacted noble landowners. While they may have secured their own subsistence, their profits from agriculture and

FIGURE 4.1 *Victims of the Black Death Being Buried at Tournai*, then part of the Netherlands, 1349. The Black Death was thought to have been an outbreak of the bubonic plague, which killed up to half the population of Europe.

peasant rents diminished. Declining resources propelled them not only to resort to warfare, brigandage, and mercenary service but also to siphon off as much of peasant production as they could. This left the overall population in a precarious position, especially during periods of famine. It also impacted the state, for governments depended on the peasant economy for tax revenues, putting them in direct competition with the landowners.

The Black Death of 1347–50 presented a new challenge. The bacterium *Yersinia pestis* first surfaced in 1346 in the urban centers of western Asia, en route from China and India. Its earliest manifestation appeared in the Genoese colony of Kaffa, in the Crimea on the shores of the Black Sea. The epidemic broke out in the army of the Mongol Khan, who had set his sights on the town. Hoping to weaken Kaffa's resistance, he ordered the afflicted corpses hurled over the city walls. Those who could, fled. Caravan ships that had been trading in the area then carried the rats, which were infested with plague-infected fleas, to Messina, Sicily, in 1347, and over the next thirty months the disease spread via the principal trade routes throughout Italy and the rest of Europe. The term "Black Death" derived from the dark-colored tumors, called *buboes*, that swelled in the limbs of the flea-bitten sick. In its pneumonic form the afflicted suffered from fever, chest pains, and the expulsion of blood, followed frequently by death. The septicemic form infected the lungs via airborne droplets and was equally as fatal. There was no known remedy for its debilitating and often lethal effects.

In addition to physical devastation, the catastrophic death tolls had a profound impact on human psychology. People did not know that the culprit transmitting the disease to humans was an infected species of flea, the *Xenopsylla cheopis*, borne by the black rat (*Rattus rattus*). Within a few hours after the bacillus enters the bloodstream, severe illness and death are almost certain. Ports, towns, and cities were filled with such rats, just as they were filled with farm animals such as goats, pigs, chickens, and cows, and it was common for ordinary people to be infested with fleas, found in bedding and clothing. However, in their ignorance they cast the blame elsewhere: on a punitive God or on minority groups such as Jews, foreigners, prostitutes, and vagabonds. They marched through the streets flagellating themselves and asking for God's forgiveness of their sins, and they persecuted minorities. Art portrayed macabre themes and the mysteries of death as well as religious fervor. Little did people know, the best defense against the plague was to avoid crowded living conditions. The groups that suffered the most were people living in tenements and working in crowded shops or residing in religious communities.

Fleas infected rich and poor alike. The rich, however, had recourse to country dwellings, away from the urban din. Such respite was famously described in Giovanni Boccaccio's *Decameron*, a collection of one hundred entertaining tales recounted against the setting of plague by noblemen and noblewomen taking refuge in a country villa outside Florence. There they told of people giving over to sensual pleasures freely as if there would be no tomorrow. Bocaccio also wrote one of the most famous literary accounts of the contagion's devastating weight on the human psyche. He related that some people isolated themselves in groups and closed themselves off from the world at large. They had the means to nourish and entertain themselves well. Other people threw themselves into public drinking, singing, and various festivities as if the plague epidemic were not serious. Many suffered from sheer terror, abandoning their kin, while mothers stopped taking care of their children.

Besides the deleterious behavior that derived from collective panic, the immediate effects of the plague included a breakdown of the food supply as harvests remained in the fields. Hand manufactures also came to a halt, and both local and long-distance commerce was interrupted. Sanitary measures, including quarantine, were inadequate to stop the ravages of the disease. The labor supply dwindled, products were scarce, and prices soared. Governments scrambled to recruit new magistrates and replace troops. Some attempted to discourage peasants from leaving farms. But these were temporary setbacks, for the dramatic decline in population in effect changed the state of the labor market for those fortunate enough to survive. The demand for workers permitted ordinary people to press for better conditions. Peasant survivors attempted to improve their sharecropping arrangements with landowners, whereby the landlords provided the heavy farm animals and tools for half the harvest. In the post–plague period farmers moved to better lands, which had been abandoned during the epidemic, and they tried to keep more produce for themselves. Skilled artisans demanded wage increases. Both old landed proprietors and urban employers were forced to negotiate or face revolts. And revolts did come to pass, provoked by excess taxation, noble demands for higher rents, and employers' refusals to grant higher wages. There were major outbursts in France in 1350s, Florence in 1378, and England in 1381. Other labor revolts in Italy took place in Lucca, Siena, Perugia, Genoa, and Verona, but they did not match the scale of uprisings in France and England. The most outstanding rebellion in Italy was that of the Ciompi, beaters and carders in the wool industry, in 1378. Some 13,000 laborers demanded a greater part in Florentine government. They took the Palazzo Vecchio for five and one half weeks before their movement collapsed. Neither in Florence nor elsewhere did the rebellions result in any deep political changes, for the ruling classes remained in power, but they made them aware of the dangers of lower-class revolt should their exploitation reach intolerable levels. Among the beneficiaries of the high levels of mortality were religious institutions, which benefited from a mass of pious bequests, some of which were used to invest in new art and architecture. Work resumed, for example, on the Duomo and Church of Santa Croce in Florence and the Cathedral in Milan. At the same time many artists expired in the plague, creating a lull in artistic innovation during the last half of the fourteenth century.

As dire as the circumstances of the mid-fourteenth century were, some of the survivors of the Black Death benefitted from the demographic reduction. The demand for new labor, especially in the cities, effected a rise in wages. There were new opportunities not only for male and female laborers, but also for merchants, who turned to luxury markets and fairs as well as providing small loans to their governments. In the north, technologies in textile production, mining, and power mills improved. States responded to the new economy by sponsoring banks and lines of navigation. Being aware that luxury markets were too small to entirely save their economies, they also expanded internal markets beyond city walls. As before, citizens continued to acquire land and invest in sharecropping and textiles and to accumulate wealth, though there were little to no improvements for agrarian workers. Higher earnings for the survivors of the contagion meant more purchasing power and capital to invest in business and property. Increased purchasing power also created a demand for higher quality goods, better housing, and more education.

The Standard of Living

The cyclical travesties of famine, malnutrition, and pestilence, followed at times by periods of growth and opportunity, raise the important subject of what daily life was like for the majority of people. Most were overwhelmingly farm laborers. A small minority filled the crafts sector. While Italy was filled with urban nuclei, the rest of Europe was more rural.

Cities and towns regularly absorbed rural workers from the countryside, where handicrafts were dispersed in cottage industries. The overwhelming majority of people went through cycles of boom and bust. Many factors shaped their experience, among them the size of the population. During the period between 1000 and 1300 the population was rising, but there was still an abundance of land to farm and in the towns and cities a demand for handicraft work, especially in textiles and construction. As population levels began to outstrip resources after 1300, land became scarcer as did openings in handicraft labor. Once the Black Death relieved demographic pressure, there were once again new opportunities for business and labor, a rise in wages, and attenuation of rural exploitation. Following general stagnation during the fifteenth century, the sixteenth century brought rising numbers of people, high inflation, and a dearth of resources to go around, similar to the early fourteenth century.

The same cyclical characteristics applied to diet and nutrition, rates of natality and mortality, and marriage. In cycles when more farmland was available and good weather prevailed, peasants could subsist and even perhaps accumulate enough surplus to have some purchasing power. However, two bad harvests in a row spelled famine and malnourishment and earnings below subsistence level. Malnutrition affected birth rates, producing temporary infertility in women. In general, infant mortality was high, especially among the lower classes. With respect to marriage, the aftermath of catastrophic mortality rates like those of the Black Death encouraged more people to wed and to wed at a younger age in order to maximize the period of human reproduction and replenish the labor force. The opposite was true in times when the population was swollen and people were experiencing a dearth of resources. In periods of population density more people postponed marriages, produced fewer children, or did not marry at all. Of course, these are broad generalizations, ones that need to be refined according to class and gender over time. Let us see how these cycles played out in the various life stages of the overall population.

Infancy

In an age when life was ridden with famine and poverty and infant mortality was high, at least 25 percent of infants failed to reach their first year of life, and another 25 percent died before reaching their teens. Registrations in the Florentine *Books of the Dead* for the years between 1385 and 1430, according to David Herlihy and Christiane Klapisch-Zuber (see later), indicated that as many as 40 percent of infants or children died during this period. Poor hygiene, filth, contaminated water, harmful bacteria, and limited medical expertise made them vulnerable to disease. There was some awareness that breast milk gave a baby better odds of survival; this was an important topic in Christian medical texts as well as among midwives and village healers. However, for a variety of reasons, including malnutrition, some mothers and wet nurses did not have enough milk.

Some of the best data regarding infancy during the fifteenth century comes from the quantitative studies of the 1427 Tuscan census that David Herlihy and Christiane Klapisch-Zuber undertook. They concluded that the infants of the rich had better chances of survival than those of the poor. Further, Klapisch-Zuber found that boys were given more care in nursing practices. Parents believed that the character of the mother or wet nurse was passed on to the child through breast milk. Consequently fathers preferred to have wet nurses for infant boys in their homes where they could be supervised, while girls might be given to countrywomen. Elite women were also more apt to entrust their children to wet nurses in order to increase their fertile years, for it was believed that nursing produced temporary infertility. Even the lower classes had wet nurses, but in general the Florentine countryside was a center of wet nursing that catered to prosperous families. Unsupervised wet nursing, however, came with risks. Countrywomen depended on this income. If their milk dried up, some were tempted to conceal the fact that they could no longer render services, and their young charges might starve.

Historians have vigorously debated whether parents were attached to their children, given the high mortality rate, especially during infancy. There is both textual and visual evidence in Italy that confirms the importance of bringing new human life into the world. While most people learned about caring for infants and young children from family members, neighbors, midwives, and perhaps physicians, both classical and Muslim medical writers produced pathologies of childhood maladies. They became more available with the advent of printing in the late fifteenth century. The first printed collection of childhood diseases, authored by Paolo Bagellardo (d. 1494) in 1472, derived mostly from the opinions of Muslim physicians. As literacy grew, such texts were read by both women and men, but it was primarily women who managed the period of gestation, childbirth, child nutrition, and health. Humanists writers also took up the subject of infant care. Francesco Barbaro (1390–1454) in Venice encouraged mothers to nurse their own babies. Besides written materials, we know that cities and towns also made provisions for abandoned infants by establishing foundling homes throughout Italy (Figure 4.2). The abandoned newborns that were deposited in these institutions were taken to countrywomen to nurse almost immediately after birth. It was believed best for a child to be nursed with breast milk until the age of two.

Material evidence also indicates how important it was to give birth to a child, especially among the ruling classes At the higher levels of society in Florence, *deschi da parto*, or birth trays (Figure 4.3), presented as gifts to a newborn's parents, illustrated heroic themes aimed to influence the child's upbringing. Childhood material culture also documents that parents tended to their babies' developmental needs with swaddling clothes, cradles, and rattles. Other evidence that suggests parents treasured their offspring are found in family portraits of Italy's great dynasties such as the Gonzaga

FIGURE 4.2 Filippo Brunelleschi (1377–1446). *Ospedale degli Innocenti* (1419–1445). Florence, Italy. Warburg/Warburgs Gallery. The hospital was a foundling home for abandoned infants.

of Mantua and the Pesaro of Venice. Paintings also illustrate the ways in which childbirth was an important event, one orchestrated by female kin and family as well as midwives (see Figure 7.20). Finally, children were assigned godparents to hold a protective place in their lives as well as to renew, expand, or solidify important social and political ties for the family.

Not all pregnancies ended with childbirth. Given its potentially criminal nature, there is scant evidence in the historical record about attempted abortion or infanticide, both crimes that included men as well as women as perpetrators. Women who were single and pregnant had no social place in Renaissance society. They left their villages or towns to give birth in secret. Among their options were to abandon the baby or give it up to a foundling home after forty days of lying in, the term for post-natal care.

Foundling homes were first established in Italy in the thirteenth century as a solution for the poor as well as the illegitimate. The fifteenth-century Hospital of the Innocent in Florence received the illegitimate offspring of nobles, many of whom had sexual relations with servants or slaves. It housed about 6 percent of all baptized children. Italian cities also founded a series of orphanages for older children. They were generally sent into service around age seven, the age both Christian (and Islamic) theorists thought

FIGURE 4.3 Masaccio (1401–1428). *Desco da Parto* (Tray Celebrating Birth), 1420. Oil on poplar wood. Gemäldegalerie der Staatlichen Museen zu Berlin, Germany.

(male) children had the powers of reason. It was common for children to lose one or both parents to war, famine, or disease. If not consigned to an orphanage, many children lived with kin substitutes, either under a religious house or in rural or domestic service.

From Infancy to Adolescence

Social class, financial means, and gender played an important part in shaping experience. In principle children remained at home for their first seven years, under parental supervision. For their first two years they were often swaddled to keep them secure; between two and five they were permitted to play without physical constrictions; from six or seven they are given small tasks appropriate to their age. In Catholic communities seven was the age when children could be held accountable for committing a mortal sin. But children could only remain at home if the household could afford it, something that once again depended on cyclical trends. Poor parents farmed their children out to work in more prosperous households, even as early as age seven. Some were apprenticed early for rural labor, the handicrafts, or trade. Orphans received vocational training. In this sense childhood was brief compared to modern standards. The poorer the family, the shorter the period of childhood. In poorer families children were given assignments early on, such as tending infant siblings, collecting firewood or worms on vines, herding livestock, weeding, sweeping, cleaning, carrying water, and doing errands. Later both boys and girls might tend fields or farm animals. Girls also served as domestics, helping with spinning, sewing, and lace making. Between seven and twelve their responsibilities grew. By age fourteen both sexes were doing the work of adults. One might argue that there was little distinction between adolescence and young adulthood. Jewish texts, for example, did not refer to adolescence as a separate phase of the life cycle. As a center of production, the household was a place where all family members participated in some form of labor. Activities revolved around planting and harvesting, furnishing raw materials for manufacture, such as flax, hemp, silk, and plants for dye; making clothing; constructing housing; and tending livestock. In artisan households some children learned trades. At times adolescent males of various social strata gathered in groups and paraded through their communities acting as social censors by committing pranks or ridiculing the behavior and lifestyles of those who did not conform to prevalent cultural norms.

For the offspring of the propertied classes childhood was under parental supervision. In legal terms, the child belonged to the paternal line. In Florence widows who remarried lost guardianship of their children, who passed to male agnatic kin. As adolescents the young were placed under the supervision of surrogate adults, whether in military companies for males or in religious institutions for either sex. Children in more prosperous or elite households began to receive some kind of formal education after age seven. The wealthy engaged tutors or enrolled sons in boarding schools. The two most famous humanist schools for males were in Ferrara and Verona, but there were also secular schools that taught Latin and mathematics throughout Italy, endowed schools run by priests, and church schools attached to cathedrals and monasteries. Teachers in vernacular schools, popular in commercial areas, not only offered instruction in reading and writing in vernacular rather than Latin, but also taught commercial mathematics, elementary bookkeeping, and literature ranging from saints' lives to chivalric poems. Jewish adolescents, on the other hand, studied in religious schools, where they learned Hebrew and religious literature.

Male children from elite circles who were tracked for marriage were trained from an early age to be family patriarchs, estate managers, and military and political leaders. Females were groomed to be household managers and mothers. Humanism (see Chapter 6) trained the ruling elites of the Italian cities and the chancery officials of Europe's growing bureaucracies. The curriculum included the constitutional histories of ancient Greece and Rome as moral and historical examples. Educators looked to antiquity for literary models, such as the writings of Virgil and Cicero. Boys also had athletic and military training and studied geography and Latin grammar to prepare them for political responsibilities. Those not destined to carry on the family line were schooled for military, bureaucratic, or religious service. Females that remained at home were generally enrolled in convents by the age of nine, where they were taught reading and writing in addition to sewing and manners. Some learned Latin and received a humanist education that enabled them to write and correspond with intellectuals. But with the exception of aristocratic women acting as regents for their husbands or sons, women could not exercise political power, nor could they teach or enter the professions. Commercialization and urbanization required more education for children. The invention of the printing press during the late fifteenth century facilitated this. Printed reading primers, grammar manuals, and classical and humanists texts could be disseminated more broadly and books acquired greater importance.

Sexuality

The baseline for regulating human sexuality was the Catholic Church, which prescribed virginity and celibacy for both sexes as the desirable states, unless intercourse was performed within marriage and for the exclusive purpose of procreation. The clergy in the Latin Church were also to remain celibate. The church also insisted that sexual relations be heterosexual, that the male be on top, and that intercourse not take place on Sundays or certain holidays. In principle, women who engaged in sexual relations outside of wedlock were stigmatized, but in practice this rule might be softened in the case of premarital relations where there was a promise of marriage. Some people did not formally marry but instead cohabited and considered their relationship to be one of marriage. However, there was no guarantee that men who had premarital sex with women would maintain their promises of marriage, and many times these cases ended up in ecclesiastical tribunals. Such relationships were also frequently regulated by the couple's community. Women's natal families often insisted on marriage for the couple, but sometimes would settle for remuneration that could be applied to the young woman's dowry. To prevent such travesties from happening, however, upper-class women were cloistered. It was largely women from the common classes, especially domestic servants, that were at risk. Again in principle, extramarital pregnancy was stigmatized and women were often constrained to give their infants up to foundling homes. There was no social place for an unmarried mother. Violators of these rules often came under the jurisdiction of the state. The male perpetrators of incest and rape, which not only violated female honor (reputation) but also brought shame to a woman's family, were severely punished. Adultery, on the other hand, had gendered consequences. While the transgressions of husbands might be overlooked, those of wives could be punished with loss of marriage and dowry and even death. Of course for every rule there was an exception, often where social class and gender were taken into account, and although sexual regulation appeared rigid in theory, in practice it was consistently violated.

BOX 4.1 THE MARRIAGE DISPUTE OF GIOVANNI AND LUSANNA

One of the persistent problems plaguing ecclesiastical courts was the multiple legal suits women filed on grounds of breach of promise to marry. Prior to the Council of Trent in 1563 there were no formal rituals for a marriage that would establish its legitimacy. Thus a variety of practices persisted, some of which led to conflict. A well-read marriage dispute introduced by the social historian of Florence Gene Brucker in 1986 was that of Giovanni and Lusanna. Brucker's presentation was one of the first micro-analyses highlighting the life of an ordinary person. Thus, the story of Giovanni and Lusanna fascinated readers.

Lusanna was the daughter of a tailor and the widow of a baker. She was engaged in a romantic and sexual relationship with Giovanni, a scion of the Florentine nobility. This was, according to contemporary standards, a mésalliance, for noblemen were tracked to marry their peers and not commoners. It was certainly not a relationship, if formalized by marriage, that Giovanni's father would approve. Giovanni, in fact, had married a woman from the aristocracy despite his relationship with Lusanna. Lusanna, however, claimed that she was already secretly married to Giovanni, in effect accusing him of bigamy. Her complaint reached the pope, who ordered the local archbishop, Antoninus, to investigate her claim. Giovanni mounted a defense structured around attacking Lusanna's sexual reputation. He claimed that prior to her husband's death she was having adulterous relationships with other men. In a parallel dispute unfolding in civil court, Giovanni claimed Lusanna had poisoned him. The archbishop Antoninus sided with Lusanna and ordered Giovanni to take her as his wife, but Giovanni, a wealthy noble, was able to appeal the ecclesiastical case, and in the end was able to abandon Lusanna for his second wife. In this case social class and gender triumphed over this ordinary woman's appeal for justice.

Further Reading: Grucker, Gene. *Giovanni and Lusanna: Love and Marriage in Renaissance Florence*. Berkeley, CA: University of California Press, 1984; republished in 2004.

Male sexuality also came under the rule of the state. Homoerotic relationships were condemned and violators were severely punished in Lucca, Florence, and Venice, where special judicial commissions for same-sex relations were established. At times the nobility were treated with more leniency than the lower classes. However, sodomy could result in execution by burning. Punishments were organized around gendered constructs and life-stages. Male youth up to the age of twenty who were passive partners in homoerotic relationships were thought to be in a temporary life stage and less severely punished than adult males. Despite the severe consequences, there were still robust subcultures in these cities. In Florence, a special magistracy, the Officials of the Night, prosecuted males engaged in homoerotic relations, the preponderance of whom were usually under thirty years of age.

Marriage

Matrimony was an important life-cycle event for two individuals (see Figure 4.4). But it was also much more, for it did not just include the bride and groom but rather a matrix of networks. It involved the establishment of a new social and economic unit, the forging of new kinship ties, and the exchange of property, whether in cash or credit, land, or simply clothing, beds, bedding, linen, pots, and pans. The betrothal and ceremony were a community affair, whereby the commitment of two people to join in wedlock was solidified by rites, such as the exchange of rings and gifts and the verbal expression of consent before a parish priest, and by festivities. In upper-class families art and artifacts, such as pendants, wedding chests, maiolica, glassware, commemorative portraits, and painted panels, also documented and legitimized the union. By its public nature, whether at a princely court, within a craft association or lay confraternity, in a humble urban neighborhood or a country village, marriage involved the surrounding community of neighbors, friends, and kin in both sustaining the commitment and maintaining prevalent moral codes.

The canonical age for marriage in Italy (and Christian Europe) was twelve for females and fourteen for males. While this might seem precipitously young by current standards it is important to note, first, that childhood was a much briefer stage of life in late medieval and early modern times, and secondly, that the human life span was shorter. Moreover, for a variety of reasons there could be considerable pressure to maximize the bride's years of fertility by having her marry as young as possible. This was the case among princely dynasts and oligarchs preoccupied with keeping or elevating family status and power over the long term. It also happened during times of population scarcity, such as in post-famine or post-plague cycles. For ordinary people age at marriage, or even the possibility of marrying, also depended on whether the couple could afford to wed. Artisan males

FIGURE 4.4 Jan Van Eyck (*c.* 1390–1441). *The Arnolfini Portrait* (1434). Oil on panel. The National Gallery, London, UK.

tended to marry earlier than men of the upper classes, and widowhood and remarriage for them were frequent.

The 1427 census in Tuscany sheds important light on marriage and household patterns for that region. It indicates that fewer than one-third of the rural male population were financially capable of marrying. Among those that did, agricultural workers married around the age of twenty-two to twenty-six. In the countryside, sons often remained under the roofs of their natal families after marrying, with several generations living in one household. Married brothers also cohabited, jointly cultivating their landholdings. Most could only afford to set up an individual household after the age of forty, but still this was rare. Rural females married earlier than males, around the age of eighteen, leaving their families for their husbands' homes. In urban environments, household formation was linked to employment opportunities, degrees of wealth, and means of production. In contrast to farming families, who needed a large pool of labor, in the towns and cities craftsmen and shopkeepers could not afford to pass their trades on to many children in a cyclical market of supply and demand. Thus sons tended to leave the family hearth, and daughters that did not marry might enter domestic service. Among urban workers that did marry, the average age for men was between twenty-six and thirty-one and for women around eighteen. It is notable that because brides were significantly younger than grooms, they might be widowed early. A number of men and women did not marry at all, becoming servants or the auxiliary members in the households of married kin.

The possibility of marriage among the families with wealth and power was critically linked to inheritance customs. In principle, in Italy Roman law followed primogeniture, whereby one male heir carried on the family dynasty and obtained a preponderance of the family's wealth. This practice prevented the dispersion of resources among multiple heirs. During the medieval period dowries, originally conceived in Roman times as a resource that covered the costs of the marriage, evolved to become a daughter's legal share of her natal family's estate. Property rights and practices, however, varied from place to place. The Florentines, for example, limited women's access to property more than the Venetians did, and the Venetians were careful to have brides formally register their dowries in order to protect them from irresponsible husbands or avaricious kin. In Brescia, a wealthy city under Venetian rule, patriarchs passed significant landholdings to their daughters, with arranged marriages that kept the real estate within their kinship circle. Such practices also invited feuds and vendettas, not just in the Bresciano but in the provinces of Parma and Piacenza as well. Popes were known to bequeath large estates to their illegitimate offspring; this was the case with Pope Alexander VI, who gave his daughter Lucrezia Borgia substantial decision-making capabilities in Spoleto and Ferrara. In some places it was possible that daughters' dowries might equal or even surpass the inheritance of their male siblings. This was often the case in the mercantile and business families of Jews, whose assets because of the nature of their activities were at greater risk. In general, however, it appears that fewer sons and daughters in elite families wed, a practice termed "restricted marriage." It meant that the upper classes produced a significant number of unmarried and displaced men and women. Not necessarily of their own will, disinherited sons joined mercenary companies or took religious vows, and daughters filled aristocratic convents.

Marriage among the ruling classes was a powerful tool for creating dynastic alliances. The princes of Italy spun advantageous political and social webs both on the Italian Peninsula and with the nobilities of Spain, the Low Countries, France, Bohemia, and Poland (see Chapter 10). Astutely arranged aristocratic marriages brought them diplomatic allies and profitable patron–client relations as well as landed wealth and resources. Thus the Sforza line of Milan were related to a number of Italian princely dynasties, as were the Este of Ferrara, the Gonzaga of Mantua, the Orsini of Rome, the Borgia of the Romagna, and the Medici of Florence. The daughters in these illustrious families were betrothed early on for strategic purposes. The Medici family in Florence began as oligarchs at the apogee of the Republic, but gradually transitioned to become virtual princes. They used aristocratic marriage as a means to consolidate their political and social ties across the Italian Peninsula. Lorenzo de Medici wed Clarice Orsini, a rich Roman heiress, and later betrothed his offspring with a number of ruling families. His daughter Maddalena married into the family of Pope Innocent VIII, his eldest son Piero married into a Neapolitan branch of the Orsini family, and his son Giuliano married a daughter of the Duke of Savoy. Lorenzo's daughters-in-law and sons-in-law gave him important diplomatic links with regional Italian powers. In Ferrara, Isabella d'Este, who served as regent for her husband during his eleven-month imprisonment to the Venetians in 1509, secured beneficial careers for her children, betrothing her daughter Eleonora to the Duke of Urbino and buying a cardinal's hat for her son Ercole.

Even for the offspring of princes that were outside the circle of primogeniture beneficiaries could profit from an astute marriage alliance within the family, bringing them positions in government and the church, careers that also helped the dynasty. Thus Pope Alexander VI married his illegitimate daughter Lucrezia Borgia to the Duke of Ferrara, and the Medici popes made important matches for their female relatives. Caterina Riario Sforza, the illegitimate daughter of Galeazzo Maria Sforza, Duke of Milan, was married at the age of fourteen to Girolamo Riario, Lord of Imola and the nephew of Pope Sixtus IV.

Like the princely courts, marriage among the ruling families of the Italian republics was also an essential tool. Hereditary elites practiced endogamy in order to maintain privileged social, economic, and political status. Overall, astute marriage ties facilitated social mobility and were a means of augmenting family resources. For these reasons, elite parents were reluctant to permit their children to choose their own spouses, instead arranging marriages for them. They held the power of disinheritance in their hands for those that disobeyed. On the other hand, recalcitrant children had the church on their side, for Catholic dogma maintained that only the consent of the spouses was need to conclude a valid marriage. As a result, some children disobeyed their parents and wed in secret.

It was not until 1563 at the ecclesiastical Council of Trent that churchmen laid down standardized rules for the rites of betrothal and marriage. The betrothal needed to be public, with the banns posted in the couple's parish in writing three times. The expression of mutual consent needed to be witnessed, at the very least by the couple's parish priest but preferably by multiple attendees. The marriage needed to be registered in the parish church, and the union had to be consummated. These rules were intended to clarify the confusion over who was married, for throughout the medieval and Renaissance period, with the exception of France, there were no standardized marriage rites. The requirements set forth were a reminder to grooms that they had to meet their obligations.

Widowhood

The state of widowhood impacted women differently than men. Men had more opportunities to remarry, and they were less affected by age. They tended to remarry quickly, for they would benefit from a new spouse's dowry, and if they had children, would acquire a new caretaker as well. Women, on the other hand, were affected by such factors as social class, wealth, and age. Those at the middle and bottom rungs of society often lost their means of financial support when their husbands died, leaving them dependent on charity or some form of work. The more fortunate, usually in the upper classes or among the professions, with inherited property and assets, enjoyed more choices. They might remarry, but this was problematic. In Florence, it meant the woman severed her allegiance with her first husband's family and with her children, who remained in their father's house. But added to that, it meant taking her dowry to another family. Some women chose not to remarry, enjoying their new independence. Others, especially the young and wealthy, fell vulnerable to the designs of their male kin, who were eager to conclude alliances of social, political, and economic benefit. Older women beyond the childbearing stage often chose to live their remaining years in convents.

Death

The end of a life under normal circumstances was surrounded by ritual. That might not be the case during periods of catastrophic mortality, such as the bubonic plague, when even parents dared not touch the bodies of their dead children let alone bury them. Funerals were at best quick or nonexistent, and many of the deceased ended up in mass graves. Under normal circumstances, families took care of their loved ones, first in their homes where they washed and dressed the corpse and privately mourned their loss. Sometimes there might be professional handlers that took on the more practical tasks. Next the body was transported to a church, generally by the day after death or as quickly as possible. The famous might arrive at the church with elaborate public rites, pomp, and circumstance, but ordinary people could not afford such rituals. They might be assisted by the local guilds and confraternities, which helped with burials and some financial assistance as well as providing mourners. In church the cleric said a requiem on behalf of the deceased and the dead, and then the body was buried. Famous people were interred in churches or family chapels, and later commemorated with elaborate tombs and altars. Ordinary people simply ended up buried in the churchyard.

BOX 4.2 THE MISERICORDIA OF FLORENCE

At a time when families feared burying their dead because of contagion, one group put their lives at risk to help. They were the members of the lay confraternity of the Misericordia. The brotherhood, founded around 1244, was devoted to assisting the sick and poor. Its membership drew from the ranks of Florence's more prosperous men. The municipal government formally recognized the Misericordia in 1329, permitting the brothers to elect their own leaders. They were at the forefront of relief work during the plague epidemic of 1348–50. Dressed in black and hooded to assure their anonymity, they wandered through the streets transporting plague victims to hospitals and burying the dead. Their work earned wide admiration, and by the fifteenth century the brotherhood began to receive a host of donations and bequests. In addition to their relief work during the repeated plague epidemics, they carried out other charitable duties, such as collecting alms to provide dowries for poor girls and giving assistance to the destitute. The brotherhood is still active during the twenty-first century.

Health Care

The precarious nature of human survival not only in times of warfare, pestilence, and famine but also during the everyday travails of life raises the question of health-care practices during this period. People sought assistance on many levels, depending on their financial means, their gender, and the opportunities that were available to them. Historians have identified at least four if not more levels of health care in operation simultaneously. The first was organized under licensed physicians, primarily men who were university-educated in Latin study and well-read in ancient Greek and Arabic texts. Europe had great medical centers from the thirteenth century in Padua, Bologna, Montpellier, and Paris. The physicians' canon of study included Hippocratic writings (fifth century and fourth century BCE) and Galen (second century BCE) as well as the Arabic writings of Avicenna and Averroës. As the humanist movement grew, with more scholars adept at ancient languages, the fifteenth century witnessed a flurry of new translations of medical texts and surgical treatises in Italy, and after 1530 in Paris. The Aldine Press in Venice published the complete works of Galen in Greek in 1525 and the Hippocratic corpus in Latin in 1525 and in Greek in 1526. The sixteenth century witnessed hundreds of new printed editions of Galen, including translations from the Greek into Latin by the English humanist Thomas Linacre (1523) and the German Johann Guinther von Andernach (1531). The botanical works of the ancients, such as Dioscorides (*c.* 40– *c.* 90 CE) and Theophrastus (*c.* 371–*c.* 287 BCE), were also put into print, in addition to Galen's pharmacological works for physicians who used plants, animals, and minerals to cure diseases. Galenic physicians followed the humoral theory of health and illness found in Hippocratic treatises. Galen, however, also prescribed not just looking at the cause of disease but also considering the constitution, lifestyle, and environment of the patient. Greek and Muslim science aimed to restore the balance of four bodily fluids: blood, phlegm, red or yellow bile, and black bile. Regimens for daily living and lifestyle were based on this. One medical treatment used to this end was bloodletting.

Medicine during this time was a blend of practices ranging from learned physicians who drew on ancient texts to astrologers and alchemists. Horoscopes, for example, were still important because it was thought that generation was linked to the heavenly bodies. More importantly, both astrologers and alchemists encouraged observation, experiment, and new theories of nature that, beyond the study of ancient texts, broadened understanding of the natural world. Physicians not only tended to the ailments of princes and oligarchs, cardinals, and popes but also to the occupants of hospitals and monasteries and the members of guilds and confraternities. They enrolled in professional colleges in their respective cities and were almost always male because females were not admitted to universities. Nonetheless, Naples did have some women physicians who generally tended to female patients for female maladies. The central and northern regions of the peninsula, on the other hand, had only a very few female physicians. Among them were the daughters or wives of doctors who already had a practice. A great many learned physicians were Jews.

The second group of health-care workers were called "empirics." They were licensed healers of both sexes that were matriculated in guilds and had learned their crafts through oral traditions and hands-on experience. Like physicians they relied upon naturalistic remedies made from animal, vegetable, or mineral ingredients. Among them were apothecaries, who dispensed remedies and gave advice, and barber surgeons, who did such things as bleed people and pull teeth. Empirics, like physicians, worked for monasteries, hospitals, confraternities, and others.

The third group of individuals involved in the healing arts relied upon nonnatural remedies such as prayers, written incantations, and magical charms. Women were the most active in this group, combining their domestic and handicraft skills with the healing arts. A homemaker might be an herbalist, a mother or grandmother or a midwife. Healers tended to friends and neighbors, often in rural villages where people had less access to physicians and empirics. Their training came from experience, from village lore, and from popular recipes. When things went awry they were often disciplined by clerics and magistrates who viewed them as witches operating in a supernatural realm. Both men and women practiced what were perceived to be the magical arts, with the former often tending to the male body while the latter helping women with reproduction and sexual matters. There was not a hard line between those who offered naturalistic remedies and those who practiced magic. The Florentine philosopher Marsilio Ficino, for example, drew upon both medieval medical theory and Hellenistic magical lore. Still, more women were prosecuted than men, for their healing powers were suspect, especially not only among male physicians but also among clerics who coveted their own influence and powers in the various communities. The figure of the witch was formally codified in 1486 when two Dominican inquisitors, Heinrich Kramer and Jakob Sprenger, wrote the *Hammer of Witches*, an encyclopedia of witchcraft that stereotyped and ultimately stigmatized female healers, making them the target of judicial discipline.

The fourth approach to healing, one fostered by clerics, advocated prayer, appeals to the saints, processions, and various acts of Christian piety. This group came directly into conflict with women healers in rural communities. It became more formalized with the establishment of the Roman and Venetian Inquisitions during the sixteenth century, both of which not only targeted heresy but also superstition and magical healing. In general, people did not rely exclusively on one category of health care over another, but rather on what was readily available. The poor, nonetheless, were more inclined to rely on those who offered the nonnatural, magical remedies circulating in their environments.

By the fifteenth century there was an effort on the part of public authorities in cities and towns to control public health. They devised sanitary regulations to ensure better hygiene and sanitary conditions. They enforced quarantine measures in times of epidemics, and they built hospitals to care for the sick. Italian cities like Florence, Milan, and Venice were in the forefront of designing institutions of public health.

BOX 4.3 THE CONTROL OF PLAGUE AND STATE-BUILDING IN FIFTEENTH-CENTURY MILAN

The supervision of the sick during the recurring plague epidemics in the last half of the fifteenth century became an important aspect of state-building in Milan under the leadership of Duke Francesco Sforza (ruled 1450–1466) and one of his principal physicians, Giovanni Catelano (d. 1497). Plague visited the city three times over three decades—1451-2, 1461, and 1483-5—the last outbreak inflicting exceptional hardship. Catelano, a member of Milan's prestigious College of Physicians, which was comprised primarily of graduates from the University of Pavia, was instrumental in devising the state's surveillance and management system. Milan thus became the first Italian city-state to establish government offices that collected information about plague victims, the first to design quarantine locations, and the first to engage specialized plague physicians. Milan had an official plague office, with physicians that monitored state health and reported to the Senate and the duke. At first victims were shipped out of the city to temporary cabins in outlying areas. Later in the century a permanent pesthouse (termed *lazzaretto*) was built. It was evident from the outset that diagnosing illness and mortality due to plague was complicated. It was difficult to distinguish plague symptoms from other illnesses, such as influenza. As state medicine evolved over the last half of the fifteenth century, the dukes and their advisors came more and more to determine how physicians diagnosed and reported plague. Their strategies coincided with efforts to control the poor and ailing during epidemics, which they wished to confine and extricate from the city.

Further Reading: Carmichael, Ann G. "Epidemics and State Medicine in Fifteenth-Century Milan." In *Medicine from the Black Death to the French Disease*. Edited by Roger French, Jon Arrizabalaga, Andrew Cunningham, and Luis García-Ballester, 221–7. London: Routledge, 1998, Ebook 2020.

Modes of Socialization

By 1350 a wide range of economic affiliations linked people of different social stations together in town and countryside, even though contemporaries were acutely aware of differences in class, age, sources of wealth, legal privileges, and gender. In addition to the discussion earlier, women were also categorized in terms of their marital status, that is, either single, married, or widowed. If we were to tour the Italian Peninsula from north to south and east to west, or the rest of Europe for that matter, we would discover that no one urban or rural microcosm was alike, due in no small part to the nature of their economic activities. Moreover, as various segments of society accumulated wealth, social definitions remained fluid, with perhaps less flexibility at the top or bottom but a great deal of latitude in the middle. On the Italian Peninsula city dwellers viewed themselves in broad terms as nobles, citizens, and commoners. The first group, originally termed "magnates," descended from the great medieval, landowning families. The second was defined hierarchically according to length of urban residency and usually embraced men in the professions, such as notaries, lawyers, judges, and physicians; government functionaries; and people in finance, large manufacture, and commerce. It was the first two groups that largely vied for civic power, with different outcomes depending on locale. In this sense the upper stratum of Italian society was far more diverse than any other part of Europe. On one hand were the nobles of the blood whose status was based on ancestry rather than wealth and on the other were the prosperous civil magistrates who rose to power via civic office. Each locale categorized and named its ruling classes differently. In Genoa the blood nobility shared power with the rich merchants, while in Venice a new nobility, called patricians and rooted in commercial wealth, arose out of the various closings of the civic council. Florence legislated early on in its history to prevent noble magnates from taking office, yet civil magistrates resembled a nobility, distinguishing themselves from the landed elites by virtue of their doing good works for their city. Rome and Naples were dominated by the great landed families and by the sixteenth century by the papacy as well. A third group of urban dwellers was filled with artisans, shopkeepers, skilled and unskilled laborers, midwives, wet nurses, and servants ranging from coachmen to chamber maids. The last group—itinerant beggars, thieves, peddlers, and sex workers—moved from place to place and occupied the margins of urban life.

In a parallel microcosm—as a separate order of society in a separate jurisdiction from lay taxation or the jurisdiction of the civil courts—was a broad assortment of religious people, again arranged hierarchically according to social origins, with those whose families were tied to the nobility or old citizenry in the high clerical offices of popes, cardinals, bishops, abbots, and abbesses, and commoners occupying positions in the everyday priesthood or monastic orders. The clergy were also categorized as regular, in monastic or mendicant orders, or secular, living among laypeople. Monasteries, convents, and various other religious associations set apart from the outside world often represented specific social classes, such as the aristocracy or wealthy citizens. They answered to Rome and derived their income from lands and the revenues their abbeys or convents produced. Men and women in monasteries and convents took vows of celibacy, were devoted to prayer, study, and good works, and in theory were more secluded, while friars in the emerging Franciscan, Dominican, and Augustinian orders of the thirteenth and fourteenth centuries performed such social services as aiding the poor and wayward, preaching, and counseling. Among the most popular friars with the urban and rural masses was the Franciscan friar Bernardino of Siena (1380–1444). He proposed municipal pawnshops (*monti*) to provide low-interest loans to the poor. Unfortunately he also stirred hostility toward the Jews. Yet another famous friar toward the end of the fifteenth century was the Dominican Girolamo Savonarola (1452–1498), who briefly assumed political power in Florence in the years between 1494 and 1498. However, popular opinion turned against him, and he was ultimately condemned by civil and religious authorities and executed.

Women were also members of many religious orders. They were barred from the priesthood and could not administer the sacraments; nor did they have access to the institutions of higher learning. Nonetheless, many of them achieved prominence during the twelfth to sixteenth centuries by demonstrating sacred charisma. Moreover, they produced significant cultural output in the way of music, theater, and art. While the female religious did not have access to the formal avenues to power, they nonetheless did exercise some personal agency. Clare of Assisi (see Chapter 3) and the members of the Poor Clares refused to obey episcopal orders or accept material benefits from the popes. Others, like the wealthy widow Umiliana de' Cerchi (1219–1246), joined Third Orders (called tertiaries, and set apart from friars—First Order—and nuns—Second Order) chose complete reclusiveness, breaking off from their families. Tertiaries worked among the poor, sick, and dying. One of the most famous was Catherine of Siena (1347–1480), the uneducated daughter of a Sienese dyer. Rejecting marriage and cloister, Catherine became a Dominican tertiary. She was considered a mystic and prophet in her time and was beatified after her death. Under the supervision of a Dominican friar, Raymond of Capua (*c.* 1330–1399), Catherine quickly surpassed her master as a model of spirituality. Raymond put himself under her guidance. He went on to write her biography, making her well-known to posterity. Catherine is an example of the religious and lay world's openness to female influence.

Like pious layfolk, the secular clergy also lived among the laypeople. Their hierarchy included bishops, whose duties included consecrating buildings, visiting parishes, monitoring the behavior of the priesthood, and guarding against heresy, and the overall priesthood, who were assigned to parishes where they performed the religious rites associated with baptism, marriage, and death and presided over daily religious services. Bishops, and their superiors the cardinals, normally derived from wealthy aristocratic families. They received great benefices of landed revenue, wealth that remained exempt from secular taxation. Receiving a bishopric was an avenue of wealth for an aristocratic family and was often kept within the dynasty for centuries.

Each of these lay and religious social divisions also spilled over into the countryside, with its mass of landless workers and peasant sharecroppers at the bottom of the social hierarchy, village elites in the middle, and large landlords at the top, for the life of the Italian city was intimately intertwined with its hinterland. Sharecropping was introduced in the fourteenth and fifteenth centuries, but some forms of vassalage still prevailed, mostly in the South. Landlords, often city dwellers, held the advantages in terms of owning property, tools, goods, and livestock. The better-off peasants had more favorable leasing arrangements and higher-yielding farms, but in general rural life for most was hard. It is also accurate to state that rural dwellers spilled into the city, not only bringing food and finished products to market but in addition taking up residence and providing seasonal or more permanent labor as needed. Cities and towns also depended on their rural neighbors to replenish their numbers in periods following high mortality. Thus the urban–rural dynamic was fluid, but at the same time city dwellers distinguished themselves socially from their country laborers, especially those who worked the land.

At the bottom of the social hierarchy were the masses of propertyless vagabonds, some finding piecework or seasonal labor and others simply unemployed. The peninsula's cities were filled with beggars, whom civic authorities frequently treated as criminals. The problem of confining, or getting rid of, the poor grew exponentially during the sixteenth century, a period of high inflation and frequent food shortages that triggered riots. But even in times of plenty, cities devised complex judicial systems to supervise and control the poor, who mostly had to depend on religious institutions for charity. Civic magistrates also took measures to compel grain growers to bring their cereals to the urban storehouses in times of famine so as to ensure a quantity of food at accessible prices.

The Italian cities and towns were also regularly replenished with immigrants from abroad. Rome and Venice were major tourist and pilgrim centers, activities that attracted a wide range of peoples in the service industries. They also attracted merchants, artists, and musicians. By the sixteenth century Rome, dominated by the papacy, also became the home of one of the largest bureaucracies in Europe, the Roman Curia, with its functionaries and dignitaries. The city thus was filled with Spanish officials in the Roman court and cardinals and ambassadors from all of Europe. They in turn attracted notaries, artists, architects, and musicians to their palaces. Rome also housed communities of people from throughout the Italian Peninsula, such as the Florentines at the church of San Giovanni. The maritime cities were home to merchants and sailors from the Adriatic, the Mediterranean, and the Levant, and German and Flemish merchants settled near the sites of commerce and handicrafts and were linked by their commonplaces of origin. Venice housed German merchants at the trading post of the Fondaco dei Tedeschi. In university towns like Bologna or Padua, many students gathered from abroad. The urban centers under Iberian rule, such as Milan and much of southern Italy and Sicily, were filled with Spanish nobles, officials, and curia. The Hapsburg wars also brought many soldiers to Italy, from France, Germany, Switzerland, and Iberia.

Jewish communities had resided in Italy since ancient times. They had their own schools for boys; rabbinical courts, where they followed Jewish law; and temples of worship. As the Italian towns and cities expanded between the eleventh and fourteenth centuries they made their living from moneylending, selling used clothing, and the textile trades. Many were also important translators and scholars of classical learning; others were physicians. During the fifteenth and sixteenth centuries several towns on the Italian Peninsula attracted new Jewish migration because of important events like the fall of Constantinople to the Ottomans in 1453, the Spanish expulsion from Iberia in 1492, and the expulsion from Sicily in 1493. This was especially true of Naples under Alfonso III, Ferrara under Ercole d'Este, Rome under Pope Alexander VI, and the Venetian Republic. The latter established the first Jewish Ghetto in 1516, housing several Jewish nations from both Western and Eastern Europe. While Jews had lived and circulated in the towns of the Veneto, it was only in 1516 that the republic permitted them to reside in the city. Engaged in costly wars, Venice was motivated to accommodate the Jews for financial reasons, for they were important moneylenders and merchants. However, the republic confined them to a circumscribed area in the city whose gates were closed and guarded at night. Jews were engaged during the late fifteenth and sixteenth centuries as creditors to princes, traders, pawnbrokers, moneylenders, textile merchants, printers, vendors of used articles, art patrons, musicians, and intellectuals. When the maritime city became a center of printing during the sixteenth century, the Jewish diaspora created a demand for texts in Hebrew, Ladino, and Yiddish. In Tuscany, Duke Cosimo I de' Medici created a new free port for Jews in Leghorn (Livorno). Greek scholars also arrived in Italy from the Ottoman Empire. Elite Muslims, such as Leo Africanus (Al-Wazzan al Fasi, 1494–1554), also came to Italy after their expulsion from Iberia during the late fifteenth century.

The slave trade was also a source of immigration. Very few slaves were sub-Saharan Africans; to the mid fifteenth century they were predominantly white. Most were women from the Balkans, the Crimea, and the Caucasus who were engaged in domestic service or wet nursing. The Black Sea had been a marketplace for slaves since the fourteenth century. Venice, Ancona, Pisa, and Genoa all had slave markets at one time or another. The Portuguese voyages to West Africa brought some sub-Saharan Africans to Venice, some of whom became pages, coachmen, or gondoliers and eventually won their freedom. The sixteenth century also witnessed an influx of prisoners of war and piracy, marketed in Malta, Naples, and Genoa. The society of the Italian Peninsula, thus, continued to be a mix of indigenous and foreign peoples with multicultural traditions.

Rather than attempt to define the myriad of social categories that populated Renaissance cities, this section will examine the ways in which women and men were linked together through their modes of socialization, whether in public or private life, in the workplace, or through their religious associations. Viewing people through that optic breaks down the sharp social divisions described earlier and illuminates their more visible vertical and horizontal ties, for women and men were linked through a variety of overlapping associations. For example, women cultivated social ties with both their natal and married families as well as in their neighborhoods and parishes. They also had affiliations tied to their work as domestic servants, wet nurses, midwives, and prostitutes, or as caretakers in hospitals, pesthouses, and orphanages. Men too circulated with others through their families, vocations, and professions as well as religious affiliations. People were bound together via family—the basic unit of social organization—friendship, work, politics, brotherhoods, charity, and religious rites like baptism, godparenting, guardianships, marriages, funerals, and burials. Feasts, processions, games, and brawls were central occasions that also brought them together.

Guilds

Guilds, or secular corporations whose purpose was to protect its members, encompassed a broad segment of society, arranged hierarchically with the professions, finance, manufacture and commerce on top, and skilled laborers underneath. In Florence, for example, between the twelfth and sixteenth centuries guilds were expressly categorized as major, middling, and minor. The major guilds included foreign cloth merchants, finishers, and dyers; wool merchants and manufacturers; silk merchants and weavers; bankers and money changers; judges and notaries; apothecaries and physicians; and furriers and skinners. Among the middle-ranging guilds were butchers; shoemakers; blacksmiths; stone masons and woodcarvers; and retail cloth-dealers and linen manufacturers. The minor guilds encompassed vintners; innkeepers; curriers and tanners; olive oil merchants; saddlers and harness-makers; locksmiths, toolmakers, and braziers; armorers and swordsmiths; carpenters; and bakers and millers. According to the Florentine *catasto* (census) of 1427, a small portion of women were matriculated in these guilds as carpenters, goldsmiths, butchers, grain dealers, painters, and cobblers.[1] Common people such as weavers, spinners, and dyers were forbidden from forming guilds, which not only controlled the quality of the professional or occupational activity but also held considerable weight in the Florentine body politic. Seven of the major guilds and two of the minor guilds were represented in government. In Venice, in contrast, guild members held no place in formal political life, which was monopolized solely by the patrician class. Nonetheless, they were at the forefront of urban life. From the thirteenth century the members of guilds formed confraternities, or pious federations, related to the trades. There were both great and small confraternities in a range of professionals and occupations, respectively. Because Venice was an international, commercial hub, its confraternities also included ethnic brotherhoods of Greeks, Albanians, and Dalmatians as well as migrants from Milan, Florence, Bergamo, and Lucca. Rome also housed a great number of trade organizations, though they did not wield much political power. Especially with the return of the papacy during the fifteenth century, and throughout the sixteenth century, suppliers and skilled workers in the building trades and decorative arts were a dominant presence in the city. Many came from Florence and Lombardy. The stock breeders, controlled by country magnates, were also a powerful association. Like many other cities Rome was also filled with artisans in the luxury trades, booksellers, millers, bakers, and others associated with the food industry. Because the capital city hosted visitors from around Europe, it also had a number of service industries that catered to an international clientele.

Besides organizing economic life, guilds provided social networks. Some guilds were exclusive male brotherhoods, but others included women. In Venice, for example, women joined the textile workers, fustian weavers, combmakers, coppers, tailors, doublet-makers, secondhand clothing dealers, ironmongers, and haberdashers. Elsewhere in Italy women's work depended on notions of gender rather than biology. In the Tuscan wool industry, for example, women were low-paid skinners, carders, stretchers, and spinners. These corporations were important places of sociability, aiding their members in times of feast and famine and in conjunction with the life-cycle rites that accompanied baptism, marriage, childbirth and godparenting, and death. Further, they were at the forefront of urban life, assisting in the foundation of hospitals, providing charity, and participating in religious feasts, festivals, parades, horse races and bull or oxen runs, musical events, public rituals, and games, and sponsoring major art works.

BOX 4.4 THE WARS OF THE FISTS

In Venice, thousands of workers together with their spouses, kin, and friends would enact violent dramas on the city's bridges generally following official state celebrations and religious feast days. They wrestled and used their fists to knock their opponents in the water. The wars of the fists, as they came to be known, have been documented since 1369, but they may have begun even earlier, along with stick battles and brawls. They are a good example of the kind factionalism that divided Venice's laboring classes into segments. The government did not necessarily discourage these violent spectacles, for they afforded menfolk the opportunity to develop their skills in martial arts and therefore potentially come to the defense of the city. By the late fourteenth century Venice had two great factions, the Nicolotti, who were composed of and led primarily by fishermen, and the Castellani, representing the shipbuilders. They gradually divided city loyalties between them. The wars of the fists attracted large crowds of spectators, including members of the nobility as well as visitors to the city. This customary, ritualized violence became a popular form of entertainment. But at the same time it constituted a primary mode of socialization, for it not only marked the geographical divisions in the city between seafarers and landed laborers but also fostered social cohesion through marital endogamy (the practice of marrying within the same faction) and godparenting.

Further Reading: Davis, Robert C. *The War of the Fists. Popular Culture and Public Violence in Late Renaissance Venice*. Oxford, UK: Oxford University Press, 1994.

Confraternities

Confraternities, often attached to federated trades, were essentially devotional associations of pious Christians. They were not organized by the church but rather were a communal expression of the laity. They held legal status and access to the courts. Among their activities were distributing alms to the poor, bequeathing monies, commemorating the dead, and assisting one another at funerals or burials. Some even founded hospitals. Confraternities played a major role in social life as hubs for banqueting, the commemoration of patron saints, the staging of public processions, and the commissioning of artistic works and reliquaries for churches. They often sponsored religious feasts, festivals, and parades and were important patrons of composers and musicians who were at the forefront of musical developments. Confraternities fostered civic solidarity and were important sites of human bonding.

Neighborhoods and Parishes

Renaissance people took their identity as much from their neighborhood and parish associations as they did from their city. Perhaps the most outstanding example is from the town of Siena in Tuscany, where the parishes held an annual horse race called the *palio* to celebrate their neighborhood pride. Neighborhoods were also the sites of important meeting places, such as the local church, markets, taverns, and wells. They were also a place to express common values through public rituals. They hosted the religious feast days of the Christian calendar, ceremonies commemorating heroes and past events, games, and brawls as well as the important life-cycle events of baptisms, marriages, funerals, and burials. Neighborhoods were a place where friendships were formed, and people chose godparents or guardians for their children. They were also the place where work relationships were grounded.

Households

Households varied in size, depending in part on custom and in part on financial means. Most households were small, and the majority of people lived in poverty. Noble households, however, consisted of large, extended families that included servants and slaves. These large households are among the best to examine vertical ties among social classes. Masters had valets and coachmen (and gondoliers in Venice) and mistresses had chamber and kitchen maids, and scholars have discovered through their testaments that they often held ties of respect and affection with one another. Masters and mistresses served as godparents, provided dowries for their female servants, and gave servants of both sexes gifts. Nobles also housed domestic slaves. Venetian patricians preferred Russian, Tatar, Mongolian, and Circassian women, but other slaves were captured in war or Mediterranean piracy or were bought in markets on the Black Sea. From the fifteenth century slaves were also brought to the city from Africa.

Gendered Associations

Women formed friendships through their occupational activities, such as cooking, cleaning, laundering, sewing, spinning, room letting, wet nursing, obstetrics, and the sex trade. They forged bonds in households, which were not only sites of reproduction but also of home manufacture, in neighborhoods and markets, in churches, in doorways, and at wells. Men socialized in more public urban spaces, where politics and competitive games and sports such as bull chasing or fistfighting took place. They also met in taverns and at marketplaces.

Conclusion

The Italian Peninsula, and Europe as a whole, entered a temporary slump during the fourteenth century, characterized by a series of famines, the devastating Black Death, and labor unrest. For the survivors, however, recovery brought new opportunities in employment and the possibility of marriage and establishing new households. Keeping in mind differences according to class and gender, childhood was a precarious stage of the human life cycle, adolescence was brief, and adulthood could begin as early as twelve for girls and fourteen for boys. People socialized in a variety of ways, first and foremost through their family ties but also through their associations at work, in the neighborhood, or within their parish. While society was organized formally in hierarchical terms, the various modes of socialization fostered common ground among men and women of different social stations.

Think Critically

1. What factors impacted the health of the agrarian economy?
2. What was the impact of the Black Death on the quality of life for the various social classes?
3. How did gender and class shape the experiences of ordinary people?
4. What was the function of marriage?
5. What were the various modes of socialization?

Further Exploration

1. What can Boccaccio's *Decameron* teach us about how fourteenth-century people reacted to catastrophic developments like the bubonic plague?
2. What effect did the Black Death have on fourteenth-century painting in Italy?

Note

1 Samuel K. Cohn, "Women and Work in Renaissance Italy," in *Gender and Society in Renaissance Italy*, edited by Judith C. Brown and Robert C. Davis (London: Longman, 1998), 115–17.

Further Reading

Primary Sources

Boccaccio, Giovanni. *The Decameron*. Middlesex, England: Penguin Books, 1972.
Datini, Margarita. *Letters to Francesco Datini*. Translated by Carolyn James and Antonio Pagliaro. *The Other Voice in Early Modern Europe: The Toronto Series*. New York: Iter Press, 2012.

Raymond of Capua. *The Life of St. Catherine of Siena: The Classic on Her Life and Accomplishments as Recorded by Her Spiritual Director*. Gastonia, NC: Tan Books, 2009.

Savonarola, Michele. *A Mother's Manual for the Women of Ferrara. A Fifteenth-Century Guide to Pregnancy and Pediatrics*. Edited by Gabriella Zuccolin. Translated by Martin Marafioti. *The Other Voice in Early Modern Europe: The Toronto Series*. New York: Iter Press, 2022.

Secondary Sources

Bonfil, Robert. *Jewish Life in Renaissance Italy*. Translated by Anthony Oldcorn. Berkeley: University of California Press, 1994. A seminal work that assesses the experience of this religious minority in Renaissance Italy from the point of view of the Jews themselves.

Bornstein, Daniel, and Roberto Rusconi. *Women and Religion in Medieval and Renaissance Italy*. Translated by Margery J. Schneider. Chicago: University of Chicago Press, 1996. A collection of essays that explores the involvement and influence of women in religious life in central and northern Italy during the twelfth to sixteenth centuries.

Boswell, John. *The Kindness of Strangers: The Abandonment of Children in Western Europe from Antiquity to the Renaissance*. New York, NY: Pantheon Books, 1988. Examines the phenomenon of child abandonment from antiquity to the Renaissance, drawing evidence from drama, mythological-literary texts, and demographic data.

Brown, Judith C., and Robert C. Davis. *Gender and Society in Renaissance Italy*. Harlow, Essex: Addison Wesley Longman, 1998. A collection of scholarly essays all of which use gender as an analytic tool to dissect Renaissance politics, economy, social life, religion, medicine, and art.

Cohn, Samuel Kline. *The Cult of Remembrance and the Black Death: Six Renaissance Cities in Central Italy*. Baltimore, MD: Johns Hopkins University Press, 1992. Through an analysis of testaments, the author reconstructs various modes of remembering the deceased in six Renaissance towns: Arezzo, Florence, Perugia, Assisi, Pisa, and Siena.

Cohn, Samuel Kline. *Popular Protest in Late-Medieval Europe: Italy, France and Flanders*. Manchester, UK: Manchester University Press, 2004. A collection of primary documents covering protests in a variety of circumstances and settings, primarily in the post-plague years between 1355 and 1382.

Cohn, Samuel Kline. "Women and Work in Renaissance Italy." In *Gender and Society in Renaissance Italy*. Edited by Judith C. Brown and Robert C. Davis, 107–26. Harlow, Essex: Addison Wesley Longman, 1998. A survey of women's role in the labor force.

Ferraro, Joanne M. "Childhood in Medieval and Early Modern Times." In *The Routledge History of Childhood in the Western World*. Edited by Paula S. Fass, 61–77. New York: Routledge, 2013. A general survey of childhood experience from the eleventh to eighteenth centuries.

Ferraro, Joanne M. "Family and Clan in the Renaissance World." In *A Companion to the Worlds of the Renaissance*. Edited by Guido Ruggiero, 173–87. Oxford,

UK: Blackwell Publishing, 2002. An examination of the way families networked, cohered, and divided in European politics and society.
Ferraro, Joanne M. *Marriage Wars in Late Renaissance Venice*. Oxford, UK: Oxford University Press, 2001. A series of micro-stories that tell the plight of women and men who go before the church court in Venice to have their marriages dissolved.
Finucci, Valeria. *The Manly Masquerade: Masculinity, Paternity, and Castration in the Italian Renaissance*. Durham, NC: Duke University Press, 2003. A sweeping examination of the ways in which men were defined in sixteenth- and seventeenth-century medical and travel literature; theology; law; myth; conduct books; and plays, chivalric romances, and novellas.
Gavitt, Philip. *Charity and Children in Renaissance Florence: The Ospedale degli Innocenti, 1410–1536*. Ann Arbor, MI: University of Michigan Press, 1990. An attentive analysis of the lives of poor children deposited in Florence's asylum for children and the ambivalence and concerns of the parents who left them.
Giannetti, Laura. *Lelia's Kiss. Imagining Gender, Sex, and Marriage in Italian Renaissance Comedy*. Toronto: University of Toronto Press, 2009. A study of the ways in which gender and marriage were portrayed, imagined, and critiqued in comedies and on stage during the Italian Renaissance.
Grendler, Paul F. *Schooling in Renaissance Italy: Literacy and Learning, 1300–1600*. Baltimore, MD: Johns Hopkins University Press, 1989. An important history of the schools and curricula that brought about Renaissance humanism.
Herlihy, David. *The Black Death and the Transformation of the West*. Edited by Samuel K. Cohn. Cambridge, MA: Harvard University Press, 1997. Examines the broader implications of the Black Death's impact, including methods of population control, the establishment of universities, the spread of Christianity, and the growth of vernacular cultures.
Herlihy, David, and Christiane Klapisch-Zuber. *Tuscans and Their Families: A Study of the Florentine Catasto of 1427*. Translated by David Herlihy and Christiane Klapish-Zuber. New Haven, CT: Yale University Press, 1985. A magisterial study of the Florentine census of 1427, which sheds light on population movement, household composition, levels of wealth, kinships, and the life stages of birth, marriage, and death.
King, Margaret. *The Death of the Child Valerio Marcello*. Chicago, IL: University of Chicago Press, 1994. Through the death of the noble child Valerio, the despair of his father, and the letters of consolation that pour into the family, the author offers important insights into the political, cultural, and private life of fifteenth-century Venice.
Klapisch-Zuber, Christiane. *Women, Family, and Ritual in Renaissance Italy*. Translated by Lydia G. Cochrane. Chicago, IL: University of Chicago Press, 1985. A study of women, childhood, marriage, and family systems in fourteenth-century and fifteenth-century Tuscany, based on diaries, laws, treatises, and tax records.
Meiss, Millard. *Painting in Florence and Siena after the Black Death*. New York: Harper & Roe, 1951. A social and cultural history of painting in late fourteenth-century Florence and Siena that examines patronage, style, iconography, and historical events.

Muir, Edward. *Civic Ritual in Renaissance Venice*. Rutgers, NJ: Princeton University Press, 1986. An important study of the ritualization of politics and society in Venice and the ways in which these practices contributed to its stability.

Musacchio, Jacqueline. *The Art and Ritual of Childbirth in Renaissance Italy*. New Haven, CT: Yale University Press, 1999. A detailed examination of the material culture and artistic working surrounding childbirth in Renaissance Italy.

Park, Katharine. "Medicine and Magic: The Healing Arts." In *Gender and Society in Renaissance Italy*. Edited by Judith C. Brown and Robert C. Davis, 129–49. London: Longman, 1998. A detailed examination of the various options ranging from learned medicine to popular magic open to Renaissance Italians seeking health care.

Rocke, Michael. *Forbidden Friendships. Homosexuality and Male Culture in Renaissance Florence*. Oxford, UK: Oxford University Press, 1998. Through an examination of the criminal records of the Florentine Officers of the Night, the author illuminates the homoerotic sexual culture of a Renaissance city.

Rocke, Michael. "Gender and Sexual Culture in Renaissance Italy." In *Gender and Society in Renaissance Italy*. Edited by Judith C. Brown and Robert C. Davis, 150–70. London: Longman, 1998. Examines a range of sexual behaviors, including homoeroticism, in its social and legal context.

Romano, Dennis. *Household and Statecraft. Domestic Service in Renaissance Venice*. Baltimore: Johns Hopkins University Press, 1996. A comprehensive study of domestic service in fifteenth- and sixteenth-century Venice, based on treatises on household management, books of costumes, civic statutes, census data, contracts, wills, and court records.

Ruggiero, Guido. *The Boundaries of Eros. Sex Crime and Sexuality in Renaissance Venice*. Oxford, UK: Oxford University Press, 1985. A study of licit and illicit sexual practices in Venice during the fourteenth and fifteenth centuries.

Siraisi, Nancy. *Medieval and Early Renaissance Medicine*. Chicago: University of Chicago Press, 1990. A foundational study for the subject of Renaissance medicine.

Storey, Tessa. *Carnal Commerce in Counter-Reformation Rome*. Cambridge, UK: Cambridge University Press, 2008. Based on a range of archival sources, a detailed analysis of the daily lives of Rome's prostitutes between 1566 and 1656.

Strocchia, Sharon. "Learning the Virtues: Convent Schools and Female Culture in Renaissance Florence." In *Women's Education in Early Modern Europe: A History, 1500–1800*. Edited by Barbara J. Whitehead, 5–46. New York, NY: Routledge, 1999. An enlightening study of the education of women in convents in Renaissance Florence.

Terpstra, Nicholas. *Abandoned Children of the Italian Renaissance. Orphan Care in Florence and Bologna*. Baltimore, MD: Johns Hopkins University Press, 2005. A study of the institutions in Florence and Bologna that cared for orphans and an insightful view into the quality of their daily lives.

5

Fifteenth-Century Politics

Timeline

1347	Cola di Rienzo (1313–1354) becomes tribune of Rome
1378–1417	Great Western Schism of the papacy
1399–1406	Florence takes control of Pisa, Siena, Perugia, and Bologna
1402	Giangaleazzo Visconti lays siege to Florence; Coluccio Salutati praises Florentine republicanism
1405	Venice annexes Padua and Verona
1409	Third pope, Alexander V, elected at Council of Pisa (to 1410)
1414	Joanna II of Naples (1373–1435) becomes queen (r. to 1435)
1414–8	Schism resolved at Council of Constance
1417	Election of Pope Martin V (1369–1431)
1419–20	Venice controls the Friuli
1421	Florence controls Livorno
1428	Venice annexes Bergamo and Brescia
1431	Election of Pope Eugenius IV (r. to 1447)
1434	Cosimo de' Medici established in Florence
1435	René of Anjou (1409–1480) succeeds Joanna II of Naples (to 1442)
1442	Alfonso I of Aragon rules Naples and Sicily (r. to 1458)
1453	Mehmed II conquers Constantinople, renamed Istanbul
1454	Peace of Lodi
1455	Italian League of Venice, Florence, Milan, Naples, and the Papal States

1458	Ferrante I (Ferdinand I, b. 1423) succeeds Alfonso I of Aragon as king of Naples (d. 1494)
1464	Piero de' Medici succeeds Cosimo in Florence
1469	Lorenzo de' Medici succeeds Piero in Florence
1488	Caterina Sforza (1463–1509) regent of Forli
1492	Piero II de Medici succeeds Lorenzo as ruler of Florence
1492	Election of Pope Alexander VI (b. 1431, Rodrigo Borgia (r. to 1503))
1494	Charles VIII (1470–1498), king of France, invades Italy
1494	Ludovico Sforza (1452–1508), Duke of Milan (to 1499)
1495	Charles VIII occupies Naples; then defeated by Italian forces
1499	Louis XII (1462–1515), king of France takes Milan
1503	Pope Julius II della Rovere succeeds Alexander VI (r. to 1513)

FIGURE 5.1 Ducal Palace, Urbino, Italy. Mid-fifteenth century. This palace, built in the center of the city for duke Federico III da Montefeltro, was a symbol of the wealth and power of his princely family.

Republics and Principalities

Free from papal and imperial interference, five large but separate powers consolidated their territorial bases in Italy by 1454 amid a myriad of smaller centers. The principal Italian city-states included the Republics of Venice and Florence, the Duchy of Milan, the Papal States, and the Kingdom of Naples, each with approximately 800,000 to 2 million subjects. The republics of Genoa, Lucca, Pisa, and Siena and the lordships of Mantua, Ferrara, and Monferrato remained in their shadow. Each of the five major city-states developed their own internal paths to political hegemony, whether by election, inheritance, or outright usurpation. Each fashioned its own brand of self-government, and each made its own shifting coalitions in such a manner than no one state dominated political affairs or overwhelmed another, a phenomenon that was later termed "balance of power."

The republics were ruled by standing councils of varying sizes as well as ad hoc committees that composed and recomposed. Ostensibly officeholders were elected and rotated the various administrative competencies. However the same families stood at the helm of government repeatedly. From the fourteenth to fifteenth centuries power narrowed to a few dynastic family lines whose wealth, marriage connections, and alliances gave them hegemony over the remainder of the enfranchised body. Their councils and committees decided internal matters such as food provisioning, construction projects, and the administration of justice. They designed fiscal policies, such as taxes on commodities as well as on immobile assets (property and credit), tolls, and forced loans. They also weighed heavily on policies of war and peace and developed systems of diplomacy.

The principalities also availed themselves of councils and committees, preserving some of the sociopolitical structures of earlier centuries when they came to power. However, these government bodies were stocked with the clients and kin of the lord or his female regent, whose power was initially illegitimate. Over time the lordships evolved into hereditary princedoms (or duchies) as the sovereign conferred material benefits on loyal followers and promised the populace some degree of political stability. Italy was filled with these princely courts. Up until 1500 Milan, Papal Rome, Naples, Ferrara, Savoy (including the marquisates of Saluzzo and Monferrato), and Mantua were the major centers under dynastic rule. The Papal State availed of its own Curia, a system of committees and councils that included both laymen (some of whom bought their offices) and clerics who were in charge of church administration as well as diplomatic missions throughout Europe. The Papal State also included a number of minor courts under noble vicars like the Malatesta of Rimini, the Manfredi of Faenza, the Sforza of Pesaro, the Varano of Camerino, the Ordelaffi of Forlì, and the Bentivolgio of Bologna. From the late fifteenth century the popes intensified their efforts to achieve regional sovereignty in these areas. In Rome itself the Colonna and the Orsini clans held their own courts. Further, cardinals, the highest prelates under the pope, were also ranked as princes, equal to dukes, and with a number of important jurisdictions, such as episcopal courts of law. Their college, established during the eleventh century to elect the pope, grew in size over the fifteenth and sixteenth centuries. From 1460 a group of cardinals came from the major princely houses of Italy, including the Gonzaga, Este, Sforza, Medici, Colonna, Farnese, Pallavincini, and Trivulzio. Others came from wealthy European families who restricted the marriages of their offspring and designated certain sons for the church, whereby the family could benefit from lucrative offices. Cardinals, and bishops or archbishops for that matter, were great lords, with many servitors, secretaries, and servants as well as entertainers and artists. They were among the greatest art and literary patrons of the age.

The lords, and in some cases their wives or daughters, held government authority, legislated, administered justice, made appointments to civic government, bestowed honors, and formally received ambassadors. They also farmed taxes, imposed indirect levies on the populace, and pledged trade monopolies to fund their lavish lifestyles and sponsor literature, the arts, and ideas. Their dynasties were among the richest families in Italy, with income from a variety of commodity and income taxes, tolls, and forced loans as well as the proceeds from their extensive property holdings and the rural economy in general. They were surrounded by mercenary soldiers and lived in fortified complexes designed to withstand sieges and rebellions. Their war machines still stand in places like Rome, Milan, and Ferrara, with castles in the center of town. Many led huge armies, which they recruited from the impoverished lower classes as well as from territories abroad and which they hired out to other city-states. Ercole and Alfonso d'Este, the dukes of Ferrara; Guidobaldo da Montefeltro and Francesco Maria della Rovere, the dukes of Urbino; and Francesco and Federico Gonzaga, the marquises of Mantua were among the principal *condottieri*, or mercenary captains, that used war as a business enterprise.

In medieval theory but not necessarily in contemporary practice these princes were feudal lords who owed military service to a sovereign. The dukes of Milan and the marquises of Mantua and Monferrato owed allegiance to the emperor; the dukes of Ferrara and Urbino and the Aragonese kings of Naples were vassals of the pope. To round out their incomes and to finance their soldiers, however, princes in some of the lesser courts accepted external military commissions, offering their men as mercenaries under contract to the larger and wealthier city-states. Federico da Montefeltro of Urbino, for example, served as the mercenary captain general to three popes, two kings of Naples, two dukes of Milan, and several Italian leagues.

The costly expenditures of princes—on new dwellings, apparel and jewelry, liveries, grooms and footmen, ladies in waiting, cooks and waiters, secretaries, the purchase of ducal titles or ecclesiastical offices, state visits, dowries for their daughters, and auspicious marriage ceremonies, artists and craftsmen as well as musicians—rendered them frequently troubled by financial difficulties, some serious enough to bring down their dynasties. To stay afloat, they hocked their jewels and borrowed large sums of money, farmed taxes, bought on credit, and paid workers with devalued coinage or vouchers. They also exploited subjects without noble privileges with excessive taxation on staples and tariffs on trade as well as obliging labor from certain segments of the peasantry to maintain buildings, roads, fortifications, and irrigation. Princes also drew income from their vast landed estates, where they collected taxes and demanded services.

Regional Rivalries and Political Consolidation

From the second half of the fourteenth century, regional rivalries among the five major Italian states centered on a struggle to control one another in an effort to net natural resources, tax revenues, and nearby trade routes. They maintained a fragile balance of power. By the beginning of the fifteenth century there was also an ideological dimension to their conflicts, with the city-states and towns under corporate rule championing republicanism (rule by councils and committees) over one-person or dynastic rule, particularly that of the Visconti in Milan and the monarchs of Naples, respectively. There was an additional element to these interregional rivalries that made the competition for resources even more complex: ecclesiastical entities siphoned off significant wealth from the secular state in the form of church benefices and pious donations from the faithful. Many wealthy families, with relatives filling the church's highest ranks, alienated their property to local ecclesiastical institutions to avoid taxation. In all, these practices placed additional pressures on the financial resources of secular governments.

The peninsula's economy had experienced a temporary slump during the mid-fourteenth century, exacerbated by the Black Death of 1348–50 (see Chapter 4). The catastrophic demographic losses stemming from the plague epidemic had changed the state of the labor market. Peasants and craftsmen became scarcer, giving them more leverage to demand higher remuneration from their employers. There was widespread unrest among textile workers in a number of areas in Europe, including Flanders, the Rhineland, and the Tuscan cities of Italy. A segment of the clothworkers in Florence, called Ciompi, for example, rose up against the government in 1378 and temporarily took power to the consternation of the established elites. Venice experienced rumblings with its wool workers as well during the years between 1375 and 1418, with grievances related to work and pay. There were also signs of economic disorder in international commerce, banking, and textile production. Cities tried to remedy these problems by establishing state banks and state navigation. They also focused on luxury production, although it only reached a limited market. Warfare, which was almost chronic, also dislocated trade centers and routes. Under these conditions, land and agriculture remained essential commodities and formed the economic imperative behind territorial expansion, not just for the cities but also for the landlords who resorted to mercenary service to make up for their losses in peasant rents and services. Both the citizenry and the landed classes attempted to siphon off as much of peasant production as they could in rent, services, and taxes.

Territorial states were constrained to develop more efficient government machinery and state finances as well as civil law and a diplomatic system that included permanent resident ambassadors. At the same time, methods of warfare also changed significantly. Whereas armed horsemen with entourages of servants—termed "lances"—continued to be engaged as fighting units, city-states like Milan and Venice also used infantry forces, particularly Swiss pike square formations, from the end of the fourteenth century. Moreover, both the size of infantries and the engagement of foreign mercenary companies grew. The introduction of gunpowder, which originated in China and was transmitted by the Muslims, transformed military tactics through the use of firearms and cannon as well as the construction of new fortifications. Guns, both arquebuses and muskets, were employed to assault and to defend cities. Artillery trains were designed for rapid deployment, and infantry were armed. Heavy cannon, capable of destroying city gates and walls, made the vertical curtain walls of medieval castles obsolete. New designs included sloping walls in polygonal or pentagonal shapes, defended by bastions. The trend over the fifteenth century was, thus, toward permanent standing forces, led both by Italian military captain from the various republics and principalities (such as Bartolomeo Colleoni, the mercenary captain for the Republic of Venice shown in Figure 5.2) and by foreign mercenaries. Military bureaucracies emerged to both organize and finance these new systems. Over the fifteenth century each of the five principal city-states consolidated its political, fiscal, and military structures to meet the demands of regional rivalries.

Milan

Among the primary aggressors in the race for territory were the Visconti family in Milan. Giangaleazzo Visconti (1351–1402; Duke of Milan, 1395) set his sights on the neighboring territories to the east and the south. Among the former were Verona and Padua. Farther east was the Friuli region, a gateway to Austria and Hungary that was essential to Venice as an entrepôt between central Europe and the Levant. To the south, the Visconti sought parts of Tuscany and the Romagna. Their ambitions to net Bologna put them in rivalry with the papacy, whose territories stretched from Rome northward along the eastern slopes of the Apennines. Meanwhile closer to home they began to build a regional state, promising peace to

FIGURE 5.2 Andrea del Verrocchio (1435–1488). *Monument to Bartolomeo Colleoni* (c. 1481–1488). Campo SS. Giovanni e Paolo, Venice, Italy. Statue cast in bronze by Alessandro Leopardi (1466–1512). Colleoni, the son of a minor noble, fought for Milan and then Venice in 1454. A wealthy man at the end of his career, he financed his own equestrian monument, situated in Venice in Campo SS. Giovanni e Paolo. Verocchio and Leopardi convey an emotional moment when Colleoni, a helmeted warrior armed with a mace, leads his company into battle.

the territories they annexed, such as Como, Vercelli, and Bergamo. The Visconti attempted to eradicate factionalism in the smaller cities under their tutelage, encouraging the landed nobility to collaborate with officeholders, but their efforts were largely ineffectual. The Visconti lords also aspired to tighten their administration, appointing *podestà* (provincial governors) over the subject cities to keep watch over finance, administration, and law and order. With this, a provincial organization began to rise over the communal institutions and their surrounding jurisdictional areas. The dukes also provided a path to promotion and social mobility for their subjects all over the territorial state, unlike the Venetians or the Florentines. Nonetheless, the Lombard hinterland was also the home of many feudal lordships, like the Trivulzio and the Borromeo, who kept a firm grip on their fiscal immunities and jurisdictions and were powerful enough to raise armies and rebel against the ruling dynasty. The dukes did not have complete control over their vast region, which extended from the Apennines to the Alps.

The Visconti were also briefly lords of Genoa in the 1350s and again in 1421 and 1436, but the Genoese managed to throw off their rule. A number of great families held local dominance over the Ligurian countryside, among them the Doria, Spinola di Luccoli, Grimaldi, Fieschi, and Malaspina, who exploited their rights over the land, and over fulling mills, tolls, and forges. They also had businesses in the city of Genoa, rivaling the urban aristocracy and the populace. The Genoese, who dominated the Ligurian coast and enjoyed vast wealth from their banking and maritime enterprises, thus, were able to keep the Milanese at bay. This was also the case with Florence and Venice. War parties rose up in these republics during the 1420s to counterbalance the Milanese aggression under Filippo Maria Visconti (Duke of Milan, 1412–1447). The Venetians, for example, managed to establish a frontier on the banks of the Adda River by the mid-fifteenth century.

When Filippo Maria Visconti died in 1447 he bequeathed the Lombard dukedom to Alfonso I of Naples (1396–1458), a move that put the leadership of the Milanese regional state in contestation. The mercenary captain Francesco Sforza had married Visconti's daughter, Bianca Maria, who brought the smaller towns of Cremona and Pontremoli with her dowry. Sforza expected to be the heir to the Visconti dynasty. Instead a small group of Milanese patricians usurped leadership, declaring themselves the Republic of St. Ambrose. It took Sforza three years to topple the republic and win the dukedom. He made what was to be a temporary peace with Venice as well as the other Italian states in 1454, betrothing his daughter Ippolita at the age of nine to Alfonso of Naples in order to solidify the alliance. The Peace of Lodi, closing a half century of interregional warfare, endured tenuously for approximately three decades.

Venice

Between 1288 and 1323 the political class of Venice consolidated, limiting the entry of new families into civic government. A Great Council of some 2,000 members held the general membership with smaller committees and ad hoc councils effectively ruling. A first closing took place between 1297 and 1298, privileging merchants and bankers. Then in 1323 the patriciate required new claimants to their political body to have a male ancestor that was or had been a member of the Great Council. They established a Book of Gold in 1328, listing the family dynasties in their membership. An attempt to establish a ducal monarchy, the Falier–Tiepolo conspiracy, failed in 1355. A second closing took place between 1414 and 1430, when fathers had to provide proof of their sons' maternal ancestry within the nobility to be admitted to the patriciate. The state, thus, became the guardian of nobility by birth, and noble marriage through endogamy was encouraged. Further hoops led to a third closing during the early years of the sixteenth century, in all making the Venetian ruling class a constitutional hereditary elite, with some forty clans or dynasties among 190 families holding preponderant places in internal and external affairs.

Although the Great Council was closed to newcomers, save for a brief exception during the eighteenth century, such exclusivity did not signify that the state was immune to political conflict or social contestation,[1] nor did it signify that there was no popular political participation. Scholars of late have found areas of political interaction between the ruling class and the populace where the latter had some representative duties in the city's institutions. Moreover, they have identified areas of negotiation and confrontation. Boatmen and fishermen, for example, jealously guarded and defended their economic interests. Guilds, an important component in the city's economic life, created pathways of political pressure in opposition to the aristocratic state. Both women and men found ways to resist social and political regulation. The Council of Ten, Venice's supreme organ of criminal justice, was constantly on the watch for sedition and acts of subordination, a fact that points to political contestation.

Beyond Venice by 1400 the republic enjoyed a vast sea-born empire, which extended from the Dalmatian coast as far as Ragusa and from the Greek Islands to the Black Sea. In responding to Milanese aggression between 1405 and 1441, it took advantage of the opportunity to create landed resources and tax bases by creating a buffer state to keep the Visconti at bay. In 1405 the Venetians seized the lands of the Carrara in Padua as well as the province of Verona. In 1419–20 they took the Friuli, an important region for transit to central Europe. The maritime republic went on in 1427–8 to annex Brescia, a metal-working and arms manufacturing region, and Bergamo, a textile center, pushing to the eastern boarders of the Milanese state. The newly annexed provinces brought in significant revenues to the Venetian state, with their great natural resources, dense population, and prosperous towns. During the annexation process the ruling class replaced the idea of communal government with that of a signoria, in some dimension equivalent to a lordship, with the Senate becoming the main legislative body in 1423. By the mid-fifteenth century Venetian power on the peninsula rivaled that of Naples. Territorial expansion magnified the number of government offices dramatically. As families gradually shifted out of trade in favor of landowning and lending, officeholding became a new source of income. Magistracies were created to oversee water distribution, the jurisdictions of fiefs, sanitation, grain, forests, mines, common lands in rural districts, borders, fortresses, and artillery. The Republic of Venice kept its hinterland by balancing off the feudal potentates, the urban councils, and the more prosperous rural peasantry. The city-state needed to control its transit trade along the Po, Brenta, and Adige rivers, protecting it from Lombardy and the Julian Alps and securing its communications both down the peninsula and in northern Europe. This necessitated the creation of permanent standing landed forces in addition to the Venetian navy.

Venice permitted its subject elites to retain their local privileges and machinery of government in exchange for tax revenues, fostering some sort of voluntarism rather than brute usurpation. It installed its own podestà and captains to watch over communal affairs. Venetian noblemen would rule over the cities in consultation with prominent local officeholders. They relied heavily on local oligarchs and local administrative organs, not only respecting local statutes but also retaining the right to alter them. The various councils in the subject cities continued to be dominated by the families that had been prominent during the days of the communes. The farther away these local elites were from the capital city, the less they were disrupted by Venetian absorption into the signoria. The subject cities were ruled by self-contained and self-perpetuating oligarchies that were closed and hereditary, similar to the Venetian patriciate. Most of the officeholders were rentiers rather than merchants or manufacturers who profited from grain speculation and tax structures that favored their own interests.

Florence

Florence, also threatened by the Visconti, annexed a series of small towns in Tuscany, like Pisa and Siena, Perugia in Umbria, and Bologna in the Romagna between 1399 and 1402. Florence's subject territories were heavily taxed, and their industries and crafts were controlled through protectionism. The Florentines vaunted the republican way of life, using the political rhetoric of civic humanism. Their chancellor Coluccio Salutati penned a patriotic invective against Visconti aggression in 1402, praising Florentine liberty over Milanese despotism. Humanist writers like Salutati also used oration and letters to legitimize the privileged status of the Florentine ruling oligarchy, invoking the Roman Republic as a model for their politics and culture. A small group of families had consistently dominated the commune, including the Albizzi, Capponi, and Uzzano. Guild membership was required in order to serve in government. After the revolt of the Ciompi wool workers in 1378 the government set up a network of spies, the Guardia or Eight of Ward, and the ruling oligarchy proceeded to control the guilds. Power, through officeholding, was concentrated in the major guilds of bankers, manufacturers, and merchants. The oligarchs began the process of constructing a bureaucratic state, with skilled professional statesmen. They also attempted to curb the privileges and immunities of the church and to keep control of courts. They enlisted professional groups in society—humanist notaries and lawyers to generate civic loyalty. Special executive commissions were set up to impose taxes and make decisions in times of crisis; their terms became longer and longer, effecting an overall narrowing of the state and the strengthening of the executive council. At the same time Florence's involvements in war and the threat of marauding mercenary armies resulted in the formation of an executive commissioned to make rapid decisions in times of crisis. The commission could impose taxes and impose forced loans. Generally, government was becoming more consolidated. It made creative efforts in the 1420s to extinguish the public debt, first by introducing a great census, or *catasto*, to take account of its taxable resources and then by establishing a state repository for dowry funds, encouraging families to invest for their daughters' eventual marriages.

The unsuccessful attempt to subdue Lucca in 1429–33, coupled with unpopular tax policies and a disgruntled mass of lesser guildsmen, brought down the dominance of the Albizzi family in Florence. They were replaced by the Medici (Cosimo, r. 1434–1464; Piero, r. 1464–1469; Lorenzo, r. 1469–1492), one of the richest family dynasties in the city, with immense private wealth from their banking network and various other investments. Founded in 1397 by Giovanni di Bicci di Medici, the bank had seven branches outside of Florence by 1451. Medici wealth also derived from textile manufacturing and from international trade. Through a variety of strategies they were able to win broad support. Giovanni di Bicci had been a voice for the lesser guilds. Later the family extended its influence through astute marriage strategies. Perhaps most important of all, their enormous resources enabled them to build up a network of clients with mutual interests who were willing to collaborate with them in government. The family would dominate urban government by shrewdly manipulating elections and controlling justice and taxation. By 1458 they were introducing special councils of their own into the Florentine constitution. They acted as unofficial rulers, who did not openly monopolize office or claim titles as *signori*, but in effect were unofficial princes.

Rome and the Papal States

The status of the popes, both as spiritual leaders and as rulers of central Italy, was weakened by the Great Schism of the fourteenth century (1378–1417). A rival pope to Urban VI, Clement VII was elected and installed in Avignon, creating a cleft in Latin Christendom. The schism called into dispute the entire legitimacy of papal sovereignty. Some of the high clergy were in favor of replacing the institution with a council. At the same time the Papal States—a midsection of the peninsula that included parts of Lazio, Umbria, Emilia-Romagna, and the Marche—were threatened with dismemberment. Besides the imminent threat of King Ladislao of Naples (1377–1414), the region fell to local potentates like the Malatesta of Rimini, the Bentivoglio of Bologna, and a branch of the Sforza in Pesaro. When a third pope was elected at Pisa in 1409, the divisions were exacerbated even further. The schism was ultimately resolved at the Council of Constance between 1414 and 1418. The sovereignty of the church, however, was still in question. The schism had deprived the Papal Curia of collecting revenues and had diminished the prestige of the Papal Office. Great Roman families like the Orsini, Savelli, and Colonna still held political sway in city and countryside, with extensive landholdings and a subservient peasantry. At times they were strong enough to form separate alliances with other Italian powers, in opposition to papal interests. The popes, however, exerting temporal power similar to that of native princes, were intent on enlarging their territorial base in central Italy and the Romagna. They used their north-central territories as pawns in the power struggle, gradually appointing loyal clients to power and fiscally exploiting the towns and countryside under their jurisdiction. With Pope Martin V (r. 1417–1431) the institution grew stronger. A member of the powerful Colonna family that held sway in the Papal States and the Kingdom of Naples, Martin managed to build his own bureaucracy. Later popes like Alexander VI (Rodrigo Borgia, r. 1492–1503) and Julius II (r. 1503–1513) were able to develop their own armies and to tighten their grip over baronial independence. They availed themselves of diplomats and governors as well as courts of law and tax revenues. Notably, Alexander VI made his son Cesare Borgia a chief papal legate and dominant power in the Romagna region.

BOX 5.1 COLA DI RIENZO (1313–1354)

Rome experienced a brief flirtation with popular rule in the figure of Cola di Rienzo (1313–1354), the son of a washerwoman and tavern keeper. Rienzo managed to become educated and enter the notarial profession. Inspired by the ancient glory of Rome, he wanted to restore both the city's reputation and its status as the leader of a unified Italy. Rienzo advocated for both the abolition of papal power and noble hegemony. For a brief time he was able to galvanize the city's landowning merchants and in 1347 have himself made Tribune, the officer in ancient Rome that protected the plebeian class against the senatorial nobility. One may view this as a call for rebirth and thus in alignment with Renaissance aspirations, yet one must keep in mind that ancient Rome was never entirely ruled by the people. During Rienzo's time neither Rome's noble families nor the pope (stationed in Avignon) were willing to share their power with this popular demagogue. For a few months in 1347 Rienzo began to restore public works and renovate the city, costly endeavors that required heavy, and unpopular, taxation. He also attempted, with little success, to summon representatives from the peninsula's cities and provinces in order to plan for the unification of Italy. Additionally Rienzo began to make messianic claims about his powers, claims that alienated Pope Clement VI (r. 1342–1352). Nor was the pope receptive to Rienzo's notions of a property-less church. Moreover, while the Roman baronage temporarily remained at bay, soon they would put their resources together to drive the would-be Tribune out. As Rienzo's favor waned, he abdicated and fled the city in December 1347. In 1354 he had regained the favor of the pope, who endorsed him as a Roman senator. When he entered the city, however, the Roman nobility had him assassinated.

Naples

With the demise of the Angevin dynasty in 1414, the kingdom was ridden with succession disputes. Queen Joanna I of Naples (r. 1343–1382), who had followed King Ladislao (r. 1386–1414), died childless in 1435, leaving a power vacuum that invited division. There were succession disputes until 1442, when Alfonso of Aragon ascended the throne and through a series of negotiations normalized relations with Pope Eugenius IV (r. 1431–1447) to curry his support. His reign included the mainland south and Sicily, which together with Naples was called the Kingdom of the Two Sicilies. It became part of the Aragonese's western Mediterranean empire, which also included Aragon, Valencia, Majorca, Sardinia, and Corsica. The Aragonese established naval bases in the south, becoming commercial competitors of Genoa, Venice, and Florence. Throughout the kingdom a strong baronage of diverse origins, some twenty or thirty family dynasties, held substantial local juridical jurisdictions and political authority. Alfonso agreed to let them rule their own lands. Moreover, he exempted them from the direct tax that financed his standing royal army. In this way he was able to make Naples the capital of a Mediterranean empire and the seat of judicial and financial organs, building up an educated bureaucracy of Spanish origin to counterbalance the barons. Alfonso financed his wars with various Italian states by fostering interregional commerce. Despite the strides he made in building a fledgling central administration and a regional capital, he was unable to improve the security of his kingdom, leaving his illegitimate son and successor, Ferrante I (also called Ferdinand I; r. 1458–1494), with serious diplomatic and military difficulties.

Family and Power

In our discussion of political consolidation earlier, the notion of family, whether as a single ruling dynasty or as one hereditary line among several with membership in republican government, comes up repeatedly. One could argue that the family was the real protagonist of Italian political development. From the fourteenth century, the number of men who formally participated in politics shrank. Moreover, within the ruling classes the disparity in wealth grew. Both rich and poor were enfranchised in ruling bodies, but only the rich monopolized the major administrative responsibilities, such as overseeing city revenues, food provisioning, and the organs of justice. We must examine elite family behavior in order to understand Italy's overall political consolidation, for it played a critical role in shaping systems of power. Close study of families participating in the governments of Florence, Venice, Milan, Siena, Cremona, Genoa, Lucca, and Verona illuminates the variables that propelled some to the apogee of power, where they monopolized the most lucrative offices. In principle, these

FIGURE 5.3 Andrea Mantegna (1465–1474). *Decoration of the Camera degli Sposi*. Fresco and dry tempera. Detail. Northern wall or wall of the fireplace. Ducal Palace, Mantua, Italy. The court of the entire Gonzaga family with its courtiers is displayed. The painting is a symbol of the power and pride of an important princely dynasty.

factors included the size and continuity of the family dynasty, its wealth and economic strength over the long term, astute marriage alliances and kinship ties, and membership in the legal or notarial professions. Size was perhaps the least controllable factor, for it depended on biological fortune, but council members could compensate for this by co-opting consanguineous kinsmen, by making alliances with their wives' relatives, and by forming clientage networks so that they could retain high offices over the long term. Endogamy, the intermarrying among families in an urban council, helped solidify control of offices among fathers and sons-in-law and among brothers-in-law as well as kin to other degrees, and it forged complex webs of social and financial relations.

By law the female kin of urban council members could not serve in office. However, they played an important part in this patriarchal framework. To begin, wives came to their marriages with dowries that were critical to land accumulation, credit, and personal loans, significantly contributing to the family's economic substance. But women themselves were very influential in the marriage market, for they inherited from their mothers, grandmothers, and aunts and were thus able to contribute to their daughters', granddaughters', and nieces' dowries. In Venice, for example, between 1420 and 1535 some of the poorer noble families went to great lengths to set limits on women's dotal wealth and inheritance in an effort to prevent themselves from being priced out of the marriage market. They were ultimately unsuccessful: between 1425 and 1524 dowries rose as much as 83 percent. Marriage had become an important business of state, essential to the family dynasty's capital accumulation. Thus the politically astute maximized their kinship connections within the ruling group through endogamy. It is important to note, however, that not every noble daughter or son married. In an effort to maximize capital accumulation and conserve wealth over the long term, families practiced restricted marriage, where perhaps one daughter or son married. The result was a large pool of unmarried male nobles and a great number of noblewomen who were shuffled into convents.

As the Italian elites closed ranks and judiciously guarded their family patrimony, the clerical population grew. The city of Florence provides an excellent example: by the mid-sixteenth century one of every nineteen Florentine residents lived in convents.[2] These institutions served not only the church but also the family and the state. During the fifteenth century the Florentine mercantile elite built some of their political clientage networks and connections within the church through the placement of their daughters in convents. Thus women in nunneries played some role in the formation and development of the Florentine state.

While patriarchy prevailed as the dominant principle driving family inheritance and dynastic succession, in the courts of the peninsula some women were able to reach the helm of power, at times through direct inheritance, such as Joanna II of Naples (r. 1414–1435), or through regency, when their sons were too young to succeed their deceased husbands. Among Italy's notable female regents was Caterina Sforza of Forli (r. 1488–c. 1500) and Caterina Corner, the queen of Cyprus (r. 1474–1489), who ruled the island for fifteen years upon her husband King Jacques II's death. Forced by the Venetian state to abdicate and move to the small Veneto town of Asolo, Caterina still held considerable influence in Venetian affairs. Other women, including Maria of Castile (r. c. 1420–1423; 1432–1458), queen of Aragon and Naples and the wife of King Alfonso I of Naples; the Duchess Eleonora of Naples (1450–1493), the wife of Duke Ercole d'Este of Ferrara; and Eleonor's daughter Isabella d'Este ((1474–1539), the wife of the Duke of Mantua, were entrusted with the power to rule while their husbands were off at war. Still others, such as Eleonora Gonzaga (1493–1550), Duchess of Urbino, held no formal power but were in positions of great influence. They might advise their husbands or help clients seeking political office or contracts for services or artistic commissions. Among the examples in this last case were Alessandra Macinghi Strozzi and Lucrezia Tornabuoni, both from Florence.

Alessandra Macinghi (c. 1408–1471), the wife of Matteo Strozzi (1422), married into one of Florence's most illustrious families. She is well known through the preserved correspondence of some seventy-three letters to her husband Matteo and her sons Filippo and Lorenzo. The letters, a conventional means of communication during this period, are an important source of information for her family's financial struggles and political rivalries with the Medici; they are also a window into aristocratic family life and culture. Cosimo de Medici (1389–1464), the informal head of the Florentine state, exiled Matteo Strozzi and several other members of his family to Pesaro on the Adriatic coast in 1434. Alessandra followed Matteo into exile, together with their children. Shortly thereafter both Matteo and three of their nine children perished in the plague of 1435. The tragic event inaugurated Alessandra's new life in widowhood, a status for which she and her husband had astutely prepared. To circumvent Florentine legal norms and retain a degree of independence, she deliberately chose not to remarry. In Florence a widow's children were to be raised by their father's extended family should their mother take a new husband. Remaining unmarried, Alessandra was able to become the guardian of their children per her husband's will. She was also permitted to choose her own male representative, also a Florentine legal norm for women, when handling the family's legal affairs. Returning to Florence from Pesaro, the newly widowed Alessandra acted as the head of her household, overseeing her children's education, working to place her sons in banking positions in Naples, and negotiating beneficial marriages for her sons and daughters. Further, she oversaw her sons' political alliances and financial investments as well as influencing where the family lived and to whom they rented farmland properties. Alessandra proved to be an able bookkeeper and financial manager of the family's activities in flax, silk, cheese, and fruit sales and distribution as well as the production of linen. When Cosimo de Medici lifted the exile of male family members in the Strozzi line in 1466, the standing of Alessandra's family rose, and Alessandra continued to play an influential role in her children's affairs until her death in 1471.

Lucrezia Tornabuoni (1427–1482), from an elite Florentine banking family, married Piero di Cosimo de Medici in 1444 at the age of seventeen. The marriage was essentially a business merger between the clans of two powerful banking families. It placed Lucrezia not only at the center of Florentine political, cultural, and religious life, but also in a position to help her husband in matters of state and diplomatic affairs. She is credited with arranging a profitable marriage alliance for her son, Lorenzo, with Clarice Orsini, a member of a powerful Roman family. The betrothal would afford the Medici family beneficial connections with the papacy. In fact her grandson, the fruit of this marriage that concluded in 1469, became Pope Leo X. Lucrezia had perhaps learned her business acumen from her family, for she was a profitable investor. Among her business enterprises was the installation of a hot spring some ten miles south of Volterra, complete with thermo-hydraulic equipment. When her husband Piero died in 1469 she spent more time writing and sponsoring writers, corresponding with the leading humanists. Profoundly religious, she was also devoted to a number of Florentine charities.

The Collapse of the Italian League

The truce of 1454 conferred relative peace on the five Italian powers for some forty years, save for Florence's war with Pope Sixtus IV in 1478 and the War of Ferrara between 1482 and 1484, which pitted Milan and Naples against Venice. But alliances continued to be fragile at best. During this hiatus a number of shrewd rulers attempted to protect the Italian League's cohesion, among them the Florentine Lorenzo de Medici, who mediated between Naples and Milan, and Pope Alexander VI (r. 1492–1503), the Spanish Borgia pope who concluded a number of calculated marriage alliances among his illegitimate children in order to avoid engaging in conflict. Ultimately these strategies to balance interstate rivalries failed, and as the century drew to a close various city-states conspired with foreign powers, offering them opportunities to intervene. A newly revived French monarchy, free from its wars with England, took advantage of the invitation. The Spanish monarchs followed on their heels. France justified its intervention through dynastic claims to the Kingdom of Naples and later through its claims through inheritance to the Duchy of Milan. Thus between 1494 and 1559 the Italian Peninsula became a principal battleground (Map 5.1 shows the Italian Peninsula in 1494)for French and Spanish efforts at territorial aggrandizement (see Chapter 8).

The Italian League began to unravel when Ludovico Sforza (1452–1508) of Milan, facing hostilities from Naples to the south and territorial competition from the Venetian Republic to the east, turned to the French king for support. Ludovico's own political status at home was also a source of tension: he had usurped power from his nephew, Giangaleazzo Maria Sforza (1469–1494), the rightful heir to the Duchy whose father had died when he was only seven years old. When Giangaleazzo came of age, he married the daughter of the king of Naples, Isabella of Aragon (also Isabella of Naples and Duchess of Milan, 1470–1524), who pressured her father Alfonso II (king of Naples, 1494–1495) to help the newlyweds assume the reins of power. Giangaleazzo mysteriously died in the autumn of 1494, and it was rumored that his uncle Ludovico had poisoned him. Relations between Milan and Naples thus deteriorated. Nor were Milan's relations with Venice to the east any better. The Venetians, ever seeking further conquests on the Italian mainland, were open to a French invasion of Naples. At the same time, the Duke of Ferrara hoped with French interference to regain the lands of Polesine di Rovigo, which had been lost to the Venetians in 1484. Thus Ludovico reached out to King Charles VIII Valois (1470–1498) of France, against his Neapolitan enemy.

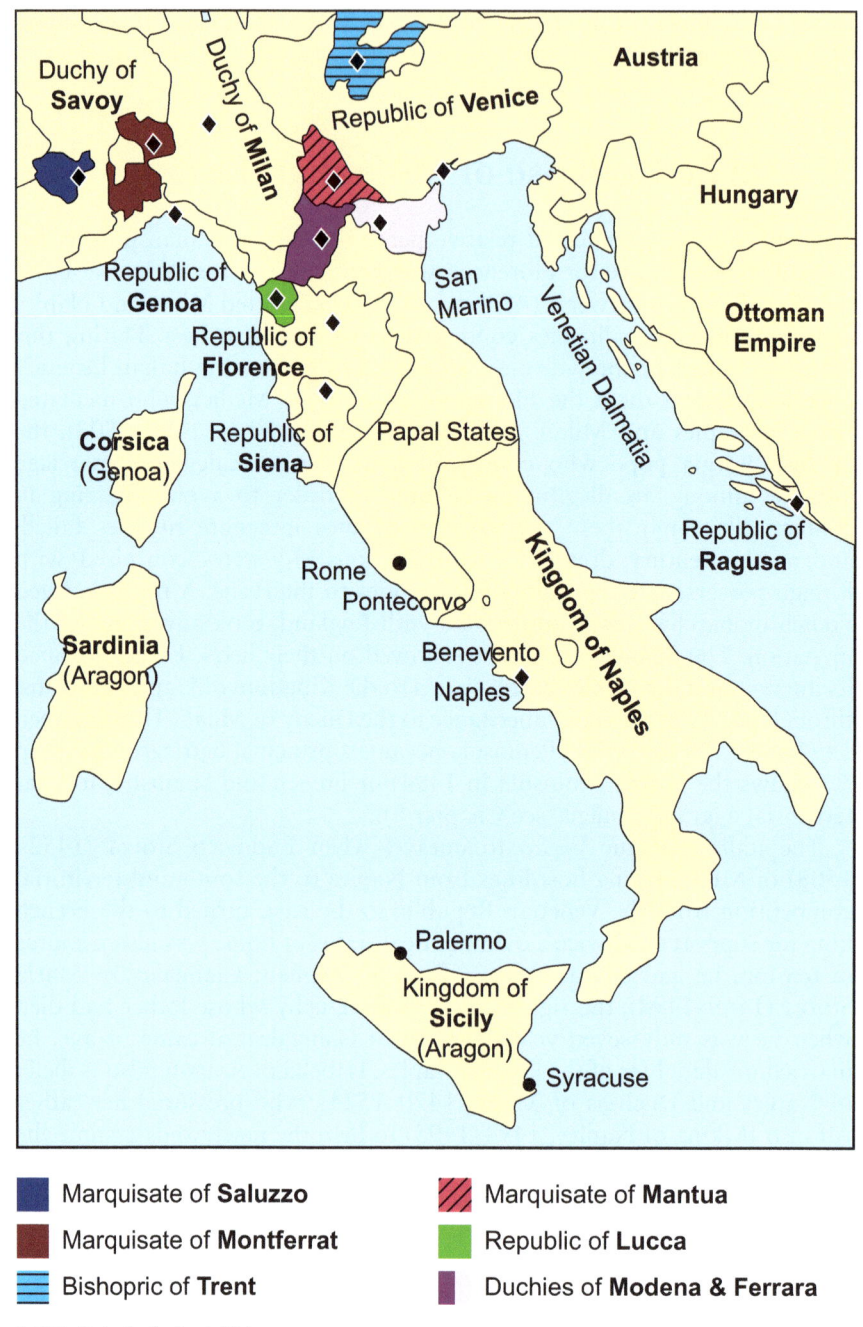

- ■ Marquisate of **Saluzzo**
- ■ Marquisate of **Montferrat**
- ≡ Bishopric of **Trent**
- ▨ Marquisate of **Mantua**
- ■ Republic of **Lucca**
- ■ Duchies of **Modena & Ferrara**

MAP 5.1 Italy in 1494.

Charles VIII held a dynastic claim to the crown of Naples through the Angevin dynasty, which had ruled Naples prior to its fall in 1442 to the Aragonese. Charles was keen on seizing Naples, a strategic southern port on the Mediterranean. His own kingdom had reached a point by 1494, with the revival of a royal bureaucracy and a strong army, where it was ready to accumulate new territories. The plan to attack Naples was set.

Pope Alexander VI (1431–1503), the Spanish Rodrigo Borgia, also sided with the French. He had attempted to ward off confrontations with Milan and Naples by concluding marriage alliances with both Italian powers for his illegitimate children. He arranged a marriage for his daughter Lucrezia (1480–1519) at the age of thirteen to Ludovico Sforza's cousin in June 1493, sealing an alliance between the Papal States and Milan. He then married his son Jofrè (*c.* 1481/82–*c.* 1517) to the Neapolitan king's daughter. Neither marriage, however, put the pope in a position of neutrality. Moreover, he faced serious hostilities from the Roman nobility because he had created many Spanish cardinals. In the end Alexander was forced to take sides.

The French crossed the Alps into Italy in 1494, fortified with an international array of Swiss, Dalmatian, and Scottish soldiers and heavy artillery, while naval forces approached Naples from the sea. The French barely encountered any resistance as they marched down the peninsula, an indication of the Italian people's lack of cohesion. Persistent exploitation of the countryside by Italy's landed elites, with heavy taxation and forced labor, as well as urban disenfranchisement of the majority of people in the peninsula's cities and towns had not fostered any loyalty.

In Florence, the Medici fled, and the theocrat Savonarola (1452–1498) who replaced them opened the city to the French. The charismatic friar, a firebrand with a penchant for apocalyptic preaching, tried to cleanse the city with the repudiation of secular art and drama. He also expelled the Jews as well as prostitutes and punished blasphemy and homoerotic relations. In his program of moral reform, Savonarola claimed that the arrival of Charles VIII was God's way of punishing the corrupt and sinful. His words resonated with a segment of the population long rooted in prophetic traditions and that was inclined to replace the elite patronage networks with a broader, republican government. Savonarola managed to establish a Great Council with citizen participation. However, the upper classes soon retaliated. They charged the friar with overthrowing the constitution and had him hanged and burned in 1498. Savonarola's popularity is a reminder that alongside intellectuals from the ruling class who were glorifying the ancients was a mass of people mesmerized by apocalyptic prophecy and predictions and against oligarchic rule.

Naples succumbed to Charles VIII in 1495. Ludovico Sforza, who had initiated the invitation to the French in order to retaliate against his Neapolitan rival, had not calculated that his foreign ally would in a few months attempt to conquer the entire peninsula. The invasion, thus, alarmed Venice, Milan, and the pope, who, with the support of Ferdinand II (r.

1479–1516) of Spain and the Holy Roman Emperor Maximilian I (r. 1508–1519), formed the League of Venice to drive the French out. Occupying Naples for less than six months, Charles's army left Naples in the summer of 1495. Eventually King Ferdinand II restored the city to Ferrante (Ferdinand) II (r. 1495–1496).

The French invasion of 1494 was only the beginning of a series of foreign intrusions onto the Italian Peninsula. The Italian city-states were rich but at the same time they were divided and thus a tempting prize. In 1499 the French made a second attempt at conquest. The second round, like the first, was made on pretense of hereditary right. The French king, Louis XII (1462–1515), claimed the Duchy of Milan as the grandson of Valentina Visconti. He curried the support of Pope Alexander VI, who was plotting to have his illegitimate son Cesare Borgia (c. 1475/76–1507) conquer the Romagna region. King Louis made Borgia Duke of Valence and arranged for his marriage to Charlotte d' Albret, the sister of the king of Navarre. In exchange the pope granted Louis XII a dispensation to divorce his wife so that he could marry the widow of the deceased King Charles VIII. Borgia helped Louis to attack Milan, and Louis gave Borgia troops to conquer the Romagna. The French thus took Milan and the region of Lombardy in 1499, and Borgia went on to net both the Romagna and several Tuscan towns.

Inheritance underlay yet a third claim to Italian territory in 1500, when Ferdinand II of Spain used his Aragonese lineage to seize Naples with the support of the French king Louis XII. Like France, Spain as well was ready to embark upon territorial conquests by the end of the fifteenth century. Two large Spanish territories were united into one with the marriage of Ferdinand II of Aragon (r. 1479–1516) and Isabella of Castile (r. 1474–1504). By 1492 the monarchs had driven the Jews and Muslims out of Spain and were planning Columbus's voyages, to be financed with the gold and silver the monarchs confiscated from religious minorities. The Italian territories were thus a tempting prize. In the Treaty of Granada in 1500 the French and Spanish agreed to split the Kingdom of Naples. The French occupied Naples and the regions of Campania and Abruzzi; the Spanish assumed the Puglia and Calabria. When the French broke the treaty the Spanish occupied the entire southern mainland and Sicily in 1503, remaining until Italian unification in 1860.

Warfare

Land-based military technology was rapidly transformed from the mid-fifteenth century. Armies still relied on cavalrymen, a medieval precedent, whereby the fighter carried a lance and sword and charged in formation on an armored horse. Around 1450 soldiers on foot used both longbows and steel crossbows drawn by a windlass. The adoption of the pike was effective in disrupted cavalry lines.

From the mid-fifteenth century gunpowder and siege cannons with cast-iron balls replaced catapults as siege weapons. Cities also built elaborate fortifications, placing cannons in their bastions for stronger defense. By the sixteenth century self-igniting firearms were common, including muskets, arquebuses, matchlocks, and pistols. Iron cannons played a decisive role in battles. The Bresciano, Venice's Lombard territory, was an important center for arms manufacture, marketing its cuirasses, swords, pikes, harquebuses, cannons, and iron bullets to Lombard and northern European areas. All of these weapons were expensive, making it increasingly rare that they were financed by nobles. They became the domain of European states, who funded larger and more permanent armies. The Ottomans had led the way, becoming among the first to train standing armies, using Janissaries—non-Muslim captives—for their troops. The various warring states also engaged mercenary companies from Switzerland and Germany in seasonal activity, generally from March to October, and soldiers were often accompanied by wives, other female companions, and family.

Intense political rivalries from the last years of the fifteenth century propelled both the republics and the principalities into the investment of improved technology. Among the prime examples is the duke Ludovico Sforza in Milan and the signoria in Florence who both engaged Leonardo da Vinci (1452–1519) as a civil and military engineer to design bridges, trench drainage, and portable trench mortars. Leonardo also drew hundreds of plans for war machines like armored vehicles, multifiring guns, and prefabricated cartridges. He also imagined parachutes, gliders, and diving suits. Most of these ideas remained in sketches. Nonetheless, scientists and other thinkers of the period remained wholly engaged in applying geometry and trigonometry to civil and military architecture, ballistics, and ocean navigation.

Naval technology and armament improved during the fifteenth and sixteenth centuries, with sailing ships designed for extended oceanic voyages. Among the most important innovations was the adoption of the Arab lateen sail that had been in use on the Indian Ocean for centuries. European shipbuilders such as the Portuguese, Spanish, and the Venetians improved upon it, adding masts and multiple square and lateen sails. The large Spanish galleons were among the best. Larger trading ships carried not only cargo but also more gunners, archers, and heavy cannon along with a skilled crew of carpenters and sailmakers. Gun platforms were constructed for greater fire power. Venice was one of Europe's biggest industrial centers for shipbuilding through the seventeenth century, producing armed warships and auxiliary craft. Women in Venice made cloth sails. In the course of the sixteenth and seventeenth centuries casting bronze made great strides in England and then Holland and Sweden, and the metal was used to produce iron buns, which were less expensive than bronze cannon. Thus their ships could carry larger numbers of armaments at a lower expense.

Improvements in navigation were also implemented during the fifteenth century. The compass evolved from a simple needle floating on a block of wood in a container of water to the pivot needle and compass card that marked directional degrees. By the end of the fifteenth century gimbal rings were added for better balance. Navigational techniques were adopted from the Arabs' astrolabe of the Middle Ages, an instrument that calculated latitude. In the sixteenth century the quadrant was used for solar sighting. With greater knowledge of spherical trigonometry, cartographers in Nuremberg constructed terrestrial globes and map projections.

Statecraft and Diplomacy

The Italian regimes of the fifteenth century may be credited with planting the seeds for what would later become the modern state. Driven by incessant warfare, they developed elaborate systems of finance and administration as well as courts of law. They also pioneered diplomacy, for the complex international relations of the period demanded representatives with deep knowledge of rivals' resources, tactics, goals, and shifting alliances. The Italian states were the first to establish permanent representatives and embassies. Moreover, they provided models for diplomatic relations and skills for maintaining a balance of power, models that other monarchs would learn from, and adapt to their own needs and techniques, during the sixteenth century.

Conclusion

The political and diplomatic relations among the Italian regional states throughout the fifteenth century remained volatile, with alignments and realignments continually changing. The internal politics within each city-state also generated group rivalries and regroupings of power. However, unlike the eleventh to thirteenth centuries, the claimants to imperial and papal powers (Holy Roman Emperors and popes, respectively) became a much less serious threat to the authority and property of the oligarchies or principalities. Even though some potentates believed the Holy Roman Emperor was still the ultimate source of legal authority, his role was reduced to the dispenser of privileges or titles in exchange for financial support. During this period the major city-states turned on each other to net landed resources and major transit routes. The lords of the principalities, trained in arms, availed of their own private armies in this competition, while the republics tended to contract out to professional mercenaries. The period between 1425 and 1454 witnessed almost chronic warfare. However, the Fall of Constantinople in 1453 and the rise of the Ottomans encouraged the pacification of the Italian states, whose focus became the looming external enemy. With the Peace of Lodi in 1454 all five Italian major powers signed a twenty-five-year peace treaty, forming the Italian League. The peninsula then experienced a forty-year hiatus before the next wave of military engagements commenced in 1494, this time with transalpine powers taking advantage of the regional rivalries.

Think Critically

1. What motivated the political consolidation of the Italian Peninsula?
2. What were the causes of regional rivalries?
3. What is the relationship between family and public life?
4. What were the social and political roles of aristocratic wives and mothers? How did they advance the family dynasty's political interests?

Further Exploration

1. As Florence defended its republican liberty against Milan and then Naples the city's guilds sponsored a series of thirty-two heroic statues to decorate the niches of Orsanmichele, the granary of the republic. What was the civic purpose of these statues?
2. Great mercenary captains were the heroes of the Renaissance, celebrated in humanist orations and with equestrian statues commemorating their valor. What ideological messages does Verocchio's equestrian monument to Bartolomeo Colleoni in Figure 5.2 convey?

Notes

1. See the essays by Dennis Romano and Claire Judde in: *Popular Politics in an Aristocratic Republic. Political Conflict and Social Contestation in Late Medieval and Early Modern Venice*, edited by Maartje Gelder and Claire Judde de Larivière (New York: Routledge, 2020).
2. Sharon T. Strocchia, *Nuns and Nunneries in Renaissance Florence* (Baltimore: Johns Hopkins University Press, 2009), 1.

Further Reading

Primary Sources

d'Este, Isabella. *Selected Letters*. Edited and Translated by Deanna Shemek. *The Other Voice in Early Modern Europe: The Toronto Series*. Toronto: Iter Press, 2017.

Strozzi, Alessandra Macinghi. *Letters to Her Sons, 1447–1470*. Edited and Translated by Judith Bryce. *The Other Voice in Early Modern Europe: The Toronto Series*. Toronto: Iter Press; 1st edition, 2016.

Secondary Sources

Chojnacki, Stanley. *Women and Men in Renaissance Venice*. Baltimore, MD: Johns Hopkins University Press, 2000. Twelve essays that explore the role of patrician women and the state in the areas of family relations, marriage, and dowries.

Ferraro, Joanne. *Family and Public Life in Brescia. The Foundations of Power in the Venetian State, 1580–1650*. Cambridge, UK: Cambridge University Press, 1983. Explores the officeholding, family relations, marriage, and dowries of the Brescian ruling class and their relationship with the Venetian state.

Ferraro, Joanne. *Venice: History of the Floating City*. Cambridge, UK: Cambridge University Press, 2012. Traces the history of Venice from its sixth-century beginnings to the twenty-first century.

Gelder, Maartje, and Claire Judde de Larivière. *Unrest in Venice. Popular Politics in an Aristocratic Republic*. New York: Routledge, 2020. A group of essays that identifies and examines political interaction and social contestation outside the formal institutions of power.

Goldstone, Nancy. *The Lady Queen. The Notorious Reign of Joanna I, Queen of Naples, Jerusalem, and Sicily*. London: Walker Books, 2009. A spell-binding account of the life and times of a female monarch.

Hartt, Frederick. *A History of Painting, Sculpture, Architecture, Vol. II. Renaissance, Baroque, Modern World*. New Jersey: Prentice-Hall, 1976. An authoritative survey of Renaissance and Baroque art history.

Judd de Larivière, Claire. "Political Participation and Ordinary Politicization in Renaissance Venice. Was the Popolo a Political Actor?" In *Popular Politics in an Aristocratic Republic. Political Conflict and Social Contestation in Late Medieval and Early Modern Venice*. Edited by Maartje Gelder and Claire Judde de Larivière, 69–87. New York: Routledge, 2020. An exploration of lower-class resistance to Venetian rule.

Kirshner, Julius, ed. *The Origins of the State in Italy, 1300–1600*. Chicago: The University of Chicago Press, 1995. A series of essays that examines the making of the early modern Italian regional states.

Mallet, Michael Edward, and John R. Hale. *The Military Organisation of a Renaissance State. Venice c. 1400–1617*. Cambridge, UK: Cambridge University Press, 1984. A thorough study of the role and organization of Venice's land forces.

Martines, Lauro. *Power and the Imagination: City-States in Renaissance Italy*. Baltimore, MD: Johns Hopkins University Press, 1988. A magisterial survey of medieval and Renaissance Italian developments that draws connections between cultural patrons and power.

Pullan, Brian. *A History of Early Renaissance Italy: From the Mid-Thirteenth to the Mid-Fifteenth Century*. New York: St. Martin's Press, 1972. An informative survey of political, economic, and social developments during the early Renaissance.

Romano, Dennis. *The Likeness of Venice: A Life of Doge Francesco Foscari.* New Haven, CT: Yale University Press, 2007. A biography of the ruling Doge between 1423 and 1457, which documents the history and culture of Venice during the bellicose years of the second quarter of the fifteenth century.

Romano, Dennis. "Popular Protest and Alternative Visions of the Venetian Polity, c. 1260 to 1423." In *Popular Politics in an Aristocratic Republic. Political Conflict and Social Contestation in Late Medieval and Early Modern Venice.* Edited by Maartje Gelder and Claire Judde de Larivière, 22–44. New York: Routledge, 2020. An essay that reveals areas of Venice's exclusive political system that were facing challenges from below.

Strocchia, Sharon T. *Nuns and Nunneries in Renaissance Florence.* Baltimore, MD: Johns Hopkins University Press, 2009. An analysis of the growth of female monasticism during the fifteenth and sixteenth centuries and the roles that religious women played in the social, economic, and religious history of Florence.

6

Humanism and the Circulation of Knowledge

FIGURE 6.1 Vittore Carpaccio (1465–1526). *The Vision of St. Augustine* (1502–1504). Oil on canvas. Scuola di San Giorgio degli Schiavoni, Venice, Italy. During the fifteenth century, the study as a separate room in the homes of the learned appeared, as exemplified in this painting.

Humanism in Italy

Interest in classical Latin is evident as early as the late twelfth century, with the secular magistrates of the Italian communes. Every urban government relied on notaries and lawyers to record their business transactions and political affairs. Twelfth-century notaries, exploring French works of Latin grammar and poetry, began to write their own grammar manuals in order to bring clarity to the contracts and records they produced for private and public purposes. During the thirteenth century, as more laymen became involved in urban government and in sponsoring urban culture, notaries and the citizens they served developed an appreciation for the style and grammar of the Latin language as well as the history and literature of the Roman past. Writers such as the Paduan judge Lovato de Lovati (1240–1309) emulated ancient models of poetry, while the Florentine Bruneto Latini (1212–1294) translated the Roman orator Cicero. Petrarch (1304–1374), a Tuscan lawyer whose father was a notary, became a founding figure in the study of classical Latin literature, especially the poetry of Virgil (see also Chapter 3). While Petrarch wrote on piety, dignity, and faith and was influenced by the Franciscans, he thought that Roman law was the best means of administering the state. Men in civic government from Naples to northern Italy began to cultivate the art of rhetoric. With Piero Paolo Vergerio (1370–1444), a statesman and canon lawyer born in the Venetian seaborne possession of Istria, it became an important art form at the end of the fourteenth century, consummated with the revival of Ciceronian oration in the works of Leonardo Bruni (1370–1444) and Poggio Bracciolini (1380–1459) in Florence. Rhetorical skill was essential for the ruling elites, in order to persuade their peers in government and as a means of defending the dignity of their families and allies. Verbal dexterity and the ability to demonstrate learning and wisdom became standards for the families at the helm of government throughout the Italian Peninsula.

Humanists were keenly interested in literary and linguistic scholarship. Their new educational program, first emphasizing Latin and then including Greek, began in Florence in 1375 with the efforts of Coluccio Salutati (1331–1404), the chancellor of the city, who had originally been trained as a notary. Salutati brought in humanists from far and wide to copy manuscripts of classical texts, especially those essential to the art of rhetoric. Importantly, he also invited Manuel Chrysoloras (*c.* 1353–1415) of Constantinople in 1397 to reside in Florence and teach Greek. Greek texts had been translated into Latin by way of Arabic or Hebrew in al-Andalus and Sicily during the eleventh and twelfth centuries. However, once Italian humanists learned the ancient Greek language they retranslated many of the original texts, including the works of Aristotle, purifying them from medieval accretions. Interest in the Greek language also spread to Lombardy by the beginning of the fifteenth century. Chrysoloras taught there between 1400 and 1403. Another humanist, Francesco Filelfo (1398–1481), who had served as a notary and chancellor to the Venetian diplomatic representative in Constantinople, became Milan's principal Hellenist, composing panegyrics and orations for Duke Francesco Sforza. The body of Greek literature available to humanist scholars in Italy greatly expanded when Cardinal Bessarion (1403–1472), the titular Latin Patriarch of Constantinople, created an enormous library of manuscripts and donated them to the Republic of Venice. From Salutati's chancellery in Florence, thus, the interest in linguistic scholarship quickly spread to the courts of Lombardy and the Veneto as well as to the Kingdom of Naples and the Republic of Venice.

Classical humanism came to serve the social and political needs of Italy's ruling elites between 1400 and 1460. Rich and influential power holders sponsored a new educational curriculum to fit their governing needs. While universities in Italy and throughout Europe continued to be the place where lawyers, physicians, and theologians trained, and where mathematics and science were emphasized, the liberal arts curriculum, based on reading classical authors, was deemed necessary to develop the virtue and eloquence of men in public life. It was taught in private schools for upper-class boys, while girls and women of the upper classes—who were generally not permitted to serve in public life—learned basic Latin in convents and other literary skills from their formally educated male kinsmen as well as tutors. Among the most notable classical teachers was Pier Paolo Vergerio, who taught the son of the despot Francesco Carrara in Padua. Elsewhere, two important elite schools for boys were founded, one by Vittorino da Feltre (1378–1446) that was commissioned by the Mantuan marques and *condottiere* (mercenary captain) Gianfrancesco Gonzaga (r. 1407–1444) and the other in Ferrara by Guarino Guarini under the tutelage of the duke Niccolo III d'Este. Guarini had studied classical languages in Constantinople. In Naples, another notable humanist adept at Latin, Greek, and Hebrew was Lorenzo Valla (1407–1457), who taught Latin grammar and philology under the sponsorship of King Alfonso. Students came from all of Italy and Europe to study in these Italian schools.

The new educational program equipped rulers and thinkers to express their contemporary concerns and experience through classical thought. The curriculum emphasized Latin grammar, poetry, rhetoric, history, and ethics. Ancient, rather than medieval, Latin grammar became an essential part of the program, while rhetoric trained orators to be eloquent and persuasive; to convince their peers of the proper course in government and to justify the places of privilege they enjoyed in society. Poetry, like Latin grammar, served as a means to sharpen communication skills. Thus, humanist pupils and teachers avidly read Homer, Virgil, Horace, Juvenal, Seneca, Ovid, and Terence and wrote poetry themselves. To write poetry was the mark of a civilized, educated human being. History, specifically Greek and Roman history, not only provided political lessons from the past but also was used as a heuristic device to express the political values of the present. A solid knowledge of history prepared advisors and rulers for political decisions and astute statecraft. History was also a font for moral lessons and moral philosophy, another subset of humanist study which included such discussions as the nature of human dignity and the human capacity for wisdom (Gianozzo Manetti, 1396–1459, and Giovanni Pico della Mirandola, 1463–1494); the freedom of human will to determine one's own nature (Salutati and Pico della Mirandola); the merits of pleasure over stoicism (Lorenzo Valla); whether social distinction derived from birthright, wealth, or public service; the corrupting influence of money; the importance of family life; the relative weight of public service versus a life of contemplation (Salutati and Bruni). The debates were meant to be essential guides to human nature, to grooming good citizens, and to shaping civil society. They also furnished the social and economic context of political life during their time, for the rulers of the various cities had come from disparate origins—old noble houses, old citizenry, and new wealth. What criteria would be used to justify their status and distinction? Their virtue? Some like Poggio Bracciolini argued, counter to the church, that private wealth did not have to corrupt the soul; if the Christian sin of avarice was avoided it could both improve the quality of life and perform the public service of beautifying cities and giving employment to the community. Nurtured by chancellors and secretaries as well as teachers in private schools and by tutorial, humanism was advanced by the papal curia, oligarchs, despots, princes, prelates, and entrepreneurial and professional men who led in civic government, both in the major cities of Florence, Venice, Milan, the papal territories, and Naples, and in the lesser cities and courts of Italy. These rulers were served by a fleet of chancellors, administrators, secretaries, advisors, and teachers whose training was also grounded in humanistic study. The humanists of the fifteenth century spoke for urban elites, describing their condition and worldly values.

In the first half of the fifteenth century humanism functioned, at least among elite men, as a means to interpret fifteenth-century political and social experience, often through propaganda and panegyrics as well as letters, poetry, speeches, treatises, dialogues, dramas, and histories. When the despotic Visconti in Milan aggressively threatened the liberty of the Florentine Republic between 1397 and 1402, for example, the Florentine chancellors Leonardo Bruni and Coluccio Salutati engaged Ciceronian oration to defend Florence's republican form of government over monarchy. They looked back to ancient models, with particular admiration for the Roman Republic. At the same time, Salutati's pupil Antonio Loschi (1368–1441) was making counter arguments in defense of Milan. In Naples Antonio Beccadelli (1394–1471), known as the man from Palermo, wrote propaganda for King Alfonso.

Humanism was put to other uses besides praising rulers and justifying their power. Importantly, scholars developed strategies for achieving some level of objectivity in scholarly inquiry. This was evident in their study of texts, where they developed a sense of the history of words and evaluated their meaning in historical context. Poggio Bracciolini, for example, recovered the ancient writer Vitruvius, which was important for architects, and in Rome Flavio Biondo (1392–1463) wrote the archeological history of the city between 1444 and 1446. In 1440 Lorenzo Valla, under the sponsorship of Alfonso of Naples, debunked *The Donation of Constantine*, purportedly a fourth-century document justifying papal jurisdiction over central Italy, by demonstrating that it was a ninth-century forgery. There was an emphasis, thus, on ascertaining facts in history and biography, separate from notions of divine intervention. Moreover, this was the moment when humanists made a conscious attempt to separate themselves from the medieval past and to see themselves as part of a new age. In this sense they were the first inventers of the concept of the Renaissance as a historical period, a concept with a distinctly western European bias.

With the rise of a more courtly and aristocratic society, civic humanism subsided during the last half of the fifteenth century. The preference for philosophers and poets over social activists coincided with the gradual consolidation of political power and aspirations to nobility. The next generation of humanists began to compose poems and orations that exalted princely power. In Naples under King Alfonso I (1442–1458) the Neapolitan Academy, led by the Latinist Giovanni Pontano (1422–1503), became a renowned center of poetry with an illustrious royal library. Even in republics humanists exalted princely magnificence. In Florence, when the Medici family took control of government in 1434, they were less concerned with civic humanism and more interested in stressing a contemplative life with themes of love, beauty, honor, the immortality of the soul, and Platonic ideals. The family founded the Platonic Academy in 1462, endowing the humanist Marsilio Ficino (1433–1499) with a villa near Careggi that was well-furnished with a library of Greek manuscripts. Ficino devoted a great deal of his career to translating the *Dialogues of Plato* and the writings of Plotinus from the Greek into Latin, as well as a body of texts preceding Plato, from the Hellenistic period. Later these works were incorporated into a standard Latin version published in Venice in 1491. Prior to Ficino's translations of Plato, an earlier generation of humanists with an interest in moral and political philosophy had focused on the works of Aristotle that the humanist Leonardo Bruni had translated from the Greek. With Ficino, however, the concepts of Plato, which had been little known in the West, offered a new platform of study and thought. Scholastic philosophers had incorporated Aristotelian thought in Christian theology. Now other scholars would grapple with how Plato and Christian thought could be harmonized. With this purpose in mind in 1474 Ficino published his *Platonic Theology*. In Plato's writings Ficino understood that material things in this world have no permanence, but that the immaterial world is instead eternally unchanging. The Holy Trinity, for example, was unchanging. The disciples of Ficino determined that Platonic texts were in harmony with Christian revelation. Among the principal ideas was that man was the center of the universe and that his soul was part of the divine being, a free agent who could chart the course of his life and free his soul. Neoplatonists exalted reason, a force that enabled humans to direct their own destinies. Other scholars who had studied Plato went on to explore additional philosophical ideas, including those in Arabic and Hebrew texts. Giovanni Pico della Mirandola (1463–1494) drew his ideas from Christian and Muslim philosophy, the Jewish mystical tradition of the Kabbalah, and the ancient traditions of the occult, arguing that the human being—mainly men—had infinite mental capacity to know, a stance that the papacy, however, found to be heretical.

Women from the middle and upper ranks of society were also important participants in late fourteenth- and fifteenth-century intellectual discourse, albeit with a different perspective than that of men. Because girls were formally educated even less than boys, there were far fewer women humanists than men. Relatively speaking, however, women in Italy had a higher literacy rate than women in other areas of Europe. Women of the upper classes were often sent to convent boarding schools around the age of seven or eight, in order to learn domestic skills like sewing or needlework. They also learned basic reading and writing, but their overall education was designed to fit the circumscribed social roles they were given by their parents or guardians as future wives or nuns. Moralists, whether Christian or Jewish, frequently argued that too much education was dangerous for the female sex and that limiting girls' reading to religious works was better than exposing them to Greek and Latin texts. Jewish girls were discouraged from learning Hebrew, the language of scholarship and scripture, for it might distract them from their duties as wives and mothers. But even if they learned Hebrew letters, the business of translation and commentary should be left to males. Whether Christian or Jewish, moralists overall were concerned with the chastity of women, fearing that certain writings would have a corrupting influence. Christian girls from well-off families were tracked to either marry or join a convent.

The reality of experience, however, did not always match the aspirations and fears expressed in prescriptive writings. Some girls learned to read and write, to do figures, and to learn music and dance. Both Christian and Jewish women also learned Hebrew and Greek philosophy as well as Latin poetry and rhetoric. Most belonged either to the nobility or to prominent wealthy families. Many enjoyed the freedom to study in convents. Thus it is important at the outset to underline the importance of social class as a determinant of women's educational experience. Moreover, it is important to distinguish between noblewomen educated and writing at the peninsula's courts from those who were in the oligarchic republics. In the latter case, women held no formal political roles. They could neither serve as notaries or chancellors, nor be in government service. In courtly society, however, noblewomen were able to serve as regents in their husbands' absences, and this gave them more political and social leverage.

The most notable female writers were exposed to more advanced humanistic study by their grandmothers, mothers, aunts, fathers, brothers, and/or family tutors. The first generation generally wrote in benefit of their families or clans. Among them was Maddalena degli Scrovegni (1356–1429), from a wealthy background in Padua, who wrote to the Carrara lord of her city asking him to exonerate her family from their exile in Venice. The Carrara family had usurped power in Padua during the early fourteenth century, confiscating the properties of their enemies and exiling them from the region. Toward the end of the century Maddalena's family aligned with the powerful Visconti family in Milan who would temporarily drive out the Carrara in 1388. The young humanist then used her Latin skills to write the mercenary captain of Giangaleazzo Visconti and express her family's appreciation of the Milanese duke's attempts to drive out the Scrovegni's hated enemies.

Many early writers were from the courts of Italy and availed of privileged positions as the wives or daughters of powerful dynasts disposed to educating their female family members in the erudite humanistic tradition. Their social positions contributed to their visibility and fame and gave them opportunities to write for official public occasions and for diplomatic ends. Among them was Battista da Montefeltro (1383–1450), the wife of Galeazzo Malatesta, lord of Pesaro. When her husband was deposed, she composed a Latin oration for the Holy Roman Emperor Sigismund's (1368–1437) visit to Urbino in 1433, requesting he restore her husband to power and that he release her son-in-law from prison. The oration won the praise of the chancellor and humanist Leonardo Bruni in Florence. After Battista's unhappy marriage ended in widowhood, she took vows with the Franciscan Order of Santa Chiara and devoted herself to the study and writing of Latin poetry and prose. She also taught her granddaughter, Costanza Varano (1428–1447), to write Latin oration, letters, and poems. Varano, like her grandmother, was also well-positioned as the daughter of the deposed lord of Camerino and the wife of Alessandro Sforza, lord of Pesaro. When she died in childbirth, her daughter Battista Sforza (1446–1472) went to live with her powerful uncle and aunt, Francesco Sforza and Bianca Maria Visconti, at their court in Milan. Battista too was educated in the humanist tradition, like her mother, grandmother, and aunt before her. When Battista became the second wife of the Duke of Montefeltro (see Figure 7.15), who was forty years her senior, her husband permitted her to act as regent during his absences. Like the women in her family before her, she educated her daughters. Her cousin Ippolita Sforza, daughter of Francesco Sforza of Milan and wife to Alfonso, Duke of Calabria and crown prince of the Kingdom of Naples, was also a notable humanist. What is more, her granddaughter, Vittoria Colonna, became a famous poet. Thus we see in this instance that humanism among married noblewomen with the potential to rule as regents for their husbands was a multigenerational tradition in alignment with their social positions and the cultural traditions of their families. Not all women writers enjoyed such status, but their parents' decision to educate them in the humanist tradition became a means of elevating the family's social currency in society.

Most male humanists championed the call for women to be obedient and virtuous and to marry and procreate. They generally accepted the misogynist discussions of woman's nature in ancient and clerical texts that described the female sex as weak and limited. Early female humanists began to reassess homosocial humanist culture and to push back. In France, Christine de Pisan (1365–1431) challenged the notion of gender difference, breaking with Plato and Aristotle to advocate the equality of women. Born in Venice, Pisan spent much of her life in France, where her father, a physician from Bologna, served the French king. Pisan wrote in many genres, including ballads, elegies, poems, and advice on government, but what stood out the most were her assertions about the status of women as well as their potential to contribute to social and cultural life. In 1405 she wrote the *Book of the City of Ladies*, an exposition on the ideal environment for women, establishing an enduring literary genre, called the Querelle des Femmes, that argued for the equal education of women and redefined their domestic and public roles. Pisan was in fact responding in the *Book of the City of Ladies* to Boccaccio's *Concerning Famous Women*, penned in 1365. In that work he praised some one hundred women from Greek and Roman antiquity and a few from the religious and cultural traditions of the Middle Ages. Boccaccio's role for women, with the exception of his entertaining *Decameron*, fit with both ancient and religious authors: they were to be chaste, silent, and obedient. Pisan challenged this, arguing that the figures that Boccaccio had described demonstrated heroic virtues, as did many other women of the past. She generated a long-lasting debate among humanist writers that envisioned women as heroic and equal to men, though they had not been afforded the same opportunities as the male sex.

Male humanists had not ignored the issue of women's role in society. Like Boccaccio, however, they constructed visions of women that fulfilled their own interests. The Venetian humanists Giovanni Caldiera and Francesco and Ermalao Barbaro viewed the family as a microcosm of the state, where women were in a subordinate position. In his treatise on marriage (1415), Francesco Barbaro specified that women's place was in the household, where they reared children and managed domestic affairs. He offered detailed advice to upper-class men about how to choose a wife, emphasizing the importance of character over wealth and beauty. Barbaro also stressed the importance of marrying within one's own social class. Another humanist, the Florentine Leon Battista Alberti (1434–1437), held similar views. Where, then, did unmarried female intellectuals fit in? They were treated with suspicion, as not fulfilling their natural roles in society. Erudite noblewomen from courtly society, however, seemed to have passed unscathed, in all likelihood because they were connected to power and privilege.

Three major female writers during the fifteenth century marshalled evidence for women's worth, citing their major achievements, honor, and human dignity. All three came from social stations beneath the high nobility, writing and speaking for courtly society. Isotta Nogarola (1418–1466), from an upper-class family in Verona, was neither married nor enrolled in a convent, a position that made her the object of hostile invective. Nonetheless, she argued that women had a place within the literary world. Her mother had sent her and her sister Battista to private teachers to learn Latin and the classics. Isotta was especially interested in studying philosophy. She wrote a series of letters to famous male scholars. At one point, writing to the Venetian statesman Ludovico Foscarini (1409–1480), she argued, cleverly using biblical, legal, and theological texts, that if women were indeed the weaker sex, as Aristotle and a long line of medieval clerics had asserted, then one could not blame Eve for the Fall. Another notable humanist in the fifteenth-century mainstream, Cassandra Fedele (1465–1558), expounded on the virtues of the female sex and their capacity for education, with a wide net of readers that included the Duchess of Ferrara, the Marquise of Mantua, the Duchess of Milan, and the queens of Hungary and Spain. She was highly praised by the humanist Angelo Poliziano as an amazing scholar conversant in both Italian and Latin and became one of the most notable female public intellectuals of her generation. From the prestigious citizen class in Venice, a hereditary group of males who served in the Venetian bureaucracy, Fedele was not a noble but rather came from a family of professionals. She was tutored privately in Latin and Greek and trained in rhetoric and the natural sciences. Because of her social status as well as her abilities, she was able to circulate with intellectuals at the University of Padua and at one point almost obtained a university post in Spain. She was also invited to write orations of the Doge of Venice. But Fedele retired from intellectual life at the age of thirty-four when she married a physician and devoted her efforts to being a wife. Marriage was often an impediment to the scholarly productivity of married women, as domestic duties and child-rearing occupied a great deal of their time. In fact when Fedele was asked by the young daughter of a Florentine chancellor, Alessandra Scala (1430–1497), whether to marry or to write, she offered no position but rather urged the younger woman to think over what she was more naturally inclined to prefer. In widowhood Pope Paul III assigned Fedele the position of director at the orphanage of San Domenico in Venice, where she resided until her death. Yet a third woman writer, Laura Cereta (1469–1499), the daughter of a Brescian lawyer married to a merchant, also gave orations and wrote letters to scholars arguing for the rights of women to be educated. Widowed young and apparently dissatisfied with her marital experience, she characterized the institution as a trap for women. Discussions of women's worth, limitations on their freedom, and reactions to more misogynist intellectual traditions would continue to be published throughout the sixteenth and seventeenth centuries, as the number of women writers expanded, particularly in Venice with Moderata Fonte (a pseudonym for Modesta da Pozzo, 1555–1592), Lucrezia Marinella (1571–1653), and Arcangela Tarabotti (1604–1652). By the late sixteenth century such writings, primarily in vernacular languages, enjoyed wide dissemination in multiple editions, thanks to the printing press.

Humanism: A Shared Intellectual Tradition

During the fifteenth and sixteenth centuries humanist learning took on a more international dimension, circulating throughout Europe in a variety of ways. One was via traveling scholars as rulers across Europe engaged individuals skilled in Latin to serve as secretaries or diplomats, to teach, or to help build large classical libraries filled with history of the past. The Italian humanist Poggio Bracciolini, for example, assisted in the foundation of the Oxford University manuscript collection during his visit to England between 1418 and 1423, and the prolific humanist writer Eneas Silvio Piccolomini (1405–1464) spent time in Switzerland, Scotland, England, and the court of the Holy Roman Emperor in Vienna as a diplomat of the church prior to becoming Pope Pius II. Other prominent Italian humanists found employment teaching Latin and letters at the courts of Transylvania, Poland, and Hungary. In Buda the court of Matthias Corvinus (r. 1458–1490), king of Hungary and Croatia, became an important humanist center. The king formed a circle of Italian scholars that included Pietro Ranzano, Bartolomeo Fonzio, and Francesco Bandini to discuss the ideas of Neoplatonism. Corvinus especially favored Plato's model of the philosopher-king, an ideal he embraced for himself as a royal patron of the arts and learning. His aristocratic wife, Beatrice of Naples (1476), joined him in cultivating classical culture and encouraged Matthias to sponsor workshops of scribes, illuminators, and bookbinders to preserve, transcribe, and translate (from Greek to Latin) classical literature and science. Engaging two Italian librarians, first Galeotto Marzio and then Tadeo Ugoletto, the king amassed more than 500 books and illuminated manuscripts.

Humanist learning also spread via scholars who had studied in Italian intellectual centers and then returned to their places of origin to establish programs of educational and religious renewal. As a result, across Europe, but especially in the northwest, grammar schools began to emphasize the classical standards of Latin expression and Greek, while scholars wrote new textbooks. They drew from Greek, Roman, Hebrew, and Christian writers to invigorate school curricula and religious study. In biblical scholarship they applied their knowledge of ancient languages to study the scriptures in their original languages. In that context, humanism eventually coincided with the sixteenth-century religious debates between Protestants and Catholics. Sectarian apologists, critics, and reformers turned to biblical theology and to improved translations of Greek and Hebrew texts in order to defend their ideas and to revitalize their respective religions. The result was an outpouring of treatises, letters, and dialogues, genres that had first been developed in Italy, as well as improved biblical texts. Their rapid circulation was accelerated by the printing press. Besides classical scholarship, humanists also promoted popular vernacular literature, with stories and plays drawing themes from the classical past as well as the forms of poetry that had circulated in the Italian courts. Dante's *Divine Comedy*, Petrarch's sonnets, and Boccaccio's stories were all strong models.

While humanist learning spread across Europe, it was also deeply embedded in the Mediterranean world, with its shared Greco-Roman legacy and its deep medieval Arabic roots. From the tenth century Jewish scholars in Palermo and Toledo had been engaged in the translation of Greek, Hebrew, and Arabic texts into Latin. That work was invigorated during the fifteenth century when humanist scholars, trained in ancient languages, criticized medieval translations and reproduced texts in their original languages. The result was a proliferation of new scholarship in the sciences and the humanities. Much of the translation and editing work took place in Italian venues, but the Ottoman court of the Sultan Mehmed II was also an important center of scholarship at this time. The sultan had attracted an international community of Christians, Muslims, and Jews who were translating ancient texts and writing commentaries. The Bible, the Kabbalah, and the Hebrew language were areas of study, especially from a philological perspective, that generated trans-Mediterranean discussions from Iberia to Naples and from Rome and Florence to Istanbul. Humanists like Giovanni Pico Della Mirandola, in his *Oration on the Dignity of Man*, maintained that all learning—Islamic, Jewish, and Christian—was part of divine revelation, and Giannozzo Manetti joined Jews and Ottomans in discussing the reliability of the Latin Vulgate translation of the Bible. Among the most important products of this international discussion was the Spanish printing in 1517 of the *Complutensian Polyglot*, a scholarly edition of the Bible in its four original languages: Greek, Hebrew, Chaldean, and Latin.

As in the study of religious thought, so too in science, translation and inquiry generated a trans-Mediterranean and trans-European intellectual exchange. Humanism's emphasis on going back to original classical sources played a fundamental role in scientific advancement. The process had begun with the labors of medieval translators and commentators, but fifteenth-century humanist scholars sought more reliable translations of ancient Greek writings. No longer entirely satisfied with Aristotle, who had defined the core university curriculum in Europe since the fourteenth century, they began to question which translations of the natural philosopher were best and how they should be interpreted. They also searched for alternatives to Aristotle. One example among many was Poggio Bracciolini's rediscovery in 1417 of Lucretius's *On the Nature of Things*, a work that asserted that the world could be explained by the operation of material forces and natural laws.

The quest to find new classical sources in natural science propelled humanists to scour European monasteries and cathedral repositories from England to Istanbul and to establish new libraries with their findings. In Rome

Pope Nicolas V (r. 1447–1455) amassed an enormous collection of Greek manuscripts on philosophy, mathematics, and medicine and commissioned scholars to translate them into Latin. Florentines like Pico della Mirandola also established a number of important libraries. So too did Cosimo de Medici, who in the 1460s commissioned Marsilio Ficino to translate Plato's works into Latin for his new Platonic Academy. At about the same time in Venice, in 1468, the great library of Greek science was established with the manuscript collection of Cardinal Bessarion, affording scholars the opportunity to develop new understandings of Ptolemaic astronomy and trigonometry. Venice also became home to a center of Hebrew scholarship after the Iberian-Jewish diaspora of 1492. Scholars from all of Europe came to study in these Italian libraries and centers.

The advent of printing from the late fifteenth century facilitated publishing projects in multiple languages and the wide circulation of classical texts throughout Europe and parts of the Ottoman Empire. Palermo, Padua, Paris, Lyon, Venice, Rome, Milan, Spain, and Istanbul all housed important centers of printing. Among them was the Aldine Press in Venice, which specialized in Greek works, including the complete medical works of Galen (1525) and the Hippocratic corpus (in Latin in 1525 and in Greek in 1526), a collection of medical texts written in the fourth and fifth centuries BCE. Rome became a center of Hebrew printing, while various European presses published gospels, grammars, and scientific works in the Arabic language. Among the ancient works put into print were Aristotle's natural philosophy, Euclid's geometry, Ptolemy's geography, and Dioscoride's *On Materia Medica*, a source for natural remedies. Wealthy patrons across the Mediterranean became avid collectors of Hebrew, Arabic, and Ottoman books and manuscripts.

The proliferation of new humanist translations of Greek scientific texts in print magnified the size of Renaissance libraries and, importantly, provided the impetus for further scientific investigation in a wide range of subjects, including surgery, geography, mathematics; and in the practical arts of mechanics, metallurgy, distillation, architecture, and engineering. In the realm of astronomy, however, it is important to note that Islamic scholars had already been engaged for several hundred years in making corrections to some of Ptolemy's geocentric ideas and had expanded on them. The sixteenth-century Polish astronomer Copernicus was not the first to theorize or calculate a heliocentric conception of the universe. It had already been anticipated by astronomers such as Nasir al-Din al-Tusi (1201–1274) and Ibu al-Shatir (1304–1375). Furthermore, there was an important Ottoman tradition in astronomical observation in Istanbul where the Persian Ali Qushji (1403–1474) had done important work.

In northern Europe and Spain the humanist approach to learning came to occupy a central place in educational and religious reform by the early sixteenth century. Initially it spread through students who had studied in Italy, and through the Brothers of the Common Life, a lay religious movement that began in the Netherlands and fostered religious reform on the eve of the Protestant Reformation. Intellectuals drew on a large repository of classical Greek and Latin texts; the Church Fathers; and the Arabic, Hebrew, and Byzantine scholarship of the Middle Ages to form new theoretical and practical approaches to school curricula and the interpretation of texts. The new translations into the vernacular of such writers as Aristotle, Thucydides, Cicero, Livy, and Ovid, put into print, reached a broad readership, fostering a general knowledge and appreciation of these works.

Humanism, thus, was a shared tradition, reaching from the Mediterranean world to northwestern Europe. Whether they fostered classical studies, promoted greater literacy, praised rulers, advocated for religious reform, or delved into science and medicine, humanist teachers and writers held certain commonalities. One was their command of the languages and literatures of antiquity, whether Greek, Latin, or Hebrew. A second was their familiarity with the genres of exposition developed by Italian humanists, such as treatises, orations, and letters. The third was their commitment to humanist methods of inquiry, which called for the study of ancient texts in their original languages and their analysis in historical context. This inevitably led to the critical review of previous scholarship. The conclusions of Aristotle, the educational methods of scholastics, and the canon of endorsed authorities promoted by the church, all came under scrutiny. The last commonality among humanists was their promotion of school curricula centered on classical languages and literature and analysis that encouraged independent, critical inquiry. It must be said, however, that this final aspiration remained largely in male hands, for secular grammar schools and universities were generally not open to women. Nor did women have many opportunities to undertake public duties or to preach. Only a small number, mostly in the princely courts, had the opportunity to rule or to engage in diplomacy, and the appropriateness of women taking the helm of government was a subject of vigorous debate among political thinkers. Upper-class women, however, did have opportunities to obtain a humanist education through private tutors, and they had access to private intellectual circles, particularly ones that addressed lay audiences with poetry, plays, and letters.

Humanism developed over the fifteenth and sixteenth centuries in a variety of political, social, and cultural contexts; in a panoply of kingdoms, sultanates, princely and ecclesiastical courts, commercial cities; in some universities; and in less formal, private cultural circles. It flowered in the courts of Mantua, Ferrara, Urbino, and Milan; in the resurging papacy in Rome; in Hungary, Bohemia, and Austria; in the monarchies of Spain and France; and later in Elizabethan England. It became part of the curricula at some monastic and private colleges and at various universities, such as Poitiers in 1431, Freiburg in 1457, Ingolstadt in 1472, Wittenberg in 1502, and Leiden in 1575. What began in the Italian city-states became a

European-wide intellectual current. The result, as we shall see in the brief survey later, was a broad and varied expression of ideas about education, politics, history, religion, philosophy, and even conduct.

Humanism across the Alps

Spain

In the fifteenth century Spanish rulers called upon humanists prized for their Latin skills to serve as secretaries and diplomats in their courts. Rulers also encouraged the study of ancient texts, the collection of books and manuscripts, and the establishment of classical libraries. Humanists responded by producing translations that would both advance the classical tradition and make available new editions of the Bible. Among the most important scholars was Antonio de Nebrija (1444–1522). The historian of the royal crown, Nebrija, authored a Latin grammar (1481), a Latin-Spanish dictionary (1492), a Spanish grammar (1492), and works on Spanish history and rhetoric. Like the Italian humanist Lorenzo Valla, who had questioned the standard Latin (Vulgate) translation of the Bible, and the Dutch religious reformer Desiderius Erasmus (1466–1536), Nebrija worked on Greek texts that would improve the vulgate translation of the New Testament. He also called for Hebrew scholars to use a similar approach in perfecting an edition of the Old Testament. Nebrija contributed to the collective project undertaken by European scholars to produce a polyglot edition of the Bible, the *Complutensian Polyglot* (completed 1517; published 1521). This important work, which brought many European humanists to Spain, was based on translations from all four original languages: Greek, Hebrew, Chaldean, and Latin. As new editions of the Bible became available, discussion of Christian reform arose. The writings of Erasmus in this regard became very popular, especially among the royal administrators and advisers of Charles V (r. 1516–1556), a native of the Low Countries who became Holy Roman Emperor in 1519. Erasmus's *Handbook of the Militant Christian*, which encouraged readers to study and meditate on the Scriptures, was widely read. The Spanish theologian Juan de Valdés (1500–1541) and Spanish scholar Juan Luis Vives (1492–1540), like Erasmus, regarded humanist education as a means to deepen the spiritual lives of the people. However, after Charles retired in 1555 and the Inquisition began to purge Catholic Europe of publications deemed a threat to orthodoxy, Erasmus's works were officially forbidden and placed on the *Index of Banned Books* (1559).

The most influential Spanish humanist of the early sixteenth century was the Valencian writer Juan Luis Vives. The embodiment of an international scholar, Vives spent most of his life circulating in northwestern Europe in order to escape the repression of the Spanish Inquisition. The son of Jews who had converted to Christianity and were eventually executed as Judaizers, he favored classical learning over the church-endorsed scholastic method he had been taught at the University of Valencia. Vives studied at the University of Paris in 1509 and 1512 and then received an appointment as professor of the humanities at the University of Leuven in 1519. He was invited to England in 1527 to tutor the princess Mary, the daughter of Henry VIII and Catherine of Aragon, an assignment he believed was important only for women who might be called upon to rule. Vives went on to lecture in philosophy at Oxford University with the help of another renowned humanist and statesman, Thomas More (1478–1535), but was constrained to retreat to Bruges in 1528 after formally disapproving of Henry VIII's request to annul his marriage with Catherine of Aragon. Vives devoted the rest of his scholarly career to repudiating scholastic teaching and pedagogy, earning the admiration of both Erasmus and More for his writings on a variety of subjects across the curriculum. Among his works were books on Latin and letter-writing, on rhetoric and dialectic, on the education of (elite) women, on how to tackle poverty, and on the nature of the soul.

Beyond Vives, Spain's most significant contribution to the spread of humanism came through the activities of the Society of Jesus, whose missionary and educational work unfolded throughout the country's global empire from the sixteenth century. The movement's founder, Ignatius of Loyola (1491–1566), was grounded in humanist education, and Jesuit schools, which emphasized classical language, literature, and history, became the basis for upper- and middle-class education.

The Low Countries

Humanism in the Low Countries during the sixteenth century centered especially around calls for the reform of Catholic theology and practice. Desiderius Erasmus of Rotterdam (1466–1536) was its most influential advocate and thinker. His influence extended beyond his native land to a wide circle of scholars across Europe with whom he corresponded. A Catholic priest, educated in the classics in the Low Countries, Erasmus completed his education in Italy in 1506, receiving a doctorate in divinity from the University of Turin. Afterwards he spent time as a proofreader in the publishing house of Aldus Manutius in Venice, an experience that exposed him to an enormous body of scholarship that would circulate throughout Europe. Erasmus was influential in the foundation of the Trilingual College (Latin, Greek, and Hebrew) at the University of Leuven, which began a program in classical studies and became a center for intellectual life. Among his numerous legacies were his pedagogical writings. They included *On the Methods of Study* (1511), essential to educational institutions offering classical literature, Latin composition, and Greek; *On Copia* (1512), a manual on the art of rhetoric; and the 1508 edition of *Adages*, a compilation of Latin and Greek proverbs for humanist writers. Erasmus was also an extremely important biblical scholar. His *Novum Instrumentum* (1516), the first New Testament in Greek, became the basis for Martin Luther's (1483–1546) translation of this work (1483–1546) into German (1522) and William Tyndale's (c. 1494–1536) translation into English (1526). The translators of the King James Version of the Bible (1611) also consulted Erasmus's work.

Erasmus was a devote Catholic, but he opposed the church hierarchy. In his highly popular work, *The Praise of Folly* (1511), he amusingly rejected the worldliness of Catholic prelates and advocated for the simple teachings of Christ. Perhaps unwittingly, Erasmus laid some of the intellectual groundwork for the Protestant Reformation.

The German Lands

Humanism in the German-speaking lands focused on reforming curriculum in the schools to include the study of Greek and Latin philology and texts. At the same time it also departed from its Italian origins to place greater emphasis on religious reform. The three most instrumental founders of humanistic learning in the German-speaking lands were Rudolph Agricola (1444–1485), Johann Reuchlin (1455–1522), and Konrad Pickel, who latinized his name as Conrad Celtis (1459–1508). Agricola began his career studying law in the Italian town of Pavia in 1469 but soon switched to Latin writing and literature. In 1475 he moved to Ferrara and studied Greek. There he wrote his major work, *On Dialectical Invention* (1478), one of the most influential texts on rhetorical theory for the age. With this Agricola became an inspiration to students of the classics in Germany and the Low Countries. He returned north to Frisia in 1479, becoming the town secretary of Groningen. There he emphasized the educative functions of language, an approach that greatly influenced both Conrad Celtis, the leading poet of the German Renaissance, and Erasmus of Rotterdam.

The German scholar Johann Reuchlin (1455–1522), in line with the Italian humanists Giannozzo Manetti, Giovanni Pico della Mirandola, and Lorenzo Valla, was devoted to the study of Hebrew texts. He composed the first Christian dictionary of the Hebrew language and was a strong advocate for the creation of university positions in Hebrew. His work circulated widely in what is now modern-day Austria, Switzerland, and France as well as Italy.

Conrad Celtis (Konrad Pickel, 1459–1508), a scholar and poet from Bavaria, acquired the descriptive "Archhumanist," or greatest of the German Renaissance humanists, for his legacy in classical languages and history as well as his cartography of the German lands. Celtis lectured widely throughout his career, in Rome, Bologna, Venice, and Florence as well as

Vienna and the north German lands. In Poland between 1489 and 1491 he pursued mathematics, astronomy, and the natural sciences in addition to classical languages and history and founded a Roman academy. He also established literary societies in Hungary, Heidelberg, and Vienna. In 1497 the emperor Maximilian I gave Celtis the unique title of "teacher of the art of poetry and conversation" and endowed him with imperial privileges. In Vienna Celtis continued to lecture on Latin and the classics. He also founded a college for poets.

During the sixteenth century, a new group of German humanists, influenced by the pedagogy and ideas of Erasmus, used their humanist skills in the theological debates of the Protestant Reformation. Among them were Martin Luther (1486–1546) and Philip Melanchthan (1497–1560). Luther, by 1520 the founder of a rival theology and church that broke with Roman Catholicism, was educated in Latin schools emphasizing grammar, rhetoric, and logic. His father wanted him to become a lawyer, but the renowned reformer instead turned to theology and philosophy and became an Augustinian friar. His observance of church practices and abuses gradually led him to form anti-papal views and to propose a revision of the sacramental system. While he began by proposing Christian reform, his public debates with pro-Catholic theologians gradually led him to take his movement outside the church. The keystone of his theology was salvation by faith alone, free of the commentaries and rituals of the church or the claimed authority of priests. As a humanist, Luther was a brilliant pamphleteer whose ideas spread far and wide thanks to the printing press. Among his foremost humanist defenders was Melanchthan, a classical scholar and teacher who advocated for educational reform and authored several textbooks and a Latin grammar. Melanchthan taught Greek at the University of Wittenberg (1519) at Martin Luther's invitation. He became an important figure in the Christian humanist movement alongside Erasmus, using his classical training in the service of moral and religious education. However, unlike Erasmus, Melanchthan supported Luther, systematizing his ideas and defending them in public even though the latter's religious position put him at odds with most Christian humanists.

England

In England humanism played a fundamental role in both secular education and religious study from its very beginnings, with its emphasis on the linguistic and historical context of classical and Christian writings. It was primarily English scholars who had studied in Italy during the late fifteenth and early sixteenth centuries who introduced the various tools of scholarship that would have a permanent influence on English culture. Among them were William Grocyn (*c*. 1446–1519), who brought Greek studies to Oxford, and John Colet (*c*. 1467–1519), the founder of St. Paul's school in London. Grocyn had spent time in Florence in 1488, where he studied Greek with

Angelo Poliziano and Demetrius Chalcondylas. Upon his return to England in 1491, he taught Greek at Oxford, becoming reputedly the first Greek professor in the kingdom. Afterwards he became the rector of St. Lawrence Jewry in London, where he joined the circle of scholars associated with Erasmus. Colet traveled to Paris and Italy after graduating from Oxford in 1490. On the continent he studied canon and civil law, patristics, and Greek. During that time he became familiar with the ideas of the French lawyer Guillaume Budé, Erasmus, and the Florentine religious firebrand Girolamo Savonarola (1452–1498). Returning to England in 1496, he lectured at Oxford University on the epistles of Saint Paul and the books of the Bible. As a religious reformer Colet wished to combine scholarship with faith, advocating for a simpler commentary on the scriptures, one free from the complex expositions of the medieval scholastic writers who preceded him. He was also a strong advocate for classical education. In alignment with this, in 1512 he reformed the educational program at St. Paul's School in London. With William Lily (*c.* 1468–1522), the first headmaster of St. Paul's, and Erasmus, Colet wrote a Latin grammar that became an essential part of the English curriculum. The body of Colet's work over his career reflected his efforts to incorporate the ideas of both classical and Christian writers such as Cicero, Augustine, Jerome, John Chrysostom, Ignatius of Antioch, and others. They were also grounded in the works of the renowned Platonists Marsilio Ficino and Pico della Mirandola.

Like Colet, Thomas More (1478–1535), a lawyer and distinguished statesman who in 1529 attained the lord chancellorship of England, was trained in the classics and remained a strong proponent of humanist scholarship. In addition to his legal training, he studied Greek with Grocyn and Thomas Linacre (*c.* 1460–1524), the translator of the Greek physician Galen into Latin and the founder of medical studies in England. A follower of Pico della Mirandola, More wrote the Italian Platonist's biography in 1510 and translated some of his letters into the vernacular. He also wrote a history of the English king Richard III, modeled after the historical writings of Tacitus. His most famous work, however, was his *Utopia* (1516), an ideal, fictional construction of an egalitarian society based on reason that reflected More's readings of Platonic philosophy and Christianity. *Utopia* was meant to satirize the author's own hierarchical social and political world. Throughout his career as a statesman, More cultivated his own intellectual interests, interacting with a number of influential humanists that included Colet; Erasmus; Vives; and Sir Thomas Elyot (*c.* 1490–1546), the author of a book describing the ideal ruler (1531) in the tradition of Machiavelli's *Prince* and Castiglione's *Courtier*. More trained his own daughter and heir, Margaret More Roper (1505–1544), in Greek and Latin. He favored the education of his daughters, and women in general, but mainly in Christian texts rather than the pagan classics, satires, or comedies. Margaret More Roper wrote Latin orations, poems, and treatises, but her only published work was an English translation of Erasmus's *A Devout*

Treatise on the Pater Noster (1542). At the end of his life More became embroiled in the controversy over Henry VIII's movement to break with the Roman Church, which he opposed, arguing for the supremacy of the pope. He also adamantly opposed the ideas of Protestant theologians, and like those who took the opposite stance on these issues used his humanist training to argue his points of view. After refusing to take *the Oath of Supremacy*, a requirement to swear allegiance to the monarchy, More was convicted of treason and executed in 1535. In 1935 he was canonized as a martyr.

Throughout the sixteenth century many prominent English literary figures were trained in the classical tradition, and this was reflected in their vernacular works in combination with the medieval conventions of their native land. The use of the English language, as opposed to French, became an issue of national pride following the conclusion of the Hundred Years War with France in 1453, and sixteenth-century authors increasingly wrote in English but made use of classical forms. Among them was Sir Thomas Wyatt (1503–1542), who introduced the Italian sonnet to England; Edmund Spenser (1552/53–1599), the author of the major epic poem *The Faire Queene*; and William Shakespeare (1564–1616), the foremost playwright of the age. However, English literature and drama were not dominated by classical models but rather were a blend of classical and native traditions. The period's most famous playwright, William Shakespeare, received a Latin education. Thus he would thus have read Ovid, Virgil, Plautus, and Terrence, and his classical education is evident in such early writings as his *Comedy of Errors* and *Titus Andronicus*. Moreover, he did explore Greek and Roman history in his dramatical works *Troilus and Cressida*, *Julius Caesar*, and *Antony and Cleopatra*, but many other of his writings owed little to nothing to classical precedent. Some of his plays were set in Italy, and he may have used Italian sources for some of his plots. Shakespeare is well known for his portrayal of the self and the human condition in his comedies, tragedies, and history plays, themes that were certainly in alignment with the humanistic tradition.

France

French intellectuals interacted with and influenced Italian humanists as early as the fourteenth century, when the papal court was centered in Avignon, but only in the sixteenth century did a few individuals receive notoriety. Among them were Guillaume Budé (1467–1540), Jacques Lefèvre d' Etaples (1450–1536), and Marguerite of Angoulême (1492–1549). Budé (1467–1540), a correspondent of Erasmus, was a scholar of Roman civil law who became the founder of legal humanism. In Paris, Budé, a master of Greek, published translations of Plutarch as well as a Greek grammar. He also wrote an important book on Roman coins and essays on philology and literature. Lefèvre d' Etaples was a Catholic religious reformer educated in Greek and Latin in France who continued his intellectual pursuits in Florence, Rome, and Venice in the 1490s. He studied Aristotle and Platonic philosophy, producing commentaries on the former as well as editions of Christian writers. Lefèvre d' Etaples returned to Paris to become a professor in the Collège du Cardinal Lemoine. Like Erasmus, he was an advocate for Christian humanism as a tool to bring about reform. Lefèvre d' Etaples produced a French version of the New Testament in 1523 at about the same time as Luther published his German version. It became the basis for all subsequent French translations. He also published a version of the Bible based on the Vulgate of Jerome in 1530. A revised edition in 1534 incorporated Greek and Hebrew texts.

Marguerite of Angoulême, the sister of King Francis I and later queen of Navarre, became highly engaged in the religious reform movement in France. She not only protected protestant reformers at her court but also encouraged women to study and write. Marguerite introduced humanistic Latin and the Petrarchan sonnet into French poetry. She also wrote devotional and mystical poems. She is most famous for her *Heptameron*, or *The Seven Days*, a group of seventy-three stories filled with clever and witty characters, some irreverent and others pious. The work, in a genre similar to Boccaccio's *Decameron*, became very popular in France as well as England when it was translated. A very few other women, including the poet Louise Labé (*c.* 1520–1566), the novelist Hélisenne de Crenne (d. post 1552), and the mother–daughter poets Madelein (1520–1587) and Catherine (1550–1587) des Roches, engaged in humanist writing, but the number remained small compared to male writers. Clémont Marot (1496–1544) and François Rabelais (*c.* 1494–1553) were among the most popular French authors influenced by humanism. Marot's poetry combined courtly French with street vernacular and classical Latin. Rabelais, a former friar trained in classics who went on to study medicine, was an admirer of Erasmus and himself a Christian humanist. A critic of the Catholic Church, he combined both evangelical humanist thought with bold humor. His immensely popular comic epics, *Gargantua* and *Pantagruel*, were filled with parody and chivalry but at the same time philosophical. *Pantagruel*, the story of a giant whose philosophy was to eat, drink, and be merry, was meant to be a critique of the contemporary monastic and educational system. In this bawdy tale that had been part of French oral culture for centuries was Rabelais's vision for a humanist education. Both this book and the successive one about Pantagruel's father, Gargantua, were condemned by the church. Michel de Montaigne (1533–1592) was also an influential writer during the Renaissance period. Educated in Latin and in law, his essays were inspired by his studies in the classics. Some, such as his "On Cannibals" (1580), with reference to European colonization, addressed contemporary moral questions.

Academies

Not all humanist scholarship evolved out of chancelleries, ecclesiastical bodies, universities, or courts. Some was the product of academies, which started out as informal groups but tended to become increasingly aristocratic and elitist by the late sixteenth century. Usually established in or near cities, they were as much an aspect of Renaissance social life as an intellectual and cultural phenomenon. Generally speaking, they were gatherings of the learned. They began in Italy during the early fifteenth century but quickly proliferated during the following two hundred years. The model spread from Italy to all of Europe. Participants delved into an enormous range of subjects, including Latin and vernacular language, history, geography, poetry, rhetoric, politics, diplomacy, medicine, mathematics, physics, engineering, agriculture, music, and theater. Some academies had specialized programs that reflected local interests. In Florence, under the patronage of Duke Cosimo I, the Florentine Academy was devoted to the city's own traditions in history, the vernacular language, and customs. The Academy of Design specialized in the arts. Both academies hailed the achievements of the city's own authors and artists, setting them in the broader context of the history of the peninsula and Europe and in the process creating their own story of the Renaissance. Another Florentine academy, The Chaff, founded in 1583, was devoted to purifying the Tuscan vernacular by tracing its Etruscan rather than Latin roots and to promoting Tuscan as a literary language on a par with Latin. It ultimately aimed, with the first Italian dictionary published in 1612, to make Tuscan the formal language of Italy. Similarly, in France the Académie de France specialized in purifying French and fashioning it into the national language. In Rome and Florence academies were established to standardize painting. The Italian academies were dedicated both to learning and to intellectual play; some formed networks of publications. They took playful pseudonyms, which they used as emblematic devices. Among them, the Sleeping (Genoa), the Impassioned (Naples), and the Frozen (Bologna). The transalpine academies, on the other hand, were more structured than the Italian ones. In states with centralizing monarchies, such as France, England, and Spain, they served the growing scientific needs, and economic ambitions, of their governments.

Conclusion

Classical Latin and letters became a part of the process of Italian urban and cultural revitalization, beginning in the twelfth century. Thereafter, between the twelfth and fifteenth centuries, notaries, lawyers, and scholars in general became intensely interested in the language and literary styles of the ancient Romans. The roots of this revived interest in classical learning were also situated in the south of Italy, at the court of the Holy Roman Emperor Frederick II of Sicily, during the thirteenth century—a generation prior to Dante's birth. Scholars in his kingdom had a great familiarity with an array of ancient languages, including Arabic and Hebrew, from the ninth century. Like Frederick II, the Angevin king, Robert the Wise (1277–1343), was also a significant sponsor of prehumanist writers like Boccaccio and Petrarch, both of whom spent time in Naples. In the fifteenth century, interest in Greek, Latin, and Hebrew texts and early church writings reached its apogee, beginning with Republican Florence and then spreading to other major cultural centers. Scholars focused on producing authentic ancient texts that were placed in historical context and, in the case of early fifteenth-century Florence, on praising citizen participation in civic life. Some of these texts were already known in the Middle Ages; others were recovered during the fifteenth century.

As the humanist approach to learning in Italy evolved over the fifteenth century, it impacted other fields of study. Scholars strove for greater objectivity and combined the emphasis on the historicity of words in context with archeology, geography, epigraphy, numismatics, and legal science. By the late fifteenth century the ideals of civic participation gave way to more contemplative thought, modeled on the ideas of the Greek philosopher Plato. Fifteenth-century humanism in Italy also had a feminine dimension, characterized by debates about the worth of women and their potential and limitations in a patriarchal society. Over several centuries humanist study and writing thus embraced a broad spectrum of transitory themes, shaped by the needs of male and female scholars, statesmen, and private patrons as well as the contingent circumstances of the times.

By the sixteenth century humanism had migrated to other parts of Europe, especially the study of ancient texts in their historical and original linguistic contexts as they applied to education and religious issues but also for the ways in which new translations and newly discovered manuscripts shed light on scientific inquiry. While humanism evolved in multiple directions and in response to local circumstances, it became the central intellectual current in Europe by the sixteenth century.

Think Critically

1. What were the practical uses of humanism in the governments of the Italian commune?
2. How did humanism serve the social and political needs of Italy's ruling elites between 1400 and 1460?
3. How did the practical uses of humanism among women differ from those of men?
4. What was the *Querelle des Femmes*?

5. In what ways was humanism a shared Greco-Roman, and to a lesser degree, Muslim classical tradition in the Mediterranean world?
6. How was humanism used in religious scholarship? In educational reform? In scientific inquiry?

Further Exploration

1. What was the political importance of Lorenzo Valla's linguistic analysis of the *Donation of Constantine*?
2. What were the main lines of argument in Christine de Pisan's *Book of the City of Ladies*? Why did they initiate a centuries-long discussion about the capabilities of women?

Further Reading

Primary Sources

Pisan, Christine de. *The Book of the City of Ladies*. Edited by Rosalind Brown-Grant. London: Penguin Classics, 2000.
Sforza, Ippolita Maria. *Duchess and Hostage in Renaissance Naples. Letters and Orations*. Edited and Translated by Diana Robin and Lynn Lara Westwater. *The Other Voice in Early Modern Europe: The Toronto Series*. Toronto: ACMRS Publications, 2017.

Secondary Sources

Adelman, Howard. "The Literacy of Jewish Women in Early Modern Italy." In *Women's Education in Early Modern Europe*. Edited by Barbara J. Whitehead, 23–52. New York: Garland, 1999. An informative discussion of the education of Jewish women in the Renaissance and early modern age.
Bentley, Jerry. *Politics and Culture in Renaissance Naples*. Princeton, NJ: Princeton University Press, 1987. An examination of the cultural history of Naples, with an emphasis on Neapolitan humanists and their influence in Europe.
Brown, Meg Lota, and Kari Boyd McBride. "Education and Work." In *A Cultural History of Women in the Renaissance*. Edited by Karen Raber, 143–62. London: Bloomsbury Academic Press, 2013. A survey of the educational opportunities for European women during the Renaissance.
Celenza, Christopher. *The Intellectual World of the Italian Renaissance*. New York: Cambridge University Press, 2018. A series of case studies of humanists that examines the related issues of language and philosophy in the period between 1350 and 1525.

Cochrane, Eric W. "The Renaissance Academies in Their Italian and European Setting." In *The Fairest Flower. The Emergence of Linguistic National Consciousness in Renaissance Europe*, 21–39. Florence: Presso l' Academia della Crusca, 1985. An examination of the proliferation of academies in Renaissance Europe.

Findlen, Paula. "The Renaissance of Science." In *The Oxford Illustrated History of the Renaissance*. Edited by Gordon Campbell, 378–425. Oxford, UK: Oxford University Press, 2019. An important survey of the changing structures of scientific inquiry from the fourteenth to the sixteenth centuries.

Grafton, Anthony. *Defenders of the Text: The Traditions of Scholarship in an Age of Science, 1450–1800*. Cambridge, MA: Harvard University Press, 1991. A groundbreaking work that analyzes the critical relationship between humanism and the development of natural science from the mid-fifteenth century to the beginning of the nineteenth century.

Grafton, Anthony, and Lisa Jardine. *From Humanism to the Humanities: Education and the Liberal Arts in Fifteenth and Sixteenth Century Europe*. Cambridge, MA: Harvard University Press, 1986. The authors trace the development of classical education in Renaissance Europe from the fifteenth-century Italian school of Guarino of Verona to the French teacher Petrous Ramus and his followers.

Grendler, Paul F. *Schooling in Renaissance Italy: Literacy and Learning, 1300–1600*. Baltimore, MD: Johns Hopkins University Press, 1989. An important history of the schools and curricula that brought about Renaissance humanism.

Hankins, James. *Plato in the Italian Renaissance* (*Columbia Studies in the Classical Tradition, 17*), 2 vols. Leiden: E.J. Brill, 1990. A monumental study of the writings and reception of Plato during the Renaissance.

King, Margaret. "Book-Lined Cells: Women and Humanism in the Early Italian Renaissance." In *Beyond Their Sex: Learned Women of the European Past*. Edited by Patricia H. Labalme, 66–90. New York: New York University Press. An informative study of the limited professional options for women writers and thinkers of the Renaissance.

King, Margaret L. *Women of the Renaissance*. Chicago: University of Chicago Press, 1991. An important analysis of the condition of women based on sources in social, intellectual, and religious history during the period between 1350 and 1650.

King, Margaret L., and Albert Rabil Jr., eds. *Her Immaculate Hand: Selected Works by and about the Women Humanists of Quattrocento Italy*. Ashville, NC: Pegasus Press, 2000. This collection of twenty-four letters, orations, and encomia by and to fifteenth-century Renaissance women highlights the contribution of women to the intellectual life of the period.

Kristeller, Paul Oscar. *Renaissance Thought and Its Sources*. Edited by M. Mooney. New York: Columbia University Press, 1979. A collection of this important scholar's writings about the major themes in Renaissance philosophy, theology, science, and literature.

Mack, Peter. "Humanism and the Classical Tradition." In *The Oxford Illustrated History of the Renaissance*. Edited by Peter Mack, 11–44. Oxford, UK: Oxford University Press, 2019. An instructive survey of the humanist movement in Europe.

Martines, Lauro. *Power and the Imagination: City-States in Renaissance Italy.* Baltimore, MD: Johns Hopkins University Press, 1988. A magisterial survey of medieval and Renaissance Italian developments that draws connections between cultural patrons and power.

Moyer, Ann E. *The Intellectual World of Sixteenth Century Florence. Humanists and Culture in the Age of Cosimo I.* New York: Cambridge University Press, 2020. An important study of the ways in which Florentine humanists examined their own achievements and created their own history.

Nauert, Charles G. *Humanism and the Culture of Renaissance Europe.* Cambridge, UK: Cambridge University Press, 1995. An introduction to humanist culture.

O'Connell, Monique, and Erick R. Dursteler, *The Mediterranean World from the Fall of Rome to the Rise of Napoleon.* Baltimore, MD: Johns Hopkins University Press, 2016. A superb study of the Mediterranean's economic, cultural, and political interactions from 500 CE to 1798.

Strocchia, Sharon. *Nuns and Nunneries in Renaissance Florence.* Baltimore, MD: Johns Hopkins University Press, 2009. An analysis of the growth of female monasticism during the fifteenth and sixteenth centuries and the roles that religious women played in the social, economic, and religious history of Florence.

Witt, Ronald G. *In the Footsteps of the Ancients: The Origins of Humanism from Lovato to Bruni.* Leiden: Brill, 2000. Through a pathbreaking analysis of texts, the author examines the evolution of humanism from its early foundations in the thirteenth century to its development as a major educational movement by the fifteenth century.

7

Fifteenth-Century Art and Its Patrons

Timeline

1401	Lorenzo Ghiberti obtains commission to produce bronze doors for Florence Baptistery
1416	Discovery of Vitruvius's treatise *On Architecture*
1427	Masaccio frescoes Brancacci Chapel, Florence
1429	Filippo Brunelleschi works on Pazzi Chapel, Florence
c. 1430	Donatello sculpts *David*, first nude statue since Roman times
1432	Paolo Uccello experiments with perspective
1434–64	Cosimo de Medici, major patron in Florence
1435	Leon Battista Alberti's treatise *On Painting* explains linear perspective
1444–82	Federico da Montefeltro, art patron of Urbino's dukedom
1445	Donatello begins statue of Gattamelata
1450	Alberti's treatise *On Architecture*
1452	Ghiberti completes East Door of Florence Baptistery
c. 1455	Piero della Francesca produces *The Flagellation of Christ*
1464	Antonio Filarete's *Treatise on Architecture*
c. 1465	Piero della Francesca paints portraits of Federico da Montefeltro and Battista Sforza
1467	Brunelleschi completes dome of Florence Cathedral
1471–84	Sistine Chapel built under Pope Sixtus IV

1474	Birth of Isabela d'Este, great art patron
1482	Leonardo da Vinci works for Ludovico Sforza in Milan
c. 1485	Sandro Botticelli paints *The Birth of Venus*
1486	Vitruvius's *On Architecture* appears in print
1498	Leonardo da Vinci completes *The Last Supper* in Milan
1501	Michelangelo sculpts *The David* in Florence
1503	Leonardo da Vinci paints *The Mona Lisa*

Fifteenth-Century Stylistic and Technical Achievements

The fifteenth century ushered in the dramatically new stylistic and technical achievements in sculpture, painting, and architecture for which the Italian Renaissance is still widely acclaimed. Much of the innovation came from Tuscany and the Veneto and then spread to other areas of the Italian Peninsula. It was least represented in the south, although both the popes in Rome and the Aragonese rulers in Naples and Sicily did engage renowned masters to their north, including Tuscany and the Burgundian Netherlands. Many artists puzzled over how they could satisfy their patrons' new desires for greater realism and naturalism in the representation of tangible forms. Among the most important technical developments was the perfection of linear perspective, that is, the depiction of three-dimensional figures on a two-dimensional flat surface—a wall; marble, wood, or bronze panel; or canvas. In the Byzantine style, or *maniera greca*, that had prevailed during the medieval period and continued to be adopted through the fifteenth century, there was no notion of space in a pictorial composition, but rather two-dimensional subjects on a gold background that remained beyond the reach of the viewer. The gradual replacement of gold backgrounds with cityscapes and landscapes that took up more space in a canvas permitted the observer to reach into the pictorial frame and engage with the narrative. In Figure 7.2, Duccio di Buoninsegna's (c. 1255–1319) *Maestà* (1308–1311), and Figure 7.3, Leonardo da Vinci's *Mona Lisa* (c. 1503–1506), we can observe many of these tangible differences and grasp the dramatic technical leaps that took place between the early fourteenth and early sixteenth centuries.

The architects Filippo Brunelleschi (1377–1446) and Leon Battista Alberti (1407–1472) both theorized and wrote on how to produce accurate linear perspective as one step toward greater realism. Ultimately it was Brunelleschi who mastered this spatial challenge with the discovery of the vanishing point (c. 1415–20), the imagined point in space furthest from the viewer where all receding parallel lines meet. Later, Alberti

FIGURE 7.1 Benozzo Gozzoli (1421–1497). *Journey of the Magi* (1459–1461). Fresco. Palazzo Medici Riccardi, Florence, Italy. This painting immortalized a number of Medici patrons for all time by placing their portraits in the canvas.

FIGURE 7.2 Duccio di Buoninsegna (1255–1319). *Madonna and Child* (1285–1286). Detail. Tempura on wood. Museo Dell' Opera Metropolitana (Cathedral Museum), Siena, Italy

would make this theory more usable to artists. Various painters also experimented with perfecting the geometrical construction of space as well as with the anatomical proportions of the human body; modulations of light and shade; the qualities of color, depth perception; and the depiction of realistic objects in natural settings. Their more realistic renderings of

FIGURE 7.3 Leonardo da Vinci (1452–1519). *Mona Lisa* (1503–1506). Oil on panel. Louvre Museum, Paris, France.

both spiritual and contemporary life were the result of new studies in optics and Euclidean geometry, whose provenance was rooted in Islamic science and mathematics, as well as through the use of oils that strengthened color and composition, first advanced in the Netherlandish painting of Jan Van Eyck (1390–1441; see Figure 4.4). Atmospheric perspective, that is, creating the illusion of depth in objects seen at a distance through gradations in color, reached new levels in the late-fifteenth-century work of Leonardo da Vinci, who also developed the technique of *chiaroscuro* (light and dark), using variations of shade in the illumination of tangible forms (Figure 7.3; see also Chapter 9). Throughout the century artists strove to perfect their spatial techniques and the way they crafted pictorial narrative through the direct observation of nature as well as through intellectual inquiry and the study of theory.

The style first changed course in Florence, where painters learned from the works of sculptors like Donatello (1386–1466) and Lorenzo Ghiberti (1378–1455). Both of these masters came from the artisan world; they had first trained as goldsmiths. Donatello demonstrated remarkable skill in adjusting the proportions of statuary to fit their final resting place with his *Saint Mark* (1411–1413), commissioned by the Florentine linen guild (Figure 7.4). The sculptor recalls the "wet drapery" of fifth-century Greek sculpture in this statue ordered by the guild of linen drapers. According to the Italian artist and writer Giorgio Vasari (1511–1574), the guild initially rejected the statue because at street level the marble head and torso appeared too large. In fact, Donatello had applied the technique of optical correction, modifying the proportions of the statue so that they would appear correct to the eye when placed in the niche above ground at the granary and religious sanctuary of Orsanmichele and thus would directly engage the viewer. When Donatello's patrons ultimately saw the work in its final resting place they were satisfied. Ghiberti, who won the city's competition to cast two sets of bronze doors (1403–24; 1425–52) for the Florence Baptistery, produced a three-dimensional marvel, with scenes of the Old and New Testament that combined both the medieval Gothic tradition and ancient classical forms (Figure 7.5). In painting Masaccio (1401–1428) led the way in the 1420s in applying Brunelleschi's laws of perspective and foreshortening and used his own understanding of anatomy and light to produce a cycle of dramatic narrative paintings with solid figures set in illusionistic space (Figure 7.6).

It is important to note at this point that not all Renaissance art broke with the medieval past. Some Florentine artists, like Fra Filippo Lippi (1406–1469) and Benozzo Gozzoli (1420–1497), still adhered to the visual effects of the late fourteenth-century Tuscan International Gothic (see Figure 7.1), with its gold leaf, brilliant color, and elaborate detail, while others like Paolo Uccello (1397–1475) and Piero della Francesca (*c*. 1415–1492) amplified on the studies of Brunelleschi and Alberti to become exponents of the new geometrical construction of space (Figure 7.7). Moreover, in Venice changes

FIGURE 7.4 Donatello (1386?–1466). *Saint Mark* (1411–1413). Marble sculpture. Orsanmichele Church, Florence, Italy.

FIGURE 7.5 Lorenzo Ghiberti (1378–1455). *Joseph and the Gates of Paradise*. Gilt bronze. Baptistery, Florence, Italy.

FIGURE 7.6 Masaccio (1401–1428). *Tribute Money* (*c.* 1425–1427)). Fresco. Brancacci Chapel in the Basilica of Santa Maria del Carmine, Florence, Italy.

FIGURE 7.7 Piero della Francesca (?–1492). *The Flagellation of Christ* (1455–1460). Oil and tempera on panel. Galleria Nazionale delle Marche, Urbino, Italy.

in painting came later. The previously mentioned Byzantine style with its two-dimensional forms set on a gold background prevailed throughout the first two decades of the fifteenth century. It was not until the 1420s that the state's mainland territorial expansion brought Tuscan and classical influences to the lagoon, and the patriciate's study of humanism and antiquity began to inform their tastes in painting. The Bellini family—Jacopo (1396–1470) and Gentile (1429–1507)—as well as Vittore Carpaccio (1465–1520) were among the first to include classical antiquity and pictorial realism in their landscapes and cityscapes. Gentile's brother, Giovanni (1430–1516; see Figure 7.22), together with Giorgione (1478–1510; see Figure 9.8) and Titian (1490–1576), followed in the second. These artists were more inclined to emphasize brilliant color and tone over the geometrical painting of the Florentines. Gentile Bellini (see Figures 7.17 and 7.21) was a primary exponent of paintings depicting the natural world, ideal beauty, and the ritual ceremonies of urban life. Another painter, Antonello da Messina (*c.* 1430–1479), a Sicilian influenced by early Netherlandish painting, also enhanced the harmony of colors on canvas and introduced the new techniques of oil painting to Venice in 1475–76 (see Figure 7.8).

The demand for verisimilitude and naturalistic vocabulary, nonreligious themes in the classics and mythology, and a more worldly rendition of religious

FIGURE 7.8 Antonello da Messina (1430–1479). *Virgin Annunciate* (1476). Oil on wood. Galleria Nazionale della Sicilia, Palermo, Sicily.

subjects aligned with changes in social structure and the consolidation of power among Italy's ruling elites. The leading families had succeeded in netting substantial financial resources in both city and countryside and in accumulating unprecedented wealth, achievements according to historian

FIGURE 7.9 Donatello (1386?–1466). *Equestrian Statue of Gattamelata* (*c.* 1443–1453). Bronze. Piazza del Santo, Padua, Italy. Gattamelata (a nickname for Calico cat) was a mercenary captain whose company was called the *gatteschi*, a playful description of his soldiers meaning "catlike." Née Erasmo da Narni, the son of a miller, he fought for Florence and the pope prior to serving Venice in the early 1430s. Celebrated with humanist eulogies, Gattamelata retired to Padua, where this statue commemorates his valor. In this ideal image of a commander, Donatello, influenced by Roman statuary, has him clad in a kind of hybrid of Roman and contemporary armor.

Lauro Martines that fostered a kind of self-congratulatory confidence.[1] One outcome of this was a new interest in celebrating the dignity of the human figure, just as in the humanist movement there was an emphasis on praising human capacity and virtue. Statuary and busts as well as portraiture of individual patrons flourished as self-validation of some combination of family lineage, aristocratic standing, political hegemony, devotion, or spirituality. Here the study of Greek and Roman statuary was fundamental. In Florence, Donatello, a master of full-figure sculpture, produced a number of significant free-standing biblical figures in the Roman style, including the marble St. Mark discussed in Figure 7.4 and the St. George (*c.* 1415–17) at Orsanmichele. Later, in Padua he sculpted an equestrian monument celebrating the military prowess of the *condottiere* (mercenary captain) Erasmo da Narni (1370–1443), nicknamed Gattamelata (1453), which was the first of its kind since Roman times (Figure 7.9).

In addition to an interest in antique sculpture, Renaissance artists and patrons looked for inspiration to Roman architecture, with its rounded arches, columns with decorated capitals, pilasters, cornices, coffered ceilings, and domes in designing public buildings and private palaces as well as churches. To some degree, this was not new in either Italy or the broader Mediterranean world, for unlike the rest of northern Europe the classical tradition had endured since Roman times. Moreover, from the fourth century the medieval Byzantine style that had developed out of ancient Roman architecture, with its rounded arches and melon domes, had prevailed among the lands along the Adriatic and in the south. Fifteenth-century theorists, however, studied the ancient buildings and theoretical sources more closely and used them as examples in an attempt to understand and emulate the ancient masters and build a new style based on their achievements. A principal admirer of antiquity Leon Battista Alberti wrote an influential treatise on architecture based on the first-century civil engineer Vitruvius (*c.* 27 CE) that was recovered in 1416, printed in Latin in 1486 and subsequently translated into several vernacular languages. Alberti's theoretical work became the principal guide for Renaissance construction, characterized by the classical ideals of harmony, balance, proportion, and symmetry. His treatise was also class-specific, relegating the dwellings of the humble to the periphery and the grandeur of the wealthy to palaces in the central city. Artists also depicted Roman architecture in painting, using mathematical perspective. Masaccio's *Trinity* (1426–1428), for example, shows God the Father and the crucified Christ together with the white dove of the Holy Spirit under a coffered ceiling sustained by Corinthian pilasters in an illusionistic chapel that appears so realistic that it invites the viewer in (Figure 7.10).

The vogue for classical Greek learning, which had begun at the end of the fourteenth century and continued to be encouraged by the immigration of Byzantine scholars to Florence when Constantinople fell to the Sultan Mehmed II in 1453, found its way into painting through the interaction of artists with patrons trained in the humanities. During the 1460s the Florentine banker and politician Cosimo de' Medici (1389–1464) established the Platonic Academy under the tutelage of Marsilio Ficino (1433–1499), where a group of scholars studied and discussed ancient philosophy and literature (see Chapter 6). Ficino translated the complete works of Plato into Latin; it was published in Venice in 1491. The translation of philosophical concepts into pictorial composition is evident in the work of Sandro Botticelli (1444–1510), whose figures of classical mythology assumed an unprecedented role in Renaissance art. His *Birth of Venus* (*c.* 1480s; Figure 7.11) and *The Primavera*, or *Allegory of Spring* (1470s or 1480s) portray Olympian deities rather than angels or madonnas and, in line with Neoplatonism, glorify the beauty of the human body. The meanings of these works have been vigorously debated. Among the interpretations, the sensuous and corporeal Venus is a naked goddess, born of the sea, and representing divine love in the

FIGURE 7.10 Masaccio (1401–1428). *Trinity* (1426–1428). Fresco. Church of Santa Maria Novella, Florence, Italy.

first painting, while in the second she is fully clothed, representing human rather than celestial love. Thus, Botticelli transformed pagan mythological themes into moral and spiritual allegories. The *Primavera* (*c.* 1470s or 1480) or *Spring* has also been read, among various interpretations, as an illusive allegory on the reign of Lorenzo de Medici, the statesman and de facto ruler of Florence.

FIGURE 7.11 Sandro Botticelli (1445–1510). *Birth of Venus* (1486). Detail. Tempera on canvas. Uffizi Gallery, Florence, Italy.

Art and Political Propaganda

Painting, sculpture, and architecture were among the primary means for rulers to convey their ideological messages to their rivals and subjects, though not the only ones. Coins, seals, pennants, and banners also projected authority, and coats of arms on buildings and even on tableware signified ownership and prestige. In Florence by the fourteenth century it was primarily the individual guilds, rather than the aristocracy or the church, that fashioned the government's civic identity through artistic representation. The seven major guilds and fourteen minor guilds occupied three-fourths of the seats on government committees and took responsibility for the commissioning of public building. During the fourteenth century the wool and cloth guilds had overseen the building of the cathedral (1296–1367) and baptistery (begun in the eleventh century); the wool merchants had sponsored the Piazza della Signoria (1330) and the Loggia (c. 1376–82) in the city's political center; and the silk merchants had taken charge of constructing the grain market of Orsanmichele in 1337, which later became a church and popular sanctuary housing an icon of the Virgin believed to work miracles. In the fifteenth century the silk merchants founded the Hospital of the Innocents (begun 1419; see Figure 4.2), an orphanage that Brunelleschi fashioned as the first true Renaissance building in the new antique style, with classical round arches on Corinthian capitals recalling imperial Rome. Taking their lead

FIGURE 7.12 Filippo Brunelleschi (1377–1446). Duomo (1420–1436) of the Church of Santa Maria del Fiore, Florence, Italy.

from humanist writings that urged the wealthy to exercise virtue through an active, civic life, bankers, lawyers, and merchants represented in the guilds also sponsored the city's various churches and hospitals.

A number of Florence's artistic works during the fifteenth century were produced in response to the government's struggle with Milan for its very republican identity. The cloth merchants stood up against the forces of Visconti tyranny (see Chapter 5) by commissioning the baptistery's two sets of bronze doors (see Figure 7.5), a much-admired feat of linear perspective with scenes from the New Testament on the north side and the Old Testament on the east side of the octagonal edifice. They also sponsored the Duomo's cupola (1420–36, Brunelleschi), an engineering *tour de force* with its double shell and herring-bone brickwork and a dramatic visual statement of Florentine power towering over city and countryside (Figure 7.12). At Orsanmichele ten of the major and minor guilds commissioned free-standing bronze or marble statues of their patron saints, placed in the niches and to be seen at street level, proclaiming the dignity and freedom of the city. Under Donatello's *St. George* is a bas-relief of the saint slaying the dragon (*c*. 1415–17), whose tail in the form of a serpent is said to refer to Florence's arch-enemies in Milan.[2] Still later, Michelangelo would sculpt the remarkably lifelike *David* slaying Goliath (Figure 7.13), placed in the Piazza della Signoria in 1501 after a much-debated discussion by the leading artists of the day over the best place to proclaim once again the state's republican freedom against despotism. The careful consideration of the *David's* placement is an important testament to the influential power of statuary during this period.

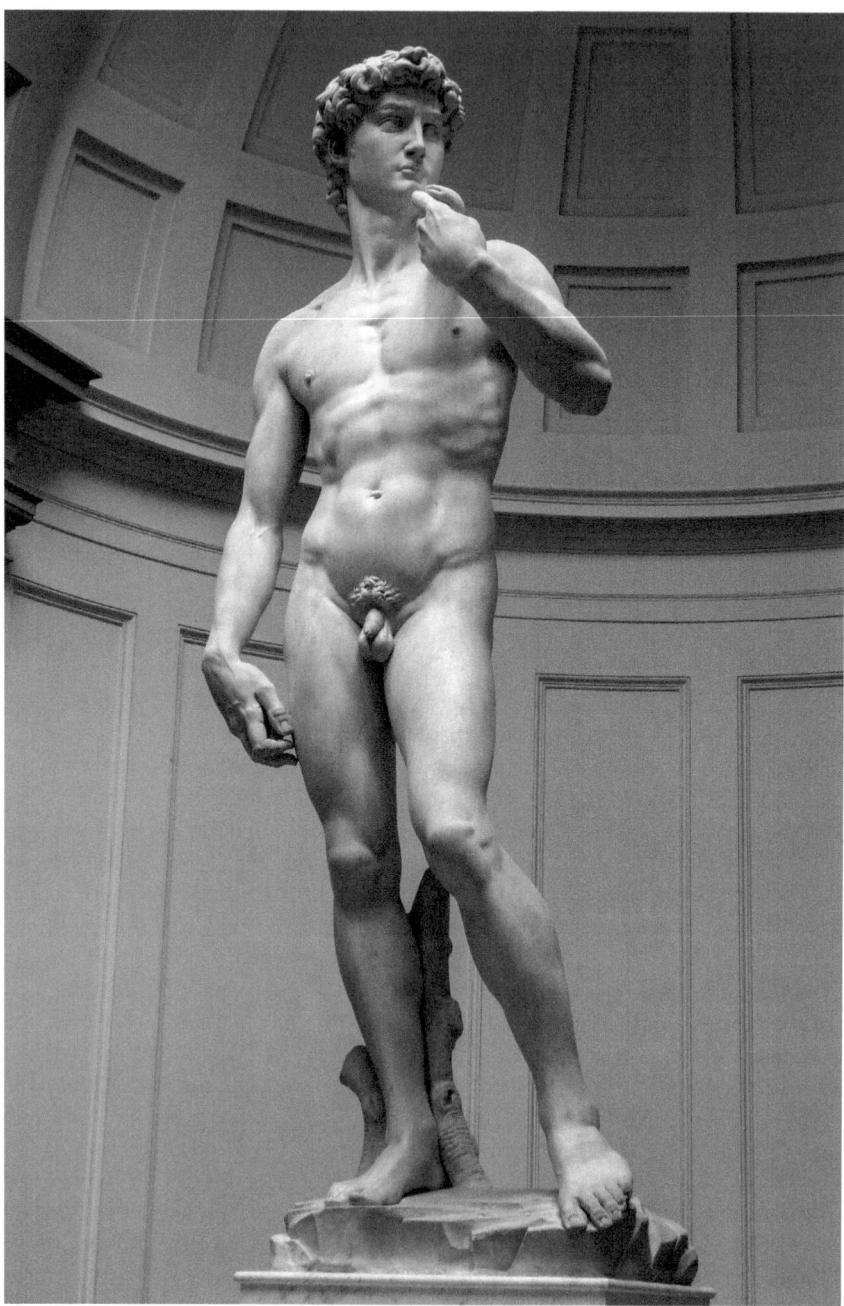

FIGURE 7.13 Michelangelo Buonarotti (1475–1564). *David* (1501–1504). Marble sculpture. Galleria dell' Academia, Florence, Italy.

Artwork was also used to foster government support in times of fiscal emergency. The city's ongoing costly wars during the 1420s and 1430s required more and more revenues. In Masaccio's painting of *The Tribute Money*, executed in 1425 (Figure 7.6), a drama between Christ and his apostles unfolds against the backdrop of a fictive landscape and Renaissance building. Christ tells Peter to find money in the mouth of a fish in order to pay the Romans, considered by some interpreters to be a strong message to the Florentines to bail out the state.[3] All of these works conspicuously displayed Florentine devotion to republican government as well as to the citizenry's commitment to beautifying the city with the enormous wealth they had accumulated through commerce, finance, and manufacture.

The other major republic, Venice, projected its power and wealth through the patrician elite that exclusively held the reins of government beginning in 1297. Some of the patriotic works that the state commissioned no longer exist, but we know about them from archival documents. Among them were the narrative paintings (1409) in the Ducal Palace that depicted Venice's mythical origins, history, and military victories as well as portraits of the doges. Both in writings and in artwork the patriciate regularly boasted that the republic, favored by God and Saints Mark and Theodore, had a perfect constitution and that its rulers were endowed with wisdom, strength, and temperance. The classical gods Mercury and Neptune also watched over the city in state iconography, and Venice was presented as a Just and Christian polity, the Queen of Virginity, as well as the Queen of the Adriatic Sea. Everywhere in the city and throughout the expanding territorial state the Lion of St. Mark, a symbol of Venetian dominion, was ubiquitous. The lion, whose form derived from an Assyrian bronze chimera, also symbolized divine protection.

Venice also commemorated ongoing important events during the fifteenth century through visual expression. Territorial expansion on the mainland from the 1420s, for example, brought new changes to the political center at Piazza San Marco. The waterfront façade of the Doge's Palace as well as the one facing the piazzetta were refashioned from their earlier Veneto-Byzantine style to that of the rich, northern European Gothic, with ogival arches. The palace was given a new ceremonial entrance, and the piazzetta façade was decorated with imagery such as Justice with Scales and Sword (Figure 7.14). From the second half of the fifteenth century, with the Ottomans threatening encroachment in Mediterranean waters, the Venetians sought to emphasize the state's naval strength, commissioning a triumphal arch (1460) at the entrance to the Arsenal, whose style linked the republic with its Byzantine and Christian heritage. They further projected the powers of the state after the 1474 battle with the Ottomans by ordering twenty-two mural paintings (destroyed in a fire in 1577) documenting important historical events in the Great Council Chamber (Gentile and Giovanni Bellini), and by the 1490s the iconography at the Ducal Palace's Barbarigo staircase fashioned Venice—rather than Rome or Constantinople-- as the heir to the fourth-century emperor Constantine's empire.

FIGURE 7.14 Giovanni and Bartolomeo Bon. *Porta della Carta* (begun 1438). Doge's Palace, Venice. The ceremonial entrance overlooking Piazza San Marco represented the new visual expression of expansionism on the Venetian mainland. The Gothic style is used to express the language of power. The top of the entrance is crowned with the allegorical figure of justice with scales and sword, a Venetian symbol of state. The lion that dominates the composition is the prime visual image of the state, a form derived from Assyrian bronze chimera, possibly part of the loot crusaders brought back from Constantinople.[4]

The iconography of the ducal courts carried a different message than that of the republics. Ruled by family dynasties rather than collective bodies, they were more in alignment with European royals who ruled by hereditary right. Among the most important tasks of the despotic regimes was to display their military potency, great wealth, Christian piety, and political legitimacy. The various rulers accomplished this by commissioning religious and military architecture and by engaging the most notable artisanal masters of the day to project their images on coins, medals, ceramics, busts, and canvas. On one hand they associated with the courtly and chivalric imagery of northern European aristocracies, especially in the decoration of their palace interiors, and on the other, from the late fifteenth century they also connected their despotic regimes with the culture of imperial Rome. As Milan's Duke Giangaleazzo Visconti (1385–1402) pushed eastward and to the south to create the Lombard territorial state, he renovated convents and monasteries and built castles. His defensive fortress in Pavia, for example, decorated with scenes of hunts and jousts and housing a rich library of Christian and classical authors, was also a powerful testament to the Lombard state's military strength during a period of aggressive expansion. At the same time Giangaleazzo associated his absolute power with the courts of northern Europe, sponsoring the flamboyant Gothic style with its windowed walls and vertical lines for the cathedral in Milan's urban center. His son, Filippo Maria (1412–47), commissioned Pisanello (1395–1455), a leading artist of the International Gothic, to make a portrait medal of himself. Like the other portrait medals popular during this time, it was based on the Imperial Roman coin portraits and served to link the ruler to the antique past for legitimacy. The Sforza, successors to the Visconti by marriage but not by bloodline, needing to establish their links with the previous regime, surrounded themselves with humanists and artists that would reinforce their right to power. Francesco Sforza (1450–1466) continued the Visconti projects at Milan's cathedral and the cloisters in Pavia, but also built a costly garrison in the Lombard capital. His son, Galeazzo Maria Sforza (1444–1476), decorated the Visconti-Sforza castle in Pavia with scenes of ambassadorial receptions that vaunted his connections with foreign powers. Later, Ludovico Sforza (1452–1508), eager to display his military potential to his competitors, employed Leonardo da Vinci to design machines of warfare, bridges, cannons, and explosives.

Like their larger counterparts, the smaller courts of Italy, ruled by *condottieri* princes, were also preoccupied with projecting their military strength as well as their wealth and prestige. The Este dukes in Ferrara built a massive castle (begun by Niccolò d'Este in 1385) in the city center, guarded by moats and defended by gateways with drawbridges. Their various building projects and paintings, adorned with images of princely power, engaged both the courtly and chivalric language of northern Europe and the symbols of classical antiquity. In Mantua the Gonzaga family made the Ducal Palace (fourteenth to seventeenth centuries) their prime symbol of hegemony. The structure opened onto the town with a Gothic façade that recalled northern European styles, but the palace's architecture, and function, was clearly defensive. Gian Francesco Gonzaga (r. 1407–1444) commissioned the Veronese artist Pisanello (1395–1455) to decorate the interior with scenes of medieval chivalry and the knights of the Round Table. After 1450 the dynasts also linked themselves with the imperial traditions of classical Rome. The court was immortalized in painting between 1465 and 1474 when the Paduan artist Andrea Mantegna (1431–1506) frescoed the *Camera degli Sposi* (the chamber where marriages were recorded; see Figure 5.3), using his skill in foreshortening and perspective to create illusionistic space intended as an extension of actual reality. Like the other princely rulers, Federigo di Montefeltro made his palace in Urbino's city center (1444–72) a symbol of his illustrious family (see Figure 5.1). The structure opened onto the hill town with a façade designed in the Roman tradition, but the western face which stood high above the countryside was decisively defensive with its loggias and tall round towers, a testament to the duchy's military strength and princely authority. The duke decorated his study (*studiolo*) with three-dimensional wood *intarsia* (mosaic) paneling and commissioned Piero della Francesca (c. 1415–1492) to paint portraits of his wife and himself. These lateral profiles (c. 1465–72) of Federigo da Montefeltro and Battista Sforza facing one another are among the most famous representations of the Renaissance focus on the human figure (Figure 7.15). Federigo's broken nose, a badge of the mercenary captain's career in battle, is realistically portrayed, while Battista is elegantly dressed and coiffed according to her social station. The couple pose nobly, their heads held high, against an ideal landscape of infinite depth and perspective, clearly conveying to the viewer their dominance over their entire environment.

This somewhat gendered picture of the Italian courts thus far has privileged the masculine priorities of male rulers. It is important to note that their wives' preferences sometimes differed. For example, the French wife of Galeazzo Maria Sforza, Bona of Savoy (1449–1503), held less spacious quarters than her husband. She shared her apartments with her ladies in waiting as well as wet nurses and children. The décor in her quarters was not political, but rather contained wedding scenes, people playing games, her arrival in Milan from Savoy, and her French origins.

In Rome, the repair of a demoralized papacy after the Great Schism (1378–1417) of the fourteenth and fifteenth centuries was undertaken after 1450 with a program of urban renewal. Popes Nicholas V (r. 1447–1455), Pius II (r. 1458–1464), and Paul II (r. 1464–1471) as well as a number of cardinals of the church sponsored lavish new palaces. The popes were intent on emphasizing their apostolic roots in the person of St. Peter, one of the first leaders of the Christian church, and the legitimacy of Rome as the international capital of Christendom. Pope Eugenius IV (1431–1447), for example, had commissioned new bronze doors for St. Peter's using his coat

FIGURE 7.15 Piero della Francesca (?–1492). *Federigo da Montefeltro and Battista Sforza, the Duke and Duchess of Urbino* (1473–1475). Tempera on wood. Uffizi Gallery, Florence, Italy.

of arms to convey the iconographic message that he was the successor of the apostle Peter. Rome became an important destination for artists from the northern courts of Italy as well as Florence. In 1480 Pope Sixtus IV (r. 1471–1484) commissioned several Florentine artists to fresco the new Sistine Chapel. Perugino's *Christ Giving Keys to St. Peter* (Figure 7.16) communicates to viewers the legitimacy of papal hegemony over Christendom within a Roman framework. Using many of the elements characteristic of early Renaissance Tuscan painting, Perugino (c. 1446/52–1523) designed a cityscape with accurate perspective and triumphal arches that referenced Rome. Christian and classical elements join in the depiction of the baptistery, which resembles a Roman mausoleum. Later, Donato Bramante (c. 1444–1514) would introduce classical vocabulary into the redesign of Saint Peter's Basilica as Rome remodeled its urban landscape around the founding figure of the apostle Peter.

In the south, King Alfonso I (r. 1443), who won the throne of Naples over his Angevin rivals, also surrounded himself with humanist propagandists and artists that would validate his status. Ruler of Aragon, Sicily, Sardinia, and southern Italy, Alfonso constructed an imposing castle on the Bay of Naples to display the power of the Aragonese regime and throughout his dominions repaired castles and other fortifications. Alfonso also drew upon the ancient Roman tradition of projecting his image on coins and medals

FIGURE 7.16 Pietro Perugino (*c.* 1446/52–1523). *Christ Delivers the Keys to St. Peter* (1481–1482). Sistine Chapel, Vatican Museums, Rome, Italy.

and commissioning portrait paintings. His cosmopolitan court, a center of humanist study, was filled with Spanish secretaries and Flemish musicians and painters.

Across the Mediterranean in the new Ottoman capital of Istanbul, another leader sought to emulate the Roman and Byzantine civilizations that had preceded him, Sultan Mehmed II. Although he ultimately sponsored a hybrid court culture that, in addition to classicism, also included Muslim Timurid-Turcoman and Persianate (Sasanian) vocabulary, he shared certain interests and goals with Italian Renaissance rulers. Among them was the use of art and architecture to validate legitimacy and power. For Mehmed, the adoption of Italian traditions would help distinguish him from the other court cultures of Greater Asia. He sat at the helm of a cosmopolitan metropole that, until his ascendancy in 1453, was both capital of the eastern half of the Roman Empire and the capital of classical civilization. The sultan was tutored in classical geography and philosophy and inspired by classical culture. He would sponsor architecture that blended Roman, Byzantine, and Italian Renaissance concepts. Mehmed, intent on displaying his new imperial powers through the visual arts, became part of the Italian patronage networks. He asked the Venetians to lend him their best artists. He petitioned the Venetian Senate to send him a painter, a sculptor, and a bronzeworker. He also requested a maker of chimney clocks and an expert in the manufacture of clear glass. Among the visitors to the new Istanbul were the portrait painter Gentile Bellini and the Paduan sculptor Bartolomeo Bellano (1437–1496). During his sojourn in Constantinople in 1479 Bellini painted Mehmet's portrait (Figure 7.17). The

FIGURE 7.17 Gentile Bellini (1429–1507). *Sultan Mehmed II The Conqueror* (1480). Oil on canvas. National Gallery, London, UK.

Lord of Rimini, Sigismondo Malatesta, also exchanged art and ideas with Mehmed, sending his court artist to Istanbul in 1461.

Domestic Space and the Enduring Memory of the Family

Because there is far more documentation for the lifestyles of the upper classes, the home has been explored primarily as a cultural reference for Italy's ruling elites. But we should note that the more prosperous artisans and shopkeepers also bought or inherited costly furniture, clothing, jewelry, specialized dinnerware, textile furnishings and painted hangings, religious items, and gilded glass, among other things. Their possessions, like those of the elite, communicated their identities and status and displayed their family honor as well as the ritual events of daily life.

The growing concentration of wealth among the peninsula's major dynasties during the fifteenth century motivated them to display their success and power through elaborate private building programs. The Medici, Rucellai, Pitti, Pazzi, and Strozzi in Florence; the Corner-Spinelli, Vendramin-Calergi, Giustiniani, and Grimani in Venice; the popes, major churchmen, and noble families like the Colonna and Orsini in Rome; and the dukes in the various courts all built lavish palaces and country villas. Ancient authors like Cicero (106–43 BCE) and Pliny the Younger (61–c. 113 CE) as well as the contemporary theorist Leon Battista Alberti recommended that these residences exhibit a grandeur commensurate with their owners' social station and success. In Florence prior to the 1440s the dwellings of the rich were constructed with great sobriety on crowded, dark streets in inconspicuous positions, a nod to Christian strictures against making or exhibiting great wealth. The attitudes of elites changed in the subsequent period. Wanting to show their affluence, they erected great blocks of stone in geometrical form, rugged and imposing in appearance, and dominating vast areas of urban space. Apologists justified the magnificence by emphasizing that the wealthy had a responsibility to enrich the beauty of their neighborhoods. Likewise in Venice on the Grand Canal noble palaces became floating symbols of Gothic and Classical magnificence (Figure 7.18).

The residences of the wealthy were filled with luxuries, rare goods, and artwork that tell us about both the elite demand for opulence and the period's material culture. In Florence, as well as other inland cities, the ground level of buildings was reserved for the patriarch's public life; in Venice the lower level received and stored cargo brought in via watercraft. Families lived on the next level above ground or water, named the *piano nobile*, in tapestried rooms filled with portraits, landscapes, and paintings commemorating important events or secular themes in the classics and

FIGURE 7.18 Palace of Ca' D' Oro, Venice, Italy.

mythology. Women's private chambers might emphasize their chastity or marital fidelity. Bedchambers were furnished with items that both bride and groom brought to their marriage. Religious images of the Virgin, Christ, and the saints in paintings made with costly pigments were common. After 1450 so were idealized male marble busts, and family lineages were represented on wellheads, facades, and tympanum reliefs.

Isabella d'Este (1474–1539), the Marchioness of Mantua, exemplifies the desire of ruling elites to stand out. Her marriage to Francesco Gonzaga in 1490 was meant to cement the alliance between the Este of Ferrara with the Gonzaga family of Mantua. Upon Francesco's death in 1519 Isabella became regent and head of state. The marchioness used her fortune to invest in material luxuries that would bring prestige as well as international benefit to her husband and children. Her expenditures included precious objects, antiquities, and paintings as well as engraved gems, gold thread, tabby silks, blue velvets from the French court, and the specialties of Parisian goldsmiths. She also worked with artisans to develop a perfume and cosmetic pharmacy that produced soaps and scents that were sent out as gifts to cement foreign alliances.

Alongside Isabella d' Este and somewhat of a rival was her sister-in-law Lucrezia Borgia (1480–1519), who arrived in Ferrara in 1502 as the new wife of Alfonso d'Este. She quickly set about renovating the chambers of the previous duchess, Eleonora of Aragon, purchasing expensive textiles and historiated tapestries to drape on walls and furniture and commissioning carved, gilded wooden ceilings that would convey the wealth and status of her family. Lucrezia's rooms were not entirely private. She kept a separate court from her husband and at times ruled in his stead when he was away at war. A blending of public and private in her self-fashioning environment was exemplified in the Islamic-style silk drapery over the cradle of her infant Ercole II, heir to the duchy. Visitors at times would be permitted to view the future ruler of Ferrara. Nor were Lucrezia's rooms entirely secular. A pious woman who often corresponded with clerics and was a patron of local convents, she commingled sacred art with secular space in her domestic interior.

Wealthy families constructed libraries and studies (see Figure 6.1) decorated with mythical and historical scenes and filled with an assortment of costly collectibles. As bookbinding and lacquer work emerged in the artisan world of mid-fifteenth-century Florence and Padua, and later in Venice, elites filled their libraries with new leather-bound books that derived from Mamluk and Ottoman ornamentation. Prosperous families also filled their chapels with relics and statuary. The marital chamber usually housed a pair of wooden chests, called *cassoni*, that stored clothing, linens, and various adornments. Their panels were decorated with narrative paintings read from left to right containing scenes of chivalry, fables from the ancient poets, or Greek and Roman history. Family arms signifying dynastic prestige adorned the ends of the chests, and the inside lid might display scenes of love. These chests often carried a moral or biblical theme encouraging the virtue, fidelity, and chastity of the wife. One of the best examples of this genre was a chest decorated with the Old Testament *Story of Esther* (Est. 2:17–19) from the workshop of Apollonia di Giovanni and Marco del Buono Giamberti around 1450–65. The front panel centers on the marriage between Esther, a Jewish woman, and the Persian king Ahasuerus, but it is placed in a contemporary Florentine setting. The king rides into the city before a palace similar to that of the Medici family and approaches a great church resembling the Duomo (Figure 7.19).

FIGURE 7.19 Marco del Buono (1402–1489). *The Story of Esther* (1422–1489). Tempura and gold on wood. Roger's Fund, 1918, Metropolitan Museum of Art, New York.

FIGURE 7.20 Vittore Carpaccio (1465–1526?). *Birth of the Virgin* (1502–1504). Oil on canvas. Guglielmo Lochis Collection, 1866, Accademia Carrara, Bergamo, Italy.

The birth of a child was also commemorated in the home. In painting, the subject was often the birth of the Virgin. Among the best examples is that of Domenico Ghirlandaio (1486–90), which shows the new mother receiving relatives bearing gifts, and the work of Vittore Carpaccio, painted in 1504–8 for the Albanian confraternity of Venice (Figure 7.20). Carpaccio's canvas depicts the home of wealthy artisans. In the foreground is St. Anne reclining in bed. On the wall, a Hebrew inscription reads, "Holy, Holy, Holy/Blessed is he who comes in the name of the Lord." Trays, called *deschi da parto*, decorated with birth scenes (see Figure 4.3) also commemorated the joyous arrival of a new child when, it is important to remember, infant and child mortality were high.

Antiquarianism and the Enduring Memory of the Renaissance

The antiquarian endeavors of Italian elites, who were filling their palaces with cabinets of curiosities containing antique coins, medals, relics, and other objects, and creating special rooms with Greek, Roman, Egyptian, and Etruscan ruins became, like the humanist movement with its reverence for ancient manuscripts and its establishment of great libraries, one of the defining activities of the Renaissance. Collecting artifacts was more than an investment or expression of pride; it was a means of establishing a cultural patrimony. Elites were creating a historical legacy that would be passed down not only to their heirs but also to posterity. By the mid-sixteenth century their collectibles also included the contemporary works of renowned artists like Leonardo in what was becoming a competitive market. The excavation of antiquities also found its way from domestic settings into public libraries and museums, such as the Public Library at San Marco in Florence (1444), Pope Sixtus IV's Capitoline Museum (1474) and Vatican Library (1475), and Julius II's Belvedere (1503). Both artists and scholars engaged in their study and attempted to place them in a historical framework. In this context, the rediscovery of Roman statuary, for example, revealed discrepancies between the ancient literary accounts of these works and their actual attributes, stirring the imagination of contemporaries to make new sense of their past. Thus the art, statuary, material objects, manuscripts, and books housed in palaces, villas, and museums both produced new areas of inquiry and at the same time contributed to the enduring memory of the Renaissance.

Art and Piety

Renaissance art was overwhelmingly religious. It reflected the important ways in which society was organized, with its Christian calendar of feast and saints' days, its celebration of the mass, its reverence for saints and religious relics, its multitude of religious orders and convents, and its lay confraternities and tertiary orders. The Roman Church wanted images that provided moral and spiritual lessons to viewers and that encouraged them to meditate on the Bible, the mystery of the incarnation (that Christ assumed a human nature), and the examples set by Christ, the saints, and the Virgin Mary. But by the fifteenth century artwork met additional needs besides professing and meditating on the faith. On one hand, it fulfilled the religious obligations of its patrons. They atoned for their material wealth and the pleasure of spending by performing charitable deeds and by embellishing the environment with works of great beauty for the glory of God and the honor of the city. On the other, it satisfied their desires to document their personal wealth and status for all posterity. Thus Benozzo

Gozzoli's *Journey of the Magi* (1459–1460) in the chapel of the Medici-Riccardi Palace (see Figure 7.1) immortalized a number of Medici patrons for all time by placing their portraits in the canvas. While the exterior of the Medici palace was austere and rustic and thus somewhat veiling the Medici family's aristocratic aspirations, Gozzoli's painting, meant for private viewing, was unrestrained. Moreover, the painting also pictured Florentine life and the Medici's global connections, displaying the dignitaries from the east who had assembled in the city for an international council in 1439. Likewise, family tombs, which reminded people to say prayers for the dead, also became immortal commemorations. Among the most notable were that of the Florentine humanist chancellor Leonardo Bruni, sculpted by the Rossellino brothers; the twenty-five Venetian doges in the Church of Giovanni e Paolo; and in Rome Pollaiuolo's (1429–1498) Pope Sixtus IV (r. 1471–1484) and Innocent VIII (r. 1484–1492) and Michelangelo's Pope Julius II (1443–1513).

Among the most famous patrons of family chapels in Florence were Palla Strozzi (1372–1462), a cloth merchant; Giovanni di Bicci de' Medici (1360–1429), a banker; and Felice Brancacci (1382–1440), a silk merchant at the churches of Santa Trinità, San Lorenzo, and Santa Maria del Carmine, respectively. Although these sanctuaries were decorated with astonishingly revolutionary works, their purpose was not to commemorate the painters or architects but rather to extol the patrons. In Santa Trinità, for example, Palla Strozzi and his father are depicted with *The Adoration of the Magi* (1423), a canvas rendered in the courtly language of the International Gothic style by Gentile da Fabriano that most likely influenced the Medici to commission Gozzoli's rendition for their chapel. The Old Sacristy of San Lorenzo, begun by Brunelleschi in 1421 and later housing the Medici tombs, projected the family's power with a new Florentine architecture that abandoned the Gothic for the more classical cubic space and melon dome. Brancacci's chapel at the Carmine, decorated by Masaccio, ushered in the new narrative style in painting already mentioned earlier, with accurate perspective, solid forms, and realistic figures whose movements conveyed feeling and personality. Family chapels were examples of their wealthy patrons' active piety and civic mindedness; they honored their lineages and expressed their hopes of achieving salvation. But they were also symbols of success.

Venice's great families also emphasized their piety through church decoration. Some of the more famous ones were commissioned in the early sixteenth century. Among them were the Pesaro family, who installed a chapel in Santa Maria Gloriosa dei Frari in 1518. There Titian painted the Pesaro Madonna (1519–1526) for his patron, Jacobo Pesaro, who kneels in a devotional pose before the Virgin Mary. Another example is in the church of San Francesco della Vigna, where Agnesina Badoer Giustinian commissioned a funerary chapel for her father Girolamo Badoer in 1508. Venetian widows also customarily adorned their family funerary chapels with the patron saints of both their natal and husbands' families.

The other great sponsors of pious art in Venice were the *scuole*, or confraternities of laypersons, which numbered in the hundreds. Controlled by the state, these associations with broad memberships of women and men played important roles in ceremony and celebration. While they were influential, both politically and in social life, they did not have any formal political authority, such as membership in the Great Council. They exercised their influence in informal ways. The five major confraternities, all male in membership, performed a number of charitable duties, providing housing for the sick and poor and dowries to indigent girls, assisting at funerals and burials, and giving alms. Each confraternity maintained an altar in a parish church, decorated with panel paintings and statues, and often commemorating the patron saint of a guild. Some of the confraternities of Venice's immigrant communities brought in artists from their native lands to embellish their meetinghouses and churches. Among them was the sculptor Donatello, who carved a wooden statue of Saint John the Baptist for the altar of the Florentine confraternity, and Albrect Dürer (1472–1528), who painted for the German Scuola del Rosario. Other immigrant confraternities used local painters like Vittore Carpaccio, who produced the *Cycle of Saint Ursula* for the scuola by that name, scenes of the life of the Virgin for the Albanian school, and *Christ, Jerome, Augustin, George Tryphon* for the Greek confraternity of San Giorgio Schiavoni.

The members of Venice's confraternities and churches sponsored works of popular devotion. Many contained venerated relics thought to possess healing properties through the power of prayer. The fragment of Christ's cross, which the confraternity of San Giovanni Evangelista was said to possess, became the subject of a cycle of narrative paintings dedicated to a history of the relic's miracles. The paintings fulfilled both religious and secular purposes, on one hand inspiring faith and hope and on the other portraying the prosperity and social stability of the Venetian state. Importantly, they also draw attention to Venice's diverse population during the time. Vittore Carpaccio's canvas of the healing of a possessed man (1494) is set within the contemporary reality of the Grand Canal, with its vibrant and thriving commercial community. In Giovanni Bellini's (*c.* 1429–1507) works, one canvas depicts a procession celebrating the *True Cross in Saint Mark's Square* (1496) with the city's religious and secular hierarchies marching around the civic center in orderly fashion (Figure 7.21). The dramatic subject of the other canvas is a group of spectators crowding onto the San Lorenzo Bridge, once again in a peaceful manner, to witness a miracle of the cross (1500). Of note is a black African, dressed only in a loin cloth, about to dive into the water, evidence of Venice's diverse population. Among the city's Renaissance-style churches with acclaimed relics attracting worshippers was Santa Maria degli Miracoli (1481–89, Pietro Lombardo), with its miraculous icon of the Virgin Mary, and San Zaccaria (1458–1515, Mauro Codussi), which housed the saint's body. The facades of both churches introduced the new Venetian passion for antiquity with their classical lines and rounded arches.

FIGURE 7.21 Gentile Bellini (1429–1507). *Procession of the True Cross in St. Mark's Square* (1496). Tempura and oil on canvas. Galleria dell' Accademia, Venice, Italy.

Beyond the more famous family dynasties, women from a range of social classes regularly endowed churches with family tombs; chapels frescoed with narrative cycles; and sacristies containing panel paintings, ornamental chalices, and reliquaries. Among them were Sibilia Cetto, the wife of a lawyer, who funded the construction of Saint Francis the Greater, a large hospital, cloister, and church complex in Padua between 1414 and 1421; Donna Brigida di Michela, a banker's wife, who commissioned a polyptych altarpiece in 1492 for the church of San Niccolò in Foligno; and Oradea Becchietti, who engaged the painter Carlo Crivelli to paint a votive image (1490) with her portrait for an altar dedicated to Holy Mary of Consolation in the church of San Francesco at Fabriano. Married laywomen in devotional orders, termed "tertiaries" or "*sante vive*" (living saints) also sponsored religious monuments, paintings, and icons of female saints. Even the humble, such as the wives of guild workers, undertook joint commissions to sponsor altarpieces and various chapel décor for churches, convents, and charitable institutions in order to express their devotion and spirituality and their hopes of earning salvation.

While artistic production for the peninsula's churches and confraternities was open to public viewing, convent and monastery art was designed for private audiences with specific, largely spiritual, needs. Its main purpose, it might be argued, was to spur contemplation and prayer. Much of the output does not fit in with the art historical master narrative about the development of style. Moreover, until the 1990s, scholars largely ignored convent art, even though it did have important religious and social functions, while the paintings of such masters as Fra Angelico (1395–1436) and Fra Filippo Lippi (1406–1469), who were members of major male religious orders, were more celebrated. Nuns from wealthy households who were shuttered in convents received an education, but they did not necessarily have the opportunity to study mathematics, and they certainly had no access to the anatomical studies that male artists enjoyed. For the most part, they were self-taught. Thus, very little of their artwork, often found in the miniatures of illuminated manuscripts, has been included in the traditional art historical canon. One female artist noted for her devotional paintings was Caterina Vergeri (1413–1463). In her tenure as part of a lay community leading a semireligious life at an Observant Poor Clare convent in Ferrara, she painted images of the Christ Child on the walls of her convent. She also illustrated her own breviary, with initials ornamented with bust portraits of Saints Clare and Francis as well as many others, images of Christ, and pictures of the infant-swaddled Christ Child.

Cloistered nuns were also patrons of the arts, obtaining images and sculpture for their convents and architects to enlarge or refashion their religious complexes. There is some debate over whether they held independent agency over the works they sponsored or were under the supervision of male administrators. Some, such as the Dominican nuns of San Domenico of Pisa, the Benedictines of Sant' Apollonia in Florence, and those of San Zaccaria in Venice, took advantage of their influential family connections. The nuns of San Domenico were able to engage renowned painters such as Benozzo Gozzoli and Fra Angelico, who adapted their iconography for a female religious audience (e.g., virgin martyrs, the mystical marriage with Christ, and female saints) within the spiritual environment of the cloister. The Benedictines of Sant' Apollonia sponsored Andrea da Castagno's painting of *The Last Supper* (1445–1450), which was not publicly known until the convent was dissolved in 1866.

Among the most renowned religious artists of the fifteenth century was Fra Angelico, a Dominican friar at the monastery of San Marco in Florence, whose major works include an altarpiece of the *Virgin and Child*, seated on a throne surrounded by saints and angels (1438–1443) and an *Annunciation* (1440–1445). Both works reflect the shared beliefs of the artist and the members of the closed community of monastic worshippers. Fra Angelico's knowledge of perspective invited viewers into the pictorial space where they could interact, through prayer and meditation, with the religious subjects.

A Worldly Artisanal Aesthetic

While the history of Renaissance art has usually been told as the history of sculptors, painters, architects, and their patrons, that is not the entire story, for it was also the history of artisans. When we examine how artworks were made we find that they involved an array of skilled craftspeople working with primary materials, such as wood and stone, marble and porphyry, clay and wax, bronze, gold, glass, precious dyes, and silk thread, among others. Artists were alchemists of color as well as practicing mathematicians learning about optics and physics who came to capture reality through various media. Many of the most renowned artists of the fifteenth century actually began as artisans. Brunelleschi, Donatello, and Ghiberti, for example, had early training as goldsmiths. Much of their artisanal skill had deep, medieval roots, and some of it came from abroad. However, up until the late fifteenth century the emphasis on authorship was ignored, despite the fact that craftsmanship and artistry were intertwined. Artisans did not just produce art, they designed it, bringing their own skill and sense of aesthetics to the product. Yet frequently it is their patrons who end up in the history books.

An examination of the decorative arts and their geographical provenance brings to the forefront some of the cross-cultural exchanges underpinning Renaissance art. The northern Italian ports, such as Pisa, Livorno, and Genoa, traded with Bruges and Ghent as well as Barcelona, Valencia, and Lisbon. The southern ports engaged with the North African coastline, while Venice was intimately intertwined with the east. As a result sculptors, goldsmiths, stained glassmakers, weavers, and embroiderers arrived from the greater European and Mediterranean world to build Italy's cathedrals; paint portraits and devotional works; produce portrait medals, reliquaries, and liturgical objects in gold and silver; cast bronze statues; carve stone; apply marquetry or inlay intarsia mosaics on wood; stain glass; reproduce Flemish tapestry, Spanish lusterware, and Ottoman pottery; bind books in stamped leather; and weave luxury cloths of wool and silk with silver and gold thread for wall-hangings, bench cushions, and bed sets. Further, painting was not just done on walls and canvases but also on fabric, playing cards, candles, and manuscripts, often with the labor of monks and nuns. Borrowing and assimilating, Italians eventually developed homegrown industries in textiles, glass, and ceramics, which they adapted to their own markets. Likewise, Italian artists also worked abroad, both in Western and in Eastern Europe as well as Greece and Turkey. Thus, it is important to keep in mind the interaction among artists and artisans on the move and to underline that they often shared Greco-Roman, Byzantine, and Islamic vocabulary in their work.

Venice presents an ideal example. The elites of this city, with a rich history in trade, embraced their classical past and their connections to Islamic Spain, North Africa, and Greater Asia. While the exteriors of various Venetian palaces, and later villas, took on Roman forms, their interiors were filled with Islamic artifacts, silk carpets, late Mamluk metalwork, inlaid brass, and leather goods. They imported porcelain from China, maiolica from Syria, and Isnik pottery from western Anatolia, and their libraries were filled with Muslim-style bookbindings for religious and classical texts. These interior furnishings testify to the city's global orientation, with foreign merchant colonies of Jews, Greeks, and Armenians in Venice itself and wide-reaching business networks and enclaves of Venetian merchants in the Mediterranean and farther east. The familiarity with material culture from abroad was not limited to the elite stratum of society. From the eleventh century international merchants as well as artisans, oarsmen, tailors, bakers, cooks, goldsmiths, pharmacists, and physicians had sojourned in Venetian colonies and in Constantinople, Aleppo, Tripoli, Cairo, and Alessandria. They brought their experiences home and displayed their goods in interior décor, collectibles, and textiles.

Venice's worldly aesthetic was also exhibited in the paintings of Gentile and Giovanni Bellini (Figure 7.22). Their *Saint Mark Preaching in Alexandria* (1504–1507), commissioned by the Confraternity of San Marco, depicts the interaction of a diverse community in a major Muslim entrepôt where Venice exchanged goods and ideas for centuries The setting blends Venetian motifs with multicultural artifacts, connecting west with east. The Byzantine basilica in the backdrop, a reference to San Marco and the Byzantine church in Constantinople that it was modeled on, Hagia Sofia, stands before an eastern bazaar. The square is Egyptian, its houses displaying Islamic carpets, grilles, and tiles, and in the skyline are minarets, columns, and pillars. The fifteenth-century contemporary world is also given classical references. Saint

FIGURE 7.22 Gentile (1429–1507) and Giovanni Bellini (c. 1430–1516). *Saint Mark Preaching in Alexandria* (1504–1507). Oil on panel. Pinacoteca di Brera, Milan, Italy.

Mark, the patron saint of Venice, is dressed as an ancient Roman. Venetian patricians stand behind him. His audience includes Middle Eastern women dressed in white, Egyptian Mamluks, North African Muslims, Ottomans, Persians, Ethiopians, and Tartars. The painting also includes a self-portrait of Gentile Bellini, important evidence that the status of the artist was changing from that of a craftsman to that of a master of note, in this case with connections to the triumphant conqueror of Constantinople, Mehmed II. Bellini had sojourned in the Bosporus citadel in 1479 at the behest of the Sultan, who wished a portrait of himself. In gratitude for painting the sultan's portrait in 1479 (Figure 7.17) Mehmed gave the artist a gold chain, which is seen in the *Saint Mark Preaching in Alexandria* in the figure of Gentile at the foot of Saint Mark's pulpit.

Besides Bellini, Egyptian and Islamic references appeared in the works of a number of painters. There was a long-standing interest in Egyptian culture, evidenced in the medieval iconography of Venice's Basilica, which housed the remains of the Egyptian Saint Mark, and in Rome, with its obelisks, pyramids, and statues of lions imported during antiquity. Egyptian architecture, hieroglyphics, and religious stories would find their way onto canvas. Among them were the frescoes of the Egyptian story of Isis, Osiris, and the bull Apis that were painted by Pinturicchio (1454–1513) and his workshop on the ceilings in the Vatican Palace in 1493 for Pope Alexander VI (Rodrigo Borgia, 1431–1503). Kufic-like or Arabic script in the halos of madonnas had been used as early as Giotto (1266/76?–1337). They also appear in the works of Gentile da Fabriano (Figure 7.23), Masaccio, and Fra Angelico during the fifteenth century. Finally, painters frequently depicted Ottoman carpets in their renderings of domestic interiors. The collections and representations of the exotic show the powerful influence of wealth through trade as well as the important connections between Europe, the Mediterranean, and the worlds father east.

Conclusion

Artistic traditions in Italy reflected both regional customs and interaction with cultures abroad. While no one stylistic formula fit the peninsula as a whole, certain innovative characteristics in sculpture, painting, and architecture emerged during the fifteenth century. These included greater verisimilitude and naturalism; a revived interest in Greek and Roman monuments and the application of classical styles to building and sculpture; the development of linear perspective in sculpture and painting; the importance of mathematical applications to the various arts; and the gradual elevation of a few individuals from anonymous status to notoriety.

It is important to understand the context of fifteenth-century stylistic and technical developments. It served propagandistic, civic, devotional, charitable, and familial purposes. While some works drew from the

FIGURE 7.23 Gentile da Fabriano (1370–?). Detail from *The Adoration of the Magi* (1423). Painting/polyptych. Tempera on panel. Uffizi Gallery, Florence, Italy. The halo of the Madonna is an example of pseudo-kufic (pseudo-Arabic) script.

classical past, their motifs also reflected contemporary life and concerns. Others were more illusionary and idealistic. Furthermore, it is necessary to consider the relationship of artistic works to observers, who included not only people in elite circles and members of civic corporations and religious orders, but also the everyday passerby, for art was a means of both cultural expression and social interaction. A mere glance or gesture might invite the viewer to take part in the world of the image, to reach the human senses, and to stimulate thought. Moreover, some people ascribed real power to the images they observed, such as the ability of religious icons to work miracles.

The visual vocabulary of fifteenth-century masters and artisans provides an indispensable window into the political, social, and religious life of the period. Artwork was a conduit and manifestation of social interaction that engaged the patron, the producer, and the audience. On a political level, art served the changing social structures that came with political consolidation throughout the Italian peninsula, whether in republics or principalities. It was used to convey political propaganda, civic identity, and the dignity of humankind. On a social level, art commemorated the status of the family, the basic unity of social organization, projecting both its material success and its piety. The enduring memory of the family was embedded in altarpieces and tombs, paintings and busts, palaces, tympanum reliefs, and wellheads. Female chastity and the joys of welcoming a new child into the family found their way into painting and the decorative arts. The art of the fifteenth century was above all religious, a testament to the deep faith that underlay and accompanied the rituals of daily life, whether for nobles or commoners. Each work of art, whether designed for a political, social, or religious function, or a combination of the three, is a testament to artisanal achievement and a powerful invitation for viewers to interact with the people of the age.

Art and artifacts documented the history of an age. Accompanying the traditional forms of art Renaissance elites commissioned in the way of paintings, sculptures, and buildings were their investments in material culture. Their collections of antique statues, coins, medals, relics, and other curiosities, together with the contemporary works of renowned artists, on the one hand shed light on the material things they valued but on another level helped create a historical memory of the Renaissance, one that would celebrate over the long term its artistic achievements.

Think Critically

1. What were the ways in which republics and principalities conveyed their ideological messages? Identify some of those messages.
2. How did artistic works define upper-class families? What stages of the life cycle did they document?
3. How did religious art serve the needs of both ordinary people and elite families?
4. What medieval and cross-cultural artisanal traditions informed fifteenth-century material culture?
5. What are the ways in which artistic patronage was gendered?

Further Exploration

1. Explore Gentile and Giovanni Bellini's *Saint Mark Preaching in Alexandria* (1504–1507; Figure 7.22). What does the painting tell you about the material culture of the age?
2. Explore how museums filled with artwork and antiquities of the Renaissance have stimulated enduring interest in the age.

Notes

1 Lauro Martines, *Power and the Imagination: City-States in Renaissance Italy* (New York: Vintage Books Edition, 1980), 262–3.
2 Ibid., 254.
3 Ibid., 254–5.
4 Mary Hollingsworth, *Patronage in Renaissance Italy. From 1400 to the Early Sixteenth Century* (London: John Murray, 1994), 12.

Further Reading

Primary Sources

Vasari, Giorgio. *The Lives of the Artists*, 2 vols. Translated by George Bull. Baltimore, MD: Penguin, 1972. A sixteenth-century biography and commentary on Renaissance artists.

Secondary Sources

Barkan, Leonard. *Unearthing the Past: Archeology and Aesthetics in the Making of Renaissance Culture*. New Haven, CT: Yale University Press, 1999. A fascinating account of how the rediscovered statues of ancient Rome influenced the way in which sixteenth-century artists and thinkers imagined and defined Renaissance culture.

Bayer, Andrea. "Representation: Art Celebrates Marriage in the Renaissance. In *A Cultural History of Marriage in the Renaissance and Early Modern Age*. Edited by Joanne M. Ferraro, 139–59. London: Bloomsbury Academic, 2020. The essay identifies paintings and material objects that celebrate Renaissance marriages.

Baxandall, Michael. *Painting and Experience in Fifteenth-Century Italy*. Oxford, UK: Oxford University Press, 1972, 2nd edition 1988. Analyzes the social context of Renaissance painting.

Belting, Hans. *Florence and Baghdad: Renaissance Art and Arab Science*. Translated by D. L. Schneider. Cambridge, MA: Harvard University Press, 2011. A study of the connection between Arab science and Florentine art, beginning with the theory of perspective advanced by the eleventh-century mathematician Ibn al Haithan.

Brottton, Jerry. *The Renaissance Bazaar. From the Silk Road to Michelangelo.* Oxford, UK: Oxford University Press, 2002. Identifies the influences of the Middle East and China on the European Renaissance.

Brown, Patricia Fortini. *Art and Life in Renaissance Venice.* New York: Harry N. Abrams, 1997. An exploration of art patronage in Venice among the guilds, the nobility, the church, and private families.

Brown, Patricia Fortini. *Venice and Antiquity. The Venetian Sense of the Past.* New Haven, CT: Yale University Press, 1996. An analysis of Venetian adaptations of Greco-Roman styles and themes.

Erichsen, Paula Hohti. *Artisans, Objects, and Everyday Life in Renaissance Italy.* Amsterdam: Amsterdam University Press, 2020. Surveys the material world of Renaissance Italy through artisanal production.

Ferraro, Joanne M. Venice. *History of the Floating City.* New York: Cambridge University Press, 2012. A history of Venice from its sixth-century beginnings to the twenty-first century.

Findlen, Paula. "Possessing the Past. The Material World of the Italian Renaissance." *The American Historical Review*, 103:1 (1998): 83–114. A groundbreaking study that demonstrates how antiquarianism and the celebration of objects were a defining feature of the Renaissance making and remaking of the past.

Grafton, Anthony. *Leon Battista Alberti: Master Builder of the Italian Renaissance.* Cambridge, MA: Harvard University Press, 2002. An engaging biography and cultural history of one of the most important Renaissance theorists of classical architecture and painting.

Grafton, Anthony, and Elisabeth Schwab. *The Art of Discovery: Digging into the Past in Renaissance Europe.* Princeton, NJ: Princeton University Press, 2022. A sweeping history of the antiquarians, and the alchemists and craftspeople they consulted, that shaped new forms of art and knowledge.

Hollingsworth, Mary. *Patronage in Renaissance Italy. From 1400 to the Early Sixteenth Century.* Baltimore, MD: Johns Hopkins University Press, 1994. An analysis of the major patrons of art in Renaissance Italy's principal cities.

Jardine, Lisa. *Worldly Goods. A New History of the Renaissance.* New York: W.W. Norton, 1998. Shows the connections between the accumulation of wealth and the creation of Renaissance culture.

King, Catherine. *Renaissance Women Patrons.* Manchester, England: Manchester University Press, 1998. Surveys laywomen's commissioning of art, and the social, political, and religious factors that enabled them to influence the Renaissance cultural world.

Mack, Rosamund E. *Bazaar to Piazza.* Berkeley, CA: University of California Press, 2002. Surveys Mediterranean trade in luxury goods from the Islamic and Asian world and their influence on the Italian decorative arts.

Martines, Lauro. *Power and the Imagination: City-States in Renaissance Italy.* Baltimore, MD: Johns Hopkins University Press, 1988. A magisterial survey of medieval and Renaissance Italian developments that draws connections between cultural patrons and power.

Miller, Stephanie R. "Parenting in the Palazzo: Images and Artifacts of Children in the Italian Renaissance Home." In *The Early Modern Italian Domestic*

Interior, 1400–1700 Objects, Spaces, Domesticities. Edited by Erin J. Campbell, Stephanie R. Miller, and Elizabeth Carroll Consavari, 67–88. London: Routledge, 2016 (e-edition). Offers a perspective on Renaissance childhood through an analysis of material culture.

Roberts, Ann. *Dominican Women and Renaissance Art: The Convent of San Domenico of Pisa*. New York: Routledge, 2008. Examines thirty works of art that originated from the convent of San Domenico of Pisa commissioned by nuns.

Sizonenko, Tatiana. "Artists as Agents: Artistic Exchange and Cultural Translation between Venice and Constantinople: The Case of Gentile Bellini, 1479–1481." PhD Dissertation, University of California San Diego, 2013. An original study of cultural exchange between Venice and Constantinople through the artwork of Gentile Bellini.

Turner, A. Richard. *Renaissance Florence. The Invention of a New Art*. New York: Harry N. Abrams, 1996. An analysis of fourteenth- and fifteenth-century Florentine art in its social, cultural, political, geographic, economic, and religious contexts.

Welch, Evelyn. *Shopping in the Renaissance*. New Haven, CT: Yale University Press, 2005. A fascinating account of what Renaissance people purchased, ranging from foodstuffs to antiquities and holy relics.

Williams, Allyson Burgess. "Silk-Clad Walls and Sleeping Cupids: A Documentary Reconstruction of the Living Quarters of Lucrezia Borgia, Duchess of Ferrara." In *The Early Modern Italian Domestic Interior, 1400–1700 Objects, Spaces, Domesticities*. Edited by Erin J. Campbell, Stephanie R. Miller, and Elizabeth Carroll Consavari, 175–90. London: Routledge, 2016 (e-edition). This gendered analysis of Lucrezia Borgia's living quarters offers important insights into how women's decorative priorities differed from men's.

8

A Shifting World: Sixteenth-Century Italy

Timeline

1453	Fall of Constantinople. End of Hundred Years' War
1454	Peace of Lodi
1455	Johann Gutenberg prints the Bible
1464	Platonic Academy established in Florence. Death of Cosimo de' Medici and succession of Piero. Printing begun in Rome
1469	Lorenzo de' Medici succeeds Piero in Florence. Marriage of Ferdinand and Isabel
1470	Printing press of Nicolas Jenson in Venice
1471	Sixtus IV becomes pope (to 1484)
1473	Printing introduced in Lyon
1478	Inquisition established in Castile
1482	Portuguese establish Elmina on the Gold Coast of Africa
1483	Charles VIII becomes king of France (to 1498)
1488	Bartolomeu Dias sailed around the Cape of Good Hope
1492	Death of Lorenzo de' Medici. Savonarola assumes power. Jews expelled from Spain. Columbus reaches Hispaniola. Alexander VI becomes pope
1493	Columbus's second voyage
1494	Aldine Press established in Venice
1494	Charles VIII invades Italy; expels the Medici
1494	Treaty of Tordesillas

1495	Holy League organized against France
1496	Forced conversion of Jews in Portugal
1497	Vasco de Gama sails to India
1498	Death of Savonarola. Columbus's third voyage. John Cabot reaches New England. Da Gama reaches Calicut. Louis XII becomes king of France
1499	Cesare Borgia begins war campaigns in the Romagna
c. 1499	Vespucci travels to South America (to 1503)
1500	Cabral reaches Brazil. Treaty of Granada
1502	Columbus's fourth voyage
1503	Julius II becomes pope (to 1513). Cesare Borgia loses power
1504	Spain conquers Naples
c. 1507	Julius II promulgates indulgences for rebuilding St. Peter's Basilica
1508	League of Cambrai against Venice
1509	Erasmus produces *The Praise of Folly*
1511	Holy League against France. Council of Pisa
1512	Fall of the Florentine Republic. The Medici return to Florence. Machiavelli is exiled. Julius II and the Swiss expel the French from Italy
1513	Machiavelli writes *The Prince*. Leo X becomes pope (to 1521)
1515	Francis I becomes king of France. Francis I defeats the Swiss at Marignano and occupies Milan. Alfonsina Orsini serves informally as regent of Florence
1516	Concordat of Bologna. Venice establishes the Jewish ghetto
1517	Luther introduces the *Ninety-Five Theses*. Oratory of Divine Love founded
1519	Charles V elected Holy Roman Emperor
1520	Suleiman the Magnificent becomes Ottoman sultan
1521	Diet and Edict of Worms: Condemnation of Luther. First Habsburg–Valois war (to 1526)
1522	Adrian VI becomes pope (to 1523). Luther's *New Testament* published; establishment of the Hospital of Incurables in Venice
1523	Clement VII becomes pope (to 1534)
1524	Francis I conquers Milan. Theatines established
1525	Imperial victory at Pavia
1526	League of Cognac
1527	Sack of Rome. Florentine Republic established for second time
1528	Capuchin order founded. Castiglione's *Book of the Courtier* published

1529   Peace of Cambrai

1530   Charles V crowned by pope in Bologna. Fall of second Florentine Republic; return of the Medici. Confession of Augsburg

1534   Paul III becomes pope; establishment of the Convertite in Venice

1535   Contarini made a cardinal. Papal authorization of the Ursulines. Charles V occupies Milan after death of last Sforza Duke

1536   Third Habsburg–Valois war. Pope makes Cosimo de Medici grand duke of Tuscany

1537   Venice establishes the Magistrates of Blasphemy

1539   Eleonora of Toledo marries Cosimo I de' Medici

1540   Papal authorization of the Jesuits. Jews expelled from Naples

1542   Fourth Habsburg–Valois war. Roman Inquisition established

1545   Beginning of the Council of Trent. Establishment of papal inquisition

1547   Venice establishes an inquisition

1550   Julius III becomes pope (to 1555)

1551   Second session of Council of Trent. Habsburg–Valois wars resume. The Ottomans capture Tripoli

1555   Holy Roman Emperor Charles V abdicates. Gian Pietro Carafa becomes Pope Paul IV (to 1559)

1559   First Index of Banned Books issued by Paul IV; Pius IV becomes pope. Catherine de Medici becomes Regent in France

1563   End of Council of Trent

1571   Christian Holy League defeats Ottoman fleet at Battle of Lepanto

1573   Venice makes peace with the Ottomans

1575   Plague in northern Italy

1577   Venice establishes the Soccorso to assist abused wives

1578   Ferrara incorporated into the Papal States with death of last Este duke

Overview

During the last decades of the fifteenth century the Italian Peninsula entered a period of turbulence and uncertainty that would gradually transform its political status and intellectual parameters over the next century. As we saw in Chapter 5, the narrow boot at the center of the Mediterranean became a major theater of conflict at the mercy of the more powerful Spanish Hapsburg and French Valois kingdoms to its southwest and north, respectively. Each of these kingdoms had embarked upon a trajectory of political consolidation that strengthened their powers and resources over those of the individual

FIGURE 8.1 Martin Waldseemüller (1470–1520). *Map of the World*, 1507. This is one of the first maps to depict the Americas clearly as a separate continent.

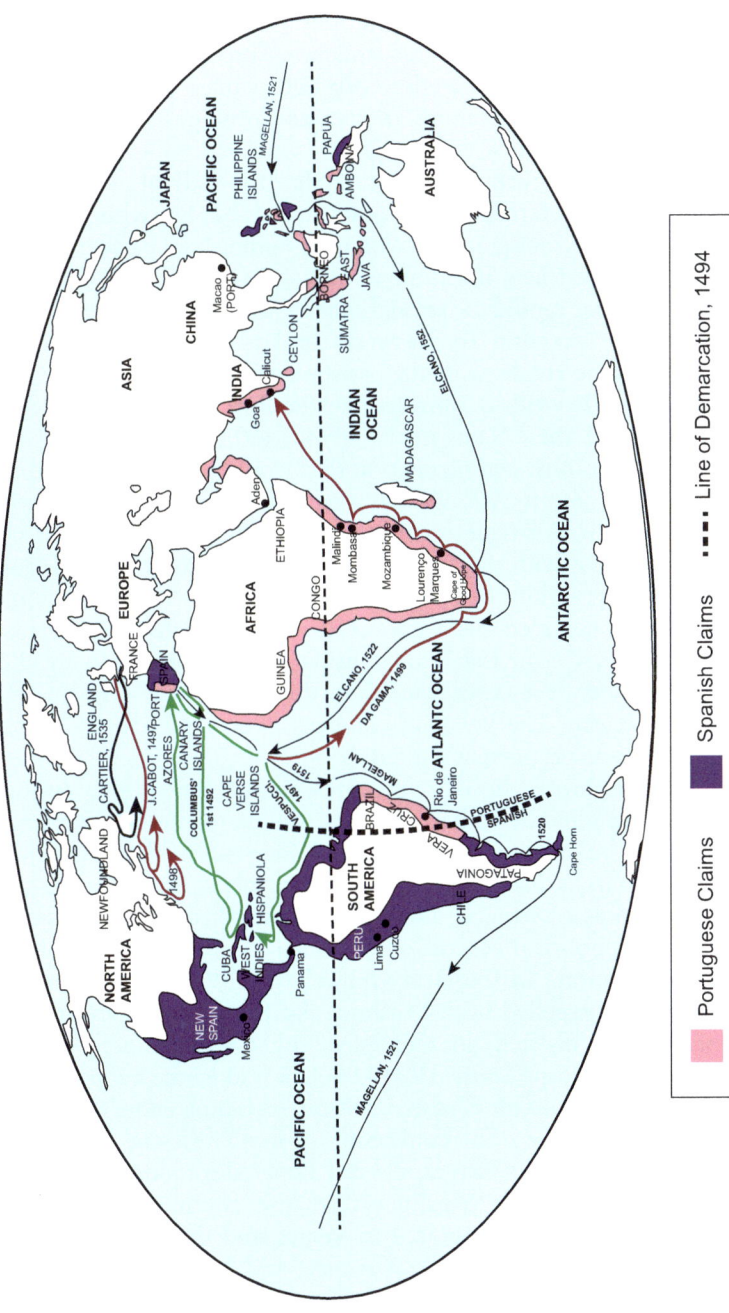

MAP 8.1 European Sea Routes and Colonial Claims of Spain and Portugal (Fifteenth and Sixteenth Centuries).

Italian city-states. Ultimately, by the mid-sixteenth century, Spain would come to dominate large areas of the peninsula, including the papacy and Papal States, Lombardy, and much of the south (see Map 8.3). Only Venice managed to maintain its political independence. Throughout the peninsula, Italian elites retreated, replacing the corporate values of the fourteenth and fifteenth centuries with a more aristocratic consciousness and courtly culture.

Despite the political turbulence during the first half of the sixteenth century, the peninsula retained its economic vitality, but not without serious challenges that required adaptation to changing commercial markets. Venice, for example, witnessed new maritime rivalries. To the east, the Ottomans began to overrun the republic's strongholds in the Mediterranean and to erode its Levantine strength. To the west, the Portuguese were becoming formidable new trade rivals, with the assistance of the Genoese (see Map 8.1). From the 1460s wealthy patrons like the Portuguese king's brother, Prince Henry, called the "Navigator" (1394–1460), were financing new shipbuilding, cartography, and navigation that would ultimately lead to the discovery of a sea route to Asia via the west coast of Africa. The Genoese merchants whom the Portuguese engaged began to forge important new commercial links: first with the Madeira islands, then with the Gold Coast (Ghana), and finally within the African interior. Then in 1488 Bartolomeu Dias (1450–1500) rounded the Cape of Good Hope, discovering a sea route to the Indian Ocean that would bring the Portuguese to the East Indies' spice markets at a faster pace than the old Venetian land circuits via the Mediterranean. The Venetian commercial economy survived these challenges, but it was permanently altered.

Political developments in late fifteenth-century Iberia also brought several new changes to the Italian cities as well as to the Mediterranean world. One was linked to the diaspora of Iberian Muslims and Jews. The Spanish monarchs Ferdinand and Isabella, whose marriage in 1469 united the kingdoms of Aragon and Castile, embarked upon a policy of both religious and political centralization. Their Christian forces defeated the last Muslim emirate in Iberia at Granada in 1492, and the Catholic monarchs officially expelled both Muslims and Jews from their kingdom. The minorities that insisted on remaining either went underground or converted. For years, Pope Sixtus IV (1414–1484) in Rome had supported the crown's policy of militant Christianization, including endorsement of a Spanish Inquisition to force the conversion of non-Christians. Sixtus IV's Spanish successor, Rodrigo Borgia, elected Pope Alexander VI (r. 1492–1503) the same year as the Muslim overthrow, continued his policies. Many of the deported Jews migrated to Venice and the Po Plain, Rome, Mantua, Ferrara, Naples, Avignon, Provence, and Istanbul as well as to Portugal and North Africa, infusing these areas with new commercial and intellectual energies. Another change, motivated by Ottoman incursions into the Mediterranean and Portuguese maritime expansion from west

Africa to Asia, was linked to the establishment of new sea routes. The Spanish monarchs, seeking an alternative route to Asia, used the land, gold, and silver they confiscated from their Muslim and Jewish deportees to fund Columbus's voyages (1492–1500) (see Map 8.1). Reaching Hispaniola, the Genoese explorer mistakenly thought he had reached India. His Florentine compatriot Amerigo Vespucci (1454–1512), however, would soon discover during his voyages to South America in 1499–1500 that Columbus had found a world previously unknown to Europeans. The impact of this discovery was profound: the earth, with its flora and fauna, its peoples and microbes, was much larger and more complex than Europeans had thought, and the Mediterranean that Italians had dominated would become by the seventeenth century one of many lucrative seas around the globe. Among those that profited from Iberian exploration and discovery were the Genoese, who enjoyed colonies in Lisbon and Seville, and with the fall of Granada in 1492, Andalusia. They slowly moved out of the Mediterranean and instead became prime organizers of commercial shipping between Seville and the Americas. After 1568 they also became the Spanish crown's primary bankers.

Religious schism during the sixteenth century added further complexity to Italian life, including social change. The Augustinian friar Martin Luther began a new church in Saxony (Germany) in the 1520s, the first of many religious confessions that would permanently fracture a thousand years of Christian unity. Some areas of Switzerland, as well as Scandinavia and England, would undergo religious reformations during the sixteenth century, splitting with the Roman Catholic Church. In the Germanic lands to the north of the Italian Peninsula the reformer managed to galvanize what had been long-standing resentment toward a lax clergy and corrupt papal bureaucracy. His success in launching a protestant movement, some of which infiltrated the Italian cities, triggered a vigorous response from the papacy and a resurgence of the Catholic Church in all aspects of Italian life.

Political Crises and Changing Regimes, 1494–1559

The first half of the sixteenth century, like the final years of the fifteenth century, brought frequent and abrupt changes in the Italian political map as the peninsula remained the focus of French and Spanish rivalries. The end of the Hundred Years' War between France and England in 1453 had allowed for a gradual strengthening of the French monarchy, while in Spain the marriage of Ferdinand of Castile and Isabella of Aragon in 1469 provided conditions for political consolidation (see Map 8.2). These kingdoms to the north and southwest, respectively, began to move in the direction of

MAP 8.2 Europe in 1500.

political centralization as townspeople opted to align with their monarchs at the expense of the nobility. Lawyers, bookkeepers, diplomats, and military advisors staffed royal bureaucracies, assisting kings and queens in the administration of taxation, law enforcement, and warfare. The monarchs gradually abandoned the medieval practice of calling upon feudal cavalry to defend their interests, instead recruiting mercenaries from Switzerland and Germany to serve in their standing armies. They financed new military technology, including artillery and cannon, both by increasing taxation and by acquiring loans from Genoese and German bankers, and embarked upon territorial expansion.

From the final years of the fifteenth century, the rulers of the various Italian regional states remained divided and continued to invite foreign intervention in their territorial conflicts (see Chapter 5). That included the papacy, which began to exert European-wide influence in political and diplomatic affairs. During the early sixteenth century, Pope Julius II (r. 1503–1513) became a principal player in the Hapsburg–Valois power

A SHIFTING WORLD: SIXTEENTH-CENTURY ITALY 231

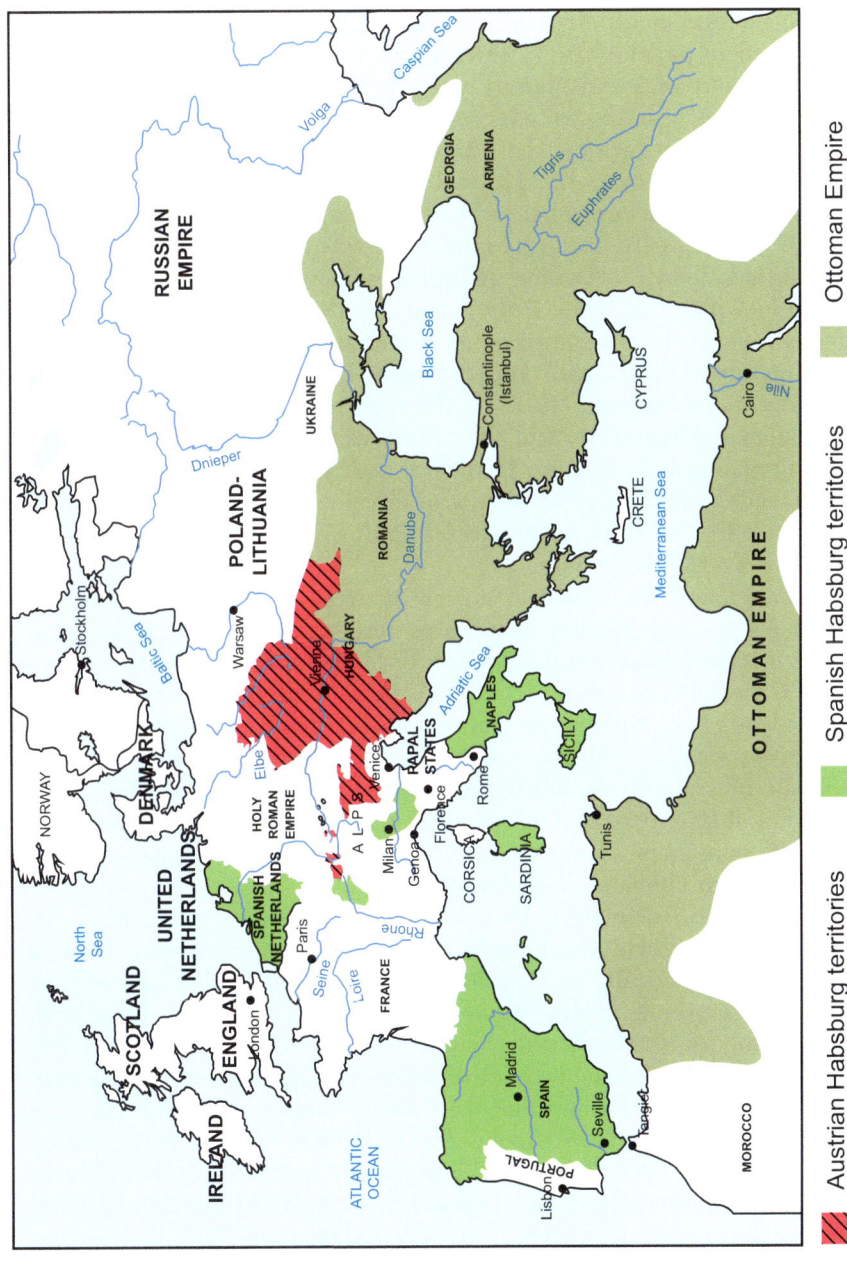

MAP 8.3 Political Divisions in 1600.

struggles. When he came to the Holy See in 1503, the Aragonese already ruled southern Italy, and the French ruled Milan. Julius, aiming to build a strong papal government, proceeded to strengthen state finances and expand his diplomatic networks. Further, he hired Swiss infantry units to supplement papal levies. In 1505–6, the warrior pope embarked upon the reconquest of Borgia family strongholds in the Romagna and the Marche. He then set out to reduce the power of the Venetian Republic in northeast Italy by forming the League of Cambrai in 1508, an alliance with Florence, France, the Holy Roman Empire, and Spain. Venice suffered a dramatic defeat before these powers at the Battle of Agnadello in 1509, temporarily losing its landed possessions. The pope, however, then shifted alliances, teaming up with Ferdinand of Aragon against the French in a pact called the Holy League. In this reshuffling, Venice was able to recoup the lost cities of its hinterland. The Venetian Republic then regrouped with Spain and the Holy Roman Empire, leaving the French at a disadvantage. In 1512, the French were forced out of Milan with Swiss enforcements, and the Sforza were restored. French power, thus, momentarily collapsed. That same year the Florentine militia that Machiavelli had recruited to defend the city fled when faced with Spanish infantry. The Florentine Republic fell, and Spain restored the Medici, making it a Spanish satellite.

Italian regimes continued to change between 1515 and 1530 as the French Valois and Spanish Hapsburgs resumed their dual rivalries in northern Italy. France captured Milan once again, but Spain, in alliance with the Medici Pope Leo X (r. 1513–1521), ultimately established a strong foothold in 1522. With its possessions in the mainland south and Sicily, and heavy influence in Genoa and Rome, the Iberian power thus became a dominant presence on the Italian Peninsula (see Map 8.3). Only Venice and its territorial state remained independent, joining Florence, the Papacy, and France in an attempt to oust the Spanish in the League of Cognac in 1526, an alliance that ultimately suffered defeat.

The Sack of Rome in 1527 by Charles V, a Spanish king from the Hapsburg dynasty who had become Holy Roman Emperor, was a defining moment both politically and psychologically for Italy's ruling classes. The emperor's Hapsburg troops, numbering some 12,000, were filled with followers of Martin Luther, the new protestant religious leader who in the midst of attacking the practice of selling indulgences—ultimately used to rebuild St. Peter's Basilica and the Vatican—began a new church. Pope Clement VII (1523–34) fled to his fortified castle while imperial troops pillaged the city. Thereafter, Spanish hegemony in Italy became definitive throughout southern Italy and Lombardy. From 1530 the Medici ruled Florence under Spanish influence. Spain shared Piedmont with France from 1535, and in 1559 it captured the Tuscan coast. In the end only Venice escaped the foreign grip.

Aristocratization

Throughout the peninsula over the sixteenth century, whether in republics or in principalities, the bases of power continued to narrow. Oligarchies slowly crystalized and princedoms consolidated around the court society of a ruler who offered patronage in exchange for loyalty and services. This aristocratization of Italy's ruling classes fell in line with the political framework found in the Kingdom of Naples, Spain, France, England, and even Switzerland. Among the oligarchies it was mostly the leading family dynasties from preceding centuries whose lineages remained at the helm of power. Some descended from the great landholding dynasties, but many had consolidated in the major professional colleges of judges, notaries, and physicians. The period of open-ended social mobility and entry into political life that had characterized the twelfth to early fifteenth centuries in Italy gradually ended by the beginning of the sixteenth century. Prior to that time merchants and manufacturers, as well as some artisans, still had the opportunity to enter civic life. By the end of the century, however, the process of exclusion had begun and was well established by 1530. The disenfranchised, whose numbers grew, were members of artisan guilds and confraternities. They may have exercised informal avenues of political pressure, but they had little to no say formally in the way civic administration was run.

Each of the towns and cities on the peninsula followed its own unique course to political consolidation, with no universal formula that describes the process. However, some general comments may be made. First, powerholders in civic councils rendered service in public office more inaccessible by changing entry requirements to exclude new aspirants who had not enjoyed citizenship over the long term. Secondly, they shut their doors to families who had engaged in manual labor or trade over at least the previous three generations. Instead the ranks of civic councils were filled more and more with men in the judiciary or in the notarial arts. Finally, they began to express a more aristocratic consciousness, demanding their members rely on agricultural income or other passive investments as well as the proceeds that derived from their privileged positions as officeholders. This last requirement was in alignment with the gradual shift in Italian economic interests, which by 1620 rendered land, commercial agriculture, and lending more secure investments than commerce or manufacture. The various powerholders, especially in the Veneto, began to build great villas, such as the one in Figure 8.2, where they devoted considerable time to expanding and improving their agricultural investments

By the mid-sixteenth century in places like Milan and Brescia in Lombardy; the various towns in the Venetian territorial state; Siena, Genoa, and parts of the Papal States, civic administrators largely came from the legal and humanistic professions. They adopted more of a rentier mentality and followed the ideals of chivalry. They met in informal, aristocratic academies dedicated to learning, particularly agrarian innovation and the mechanical sciences, and to intellectual play, in the form of theater and literature. Their

FIGURE 8.2 Andrea Palladio (1508–1580). Villa Barbaro (1554–1560). Maser (Treviso), Italy. (Built for the brothers Daniele and Marcantonio Barbaro.)

urban centers became conduits for the transmission of aristocratic values, and status was measured according to various grades of nobility that had to do with the antiquity of a lineage as well as with the professional status of its members. In areas governed by princely rule, such as the Medici dukedom in Tuscany, the Spanish viceroyalties in Lombardy and the Kingdom of Naples, the duke or duchess played a growing role in local governance. Their centralizing ambitions transformed the functions and competencies of the urban oligarchies under their sway.

In this context of aristocratization, the behavior of the family dynasty—that is, its wealth and lifestyle, became fundamental to the workings of government, and the members of these elite groups tightened their restrictions on marriage. To consolidate family wealth, fewer children within the ruling classes were permitted to marry, and those that did were carefully aligned with their social equals or better, despite at times their objections. The dowries of new brides skyrocketed among these endogamous political groups, while convents and monasteries exploded with the leftover children who were not tracked for marriage. Lives of enclosure awaited the unmarried daughters and nieces of Italy's aristocrats, albeit ones where avenues of creative activity were still open to women. Enclosure brought change to nuns' quality of living. Whereas some, as in Florence, had been able to work in the various divisions of the textile industry during the fifteenth century, and thus contribute to the urban economy, enclosure cut them off from the city's business networks. For the sons and nephews of elite families, enrollment in the clergy became ever more an avenue of social mobility and a way to preserve and expand the wealth and influence of the family dynasty. In tandem with this latter development, more and more property came under the auspices of the church, making it exempt from secular taxation.

A very few aristocratic women escaped enclosure and through their family and marriage connections were able to enter the ranks of diplomats and rulers. Betrothal and marriage were among the most important diplomatic tools in this age of political rivalry, and the highest families of the Italian aristocracy steadily intermarried with powerful European families. Perhaps the most famous was Catherine de' Medici (1519–1589), who became the wife of King Henry II of France in 1533. Catherine, the granddaughter of Lorenzo de' Medici and the niece of Pope Clement VII, had inherited a fortune, and the Medici family found it opportune to place her at the highest political levels in France. When her husband died prematurely in 1559 while her sons were very young, she virtually ruled the kingdom. A few years after Catherine's dynastic marriage, in 1539 another female aristocrat and daughter of the Spanish viceroy of Naples, Eleonora of Toledo (1522–1562), joined the powerful Medici clan as the wife of Cosimo I in Florence. During this period marriage became an important tool in the advancement of the emperor Charles V's plans to forge imperial alliances. He actively encouraged the dynastic marriages of Italian aristocratic women with the nobilities of Spain, the Low Countries, and the Hapsburg lands so as to build social and political networks. Further, he arranged marriages for his own female kin with the princely dynasties of the Italian Peninsula. Thus, Francesco de' Medici, the son of Cosimo I and Eleonora of Toledo, wed one of the emperor's nieces, as did the Dukes of Mantua and Ferrara, while the Duke of Savoy's son wed the emperor's granddaughter.

At home on the Italian Peninsula the turbulence of the invasions opened the door for aristocratic women to take charge as their husbands or sons were frequently away at war or at times held in hostage. Among the most celebrated of these exceptional women was Isabella d'Este (1494–1539), Duchess of Mantua and the daughter of Ercole I d'Este, Duke of Ferrara, and Leonora of Aragon, the daughter of King Ferrante of Naples. Isabella had grown up in the courtly society of Ferrara, where her mother Leonora, a great patron of writers and artists and an eloquent writer herself, had at times ruled the duchy in her father's absence. Isabella, like her mother, was in many ways destined to rule. She received a solid classical education and in her youth interacted with the most notable humanist scholars and artists of the day. Talented in her own right, she was well-versed in Roman history and capable of translating Greek into Latin. She was known to discuss the classics and affairs of state with ambassadors. In 1490 Isabella married the Marchese Francesco Gonzaga of Mantua (ruled 1484–1519) to whom she had been betrothed at the age of six. Her husband, a military captain, was frequently away from home. Thus Isabella became Mantua's consort co-regent, a position that both opened up the diplomatic world to the young bride and gave her the opportunity to hone her skills as a ruler. In 1500, for example, she met King Louis XII of France in Milan to persuade him not to send his troops against Mantua. When her husband was captured by the Venetians in 1509, she directed Mantua's military forces until he was released in 1512. That same year she hosted the Congress of Mantua, a diplomatic convention to study relations between Florence and Milan. In widowhood Isabella stood at the helm of the Mantuan state, a position she prepared for diligently by studying such subjects as architecture, agriculture, and industry. Known widely for her literary and artistic patronage, Isabella was also an efficient and admired ruler.

Alfonsina Orsini (1472–1520) was also given opportunities to serve as a regent, both for her husband Piero di Lorenzo de' Medici (m. 1488) of Florence and later for her son Lorenzo. A member of the high aristocracy raised in the royal court of Naples, she was a prime advocate for the Medici family during their exile from 1494 to 1512 and worked to secure the family's political position through astute marriage alliances and diplomatic connections. In addition to arranging a French royal marriage for her son, Lorenzo, she concluded an important marriage alliance for her daughter Clarice with a member of a rival Florentine family, Filippo Strozzi, in 1508. When Alfonsina's brother-in-law became Pope Leo X, she continued to maximize her family's interests by helping her son-in-law obtain the office of Depositor-General of the Vatican, a position that placed the family within reach of the Vatican's coffers. She also worked to advance her son's political stature in Florence. Lorenzo would in effect rule Florence with his mother's assistance. She served, informally, as his regent in the summer of 1515 when he led his army in support of Pope Leo X and the Spanish against France, manipulating city councils, designing war strategies, and making use of diplomatic contacts. The pope even engaged her to provide ambassadors in negotiating a treaty with France. In 1516 she helped Lorenzo secure the Duchy of Urbino, and while he was away she ruled Florence remotely from Rome. Alfonsina thus is another example of the exceptional opportunities in politics and diplomacy that became open to aristocratic women during the period of the Italian wars.

The Resurgence of the Church

By the second decade of the sixteenth century the papacy had become a formidable political and military power, with enormous influence both on the Italian Peninsula and in European affairs. The resolution of the fourteenth-century schism in 1417 had permitted the Latin Curia to return from Avignon to Rome, and over the fifteenth and early sixteenth centuries it grew larger and more cosmopolitan. Rome attracted wealthy, aristocratic clerics from all of Italy as well as Spain, making the curial administration more complex. In tandem, the popes became increasingly like the other western European monarchs and Ottoman sultans, sustained by growing bureaucracies. However, despite the growth of papal power and prestige, and the formation of an elaborate bureaucracy, the leaders of western Christendom still had to contend with long-standing challenges from the congregation of believers. For centuries people from all social classes had consistently embraced their religion and manifested their devotion, whether in good works like caring for the needy or commemorating the dead, or in constructing chapels and decorating altars, or in conducting religious processions and celebrating feast days. Religion was a fundamental component of daily life. A number of abuses on the part of the clergy, however, had remained undisciplined, fostering a persistent strain of anticlericalism. This was evident as early as when Boccaccio was writing the *Decameron* during the mid-fourteenth century, with his caricature of lusty and greedy friars. In England Chaucer as well painted critical snapshots of the clergy in his *Canterbury Tales*. In the sixteenth century the problem of a corrupt papacy and clerical abuse became central to Christian reformers with humanist training in Italy, such as Erasmus of Rotterdam (see Chapter 6). Among the clerical offenses was the absenteeism of bishops, the purchase of church offices, the moral debauchery and greed of the priesthood, and the overall failure of the clergy to tend to the devotional needs of the people. The rate of literacy had steadily risen over the fifteenth century, and Christians were looking for more meaningful sermons and model behavior to guide them in daily life. Reformers in northern Europe like Erasmus offered guidance on how to lead a pious, Christian life. They also promoted the education of youth and raising the levels of literacy, a goal that would be taken up by the religious orders of Ursulines and Jesuits as well as the northern humanists in the Germanic lands and England (see Chapter 6). Erasmus had studied with the Brethren of the Common Life, a group of Catholic laymen who devoted themselves to charity and to teaching the Scriptures, founding schools with high standards. The movement, which advocated for Modern Devotion, spread from the Netherlands to fifteenth- and sixteenth-century Germany and helped pave the way toward a Protestant Reformation.

Perhaps the greatest challenge on the table was the advent of Protestantism, which first grained ground in Saxony with Martin Luther's objections to the sale of indulgences (pardons for sins) in 1517. Luther, thanks to the printing press and the support of the German nobility, galvanized what was more than a century of discontent with Catholicism and with the behavior of the Catholic clergy. The call for reform was to some degree a call to turn back the clock to more spiritual and less material times, and in that way a repudiation of Renaissance secularism. But at the same time the reformers, most of whom were trained in humanist schools, affirmed the achievements of Renaissance philologists by applying the tools of humanist scholarship to produce new biblical editions in the vernacular (see Chapter 6) that made the scriptures more accessible to the literate masses. They also took up the humanist theme of reading the scriptures without the interpretation of the clergy in order to form a direct relationship with God. A skilled rhetorician with solid humanist training, the former Augustinian friar took his reform movement outside of the Latin Church by 1525 and effected a permanent religious schism among Christians throughout Europe. In the following decade, England under Henry VIII would follow suit, splitting from Rome and making the king the head of the Anglican Church. In Rome, the papacy was forced to confront both the criticisms of the clergy and the spread of Protestantism.

The Catholic response to religious schism took a variety of forms, which historians have described both as "reform" and as "counter-reform." The first was a revitalization of religious life through activism from within; the second, a reaction to protestant movements overall as well as to other non-Christians, such as Jews, Muslims, and social outcasts who had been relegated to the margins of society. These efforts were both comprehensive and widespread. In general terms, reformers aimed to better educate the clergy and reinforce the mandate for clerical celibacy. But perhaps most important of all was their aim to reach out to the poor and needy in order to stop the flight of Catholics to Protestantism. Leading these efforts were such auspicious nobles as Gasparo Contarini (1483–1542), a Venetian senator, diplomat, and humanist scholar who had studied at the University of Padua. Contarini had served as the Venetian ambassador to the court of the emperor Charles V (1520–25) as well as ambassador to the papal court in Rome (1528–30). He strove to enforce greater moral discipline among the clergy. Moreover, as a diplomat and humanist he advocated convening a general council to reach some degree of compromise with Protestants and reunite the Christian church. Another noble who joined the cause of reform was Gian Matteo Giberti, the son of a Genoese admiral who served as the bishop of Verona. Giberti, like Contarini, also attacked clerical abuse and focused his efforts on reaching the needy. He was instrumental in founding orphanages, schools, poor relief, and education for the priesthood.

A number of already well-established groups embraced the theme of spiritual revival during the first two decades of the sixteenth century. Among them were the Benedictines, Franciscans, and Augustinians as well as the confraternities of lay piety. In addition, new orders like the Capuchins (1528) sprung up to minister to the sick and poor, a cause that became tremendously popular with the masses. One very successful order was the Oratory of Divine Love, founded in Genoa in 1497 under the advice and inspiration of the mystic aristocrat Caterina Fieschi (1447–1510). The Oratory, which spread to several Italian cities in central and north Italy, was devoted to learning, prayer, charity, and public service. Among its members, which included laymen as well as clergy, was Gian Pietro Carafa (1476–1559), who became Pope Paul IV (1555–59). At the higher levels of the church hierarchy, prelates joined the Theatines, a brotherhood founded in 1524 that was devoted to study, meditation, preaching, and charity.

Women mystics and teachers also participated in the revitalization of the Catholic Church. The most famous was Angela Merici of Brescia (1474–1540), who devoted her career to the education of young girls. In 1535 Merici founded the first teaching order of women, the Ursulines. Unlike other female orders, the Ursulines at first were not cloistered nuns. They taught in the homes of their students. By the late sixteenth century, however, they were cloistered and in 1612 came under the Augustinian rule of celibacy, poverty, and obedience. Their movement spread throughout Europe and beyond.

The other important teaching order founded around the same time as the Ursulines was the Society of Jesus, known as the Jesuits. A hierarchical organization established by the Spaniard Ignatius Loyola (1491–1556) and endorsed by the papacy in 1540, the Jesuits demanded obedience and great discipline. Their purpose was to educate youth in the doctrine of the church and to convert pagans and non-Christians. Above all, the mission of the Jesuits was to fight Protestantism. They established schools that taught both scholasticism and humanism throughout Italy, Europe, Asia, Africa, and the Americas.

Catholic thinkers made some attempt at doctrinal compromise with the Protestants at the Council of Trent, a meeting of Europe's high clergy which convened three times between 1545 and 1563 in a small town on the southern slope of the Austrian Alps. However, the effort of Christian humanists to reach those Catholic theologians who subscribed to more traditional religious practices and thinking failed. Catholic prelates reaffirmed the status quo, which included endorsing the Vulgate bible, the seven sacraments, and the importance of performing good works. Further, they reaffirmed the infallibility of the papacy and denounced Protestantism. Where theologians at Trent made some new inroads was in the realm of marriage rites, stipulating that the banns must be published three times, the couple must express mutual consent, consent must be voiced before a parish priest and witnesses, and the marriage needed to be registered. Trentine prelates also made provisions for the education of the clergy and reiterated the church's prohibition of clerical concubinage. These were lofty aims with uneven results. Perhaps where Trent, and the Catholic Reformation in general, had its most positive results was in reaching the masses, through charitable endeavors such as foundling homes, orphanages, hospitals, and asylums for women. Reformers reached those masses both by performing good works and through the new styles in painting, sculpture, and architecture that emerged with the proliferation of new buildings to accommodate the growing number of religious orders. The purpose of this artistic output was both to teach the doctrines of the church and to generate piety by engaging the emotions of its viewers.

Targets of Oppression: Heretics and Sex Workers

The sixteenth-century church in Italy became increasingly dogmatic, disciplinary, and repressive, a stance that found support among the peninsula's secular rulers. This aspect of the Catholic response to religious change began under Pope Paul III (1534–49), whose initiatives and ultimate failure to reach some agreement with Protestants in some ways marked the end of the Renaissance papacy and the beginning of the Counter-Reformation Church. Paul III entrusted the arm of repression to his cardinal, Gian Pietro Carafa (1476–1559), who in 1542 introduced a papal inquisition to stamp out Protestantism in Italy. A tribunal of six cardinals served as inquisitors under Carafa's leadership and were assisted by informants from all social classes. The inquisitors tried heresy, sorcery, and false pretenses of sainthood throughout Italy, both in city and countryside and among the rich and the humble. When Carafa became Pope Paul IV (1555–59), he also established the Index of Banned Books, which forbade the reading of such authors as Erasmus, Machiavelli, and Rabelais as well as the Muslim Qur'an. New standards in artistic subject matter were also applied, namely the elimination of nudes in painting as well as all reference to subscribers of Protestantism. This program of repression continued under successive popes well into the seventeenth century.

BOX 8.1 THE RELIGIOUS REPUDIATION OF ART

In the final session of the Council of Trent in 1563, theologians weighed in on the subject matter and styles of Renaissance art. They exhorted artists, and implicitly their patrons, to avoid all lasciviousness, particularly in sacred settings. Moreover, they assigned bishops the task of censoring the artwork that reached their district churches. With this, the nude figures in the famous *Last Judgment* (Figure 8.3) of Michelangelo Buonarotti in the Sistine Chapel came under fire. Shortly after the meeting of the council, the Mannerist painter Daniele da Volterra painted over the genitalia in the fresco with drapery. A decade later, in 1573, the work of another famous painter underwent church censorship. Paolo Veronese faced the wrath of the Venetian Inquisition when he painted a number of disorderly scenes with buffoons, drunken Germans, and dwarfs in his *Last Supper*. To circumvent the destruction of the work and his own punishment, he renamed the painting The *Feast in the House of Levi* (Figure 8.4).

FIGURE 8.3 Michelangelo Buonarotti (1475–1564). *The Last Judgment* (1536–1541). Fresco. Sistine Chapel, Vatican Museums, Rome, Italy.

FIGURE 8.4 Paolo Veronese (1528–1588). *Feast in the House of Levi* (1573). Oil on canvas. Galleria dell' Accademia, Venice, Italy.

Venice followed Rome in 1547 with its own system of surveillance and repression, creating an inquisition for heresy, and later witchcraft. Rome staffed the Venetian tribunal with an auditor, an inquisitor, a fiscal lawyer, and a notary. However, three Venetian noblemen actually supervised the activities of the tribunal. Their first target was Lutherans and Anabaptists, considered a menace to the unity of Venetian territories. In fact the city of Venice itself was home to several protestant groups, which included itinerant priests and friars, various boarders lodged in rooming houses, and a large colony of German merchants and laborers. Many artists and writers had also come to Venice after the Imperial forces sacked Rome in 1527. They were joined by journeymen printers from France and Savoy who found gainful employment in the Venetian printing houses that were carrying protestant writings to a wide-ranging readership. The nearby town of Padua also hosted messengers of new, protestant ideas, largely among the university students arriving from northern Europe.

BOX 8.2 DOMENICO SCANDELLA (1532–1559): A SIXTEENTH-CENTURY MILLER TRIED AND BURNED FOR HERESY

Most people had not received formal instruction in the Latin catechism of the Catholic Church. Their religious beliefs and practices were grounded both in their daily material experiences and in the sermons they may have heard during religious services. As the Catholic Inquisitions in Rome and Venice gained force and interest not only in the unorthodox ideas of the learned but also in those of ordinary people, they encountered what they quickly condemned to be heretics. This was the fate of one Domenico Scandella (1532–1599), called Menocchio, a miller from Montereale Valcellina in northeast Italy. He was first tried for heresy by the Venetian Inquisition in 1583, but retracted his stated ideas in 1584 and thus was spared a death sentence. After spending 20 months in prison, he was placed under house arrest and required to wear the sign of a burning cross on his clothing that signified he was a heretic. But Menocchio did not cease to talk about his ideas with the villagers and passing travelers who visited his mill. Thus, he was arrested again in 1598 and burned in 1599.

Menocchio was not an illiterate peasant. He had reading widely, including perhaps the Muslim Qur'an. From his various readings he synthesized his beliefs. Among his unconventional ideas was a rejection of the Catholic sacraments, including baptism, the rite that brings infants into the religious congregation, and the necessity of a parish priest in order to marry. He also doubted the virginity of Christ's mother, Mary. But his views also contained a strong element of anticlericalism. He accused prelates of making their living from laws and commandments that were their own human inventions. He went as far as to call them demonic. Menocchio also attacked the wealth of the clergy, whom he thought made their living by oppressing the poor. The Latin mass and ecclesiastical court procedures conducted in Latin, he proclaimed, were a ruse, for the poor could not understand what was being said. Everyone, including heretics, Christians, Jews, and Turks, according to Menocchio, were God's children.

Further Reading: Ginzburg, Carlo. *The Cheese and the Worms. The Cosmos of a Sixteenth-Century Miller.* Baltimore, MD: Johns Hopkins University Press, reprint edition 1992.

In Venice a variety of ideas associated with religious change and deemed dangerous by the aristocratic state were circulating. For example, one group of skilled artisans with a high level of literacy began to argue for greater social equality. They were joined by the poor and illiterate who were seeking material improvements, such as holding property in common. This group began to target the wealth and privileges of the Catholic hierarchy. Meeting in biblical reading groups, they also rejected Catholicism. Another group, millenarians matriculated in Venice's more elite crafts, were less interested in overturning the social and political order and more intent on gaining religious autonomy, including the right to read and interpret Scriptures for themselves. The advocates of egalitarianism and alternative forms of worship quickly came under the scrutiny and repressive force of the Venetian Inquisition.

The Venetian Inquisition treated Jews, whose financial resources as lenders and merchants were important to the Venetian government, with more toleration, provided that they did not proselytize. However, authorities kept a vigilant eye on Christians who flirted with Judaism. Marriage between Christians and Jews was heavily frowned upon. The Venetian government had only permitted Jews to live within the city for the first time in 1516, while other Italian cities had welcomed the Jewish nation long before. Venice was motivated to change course because of the financial resources of the Jews, who lent the state money during the critical years of the Italian wars. However, the Jewish community was carefully contained in one section of the city, which came to be known as the ghetto, and required to wear yellow berets. The gates of this segregated community were closed at night, and its Jewish inhabitants were obliged by the Venetian state to pay the salaries of the officials that guarded them. Only physicians were permitted to leave the ghetto at night, in order to attend their patients.

FIGURE 8.5 School of Tintoretto (*c.* 1575). *Veronica Franco*. Oil on canvas. Worchester Art Museum, Massachusetts, USA.

By the last two decades of the sixteenth century most of the so-called heretics that were in danger of coming before the Venetian Inquisition for challenging Catholic doctrine had fled Venice. The inquisition then changed its focus and began to persecute perpetrators of witchcraft, magic, and superstition; those who blasphemed God, the saints, and the church; and those who pretended to appropriate the sacred and spiritual powers of the church. Most of these violators were women from the lower classes, who were continuing the traditions of their ancestors as folk healers. However, the inquisitors had little tolerance or understanding of folk culture, which interfered with the church and state's claims to hold ultimate authority. Secular magistrates also became particularly anxious over female incantations and potions that might deceive men of their ranks to wed women of the lower classes and thus taint the purity of the aristocratic, hereditary elite. The Venetian Senate emanated dire warnings in the form of broad sheets and laws against potential violators. Thus the anxieties over heresy gave way to fears about the powers and sexuality of women, whose urges, physicians and natural philosophers following Aristotle believed, were uncontrollable. Thenceforward unmarried women were to be segregated and cloistered, while folk healers were either driven out of the city or imprisoned.

BOX 8.3 VERONICA FRANCO (1546–1591): A SIXTEENTH-CENTURY POET AND COURTESAN

Veronica Franco (Figure 8.5) was a poet and courtesan in sixteenth-century Venice. Although born into the prestigious citizen class of the city, a second-tier hereditary elite, Franco's mother was too poor to provide her daughter with a dowry in order to wed. Instead the young woman was educated by her brother's tutor in the humanities, including classical Latin, and learned to sing, dance, and play an instrument. She was a member of the highest tier of sex workers in Venice, the courtesans, culturally refined women who associated and had sexual relations with upper-class males. They were the only women permitted to enter the libraries of the city. Franco was best known for her poetry, some of which referred to her own experiences with love, and her written letters, which were often received by the patrician elites of her time as advice. She enjoyed a wide and influential reputation with Venice's leading political figures and at one time with King Henry III of France.

Franco held no illusions about the hard life that awaited sex workers, even ones of her more elevated social station. She offered at one point to help the daughter of one of her courtesan friends to enter the Casa delle Zitelle, a refuge for girls in peril. She strongly warned the mother to protect her daughter's virtue in a dangerous world where poor girls might fall prey. Franco underlined the importance of female virginity in order for a young woman to make a decent marriage. The courtesan condemned the life of sex workers, who were vulnerable to being robbed or murdered and also to contracting debilitating diseases. Franco's fortunes changed after 1575, the year of a great plague in Venice. Many sex workers were targeted by church and state officials looking for scapegoats to blame for the onset of pestilence. Two years later the Venetian Inquisition charged the courtesan with witchcraft. She was believed to have placed members of the male aristocracy under her spell. Eventually the charges were dropped. In 1577 she petitioned the Venetian government to establish an asylum for repentant prostitutes. The government did undertake such a program, but without Franco's participation. Her later years are clouded in obscurity.

Further Reading: Rosenthal, Margaret. *The Honest Courtesan: Veronica Franco, Citizen and Writer in Sixteenth-Century Venice.* Chicago, IL: University of Chicago Press, 1992.

In the context of the Catholic Reformation and Counter-Reformation, female sex workers, who had been long tolerated in Italian cities, came under the watchful eye of religious and civic authorities. Some of these women worked in state-approved districts, for magistrates thought them a necessary evil to accommodate the sexual energies of unmarried men as well as a lucrative source of tax revenues. Other sex workers were not under legal supervision and spatial segregation, but rather operated clandestinely. Port cities attracted both an international labor force that included Poles, Germans, English, Spanish, and Dalmatians and more local migrants. Venice, for example, housed sex workers from the Friuli to its northeast; the Veneto and Lombardy to its west; and the Romagna, Tuscany, and Naples to its south. Rome housed an international workforce. In addition to these laborers on the move, however, there were also local inhabitants that sold sex as community insiders. These women were tenants, consumers, and neighbors. Some were single and without kin; still others were married and either separated from their husbands or working together with them. Many were mothers. All were constrained to support themselves and their families, either sustaining sex work over the long term or as a means to temporarily resolve their financial troubles. In general, they were deprived of an idealized patriarchal household under male supervision. For them, and the business owners that profited from their activities, sex as a commodity became more important than how it was morally perceived. Moralists, however, socially constructed them as fallen women, and governments began to exert greater discipline over them.

The problem of prostitution was intricately linked to that of dire poverty. The sixteenth century was particularly burdensome for rural peoples. It witnessed dramatic demographic pressure, periodic food shortages, and skyrocketing wheat prices. Many of the rural poor took refuge in the cities and towns of the peninsula. The alleviation of their poverty became of utmost importance. The impetus for reform came from both secular and the religious sources discussed earlier. Venice provides an ideal example. At the state level several secular institutions arose to cleanse the city of vice. Among them was a magistracy to supervise moral behavior in convents and monasteries (1521) and a tribunal called the Magistrates of Blasphemy (1537) that punished moral offenses against the state, God, and the Virgin Mary as well as gambling and prostitution. At the same time, at the community level, the confraternities as well as individual testators strove both to save lost souls and to address the urgent social needs that resulted in prostitution, poverty, and crime. Venetians founded a home for repentant prostitutes, called the Convertite, during the 1530s. The women pledged to lead lives of austerity and follow the rules of chastity and obedience laid down by St. Augustine. In 1562 the Convertite became cloistered. Another institution, the Zitelle Periclitanti, sponsored by the Paulines in Venice, took in virgins in peril between the ages of nine and twelve, some of whose mothers had resorted to selling sex. The girls learned to cook and sew and were given small dowries to either marry or enter a convent. For married women who no longer lived with their husbands and were in danger of losing their modesty, the Venetian community established the Soccorso in 1577. Women in failed marriages, wives with abusive husbands, and wives whose husbands accused them of adultery found safety there.

It must be added that women were in danger not only of losing their modesty, an important social currency, but also of contracting syphilis, a disease that had arrived in Europe following contact with the Americas and which had become endemic among both men and women throughout the peninsula after the Italian wars. In Venice some of the men and women who were afflicted with venereal disease entered a specialized hospital for the "incurable," which was established in 1522 by the Company of Divine Love. Those who refused treatment were expelled by the ministers of Public Health. Moreover, the outcasts whom the voluntary charities failed to reclaim, as well as those groups and individuals who openly exercised unorthodox ways, encountered the repressive forces of the state's tribunals as well as that of the Holy Inquisition, with whom the Venetian patriciate collaborated. A moral and disciplined society fit well with the ideals of this aristocratic state.

Economic Vitality and Material Consumption

Well into the seventeenth century some areas of the peninsula, particularly Venice and Genoa, continued to ride the wave of prosperity with economies that survived the ravages of warfare and the disruption of trade and manufacture. Iberian trade between Atlantic Europe and Asia as well as the Americas would eventually overtake Italian Mediterranean commerce by the third decade of the seventeenth century. Both the English and the Dutch also made advancements in global commerce, at the expense of the Italians. However, throughout the sixteenth century the axes of commercial development would continue to center on the Mediterranean and Greater Asia for city-states like Venice. The Genoese, on the other hand, became fruitfully anchored in economic activities outside of Italy and linked to Iberian exploration and discovery. They helped create a sugar-based economy in Madeira and financed commercial shipping to the Americas. They traded in sugar, hides, medicines, and cochineal. From London they imported low-grade textiles and from Sicily they purchased grain. After 1568 they shifted from commercial activities to handling the loans of the Spanish crown as well as financing the importation of South American silver. Genoese bankers thus experienced a kind of Golden Age until about 1650.

Venice's commercial vitality during the sixteenth century also continued to prosper thanks to the efforts of diplomats, merchants, and pilgrims. Oarsmen, tailors, bakers, cooks, smiths, pharmacists, and physicians also accompanied merchants to Venetian colonies in Constantinople, Aleppo, Tripoli, Cairo, and Alexandria, journeys and sojourns that inevitably fostered awareness of a globalized material culture. As the sixteenth century progressed, fewer Venetian nobles engaged in trade because of its risks. Competition for the Republic's Aegean possessions with the Ottomans led to some commercial losses, particularly that of Cyprus in 1571, a source of salt, cotton, sugar, and grain. However, the Ottoman threat in Mediterranean waters subsided after 1574. The republic did suffer from banking problems in the 1570s and 1580s, and it also lost some ground in the spice trade when the Portuguese discovered a route to Indonesia via the Cape of Good Hope. Thus toward the end of the century nobles allowed more of the city's Spanish and Portuguese Jews to run their eastern Mediterranean and Levantine markets. However, it is important to emphasize that Venice's geopolitical, economic, and cultural connections with the Ottoman Empire continued.

Venetian nobles turned increasingly to investments in real estate and agriculture on their mainland (see the example of Villa Barbaro in Figure 8.2). They divested the church and the peasantry of property and began intensive land reclamation, applying wind and waterpower to milling, fulling, and pumping. The Dutch had led the way in mastering swamp and marsh drainage, but in Italy canal building reached a new height not just in the Veneto but also in Lombardy. Agrarian academies in Padua and Brescia sprung up to study how to improve agricultural technology and to develop better cereal production as well as new crops to overcome the subsistence crises that were weighing on a growing population. They were places of innovation in the natural and mechanical sciences. One result of this was the importation of maize, called Turkish or west Indian grain, from the Americas. Ground into polenta, a kind of corn meal, it saved the populace from famine. There was also more intense cultivation of rice and mulberry plants for silk production. At the end of the sixteenth century

Venice hired Galileo Galilei (1564–1642) to teach both fortifications and mechanics at the University of Padua. While there the famed scientist invented a hydraulic device for improved irrigation and drainage. The agrarian academies also integrated livestock-raising with grain cultivation. Importantly, the administrative elites in Venice and its subject cities devised tools to avert famine.

Meanwhile Venice's home economy boasted among the largest industrial bases in Europe, especially in shipbuilding. The city was a magnet for migrants from various parts of Italy and abroad, male and female, seeking work in the wool and silk industries, the manufacture of glass and leather, goldsmithing, copper, and blacksmithing. Venice itself was also a major center of the printing industry, where Aldus Manutius (c. 1459/52–1515) established the Aldine Press in 1494. Elsewhere in the republic, the Bresciano, Venice's wealthiest province on the mainland border with Lombardy, also provided labor opportunities to many with its metallurgy, mining, and arms industries. Arms production was particularly lucrative in this bellicose period, with its swords, pikes, arquebuses, and cannons. Women as well as men worked in the mining industries of the Lombard Valtrompia. Other areas of the regional state gave work to mostly female laborers and their children in small cottage industries that revolved around spinning, weaving, and embroider, industries that centered on the household. This was also the case in the Kingdom of Naples, where the silk industry thrived.

Economic activity in Venice, and throughout its landed possessions on the mainland, fueled the cultural vitality of nobles and wealthy citizens. It also furnished new opportunities for work and some degree of purchasing power for artisans, shopkeepers, and merchants. Nobles adhered to the classical past and Roman traditions in their palaces and villas, but they also collected Islamic artifacts; Isnik, Turkish, and Indian wares; and Asian carpets from the Ottoman lands. Venetian manufactures made and exported their own versions of some of these items, such as Syrian glass and Islamic metalwork. Beyond the Venetian nobility, there was a high demand for textiles throughout the Italian Peninsula and abroad, which were used in both fashion and home décor, home furnishings, paintings, and other domestic goods whose production offered great potential for profit.

The marketplace became an extraordinary venue of exchange not just for nobles but also for the artisans and shopkeepers who made and sold luxury goods. At every social station there was some degree of purchasing power, or potential for inheritance, and thus some degree of material consumption. Sumptuary laws, that is, laws that regulated spending commensurate with one's social status, are a testament to this. Among the more prosperous, these hierarchical laws were often transgressed. But even servants sometimes had the good fortune to be gifted with precious treasures in the wills of their masters and mistresses. Thus Venetian homes were filled with artisanal work, including decorated beds and chests, fancy dining tables, tapestried upholsteries, painted hangings, and fancy dinnerware. Artisans did not just make material objects; they made cultural artifacts. Moreover, they experienced them in their homes, which were family places of honor and pride; in their guild halls and confraternities, which reflected the values of their working community; in their churches, where they expressed religious devotion; and in their neighborhoods when they commemorated significant events. Sixteenth-century luxury production and consumption, thus, were an important testament to their cultural awareness.

This description of sixteenth-century economic vitality, however, comes with an important caveat: the majority of the population did not thrive from the exchange taking place on the celebrated trade routes, nor on handmade luxury products. Some eked out a living as itinerant rural peddlers to cities, towns, villages, and farms, but most people relied on the raw materials that were produced at home. Wage earners largely received limited earnings in de-based coinage. They lived apart from material consumption and artistic production. Most of their income was expended on foodstuffs and a few household items. Their houses, unlike the stone palaces that were embellishing city and countryside, were made from cheap lumber and earthen materials. They wore homespun linen or coarse wool and also relied largely on used clothing. Cities were large receptacles for the rural poor. Two cases exemplify this. In the small Adriatic port of Pescara, linked with Atlantic trade, 75 percent of its population was living in makeshift shelters in 1564. In Genoa, the poor sold themselves as galley slaves. We can easily argue that the Italian Renaissance in material culture did not reach the mass of peoples but was rather a limited phenomenon.

Conclusion

The sixteenth century brought dramatic changes to the Italian Peninsula. The independent Italian regimes of the early Renaissance fell to the larger and more resourceful centralizing European states to their west, with Spain assuming predominance by mid-century. Italian elites learned to adapt to Spanish rule. At the same time, they consolidated their political power, closing their ranks to new social energies, investing in landed enterprise, and engineering marital strategies that would preserve their financial hegemony. Both oligarchic and princely regimes slowly replaced the corporate ideals of the early Renaissance with more aristocratic values and courtly lifestyles similar to those of the western European nobilities. They still enjoyed enormous wealth. Industrial enterprise, especially in textiles, continued to thrive in the major cities and some of the smaller towns, and Venice and Genoa still enjoyed formidable commercial strength. The former retained its Mediterranean trading links; the latter turned its attention to Atlantic trade and monetary lending.

The papacy rose in power during this century, becoming as much a princely court as the other monarchies of Europe, but external developments linked to the advent of Protestantism and religious splits from Catholic leadership in Rome also brought internal change within the Catholic Church. Both the clergy and the laity engaged in programs of revitalization that targeted the spiritual and material needs of a broad segment of society, while a more militant papacy trumpeted the triumph of the Catholic Church over Protestantism, a cultural stance that would spread to all of Europe and continue into the next century. At the same time, the church's demand for greater moral discipline and religious orthodoxy, largely embraced by secular authorities, bred social intolerance and division. Prelates encountered various forms of resistance to official church culture from peoples they branded as heretics, prostitutes, sodomites, witches, and sorcerers. In the midst of all these changes the sixteenth century witnessed an efflorescence of literary and artistic achievement that underlines how power and culture can develop at different rates. Italy's elites may have lost their political insularity, but they still had an abundance of wealth with which to fund the flowering culture of the High Renaissance (see Chapter 9) as well as that of the Baroque period that followed.

Think Critically

1. What vulnerabilities resulted in the fall of Italian regimes?
2. Why and how did Italy's elites move toward aristocratization? How did marriage strategies aid this process? What role did aristocratic women play in Italian politics?
3. What measures did the Catholic Church take to revitalize religious life and reform clerical laxity?
4. How and why did the Catholic Church become more intrusive and oppressive during the sixteenth century? Which groups were targeted and why?
5. Where was Italian commercial competition emerging? What accounted for Italian economic resilience?

Further Exploration

1. Compare the resources of the Spanish and French monarchies in terms of tax resources, population size, and military power and bureaucracies to those of any given Italian city-state.

2. What were the developments that gradually changed Renaissance culture? How was that culture, particularly in applying the tools of humanistic learning, taking root in Europe?

Further Reading

Brown, Patrician Fortini. *Private Lives in Renaissance Venice: Art, Architecture, and the Family*. New Haven, CT: Yale University Press, 2004. Analyzes the domestic, social, and political context of Venetian art.

Cipolla, Carlo M. *Before the Industrial Revolution. European Society and Economy, 1000–1700*. New York: Norton, 1976. A survey of the economic and cultural factors that preceded the Industrial Revolution.

Dandelet, Thomas. *Spanish Rome, 1500–1700*. New Haven, CT: Yale University Press, 2001. A study of how Spanish monarchs and their agents brought Rome and the papacy under their control.

Ericksen, Paula Hohti. *Artisans, Objects, and Everyday Life in Renaissance Italy*. Amsterdam: University of Amsterdam Press, 2020. An exploration of how artisans experienced the material and cultural world of Renaissance Italy.

Ferraro, Joanne. *Family and Public Life in Brescia. The Social Foundations of the Venetian State*. Cambridge, UK: Cambridge University Press, 1993. An exploration of family behavior among the ruling elites of Brescia and their relationships with the Venetian state.

Ferraro, Joanne. "Making a Living. The Sex Trade in Early Modern Venice." *The American Historical Review*, 123:1 (2018). A close analysis of prostitution in early modern Venice, placed in world comparative perspective.

Ferraro, Joanne. "The Manufacture and Movement of Goods." In *The Renaissance World*. Edited by John J. Martin, 87–100. New Jersey: Routledge, 2007. A general survey of hand manufacture and trade in Renaissance Italy.

Ferraro, Joanne M. *Venice: History of the Floating City*. New York: Cambridge University Press, 2012. Traces the history of Venice from its sixth-century beginnings to the twenty-first century.

Ginzburg, Carlo. *The Cheese and the Worms: The Cosmos of a Sixteenth-Century Miller*. Translated by Anne and John Tedeschi. Harmondsworth, Middlesex, England: Penguin, 1980. The story of a miller in the northeastern part of the Venetian state who faces the inquisition on charges of heresy.

Hanlon, Gregory. *Early Modern Italy, 1550–1800. Three Seasons in European History*. New York: St. Martin's Press, 2000. A thorough survey of early modern Italy.

James, Carolyn. *A Renaissance Marriage. The Political and Personal Alliance of Isabella d'Este and Francesco Gonzaga, 1490–1519*. Oxford, UK: Oxford University Press, 2020. A case study of a dynastic marriage that sheds new light on the role of the aristocratic family in the political and diplomatic dynamics of the Italian regional states.

Martin, John J. *Venice's Hidden Heretics*. Berkeley: University of California Press, 1993. A close examination of the groups that were suspected of or charged with heresy in Venice.

Rosenthal, Margaret. *The Honest Courtesan: Veronica Franco, Citizen and Writer in Sixteenth-Century Venice*. Chicago: University of Chicago Press, 1992. The biography of the famous poet who made her living as a courtesan.

Ruggiero, Guido. *Binding Passions. Tales of Magic, Marriage, and Power at the End of the Renaissance*. Oxford, UK: Oxford University Press, 1993. An analysis of popular culture in relationship to love and marriage through a series of engaging tales.

Ruggiero, Guido. *The Renaissance in Italy. A Social and Cultural History of the Rinascimento*. Cambridge, UK: Cambridge University Press, 2015. An original and important new interpretation of the Renaissance in Italy.

Strocchia, Sharon. *Nuns and Nunneries in Renaissance Florence*. Baltimore, MD: Johns Hopkins University Press, 2009. Highlights the importance of convents and nuns in shaping the social, cultural, and economic history of Florence.

Storey, Tessa. *Carnal Commerce in Counter-Reformation Rome*. Cambridge, UK: Cambridge University Press, 2008. An in-depth study of prostitution in Rome and of the lives of women who sold sex to make a living.

9

Sixteenth-Century Culture

FIGURE 9.1 Raphael (1483–1520). *The School of Athens* (1511). Fresco. Vatican Museums, Rome, Italy.

Timeline

c. 1487	Leonardo draws his *Vitruvian Man*
1494	Aldine Press established in Venice
1492	Columbus reaches Hispaniola
1493	Columbus's second voyage
c. 1495/98	Leonardo begins *The Last Supper*
1497	Vasco de Gama sails to India
c. 1499	Amerigo Vespucci travels to South America (to 1504)
1500	Cabral reaches Brazil. Treaty of Granada
1501	Michelangelo begins sculpting *The David*
1502	Columbus's fourth voyage
1502	Sultan Bayezid II begins design of bridge over the Golden Horn
c. 1503	Erasmus publishes the *Enchiridion* (*Handbook of a Christian Knight*); Leonardo begins his *Mona Lisa*
1505	Michelangelo's statue of *Moses*
c.1506/08	Giorgione paints *The Tempest*
1506	Reuchlin publishes Latin-Hebrew grammar. Bramante begins the building of St. Peter's Basilica
1507	Waldseemüller writes *Cosmographiae introduction*
1508	Raphael begins decorating the papal apartments
1509	Erasmus writes *Praise of Folly*. Raphael begins painting *The School of Athens*. Battle of Agnadello. Vittoria Colonna becomes part of the literary circle of Costanza d'Avalos, Duchess of Francavilla
1512	Michelangelo finishes the Sistine Ceiling
1513	Machiavelli writes *The Prince*
1516	Ariosto writes *Orlando Furioso*. Erasmus *New Testament* published
1517	Completion of the Polyglot New Testament; c. 1517 Machiavelli writes *The Discourses on Titus Livy*; Luther writes *The 95 Theses*
1518	Veronica Gambara begins rule of Correggio (to 1550)
1519	Death of Leonardo da Vinci
c. 1519	Michelangelo begins Medici tombs
1520s	Guicciardini writes *Dialogue on the Government of Florence*
1522	Luther's *New Testament* published
1524	Giovanni Verrazzano explored the Atlantic Coast of North America
1528	Castiglione's *Book of the Courtier* published

1534	Titian begins to paint the *Presentation of the Virgin*
1536	Michelangelo begins painting *The Last Judgment* in the Sistine Chapel (to 1541)
1537	Guicciardini begins his *History of Italy*; Jacobo Sansovino begins building Library of San Marco in Venice
1540	Tintoretto painting for Venice's artisan community
1543	Copernicus's *De Revolutionibus* published
1543	Vesalius publishes *On the Structure of the Human Body*
c. 1546	Titian paints Doge of Venice, Andrea Gritti
1550	Sinan designs the Süleymaniye in Istanbul
1554	Jacobo Sansovino begins building Ca'Corner della Ca'Grande in Venice
1555	Sofanisba Anguissola paints *The Chess Game*
1561	Sofanisba Anguissola paints a portrait of Margaret of Parma
1576	Palladio begins building Church of the Rendentore in Venice
1578	Tintoretto paints ceiling of the Sala delle Quattro Porte in Doge's Palace, Venice
1609	Galileo constructs a telescope
1610	Galileo publishes the *Starry Messenger*

The Intellectual Response to Political Change

In Italy, the repeated invasions and confusing installation of new regimes prompted some intellectuals to pen caustic satires and launch moral indictments at the peninsula's ruling classes. The fragile regimes of despots and oligarchies had caved. The subjects of the various city-states, devastated by incessant warfare and growing taxation, showed little loyalty to their Italian rulers and little inclination to defend Italian rule. They had experienced political corruption and rule by brute force. Thus, in many ways the collapse of the various republics and principalities was due to a fundamental lack of political cohesion or military solidarity. Confronted with the powerful monarchies of France and Spain, Italy's fragile regimes were easily overthrown. With larger populations and greater tax resources, the Hapsburg and Valois kings availed themselves of a monopoly of military force, bigger armies, new weapons, and new fortifications.

A witness to these momentous political changes, the famous sixteenth-century writer Niccolò Machiavelli (1469–1527) offered profound insights into the peninsula's plight. The son of a lawyer with a solid humanist education, Machiavelli had invested much of his career in Florentine politics. He had also been a first-hand witness to intercity power politics and corruption on the peninsula. In 1498 he became Florence's Secretary to the Chancellery for Foreign Affairs and War in the new republican government that followed Piero de' Medici's expulsion. He also served as Florence's diplomatic ambassador to the politician and military commander Cesare Borgia as well as to Rome and France. In 1506, he organized a citizen militia under the government of Piero Soderini, Florence's new leader. Drawing on ancient Rome as his model, Machiavelli believed Florence needed a citizen militia. Experience had taught him that mercenary companies were not sufficiently loyal. His experiment, however, failed. Florence lost its war with Pisa, the militia was disbanded, and Piero Soderini's government fell in 1512. That year the Medici returned to Florence with the help of a Spanish army, driving Soderini into exile. Machiavelli was exiled as well, his lifelong career in politics ending in disgrace. He thus set out to write about the ills of corrupt government in one of his major works, *The Discourses on Livy* (1517; published in 1531). There he advocated for a rebirth of the Roman republican model, with leaders that would practice civic morality. The Italian city-states, he lamented, had succumbed to the whims of Fortune, a classical idea whereby humans hold little control over their destiny. In this cynical period of exile from public service he also wrote *The Prince*, his most famous and influential work. It was a handbook for rulers, exhorting them to exercise *virtù*, or strong will power and skill in political affairs, and to pay little heed to moral principles. Machiavelli argued that it was *virtù* that had once made Italy great; its deterioration had produced ineffective governments and had resulted in foreign invasions. In *The Prince* Machiavelli justified lying, cheating, stealing, and even murder if these behaviors in leadership advanced the interests of the state. *The Prince*, a work of deep pessimism grounded in Italian misfortunes, became a new statement about the nature of statecraft, which, as a work in progress, needed to be understood and improved upon quite separately from the moral precepts of the church.

There has been much scholarly debate about Machiavelli's intent on writing *The Prince*. Some argue that it was supposed to be a book of instruction for Giuliano de Medici on how to govern the Romagna region and not an all-encompassing treatise. They point out that Machiavelli's views are best represented in his *Discourses on Livy*. Importantly, for the history of political thought, is the author's vision of the state as an autonomous power, controlled by its own laws and the needs of the citizenry, that must be completely secular and without church interference. This was a viewpoint that recalled the work of an earlier thinker, Marsilio of Padua (*c.* 1270–*c.* 1342), who wrote his *Defensor Pacis* in 1324 while pro-imperialists and pro-papists were vying for power in the Italian cities. An advisor to the anti-papal party, Marsilio advocated for an autonomous, secular state that would provide order and stability and would receive legitimacy from its citizens. The church soon declared him a heretic. But this strain of thought, from Marsilio to Machiavelli, was at the core of Renaissance discussions about the concept of a state during the sixteenth century. From medieval

FIGURE 9.2 Raphael Sanzio (1483–1520). *Portrait of Baldassare Castiglione* (1514–1515). Oil on canvas. Louvre Museum, Paris, France.

times it had been conceived of as a contract between the public and the private and between secular and religious jurisdictions. Secular and material interests, however, had driven state development in the various competing regions of the Italian Peninsula over the fifteenth century and included the European transalpine powers in the century's final decades. The sixteenth century brought new critics of both church and state, debating in the midst of religious reformations, to revisit the legal history of the state. Some envisioned it more as its own separate unit of government, in opposition to the church's claims of universal authority, while others supported the sovereignty of the church.

Machiavelli's contemporary, Baldassare Castiglione (1478–1529) (Figure 9.2), a trained humanist who served in the courts of Milan, Mantua, Urbino, Rome, and Spain during his career, also dealt with questions of the state and of morality. Like Machiavelli, Castiglione attempted to offer a remedy for the decline of the Italian city-states and the onslaught of foreign invasions. Also like Machiavelli, Castiglione turned to the concept of *virtù* and called for both ladies and gentlemen of the courts to apply this ideal to their lifestyles. In his *Courtier*, written in 1513–18 and published in Venice in 1528, he praised the qualities of noble birth, honor and grace, the expression of effortlessness (*sprezzatura*), and military prowess for men. The ideal courtier would be emotionally composed, adept at elegant and confident rhetoric and conversation, and noble in bearing. Both athletic and skilled in the military arts, he would also be well-grounded in the humanities, the classics, and the fine arts. Ladies, he opined, were essential, and society must love and honor them. The ideal lady was soft, delicate, sweet, and beautiful. She must be a good conversationalist and fashionably dressed. She must show courage and skill, and above all, she must be chaste. Castiglione also added that both sexes must have musical ability, artistic taste, and wit. This formula was cast in the form of a fictional conversation amid music, dancing, and games at the court of Urbino. There courtiers and prelates gathered. Among them were important political players from the courts of Italy, such as the scholar and poet Pietro Bembo, the noble prelate from Verona Ludovico da Canossa, and the exiled Medici heir, Giuliano. Castiglione ultimately advocated for rule by a prince who was to be sustained by an aristocratic hierarchy. Above all he exhorted courtiers to advise their princes to act with *virtù*. Castiglione was inspired by the work of ancient writers such as Plato, who had written on the ideal republic, and Cicero, who was the ideal orator. At the same time, his *magnum opus* was a nostalgic evocation of the court of Urbino, where Castiglione had spent some time during his youth.

The Courtier addressed the concerns of women as well as men. Among its readers were the poet Vittoria Colonna; Isabella d'Este, the marchioness of Mantua, and the author's own mother. The debate about women's worth and women's role in court society is among the discussions in this work, with the misogynous Gasparo Pallavicino advocating that the female sex focus on being beautiful, dressing fashionably, and making pleasant conversation. Other participants emphasized the importance of women in playing a civilized role in court society. Printed in multiple languages and widely distributed, *The Courtier* became a classic model for aristocratic behavior and conversation in sixteenth-century European court circles.

In contrast to Castiglione, other authors were outspoken critics of courtiers, cardinals, and princes. Among them was the satirist and writer of lusty comedies Pietro Aretino (1492–1556), who was a generation younger than Machiavelli. Under the patronage of the banker Agostino Chigi (1466–1520) and then Pope Leo X (1475–1521), Aretino wrote such biting criticisms of court society that he was known as the "scourge of princes." With his irreverent wit he insulted nobles of all ranks, attacked the institution of marriage, praised prostitution, and mocked the kind of civic morality to which Machiavelli and Castiglione had subscribed. Yet another writer, Ludovico Ariosto (1474–1553), also shunned the aristocratic and courtly world of his early adulthood. Educated first in law and then in the classics, Ariosto served as a gentleman and poet in the court of Cardinal Ippolito d'Este in Ferrara. There he also enjoyed the patronage of the cardinal's older sister, Isabella d'Este (1474–1539), famous in her own right for her erudition and artistic commissions. Later he served as a diplomat for Cardinal Ippolito's older brother, Alfonso. Under the Este's courtly patronage, Ariosto wrote the epic romance for which he is famous, *Orlando Furioso*. This chivalric satire may certainly be read as escapist literature, with its creation of an alternative world to the one Ariosto lived in. But it also served a practical purpose meant to address the challenges of war and leadership that his patrons, the Este of Ferrara, faced. *Orlando Furioso* is filled with descriptions of the brutality of warfare and the destructiveness of love. In it the *virtù* of the Italian courtier fails, becoming the victim of Fortune; so much so that the writer created a heroic woman character, Bradamante, as the new arbiter of skill and success.

Thus, a succession of writers offered their perspectives on the decline of the Italian city-state and the beginning of foreign rule. Some looked for antidotes to the continual succession of political crises; others abandoned the cause in favor of escapist literature. After 1530, some political leaders studied and praised the Venetian constitution, which had outlasted the despotic and republican regimes of the fifteenth century and had already enjoyed nearly three hundred years of continuity. They saw the Venetian constitution in ideal terms, as a mixture of monarchy, aristocracy, and democracy. Among them was Gaspare Contarini (1483–1542), a member of the Venetian Senate who had also entered the ranks of the city's most powerful council, the Ten. Contarini characterized Venetian government as mixed, but in reality the city was ruled by just a few wealthy families. Contarini repeated what has become known as the myth of Venice, that the republic endured because it had been ruled by a wise and not entirely self-interested merchant elite. His work was quickly translated from the Latin into Italian, French, and English and was read by those seeking a more perfect governmental constitution.

The Florentine aristocrat Francesco Guicciardini (1483–1540) also favored a mixed republican constitution in his *Dialogue on the Government of Florence*. However, when he retired from public life, having served the restored Medici and the papacies of Leo X and Clement VII (1478–1534), he concluded it was not possible to revive past forms of government. Instead, rulers must base their actions on the shifting circumstances of the day. In his *History of Italy, 1494–1534*, classical models of government are conspicuously absent. Nor is history employed to predict when Fortune would derail the best-laid plans. Guicciardini instead analyzes the actions of historical actors to explain the decline of the city-state tradition and then advocates for a return to republicanism and independence from a foreign yoke. If only Italy's elites would band together, divest the corrupt papacy of its temporal powers, and drive the Hapsburgs out. His wish, however, was not fulfilled. Italy's elites could not turn back the clock.

Women writers of the period, who were beginning to occupy a central place in Italian cultural life, approached the changing political fortunes of the Italian Peninsula differently. They were somewhat more practical, using their social status, their wealth, and above all their aristocratic ties and circulation at the Italian courts to advance their own political interests. Some even established their own academies in Milan, Venice, and Florence as well as Mantua, Ischia, and Siena. Although they were trained in Latin, they began to write treatises and letters in the vernacular, as well as sonnets, poems, and dialogues. Two of the most notable and frequently published female intellectuals of the time, Veronica Gambara and Vittoria Colonna, actually embraced imperial power and the new aristocratic order of the emperor Charles V.

Veronica Gambara (1485–1550), a distinguished aristocrat from one of the oldest and most important dynasties in the Lombard province of Brescia, came from a robust line of female intellectuals, including her great-aunts, the humanist poets Ginevre and Isotta Nogarola. Gambara was also the niece of Emilia Pia, one of the interlocutors in Castiglione's *Courtier*. Like her predecessors, this renowned poet received a humanist education, studying Latin, Greek, philosophy, theology, and scripture. At the age of seventeen, she began a correspondence with Pietro Bembo (1470–1547), one of Italy's leading Petrarchan poets. Her poetry and letters touched on politics, spirituality, and love for her husband, writings that earned her the accolades of her male contemporaries, Bembo and Ariosto would describe her as an important representative of Italian virtù and someone who could assist Italy in regaining its lost political and cultural stature.

Gambara's marriage in 1509 at the age of twenty-four to the Count of Correggio, a fiefdom in Emilia Romagna, put her in a position to be a key player in Italian politics, especially in widowhood (1518 and 1550). She took charge of the political and military affairs of her late husband's realm, and her court became a noted center for conversation, visited by many of the major writers of the day as well as artists, diplomats, and officials. Her political position was further strengthened by her brother, the papal governor of Bologna and host to the Holy Roman Emperor Charles V's papal crowning in 1530. Gambara astutely positioned herself in alignment with Charles, who was designing a new Spanish-dominated aristocratic order on the peninsula. In 1530 the emperor visited her estate, promising

FIGURE 9.3 Sebastiano del Piombo (1485–1547). *Portrait of Vittoria Colonna* (1520–1525). Oil on wood. Museu Nacional d' Art de Catalunya, Barcelona, Spain.

his protection to Correggio. In return she wrote sonnets celebrating his virtues and accomplishments, including his military campaigns against the Ottomans and his restoration of the Medici regime in Florence. But Gambara became more than a poet: she was also a major political figure active in the planning of the emperor's new aristocratic order for the Italian Peninsula and thus a prime example of the connection between literary figures and political leaders.

Vittoria Colonna (1492–1547) (Figure 9.3), like Gambara, also hailed from the highest aristocratic ranks of the peninsula. She was the daughter of Fabrizio Colonna, grand constable of the Kingdom of Naples, and of Agnese da Montefeltro, daughter of the Duke of Urbino. At the age of three she was betrothed to Fernando Francesco d' Ávalos, son of the Marquise di Pescara, at the behest of Ferdinand, King of Naples, who hoped to establish an alliance between the Colonna family and the Spanish throne. When Colonna was nine, her family moved to Ischia, the home of her future husband. There she received a humanist education in literature and the arts from another luminary, Costanza d' Àvalos, the aunt of her future husband. When Colonna finally married, she had little occasion to see her husband, who was frequently away in service as a military captain for Emperor Charles V. She managed to hold some sway over her husband's political career, persuading him not to join a pro-French league against the emperor after the Battle of Pavia (1525) or from accepting the crown of Naples from the French as a reward for his loyalty. Àvalos died in 1525. Now widowed, independently wealthy, and childless, Colonna retreated into a convent in Rome as a secular boarder and resisted all pressure by the Colonna family and the pope to accept a second marriage proposal. During the late 1520s and early 1530s, she lived once again in Ischia and socialized with Neapolitan intellectuals. Among them were a number of Spanish aristocrats who were discussing the new Lutheran ideas. While she may not have advocated for the new religion, she was influenced by such primary ideas as justification by faith alone to achieve salvation. By the late 1530s she was involved with reform spirituality and with Christian humanists' attempt to find some compromise between Catholic and Protestant theologies. She became devoted to spiritual writing, greatly aided by her aristocratic status, her wealth, and her widowhood, which gave her a degree of independence. Colonna remained in close correspondence with the major religious thinkers of the day. Also, it was during this period that she became a close friend of the famous artist Michelangelo, to whom she dedicated a book of sonnets. Like Veronica Gambara, she was praised by male writers of the period for her chastity, love of learning, and wifely devotion, qualities they thought would aid Italy in regaining its cultural and political stature. Like Gambara, she was willing to ally with Spanish imperial powers to protect her political interests.

New Methods of Scholarly Inquiry

During the sixteenth century the new discoveries were challenging old ways of thinking and with them the traditional authority of the Latin Church. Throughout the Middle Ages the church had served as a powerful sponsor of intellectual ideas, one that endorsed specific methods of inquiry and included a closed circle of ancient natural philosophers into its accepted canon. For nearly a millennium the purpose of studying the natural world had been to understand God, and from the eleventh century scientific inquiry revolved around church-dominated universities such as the one in Padua. Aristotle's writings had served as the foundation for speculation in natural science, but Ptolemy's corrections of Aristotle's cosmos, which were centered on a motionless earth, also enjoyed wide acceptance. During the fifteenth century, however, humanism furnished new tools for the advancement of science and mathematics when scholars transcribed texts from the original Greek into Latin. They also discovered texts from the Hellenistic period (c. 323 BCE–c. 31 CE) that had been unknown during the Middle Ages. The new translations, together with observations of how planetary objects moved, prompted some humanists to push back against the Aristotelian tradition and view nature and the physical universe as something that could be better understood and even managed. Moreover, they prioritized instrumental observation and mathematical precision, methods that had developed out of the artisanal world of the commercial cities in Italy and northern Europe.

An early example of a humanist who worked in opposition to Aristotle is Nicolas of Cusa (1401–1464), a German prelate and mystic from Heidelberg who left his hometown in 1417 to study at the University of Padua, at the time an epicenter of Greek scholarship. Nicolas became part of the Italian intellectual milieu that was seeking alternatives to Aristotelianism (see Chapter 6). He studied Platonic philosophy, Euclidian geometry, Ptolemaic astronomy, and Archimedean physics; he also wanted to learn Greek. Nicolas's approach to scientific inquiry was mathematical, based on his understandings of both Plato and Euclid. He rejected the current notion of a finite, qualitative universe and proposed approaching understanding it through experience rather than exclusively through textual interpretation. He argued, in opposition to Aristotle, that the universe was neither finite nor geocentric but rather without boundaries. Other scholars followed in Nicolas's footsteps, and Padua became an important center of new experimental methods of inquiry.

The most renowned revisionist, however, was Nicolas Copernicus (1473–1543), a Polish priest and polymath who had also studied at the University of Padua almost a century after Nicolas of Cusa. In 1514 Copernicus circulated a small pamphlet to his community of scholars that proposed an alternate understanding of the cosmos. He studied both Aristotle and Ptolemy, and in this sense was applying humanist methods of inquiry. However, he aimed to refine, if not correct, ancient astronomical practice. In the end he arrived at different conclusions through the use of mathematical calculation, positing that the earth was not the center of the universe but rather just another planet revolving around the sun. Yet he still sustained in part the Ptolemaic system, with its circular and uniform motion of the planets in crystalline spheres.

Copernicus was not the first astronomer to advance a heliocentric idea. The groundwork for his work had been laid long before. Medieval Islamic astronomers, using translations of Ptolemy's *Almagest* and *Geography* from

Greek into Arabic, had also critiqued the second-century natural philosopher. Copernicus's theories and calculations were similar to those of the Persian scholar Nasir al-Din al-Tusi (1201–1274) and the Arab astronomer Ibn al-Shatir (1304–1375), whose works had been translated into Latin and defused throughout Europe. The Polish priest's sojourn in Italy—in Bologna, Rome, and Padua—had afforded him the opportunity to consult a treasure trove of such medieval manuscripts. Moreover, he was exposed to the ideas of other scholars who were studying astronomy, astrology, and mathematics as well as the ancient Greek language. Copernicus had German predecessors who during the fifteenth century were rereading and revising Ptolemy in the original language, and across the Mediterranean in Istanbul a center for Ptolemaic studies was also designed to carry out similar studies. Copernicus thus bore the fruit of a wide body of humanistic and scientific learning.

Between 1514 and 1543 Copernicus refined his theory, rereading texts and making new calculations. However, he hesitated to publish his findings, for they contradicted both the Bible and the Latin Church's views. It was not until close to his death in 1543 that his heliocentric concept of the universe was published, as *De revolutionibus orbium coelestium* (*On the Revolutions of the Celestial Spheres*). Thanks to the printing press, Copernicus's ideas essentially brought the work of natural Greek philosophers to its conclusion, but opened the door to further scientific inquiry. Among the later scholars who made supporting calculations and found the Aristotelian-Ptolemaic system inadequate was Tycho Brahe (1546–1601), a Danish astronomer and astrologer, who accurately measured astronomical motions, and his student Johannes Kepler (1571–1630), who replaced both Copernicus's and Brahe's circular motion of the planets with an elliptical shape and orbits of variable speeds. Finally, it was Galileo Galilei (1564–1642), a mathematician who first taught in Pisa and then at the University of Padua, who during the seventeenth century demonstrated the Copernican theory with the aid of his newly devised telescope based on that of a lens grinder in Flanders. Galileo opened a new era in astronomy with his observations of the stars, currying the favor and patronage of the Florentine Grand Duke Cosimo II (1590–1621), an era, however, that would come under the critical eyes of Aristotelian theologians.

Neither Copernicus nor Galileo were alone in attempting to bring Aristotelian ideas to a conclusion. In Italy Bernardino Telesio (1509–1588) of Cosenza, in southern Italy, also opposed Aristotle, maintaining that nature worked according to laws. Another thinker, Giordano Bruno (1548–1600), a Dominican friar from Nola near Naples, accepted Copernicus and went on to suggest the universe was infinite and without a center. Both Telesio and Bruno's works were placed on the *Index of Banned Books* (1559), and Bruno was imprisoned and burned. Still another Dominican from southern Italy, Tommaso Campanella (1568–1639), following Telesio and Bruno, defended Galileo and was imprisoned for twenty-seven years, from 1599 to 1626.

A heliocentric rather than geocentric universe, thus, was the subject of a contentious debate among scholars both outside and within the church that culminated with the trial by the Roman Inquisition of Galileo in 1633. A number of crucial questions about authority were raised. Who would decide on conflicts between traditional and new theories? The church or natural philosophers? The Copernican theory that Galileo ultimately proved appeared to substitute a spiritual meaning of the universe with a mathematical one, and for this reason a number of church theologians, albeit not all, pushed back, and those in power were able to force the scientist to recant. With the trial of Galileo, the church reaffirmed its singular authority to explain the workings of the universe.

Despite the geocentric and heliocentric controversies, and the outcome of Galileo's trial, it is evident that the supremacy of Aristotelian traditions was already coming to an end with the new methods of knowing about the nature and workings of the universe initiated during the second half of the fifteenth century. This evolved in part out of humanist methods of inquiry, which involved both producing new translations from the Greek into Latin and eventually into the vernacular and questioning the usefulness of ancient texts. It also evolved out of the establishment of scientific libraries, which afforded scholars a larger assortment of texts and the opportunity to arrive at new ideas (see Chapter 6). Still further, it was a product of putting the body of scientific knowledge into print so that new works could be produced and rapidly distributed not just in astronomy or cosmology but also in natural philosophy, mathematics, medicine, and natural history. This was, then, the overarching intellectual trajectory that eventually led to such revisionist scholarship as that of Copernicus.

There was also another long term and overarching trajectory, beyond texts and their interpretation, that produced new ways of knowing about the workings of the universe: the expertise that derived from observation and practical experience. Galileo would not have come to his more precise calculations about heliocentrism without the aid of the telescope that was based on the work of a Flemish lens grinder. That innovation came out of an artisan's workshop. So too did Michelangelo's true-to-life sculptures of the human form, for the artist had deepened his knowledge of the body through engagement in human dissection. Moreover, he, and other artists of the period, also observed live models in addition to antique statues. The importance of observation was also evident in the case of the Flemish-born physician Andreas Vesalius (1514–1564), whose anatomical discoveries emerged around the same time as Copernicus was publishing his theories. Trained at the University of Padua, Vesalius became an advocate for Galenic anatomy. He had carefully read the medieval texts of Islamic physicians, but at the same time he emphasized the importance of observation, through human dissection. He wrote a series of anatomical tables in 1543, complete with detailed illustrations, that would be used widely in medical work throughout Europe.

Copernicus's and Vesalius's new theories achieved wide circulation thanks to a number of other processes that had developed over the previous centuries out of the artisan's workshop: how to produce paper and ink and how to print; how to use linear perspective to produce three-dimensional illustrations on paper, an offshoot of the better understanding of Arabic mathematics, Euclidean geometry, and Roman architecture (see Chapter 7); how to produce illustrations from woodcuts; and how to bind books and make leather covers for them. These are just a few examples of the practical expertise that contributed to the production and dissemination of new knowledge, in this case through the visual and textual messages that emanated from bookmaking. While some of these techniques were rooted in the workshops of the Italian Peninsula's commercial cities, others such as the expertise in instrument making and printing developed in northern Europe.

Copernicus's and Vesalius's discoveries were circulating at the same time that Europeans were reassessing their place on the globe. The Portuguese had found a route down the west coast of Africa and around the Cape of Good Hope to India and southeast Asia. The Spanish had made contact with the Americas. In 1494 the pope signed the Treaty of Tordesillas, assuming the authority to divide the newly discovered lands outside Europe between the Portuguese and Spanish empires, along a meridian 370 leagues west of the Cape Verde islands, off the west coast of Africa (see Map 8.1). Portuguese, Spanish, and Italian missionaries set off to these new lands to convert the indigenous peoples to Christianity, a move designed to place Rome at the center of the Catholic world.

The Iberian discoveries had generated new scientific curiosity about the natural world and the ways in which these European powers could obtain commercial benefits from the natural resources of their growing empires. New ship design (first caravels and later galleons), new cartography, better knowledge of the Atlantic winds, and a variety of navigational instruments including the Chinese magnetized needle and compass, the Arab kamal, and the ancient astrolabe had made it possible for explorers under Portuguese, Genoese, and Spanish sponsorship to reach new lands. The discoveries showed the inadequacies of ancient knowledge and prompted thinkers to reconsider how nature was to be explored. Ptolemy, Plato, and Aristotle, for example, had not known about the Americas, so how useful were they? How useful was Galenic medicine and ancient pharmacopoeia in understanding the flora, fauna, minerals, and microbes of the Americas? The immune systems of Europeans and Native Americans? How useful was the biblical account of human history? How relative were European cultural values? The New World rattled the conventional body of knowledge and conventional ways of knowing. The writings of the ancients were not as useful as employing direct observation, collection of specimens, and analysis. Scientific curiosity demanded improved understandings of astronomy, mathematics, geography, natural history, and medicine. At the same time new advancements became essential to commercial enterprise and empire building. Scientific inquiry, thus, acquired new status and a new purpose in the service of European, and Ottoman for that matter, powers.

The epistemological advancements outlined earlier were not specifically Renaissance Italian achievements. Yet they were in part rooted in the medieval and Renaissance history of the Italian Peninsula, where the translation of ancient texts and humanist methods of inquiry had first developed. They were also rooted in part in the artisanal workshops of the peninsula's commercial cities, where craftspeople learned to make things from nature, and in the demands for mathematical education associated with commerce, business, and manufacture. Other knowledge came from the observations of astrologers or the compounds of alchemists, again through hands-on, learned expertise. Yet after 1492 the world had changed. European monarchies had invaded Italian lands. Gunpowder had changed the mechanics of warfare. The magnet had changed navigation, and printing had revolutionized the way knowledge was transmitted. The Italian Peninsula was thereafter part of a larger and rapidly changing world.

Nor was the Roman Church's claim to be at the center of the Christian world secure, either. It was being challenged not just by the discoveries of natural philosophers but also by Christian scholars and their followers who refused to accept its singular authority to interpret the Bible. Once again, while such challenges were not entirely Italian phenomena, they were rooted in Italian humanism and had important consequences for Italy. Scholars challenged the way scholastic theologians applied the doctrines of ancient philosophers to religious ideas. During the medieval period several theologians, but especially Thomas Aquinas (1225–1274), strove to combine Christian faith with Aristotle and to make it more intelligible through a method of question, argument, and conclusion called disputation. Humanists found this method tedious and hard to understand; it was not in their estimation eloquent. Erasmus and his followers questioned the authority of Aristotle, instead relying more heavily on the Bible, which they had read in its original languages and then translated into the vernacular. The writings of the Church Fathers, translated from their original languages, could also be consulted as sources for Christian teaching. The translations into the vernacular made it possible for believers to simply read the Scriptures and use the teachings of Jesus for themselves, without medieval commentaries or the sermons of the Catholic clergy. Perhaps the most important development accompanying this trend of thought was the new polyglot edition of the Bible published in 1520 in Spain that included all four original languages: Greek, Hebrew, Chaldean, and Latin. Christian humanists traveled to Spain from around Europe to participate in the project. Erasmus of Rotterdam had produced his own printed edition of the Greek New Testament in 1516, and the protestant reformer Martin Luther (see later) used that edition for his German translation of the Bible, published in 1522. For Martin Luther, the Bible was the sole fount for religious understanding. Printing facilitated the circulation of additional Bibles in a variety of vernacular languages, and it was not just the Christian Bible that was being studied. Jewish intellectuals, including the grammarian, teacher, and scholar Elia Levita (1469–1549), analyzed the Hebrew tradition from a humanistic philological perspective. The new editions of the Bible, which put the scriptures in the hands of both laypeople and clerics, sparked new thinking about moral and religious matters. These various reinterpretations of scripture contributed to the fragmentation of the Christian church.

During the very decades when Copernicus was working out his theories, another independent thinker, also grounded in humanistic study, would challenge the authority of the Latin Church and the office of the papacy. The German priest and Augustinian friar Martin Luther (1483–1546), offended by the church's sale of indulgences to pardon sins, called for internal reform, and when none was forthcoming began a separate church. Thus an advocate of scholarly inquiry based on experiment, observation, and mathematical calculation and a disciple of religious reform trained in humanist critical methods helped usher in the new intellectual order, one that challenged a thousand years of medieval scholastic authority.

A new order, however, would not come without formidable resistance. What ensued over the sixteenth and seventeenth centuries was a bitter struggle between new thinkers and church authorities over competing claims for the truth. There were also independent thinkers that fell in neither camp, such as Paracelsus (c. 1493–1541), a Swiss-German physician and alchemist who rejected Greek medical theories in favor of the homeopathy of peasants and wise women, spiritualism, and chemistry. Gradually natural philosophy became a central way of inquiry, challenging centuries of medieval scholasticism and Aristotelianism as methodological guides to ways of knowing. The study of mechanization and materialism in the practical arts and as a way to serve contemporary needs would come to replace the old, medieval hierarchy. Moreover, the papacy would lose its stature as an ultimate authority. An expanding world had become more complex. Europe was no longer at its center, nor was the earth the center of the cosmos.

High and Late Renaissance in Art

While lay writers fretted over crumbling Italian regimes and the installation of French and Spanish powers and theologians sparred with scientists and religious reformers, important new styles in art emerged during the first two decades of the sixteenth century that would outlive Italy's crises in authority. The technical achievements in painting rooted in the previous century—linear perspective, realism, light and shade, and the depiction of nature and the human psyche—reached their zenith first with Leonardo da Vinci (1452–1519) and then with Michelangelo Buonarroti (1475–1564) and Raphael Sanzio (1483–1520), who each in turn established new norms for the genre. In Venice, Giorgione (1478–1510), and later his pupil Titian (c. 1488/90–1576), would usher in new palettes of bold, textured colors in oil and subject matter that broke with the classic past. Scholars view

FIGURE 9.4 Leonardo da Vinci (1452–1519). *The Last Supper* (1495–1498). Mural painting. Church of Santa Maria delle Grazie, Milan, Italy.

these groundbreaking artists as the exponents of a new phase in Western art termed the "High Renaissance" (1500–1520), one that would see the status of great artists elevated from mere craftsmen to respected professionals.

Leonardo, an apprentice of humble origins in the Florentine workshop of Verrocchio, was a pioneer of the new style in painting. Although he worked primarily in the late fifteenth century, he is included with the High Renaissance artists of the early sixteenth century because his inventiveness was considered far ahead of its time. His *Last Supper* (c. 1495–1496) (Figure 9.4), a mural painted for the refectory of the convent of Santa Maria delle Grazie in Milan completely broke with early Renaissance traditions. Its perspective is not related to the space of the room but rather seems to transcend this world for somewhere more ideal. An accomplished scientist as well as an artist, Leonardo treated painting much the same way he approached his exploration of nature, basing it on physical observation and mathematical perspective. He spent much of his time inquiring about the natural world, studying such phenomena as the anatomy of humans and animals, the structure of rocks, the properties of light, the movement of water, and the growth of flora and fauna. He applied what he learned to his painting and drawing. Among his most iconic works, the *Mona Lisa* (Figure 7.3), executed in Florence between 1503 and 1506, exhibits a new mastery of facial expression. The portrait of this Italian noblewoman whose identity is the subject of debate not only captures the human form on canvas, something fifteenth-century painters had already managed, but through the use of light and shadow Leonardo also conveys something about the inner reality and personality of the human being. The painter also introduced new portrayals of nature in his paintings, making them essential narratives rather than mere background. His hazy bluish landscapes, flowing waters, jagged peaks, and mysterious skies seem more philosophical than realistic. So too was his famous drawing of the *Vitruvian Man* (c. 1487), based on the writings of the first-century BCE architect and civil engineer who believed that squares, rectangles, and circles in buildings should be based on the proportions and measurements of the human body. The *Vitruvian Man* was an affirmation that humans hold a central place in the universe.

While the Italian wars ravaged Italian soil, the geographical axes of artistic innovation multiplied as artists looked for patrons during turbulent times. Florence was still to some degree the cradle of Renaissance art, for three of the giants ascribed to the High Renaissance—Leonardo, Michelangelo, and Raphael—began their careers there, Leonardo executing the *Mona Lisa*, Michelangelo the towering sculpture of *David*, and Raphael producing harmoniously sweet madonnas for wealthy patrons. But soon these giants were also in demand at other princely courts and republics. Rome and Venice became major centers of artistic sponsorship, the former the sphere of princes and popes; the latter the artistic domain of nobles, citizens, and charitable associations. The art patrons of these cities did not spend any time ruing political upheaval or losses. On the contrary they were keen on celebrating their past and current glories, their fame, and their fortunes. Popes and cardinals in Rome commissioned heroic and monumental forms, rich in ornamentation and grand in scale. They used art and humanist writings to emphasize their association with ancient Rome's patrician culture, combining the classical with the religious. Churches and urban palaces with lush gardens grew larger. Figures gained volume and force. Portraiture took on new dimensions, becoming ever larger, with artists paying increasing attention to the material signs of aristocratic decorum. Aristocrats were more expensively dressed, their gazes to spectators outside the pictorial plane ever more self-confident. In Venice, patricians ignored the fact that the city's foundations were rooted in the post-Roman, medieval period. Instead they invented associations with the ancient Roman Republic in architecture, painting, and sculpture. At the same time, they also became more interested in the patrician culture of antiquity, which was more orientated toward the countryside. They turned increasingly to their mainland possessions, leaving the risks of Mediterranean commerce to the Ponentine and Levantine communities in their city and concentrating more on agricultural investment and the villa culture of the ancient Roman world, with its resplendent palaces and gardens. Themes in painting thus explored the mainland landscape, growing more pastoral, poetic, and dreamy as well as more erudite.

Rome

Rome became a major center of artistic innovation under the patronage of Pope Julius II (1503–13), the delle Rovere nephew of a former pope,

Sixtus IV (1471–84). Julius benefited from enormous financial resources and was able to spend extravagantly. As a cardinal prior to becoming pope, he assembled large art collections for personal and public use and commissioned a number of civic and religious buildings. When he became pope, art became an instrument of propaganda for his office, which had fallen into disarray during the previous century amid a series of corrupt and nepotistic pontiffs. He deliberately chose the name Julius after the ancient emperor Julius Caesar who had sponsored elaborate building projects in imperial Rome. Pope Julius II chose the same classical language for his building style, undertaking considerable renovations in the city. Associating with such ancients as King Solomon, Julius aimed to renew the popular prestige of the pope. He had his image placed on medals, emblems, and other artworks showing him as a liberator and peacemaker in the midst of the Italian wars. In reality he led one of the two great European alliances as a statesman and military commander, secularizing the papal office. He stood at the hub of European diplomatic relations as Italy became the cockpit of Hapsburg and Valois rivalries. His coffers filled with both ecclesiastical and secular taxes, he had the financial means to sponsor and set the tone in culture and art.

Among Julius's most well-known commissions was the rebuilding of St. Peter's Basilica (see Figure 9.6). The Roman Church was facing serious conflicts at the time, with calls for reform from both intellectuals and the populace. The new basilica was intended to invigorate religious sentiment and become a great monument to church and state. To the shocking dismay of the Roman populace, Julius dismantled the emperor Constantine's original fourth-century church housing the remains of Saint Peter. In 1506 he engaged Donato Bramanté (1444–1514), who had been forced to leave Milan when the French ousted the Sforza in 1499, to build what was to be the largest church in Christendom, one on a massive scale similar to the monuments of ancient Rome. Based on a Greek cross plan, St. Peter's was modeled after the fourth-century Church of San Lorenzo in Milan and the imperial church architecture of the Byzantine East. Bramante, like Leonardo, was fascinated with Vitruvius's ratios and based his original plan of the new basilica on the first-century architect and civil engineer's exposition of geometric relationships. A memorial of the remains of the saint (as opposed to the actual remains) for whom the basilica was named is situated in the center of the great edifice, making the apostle essentially a Vitruvian man sitting at the heart of the Catholic world. Bramante also had plans to build a dome that would totally abandon the vertical-ribbed form Brunelleschi had executed for Florence's cathedral a century earlier in favor of a hemispheric model. However, the architect died before his plan could be realized.

Julius was also fortunate to be able to commission the artist who changed not only the course of Western art but also the role of the artist in society, Michelangelo Buonarroti (1475–1564). The son of a notary with a limited formal education in Greek and Latin, Michelangelo apprenticed in painting at the Florentine workshop of Domenico Ghirlandaio at the age of thirteen. He also trained in sculpture with a pupil of the Florentine sculptor Donatello. The young Michelangelo attracted the attention of Lorenzo de Medici, the ostensible ruler of Florence, and in 1490 was brought to live in the nobleman's palace at age of fifteen. There for the next two years he was exposed to works of art in the Medici collections as well as to the Florentine academy of scholars discussing Neoplatonism. The artist was profoundly interested in the Divine, from which he believed the creative process originated. He was also centrally focused on the human body. Like Leonardo, he spent time engaging in human dissection at a local hospital. Among the most iconic works displaying his knowledge of the body was the statue of David slaying Goliath (1501–1504), placed in the central square of Florence. The fourteen-foot-high sculpture of a muscular young man standing in bold defiance of an enemy, a veritable colossus symbolic of the Florentine Republic defending its own freedom, inaugurated the heroic style of the High Renaissance (see Figure 7.13). Michelangelo, deeply indebted to Greco-Roman sculpture which he aspired to outdo, displayed all his knowledge of anatomy as well as his belief in the human spirit through the beauty of David's body. With this magnificent work, it is not surprising that he caught the eye of Pope Julius, who in his own way wished to be portrayed in powerful partnership with both the classical and the Divine. In 1505, the pope asked Michelangelo to design a gigantic tomb for himself where St. Peter was presumed to be interred, but the work was never finished because the following year Julius redirected his funding to the building of St. Peter's. What did remain was the artist's statue of Moses, that, like the David, was a crushing figure of musculature unlike any statue since the Hellenistic period. With these works Michelangelo established a new artistic standard in sculpture.

Pope Julius also left his mark on Rome's architecture and painting. After recovering the papacy's lost lands in the Romagna and the Marche, he built the largest bureaucracy in Europe. To accommodate it, he commissioned two great palaces on the Via Giulia for his financial and legal departments. The Vatican complex, monumental in scale and classical in style, would also accommodate tournaments and theater, military parades, bull fights, and naval battles. Bramante designed the Cortile del Belvedere (begun in 1503), a courtyard modeled on classical Roman villas, to house Julius's sculpture collection. Michelangelo decorated the ceiling of the Sistine Chapel (*c.* 1508–12). Raphael Sanzio (1483–1520), also a great master in Florence and Rome during the High Renaissance, would paint the frescoes in the papal apartments, making Julius a prominent figurehead. Each artist brought significant innovations in style, though from different perspectives. Michelangelo produced heroic portrayals of bigger-than-life humans, almost transcending nature. The Sistine chapel was filled with erudite iconography, its theme based on the Old Testament with scenes from *Genesis* on the Creation and Fall. Its execution took place at the very time Julius was fighting for the independence of the Papal States against the armies of King Louis XII of France. Raphael's assignment in 1508 for the papal apartments was more temporal. The power and majesty of his figures became a paean to pontifical authority, with paintings symbolizing events of war and diplomacy and depicting the Vicar of Christ and successor to St. Peter as the guarantor of peace and stability, something he was not. In the pope's study Raphael painted the four spheres of Renaissance learning: theology, philosophy, poetry, and jurisprudence. Together they represented the humanist embrace of both worldly and spiritual wisdom, combining both Greek philosophy and Christian teaching. Among the most renowned of these paintings is *The School of Athens* (1509–1511) (see Figure 9.1), whose main subject is classical philosophy. Plato, Aristotle, and Pythagoras are gathered together on one wall, and, according to the sixteenth-century writer Giorgio Vasari, are reconciling theology with all knowledge. Raphael included the portraits of living artists in the canvas, a testament not only to the growing status of such figures as Leonardo (as Plato), Bramante (as Euclid), and Michelangelo (as Heraclitus) but also to the claim that the achievements of the Renaissance age were comparable to those of the golden age of Athens. The young painter also included a portrait of himself in the corner of the picture, gazing confidently at spectators. Other rooms portrayed Julius as a lawgiver and head of state. Raphael took his inspiration for these images from the miniatures in the pope's illuminated manuscripts, but they refer to contemporary events. Among their subjects were the wars among states, the pope's visits with dignitaries, and the liturgical, fiscal, historical, and military aspects of both the papacy and the papal curia.

BOX 9.1 SOFONISBA ANGUISSOLA (1532–1625)

Raphael was not the only one to paint important portraits. Sofonisba Anguissola (Figure 9.5) (1532–1625), born in Cremona to a minor noble family, was one of the rare women during that time period to receive an education in the fine arts. Her training was in all probability private, for standard workshops during the Renaissance were the exclusive spheres of male artisans. Her social rank also gave her the possibility of traveling, an unusual luxury for women of the age. In 1554, at age twenty-two, Anguissola traveled to Rome, where she met Michelangelo. Anguissola showed the renowned artist one of her drawings, *Boy Bitten by a Crayfish*, and he was so impressed that he gave her sketches from his notebooks to draw in her own style and then tutored her. Under Michelangelo she developed new styles of portraiture, using herself and her family as subjects. Her most famous painting was *The Chess Game* (1555), with portraits of her sisters Lucia, Minerva, and Europa in a scene

FIGURE 9.5 Sofonisba Anguissola (1532–1625). *Self Portrait*. Oil on canvas. Łańcut Castle, Łańcut, Poland.

from everyday family life. It was novel to place the family in a domestic setting rather than the more popular allegorical paintings of the period. By 1558 Anguissola's reputation was established. The Duke of Alba, in Milan, commissioned her to paint his portrait, and he was so pleased that he referred her to the Spanish court of Phillip II in Spain. She became the court painter and lady-in-waiting to Queen Elisabeth of Valois, painting several official portraits for the court during her fourteen-year residence, including Philip II's sisters and his son, Don Carlos. In 1561 she painted a portrait of Philips's sister, Margaret of Parma, for Pope Pius IV. Later she painted the king's fourth wife, Anne of Austria, after Queen Elisabeth died in childbirth in 1568. Her portraits were filled with the period's royal costumes and jewelry, in themselves historical pieces. Philip II had also been interested in engaging the Venetian Marietta Robusti (1560?–1590) as a court painter. However, her father, the renowned Jacobo Robusti, known as Tintoretto (1518–1594, see later), did not wish to part with her. Thus she remained an apprentice in her father's workshop.

Julius's successor, Leo X (Giovanni de Medici, 1475–1521; r. 1513–1521), replaced the Della Rovere pope's emblems with those of his Florentine family. The Vatican was thus adorned with Medici arms and portraits of Leo with his Florentine courtiers. (The city of Florence was also a beneficiary of Leo's position as a Medici pope. There Michelangelo designed Giuliano and Lorenzo de Medici's funerary monuments in the chapel of the Medici Church of San Lorenzo.) Pope Leo, like his predecessor, commissioned paintings alluding to diplomatic alliances, but during his term of spiritual office those relations had shifted. The Christian states of Europe had to grapple with the looming power of the Ottomans. Leo wanted King Francis I of France to lead the campaign against the Ottomans, but the French king's international interests were divided between Ottoman hegemony and that of the Hapsburg threat surrounding his kingdom. Leo commissioned imagery that was both historical and theological in nature and that portrayed himself as the supreme authority over Europe, whether in republics, principalities, or kingdoms.

Pope Leo X is also notable for his granting of indulgences, the practice of pardoning the punishment of sin. Martin Luther's critique of indulgences was the issue that started the Protestant Reformation. Leo used the donations for the reconstruction of St. Peter's Basilica, fueling protestant antipathy toward the Roman Church. The pope spent lavishly on art and charity as well as on his dynastic wars, driving the papacy into debt for years to come. During his term he was the patron of numerous altarpieces, portraits, and funerary monuments, many the work of Michelangelo and Raphael.

BOX 9.2 MICHELANGELO BUONARROTI (1475–1564) AND MIMAR SINAN (C. 1490–1588)

These two giants of sixteenth-century architecture, one working in Rome and the other in Istanbul, exemplify the cultural and artistic convergence between the Latin West and the Ottoman Empire. Both

FIGURE 9.6 St. Peter's Basilica, Rome, Italy.

worked for major political potentates, Michelangelo for Roman Catholic popes and Sinan for Ottoman sultans, both of whom in many ways were using art and architecture to advance similar programs. Both were also part of the same patronage networks. Sultan Bayezid II, for example, had consulted Leonardo da Vinci in 1502 in his construction of a bridge across the Golden Horn. He also invited Michelangelo in 1505 to submit a design. There was mutual architectural and artistic influence between Italian and Ottoman powers during this time.

Around 1550 Michelangelo and Sinan were engaged in, and perhaps competing, for the same architectural distinction: to build the biggest dome in the known world. In Michelangelo's case, in 1546 Pope Paul III asked him to complete what the deceased architect Donato Bramante had initiated, the construction of St. Peter's dome (see Figure 9.6). Sinan, on the other hand, was employed in 1550 by the sultan Süleiman the Magnificent, in many ways a rival of the Holy Roman Emperor Charles V, to construct an imperial mosque that would glorify his powers, the Süleymaniye (Figure 9.7), on a hillside overlooking the Golden Horn.

It is likely that both architects influenced one another. Sinan would have seen drawings by Italian architects throughout his career. The son of a stonemason and born Christian, he had received a technical education and become a military engineer. Later, as a Janissary commander, he had traveled extensively in Europe, an experience that contributed to his architectural and engineering skills. While his early career concentrated

FIGURE 9.7 Süleymaniye Mosque, Istanbul, Turkey.

on military infrastructure projects, he went on to become the chief royal architect for several sultans, constructing several civil and religious buildings before his commission of the great Süleymaniye Mosque. It is likely he was exposed to Michelangelo's designs for the dome of St. Peter's in Rome, for they were well-known in Istanbul. In turn, Michelangelo, was informed through diplomatic records that Sinan was building the Süleymaniye for Sultan Süleiman.

Both architects hailed from a Greco-Roman, Byzantine tradition. Sinan's Süleymaniye Mosque, like the Basilica San Marco in Venice, was heavily influenced by Hagia Sophia, a mosque that was formerly a Byzantine church. It is also probable that he was familiar with the ideas of the Italian Renaissance architect Leon Battista Alberti, a follower of the ancient engineer Vitruvius. Michelangelo was attempting to honor Bramante's plan for St. Peter's, with its perfect forms of the hemisphere and the circle as his models, and to make the dome higher than that of Hagia Sophia or other mosques. Both Michelangelo and Sinan were in some respects building the ideal religious edifice while at the same time fulfilling the similar aims of their patrons. Popes and sultans were cultural rivals as well as political ones, and each desired to have the largest amount of space under a single central dome. In the end St. Peter's height exceeded that of the Mosque, but at the time the dome of the Süleymaniye was the highest in the Ottoman Empire. For Michelangelo and Sinan, like Donato Bramante before them, the dome was based on the perfect geometrical figure of the circle, which in its own way reflected Divine perfection, for one the triumph of Christianity and for the other that of Islam. Their domes emulated the classical past, with the remains of Roman temples throughout the Mediterranean now becoming models for sacred architecture. The work of these two architects underlines the shared Greco-Roman tradition of the Mediterranean world. Whereas the West had lost its connection with the classical past during the early Middle Ages, only to recover it during the Renaissance period, the east had enjoyed uninterrupted continuity, manifest in the new architecture of the sixteenth century.

The Sack of Rome in 1527 brought the High Renaissance to a close as artists fled the city in search of more stable places to work. Michelangelo remained in Rome accepting papal commissions, but his style of painting changed, ushering in a new period in Western art called Mannerism, which in many ways was a refutation of the preceding era but still incorporated its technical achievements. Michelangelo's figures in such works as *The Last Judgment* (1536–1541) (see Figure 8.3), painted for Pope Clement VII in the Sistine Chapel, lack the ideal beauty and heroism of the Sistine ceiling, reflecting instead the gloomy atmosphere following the invasion. Other painters of the period produced figures of distorted proportions, strange colors, and bizarre subject matter. However, the diaspora of Florentine and Roman artists exported the stylistic achievements and technological innovations of High Renaissance art and architecture throughout the Italian Peninsula and all of Europe. Among the prime examples is Sansovino (1480–1570), a Florentine refugee who moved to Venice and designed the Library of San Marco in 1537, merging Gothic motifs with the Roman classical style. Later, perhaps the Veneto's greatest architect, Palladio (1508–1580), a native of Padua who had studied in Rome, adorned the Venetian mainland with classical villas and palaces (see Figure 8.2). In Venice he also revived the form of the Pantheon's central hemispheric dome in the Church of the Redentore. The Renaissance style in architecture was also exported to eastern and northern Europe over the next two centuries, and with Palladio to England and the United States.

BOX 9.3 ANDREA PALLADIO (1508–1580)

Andrea Palladio (1508–1580), a native of Padua, first apprenticed as a stonemason. He later studied in Rome and became one of the most influential individuals in the history of classical architecture. Palladio's teachings are summarized in his architectural treatise, *The Four Books of Architecture* (1570). Much of his legacy remains in Venice and the Veneto, where he designed the country villas of many families in the Venetian ruling class (see figure 8.2)—among them, the Barbaro, Cornaro, Foscari, and Pisani. One of his patrons, the humanist and scholar Gian Giorgio Trissino, gave him the name by which he became known, Palladio, an allusion to the Greek goddess of wisdom Pallas Athene and to a character in a play written by Trissino. The word *Palladio* means "wise one."

Palladio took his inspiration from Roman architecture but then selected and used the stylistic elements of this genre in innovative ways. His buildings were often constructed on elevated ground to take advantage of sweeping views of rolling hills, rivers, and gardens. Like the ancient Roman villas, they often included loggias and shaded arcades. Of note, Palladio integrated these structures into the surrounding natural environment. This style was particularly popular in English country villas. It was first adopted by Inigo Jones, who had been inspired by Palladio's ideas after visiting the Veneto countryside. Jones's first work was the Queen's House at Greenwich (1616–35). Palladio was also very influential in the United States, a country that in its formative years expressed a great affinity for the architecture and symbols of the Roman Republic. Among the most notable examples are Harvard University's Harvard Hall (1766) and Thomas Jefferson's Monticello (1772). Palladio's influence is also evident in American plantation buildings as well as many town post offices, municipal halls, and other public edifices.

Further Reading: Cooper, Tracy. *Palladio's Venice: Architecture and Society in a Renaissance Republic*. New Haven: Yale University Press, 2005.

Venice

After Raphael's death in 1520 it was the Venetians who led in oil painting, particularly with thick, vivacious colors. While the Florentines excelled in design and composition, the Venetians were more preoccupied with lush, sensuous color. The Roman and Florentine High Renaissance had taken root in Venice with the Bellini family of artists, but it was actually Giorgione (Zorzi da Castelfranco *c*. 1477–1510) who founded the Venetian school with his *Madonna Enthroned* (*c*. 1505). Similarly to Leonardo, landscape dominates his picture, but in Giorgione's case with bold-colored oils. The same applies to Giorgione's most famous painting, *The Tempest* (*c*. 1505–1510), where the landscape of the Veneto region is almost magical.

FIGURE 9.8 Giorgione (?–1510). *The Tempest* (1505). Oil on canvas. Galleria della Accademia, Venice, Italy.

Giorgione's *Tempest* (Figure 9.8) was executed at a time when Venetian patricians were turning attention to their mainland, building sumptuous country villas and spending increasingly more time as landowners rather than in commerce. The artist introduced radically new subject matter, with allegory, idyllic landscapes, and sensuous female nudes. The *Tempest*, produced around the time Venice was struggling with transalpine forces at Agnadello, still remains a mystery to art historians. It is set in the countryside, with a city in the distance. A fully clothed soldier stands next to a woman nursing a baby, who is completely nude but for a cloth covering her shoulders. The sky is lit with a bolt of lightning. The painting is both pastoral and poetic, but what did it mean? Did it presage hard times to come for the republic, which was facing a political and diplomatic crisis at the beginning of the sixteenth century? Or was it perhaps just a visual pastoral poem that really has no other meaning than to evoke the classical past with mythological-looking figures and fragments of Roman ruins? If, indeed, it has no real subject, that would make it stand out from most central Italian High Renaissance works that were often based on recognizable myths and stories. Four decades later Giorgione's pupil, Titian (Tiziano Vecelli or Vecelio, *c.* 1488/90–1576), who had also trained in the Bellini workshop, produced his celebrated portrait (*c.* 1546) of the ambitious and awe-inspiring Doge of Venice, Andrea Gritti (1455–1538; r. 1523), a political titan that has been compared to Pope Julius II. The painting is an important representation of the enduring power of the Venetian dogeship and the republic itself. Venice would ride the tide of the Italian Wars and its commercial rivalries on its seaborne Empire for yet another century. In fact, most of Venice's cultural output during the sixteenth century took no heed of contemporary political crises but rather took advantage of them to elevate the republic's status.

From the fifteenth century the ruling patricians of the Venetian Republic sharpened their myth-making images of the polity, developing an elaborate panegyric and iconography. Among their claims, advanced by the humanist Lauro Quirini, was that Venetian nobles were the direct descendants of the Romans. In fact, Venice did not hail from Roman origins, having been established on amphibious foundations in 568 CE in a lagoon. Nonetheless, by the early sixteenth century the myth was firmly embedded in humanist literature. Patricians claimed Venice was born on water the day of the Annunciation of the Virgin, that it was the new Jerusalem, and that it was the first free republic after the fall of Rome (*c.* 410 CE) in the western half of the Roman Empire. These mythical foundations were reiterated in both the sculpture and painting proudly displayed in the Palace of the Doge. Unfortunately a great fire in 1577 destroyed much of this work, which we know about from archival sources, but was the impetus for a new artistic program during the final two decades of the sixteenth century. The first-floor chambers of the Ducal Palace exhibited Venice's military victories with the canvases of Jacopo Bassano (1510–1592), Paolo Veronese (1528–1588), and Palma the Younger (1544–1628). On the third floor, Tintoretto (1518–1594) painted the ceiling of the Sala delle Quattro Porte (1577) with the story of the city's foundations. Jupiter led Venice into the Adriatic. Paolo Veronese painted Jupiter's wife Juno showering Venice with abundant riches, proclaiming that the city was blessed not only with commercial wealth but also with wise rulers. Venice was also portrayed as Justice and as Queen of Heaven throughout the city's political center as well as in the Ducal Palace with paintings by Paolo Veronese. Venice, thus, was an ideal state favored both by God and the saints as well as the ancient Roman world.

Like in sculpture and painting, the architecture of the city turned to classical magnificence, accompanied by treatises on living a noble lifestyle and emulating Rome. The turn came after the Battle of Agnadello in 1509, when the republic lost its subject cities to the Holy Roman Emperor. The devastation shook the confidence of the ruling class and became the impetus for a renovation that proclaimed their magnificence. Between 1510 and 1560 a part of the patriciate turned to ancient history. The architect Mauro Codussi's Ca' Loredan (now Vendramin-Calergi), constructed for the noble Andrea Loredan c. 1510, became the first Renaissance residence, adorned with Corinthian capitals. Other nobles followed, commissioning classical geometry and language such as the Doric, Ionic, and Corinthian orders. A prime example was Jacobo Sansovino's Ca'Corner della Ca'Grande (c. 1554–60). Monumental in size and richly ornamented, the bas-reliefs of cuirasses, shields, war trumpets, and Roman armor were designed to create a Roman genealogy for the Corner family. Again, many families, including the Dolfin and the Grimani, followed the Corner's example, portraying their families as successor of Rome.

The most significant transformation in Venetian architectural style occurred between 1530 and 1570, a time that, because of a confluence of calamities, placed various stresses on Venice. It was the period following the Sack of Rome by Imperial troops and the cementing of Spanish Hapsburg presence in Italy. It was also the time of the Catholic Counter-Reformation against the spread of Protestantism, supported by the Spanish Hapsburgs. Further, the presence of the Ottomans in the Mediterranean threatened the republic's seaborne empire. Venice was compelled to cautiously guard both its seaborne empire and its republican liberty. A pro-papal faction of the nobility undertook the Romanization of the city's political space, taking advantage of the diaspora of Rome's architects after its sack to define itself as the new Rome. Among them were Jacopo Sansovino, Michele Sanmichele (c. 1484–1559), and Sebastiano Serlio (1475–1554). Sansovino inaugurated a building program for a second Rome between 1537 and 1554, designing the Piazzetta San Marco, the construction of the Loggetta, the Library of St. Mark, and the New Mint. (Figure 3.5, left side displays the Library of St. Mark and the New Mint, juxtaposed with the right side, which displays the Gothic Palazzo Ducale.) All were reminders of ancient Rome. In turn, the nobles in the pro-papal faction, such as the Dolfin, Corner, and the Grimani mentioned earlier, built palaces in the Roman Renaissance style. It was no coincidence that the latter two families held five of Venice's eight cardinal ships between 1500 and 1550. Upon Sansovino's death, Palladio continued the classical theme, most pronounced in church building. Among the most celebrated was the Church of the Redentore (begun 1576), constructed in celebration of the end of the 1575 plague epidemic. The Redentore was a classical temple floating on water. The anti-papal faction, on the other hand, held control of the architecture of the Ducal Palace, which remained Gothic in style, in line with Venetian tradition.

The confraternities of the city, which were groups of non-nobles, also advanced iconic mythmaking, with the support of the government. Among them was the Carità (Charity), which commissioned Titian's *Presentation of the Virgin* (1534–1538), a mural that connected Venice to Rome by placing both the Doge's Palace and the Pyramid of Gaius Cestius in the composition. The confraternities also played an important role in civic life, making their presence known in their elaborate processions and works of charity. Like the patriciate, they reiterated the idea of a peaceful society governed by wise rulers. Also importantly, the confraternities emphasized their own status in the city's world of work. Nowhere is this more evident than in the works of Jacobo Tintoretto, who contributed to the artistic programs of forty-one Venetian churches. Considered a painter of the Counter-Reformation, an age when the Catholic Church was responding to the spread of Protestantism while strengthening its own internal structures, Tintoretto received commissions from some twenty-seven confraternities, making him a significant voice of in the Venetian artisan community. Among his numerous works was a painting of *Saint Barbara* for the tailors, a *Presentation of Christ at the Temple* (c. 1546–1548) for the altar of the fishmongers at the church of Santa Maria dei Carmini, a *Baptism of Christ* (1580–1582) for the boatmen at San Silvestro, and an *Adoration of the Cross* (c. 1578/81) for the linen makers' guild. Tintoretto's paintings were representative of the artisans' social world, via the patron saints of each guild. They were rendered in a vernacular language, with objects from everyday life. In *The Birth of St. John the Baptist* (late 1550s) for the Church of San Zaccaria (Figure 9.9), for example, the artist exhibits typical stone pavements and glass windows in this scene of birth from everyday life. Tintoretto's style was virtually pathbreaking, for he attached both his figures and the everyday surroundings to the space (e.g., specifically Venetian furniture and glassware) that viewers would occupy. In this way he engaged the viewer's participation in the setting, at times even bringing him or her into the pictorial space. This technique encouraged the active devotion of the masses, who observed religious images in the context of Venetian material culture.

FIGURE 9.9 Jacobo Tintoretto (1519–1594). *The Birth of St. John the Baptist* (1554). Oil on canvas. Hermitage Museum, St. Petersburg, Russia.

BOX 9.4 RENAISSANCE MUSIC

Renaissance styles in music originated in Burgundy and Flanders during the first half of the fifteenth century. The first generation of composers produced vocal and instrumental compositions with clear melodies and balanced polyphony for the Burgundian courts. At midcentury their musical styles began to spread throughout Europe, including the courts of Italy. The papacy and the princely houses of the Medici, Este, and Sforza were all competing to outdo one another in artistic production and display and that included music. Music was essential in court entertainment and in public pageantry as well as in sacred, church rituals. Each Italian prince engaged composers and musicians from both northern Europe and Italy to staff their courts and provide the city with entertainment, for musical performance was an important feature of both aristocratic and civic life, with its public weddings, civic festivals, and special events. In Medicean Florence Lorenzo de Medici founded a School of Harmony with musicians from all of Italy. Composers and vocalists adapted polyphony to both sacred and secular musical forms. Within the first were the mass and the motet, a Latin choral composition. The second included the *chanson* or song; the *frottola*, a poem set to music; and the madrigal, a song usually sung in a small group with two or three voices set to lyrics. While Italian composers borrowed from the north, they also developed their own lyricism and melodies in vocal music. Italian vernacular poetry provided the lyrics for the compositions.

By the mid-sixteenth century musical forms developed into more specific genres. Among them was sacred music, which followed the norms of the Council of Trent (1563) in emphasizing simplicity. This was best exemplified in the Roman School with the masses and motets of Pierluigi da Palestrina (c. 1525–1594). In contrast, the madrigal, cultivated at the Ferrara School of music and many of the other princely courts, became more complex. At the same time in places like Venice, church and state developed more grandiose styles of polyphonic and antiphonic music, performed in the great Basilica of San Marco between 1530 and 1600. The Venetian school also began to develop orchestration. Multiple choirs of singers together with brass and strings in various parts of the Basilica generated a musical movement that quickly spread to all of Europe. The most famous Venetian composers included Andrea (c. 1532/33–1585) and Giovanni (c. 1554/57–1612) Gabrieli and Claudio Monteverdi (1567–1643).

Conclusion

The post-invasion period on the Italian Peninsula was characterized by a series of discussions and debates that brought into question the very nature of Renaissance government and social organization as well as the traditional canon of knowledge and authority. The failure of oligarchies and despotisms to foster political cohesiveness, and to invite foreign intervention, led to an overall retreat into aristocratic lifestyles and courtly ideas. This was a tangible change from the preceding period, which had permitted more corporate participation in political and civic life. At the same time, the geographical discoveries and the new scientific findings overturned Italy's, and Europe's, place in the world as well as the earth's place in the universe. More than a thousand years of prescribed knowledge came under question. The tools of humanism aided new inquiry in science and biblical studies, calling into question scholastic learning and the infallible authority of the church. Despite all these dramatic changes, the arts, fueled by a vibrant economy, thrived. Grandeur and heroism masked the anxieties brought about by changing times. The Renaissance was giving way to new concerns, ones characterized by spiritual revival and religious controversy, by aristocratic dominance and courtly society, by leisurely lifestyles in country villas, and by the influence of Spain on Italian life.

Think Critically

1. What were the various solutions sixteenth-century writers offered to stave off the political decline of Italy?
2. How did the humanist tools of learning advance explorations in science? In biblical studies?
3. Who were the major patrons of art and architecture during the High Renaissance? What messages did the patrons of Rome and Venice wish to convey through artistic works and who was their audience?

Further Exploration

1. How did heliocentrism challenge the authority of the church?
2. What role did the artisanal workshop play in learning about the natural world?
3. How did the discovery of the Americas challenge European preeminence?

Further Reading

Primary Sources

Ariosto, Ludovico. *Orlando Furioso*. Oxford, UK: Oxford University Press, 2008.
Castiglione, Baldassare. *Book of the Courtier*. Translated by Charles S. Singleton and edited by Daniel Javitch. New York: W.W. Norton, 2002.
Cellini, Benvenuto. Introduction by George Bull. *Autobiography of Benvenuto Cellini*. London: Penguin Classics, 1999. The autobiography of a goldsmith, sculptor, and adventurer whose story describes the manners and morals of rulers and street people during the age of Michelangelo.
Colonna, Vittoria. *Sonnets for Michelangelo: A Bilingual Edition*. Edited and translated by Abigail Brundin. *The Other Voice in Early Modern Europe*. Chicago: University of Chicago Press, 2005.
Machiavelli, Niccolò. *The Prince*. Edited and translated by Peter Bondanella; Maurizio Viroli, Introduction. Oxford, UK: Oxford University Press, 2008.

Secondary Sources

Brown, Patricia Fortini. *Art and Life in Renaissance Venice*. New York: Prentice Hall and Harry N. Abrams, 1997. An exploration of art patronage among the guilds, the nobility, the church, and private families.

Brown, Patrician Fortini. *Private Lives in Renaissance Venice: Art, Architecture, and the Family*. New Haven, CT: Yale University Press, 2004. Analyzes the domestic, social, and political context of Venetian art.

Cooper, Tracy. *Palladio's Venice: Architecture and Society in a Renaissance Republic*. New Haven, CT: Yale University Press, 2005. A meticulous study of Venetian patronage of Palladio's work, including the state, charitable foundations, and convents.

Cox, Virginia. *Women's Writing in Italy*. Baltimore, MD: Johns Hopkins University Press, 2008. A comprehensive, gendered analysis of the tradition of women's writing in its broader contexts.

Ericksen, Paula Hohti. *Artisans, Objects, and Everyday Life in Renaissance Italy*. Amsterdam: University of Amsterdam Press, 2020. An in-depth study of how artisans and small local traders experienced the material and cultural Renaissance.

Ferraro, Joanne. *Venice. History of the Floating City*. Cambridge, UK: Cambridge University Press, 2012. A sweeping history of Venice from its foundations to the twenty-first century.

Findlen, Paula. "The Renaissance of Science." In *The Oxford Illustrated History of the Renaissance*. Edited by Gordon Campbell, 378–425. Oxford, UK: Oxford University Press, 2019. An important survey of the changing structures of scientific inquiry from the fourteenth to the sixteenth centuries.

Finucci, Valeria. *The Lady Vanishes: Subjectivity and Representation in Castiglione and Ariosto*. Palo Alto, CA: Stanford University Press, 1992. A study of the representation of women in Castiglione's Courtier and Ariosto's Orlando Furioso in sixteenth-century debates on women and popular narratives.

Grafton, Anthony. *Defenders of the Text: The Traditions of Scholarship in an Age of Science, 1450–1800*. Cambridge, MA: Harvard University Press, 1991. A groundbreaking work that analyzes the critical relationship between humanism and the development of natural science from the mid-fifteenth century to the beginning of the nineteenth century.

Grafton, Anthony, and April Shelford, Nancy Siraisi. *New Worlds, Ancient Texts: The Power of Tradition and the Shock of Discovery*. Cambridge, MA: Harvard University Press, 1993. A lively study of how mariners, scientists, publishers, and rulers grappled with the evidence of the New World that challenged old world texts and learning.

Hartt, Frederick, and David Wilkins. *History of Italian Art*. 7th edition. New York: Pearson, 2010. An important survey of art and architecture in Italy between *c*. 1250 and 1600.

Kempers, Bram. *Painting, Power, and Patronage. The Rise of the Professional Artist in Renaissance Italy*. London: Penguin, 1987. Traces the evolution of patronage in Italy and the professionalization of the artist.

Kirshner, Jules. *The Origins of the State in Italy, 1300–1600*. Chicago: University of Chicago Press, 1995. A collection of essays by eight distinguished scholars, who present overviews of the key problems of the emergence of the state in Europe, beginning with the Italian regional states.

Mackenney, Richard. *Venice as the Polity of Mercy. Guilds, Confraternities, and the Social order, c. 1250–1650*. Toronto: University of Toronto Press, 2019. An important study of the ordinary people of Venice, the degree to which they were empowered, and the means through which they expressed their piety and economic interests.

Richardson, Brian. *Print Culture in Renaissance Italy: The Editor and the Vernacular Text, 1470–1600.* Cambridge, UK: Cambridge University Press, 1994. Examines impact of printing and editing the texts of early writers such as Dante, Petrarch, and Boccaccio as well as contemporary works of entertainment.

Rosand, David. *Myths of Venice: The Figuration of a State.* Chapel Hill: University of North Carolina Press, 2001. Though a study of Venice's major works of art and architecture, the author illuminates how the state shaped both imagination and political thought to sustain the city's myths.

Rowland, Ingrid. *The Culture of the High Renaissance: Ancients and Moderns in Sixteenth-Century Rome.* Cambridge, UK: Cambridge University Press, 2001. This interdisciplinary study examines the culture, society, and intellectual norms between 1480 and 1520 that brought about the creativity of the High Renaissance in Italy.

Ruggiero, Guido. *The Renaissance in Italy.* New York: Cambridge University Press, 2014. An important new conceptualization and periodization of the rebirth of antique forms in Italy.

Shemek, Deanna. *Ladies Errant: Wayward Women and Social Order in Early Modern Italy.* Durham, NC: Duke University Press, 1998. With a survey of the literature devoted to the conduct of women as its starting point, this lively work analyzes the images of unruly feminine behavior in literature, paintings, legal proceedings, and public festivals.

10

Worldly Connections: The Renaissance Exchange

What Was the Renaissance in Italy?

This text envisions the Renaissance, based first in Italy but then spreading to other parts of Europe, primarily as a cultural movement focused on the revived interest in classical antiquity. It covered a broad spectrum: ancient languages and literature, art and architecture, philosophy, political and religious thought, and scientific ideas and practice. Pinpointing that movement in time and space is a complex endeavor, with no firm beginning and no certain end. It unfolded, at least on the Italian Peninsula, primarily between 1350 and 1600, while in other parts of Europe, such as England, it extended into the seventeenth century. Among the central features of Renaissance culture were a continued interest in Greco-Roman forms in language, literature, and the arts; the flowering of humanism, which included the philological study of ancient languages and the rise of the vernacular; the study of science and medicine, based both on ancient texts and direct observation and practice; and an emphasis on the nature and capabilities of humankind.

In some ways Renaissance culture during the fifteenth and sixteenth centuries built on what had come before it. The humanistic program that was so central to this culture did not clearly break with the immediate past, as Italian contemporaries claimed. On the contrary, it built upon strong medieval Mediterranean roots, first in Byzantium, then with the advent of Islamic and Jewish scholarship in Spain and Sicily, and finally with the medieval canon of study throughout Europe that embraced both classical writers and the Church Fathers, Latin philology, and the art of rhetoric. Aristotle, Seneca, and Cicero were all discussed during the Middle Ages, and rhetoric, a principal Italian humanist discipline, was also one of the seven liberal arts in the medieval educational program.

Moreover, scholasticism, the medieval approach to study that relied upon consulting ancient authorities, still thrived in universities between 1350 and 1600, both on the Italian Peninsula and throughout Europe, alongside Renaissance secularism. Scholars still turned to the Church Fathers for guidance, and some thinkers continued to write ecclesiastical history and hagiography in the medieval tradition. That is not to underestimate, however, the importance of humanist contributions to classical scholarship and to the establishment during the fifteenth and sixteenth centuries of libraries and educational programs that would have a far-reaching impact on European life.

Perhaps the clearest cultural break with the medieval age came in the realm of Italian art, with the development of perspective, a technique that not only enabled an almost mirror-like representation of the natural world but also went on to inform scientific inquiry, astronomy, cartography, mathematics, and engineering. In the art of perspective Italian artists owed a degree of their mastery to Euclidian geometry and to Arabic math and optics. They learned as well from artists in the Low Countries, where painters whose subjects ranged from botany to landscape to the material objects in domestic interiors devoted intense attention to detail and introduced the rich colors of oil paints. The artwork of the Renaissance was different than the preceding age in the way it introduced secular subjects, including portraits of individuals, classical myths, landscapes, and illustrations of daily life in addition to religious subject matter. The change was tied to the nature of patronage in Italy, which in addition to the church, also included broader segments of the middle and upper urban classes.

The Italian Peninsula also spearheaded a money culture during the thirteenth and fourteenth centuries, a momentous development that helped fund its other cultural and intellectual achievements. It was the medieval commercial revolution that made the revitalization of Italian cities possible, and with it the exposure to other cultures. Italian trading routes to the Black Sea and China and to Syria and Egypt not only funded the Renaissance in Italy but also offered the wealthy and their corps of artisan workers a treasure trove of new ideas and material artifacts from these culturally rich regions. At the same time, banking networks and trade fairs in northern Europe, which was also experiencing early urbanization but on a smaller scale, exposed Italians to additional stylistic elements, such as French Gothic architecture, Netherlandish painting, and Burgundian music. Wealthy patrons and consumers of both sexes on the Italian Peninsula absorbed these intellectual, artistic, and material traditions but then also created their own, based on a nostalgic desire to resuscitate antiquity and to reinterpret their own contemporary environment. They devised new ways of both representing and seeing reality. They hungered for new knowledge in science and medicine that would improve their lives and understanding of the naturalistic world. They created new forms of government and statecraft, for the political and economic life of the Italian city-states required civic involvement, diplomatic abilities, and training in the arts of communication and persuasion, demands that required greater skills in the humanities and that ultimately fostered a more critical attitude toward authority and tradition. The rise of the various territorial states that competed with one another for resources also demanded improved military weapons, tactics, and architecture; reliable methods of taxation; and fiscal efficiency, areas one might categorize as separate from art and ideas but that were in fact related in practical terms.

It is evident from its beginnings that there was no one history of Italian Renaissance culture, just as there is no one history of the Italian Peninsula, for Italy as a nation, or even as a concept, did not exist prior to the nineteenth century. The peninsula's various regional histories shared common threads, such as a Latinate–Christian culture, but at the same time each developed at its own pace and in its own unique way. They were to a significant degree products of their individual geographical and economic realities. Port cities such as Palermo, Naples, Pisa, and Venice as well as nodes of international trade and finance on major rivers like Florence had greater exposure to the cultures of the wider Mediterranean, North Africa, and Asia than the more insular towns and villages with agrarian economies. Milan, at the foothills of the Alps, kept strong ties with northern Europe, which was steeped in Gothic traditions. Like Milan, a number of Italian centers with princely dynasties borrowed from the medieval chivalric traditions of the north, embracing them in tandem with Greco-Roman culture. Florence was exposed to a variety of cultures throughout Europe due to its international banking networks and textile markets. Venice looked to Alexandria, Damascus, and the civilizations on the Silk Road, but it also admired ancient Rome and the cultural traditions of the north. In music, for example, the French composer Josquin des Prez (*c.* 1450–1521) made his career in Italy and led with medieval polyphonic composition, but by the late sixteenth century Venice, home to Andrea (1532–1585) and Giovanni Gabrieli (*c.* 1554–1612), became the center of innovation with polyphonic choruses and madrigal singing that made vernacular poetry into a form of word painting.

Large metropoles with superior economic resources were shaped both by indigenous peoples and by peoples on the move, whether within the Italian regions or to and from the Italian Peninsula to the other parts of the globe. Itinerant merchants, bankers, galley rowers, teachers, students, printers, painters, sculptors, architects, artisans, missionaries, mendicants, captives of war, and more all played some role in producing the society and culture of the densely populated Italian cities between 1350 and 1600. Over time historians have divided their output into high and popular categories, with the most visible actors in the first group and the less visible, or even forgotten, producers of folklore and rituals in the second. It is the patrons of writers, artists, and scientists—that is, the oligarchs, princes, dukes, popes, bishops, and cardinals, and their highly literate female kin—that dominated the Italian cities and that have been given the most credit in producing Renaissance culture during the fourteenth to sixteenth centuries; less so the laboring classes and certainly not the masses of poor struggling with subsistence and disease that existed on the margins of a very small and prosperous cultural milieu.

Yet we must not brush aide too quickly the masses of people who developed their own kinds of religious and secular culture simultaneously with the peninsula's urban elites. Profoundly religious, they too practiced their own rites of devotion, if not in church through the celebration of the Mass and the reception of the sacraments, then in their prayers to the Virgin and their favorite saints, in their purchase and sale of sacred relics, in their corporate processions and charitable works, and in their pilgrimages to holy shrines. They lived amid the art and architecture of the times and absorbed them in their own ways. Their calendars, which noble and merchant families also shared, were marked by religious feast days and the commemoration of saints, occasions on which they held their own celebrations and listened to their own popular preachers. Alongside the sacred, people from all walks of life and social classes, including philosophers, also held on to more pagan beliefs in the supernatural, such as magic and omens, or talismans and amulets. They drew on astrology, divinatory culture, and folklore, some of which became part of renowned literary and scientific works. Moreover, astrology and alchemy were important experiential and practical contributors to the advancement of scientific inquiry. A variety of instructive practices were developed out of lived experiences with natural phenomena. Commoners, whether rural or urban, also created secular culture that ranged from drama, songs, and dances to circus entertainment. Their folkloric traditions played out in village squares, urban neighborhoods, inns, and taverns, where sometimes learned individuals also participated. At times their concerns and anxieties also played out in ritualized violence. Although this text has not given equal space to the development of popular culture or popular religion, it is important to acknowledge their importance and place alongside the cultures of ecclesiastical, intellectual, and medical elites.

Renaissance culture was far from homogeneous. It applied best to upper-class, Christian patrons of the arts and humanities; less so to women, whom some male humanist writers still situated exclusively in circumscribed roles. Moreover, lots of minority groups did not fit in to this culture, including heretics, sorcerers and witches, and the poor. Secular and ecclesiastical authorities treated magic, superstition, the sexuality of women, and the homoerotic practices of men with suspicion and condemnation. Jews and Muslims made important contributions to the economic and intellectual life of the period, but nonetheless, from a social or political perspective, they did not fit in comfortably with the dominant culture. In all Renaissance culture was of limited resonance in society at large.

How Did Renaissance Culture Develop?

While this text emphasizes Renaissance culture's Italian origins, it also acknowledges the wider connections with places beyond the peninsula that shaped it. What the peoples of the various Italian urban centers transmitted to one another and what they selectively imparted and received from others abroad is difficult to measure in hindsight, but it is important to acknowledge their wider relations and point to some, albeit not all, of the many events and innovations that brought them together. Among the major catalysts for the exchange of knowledge, as we saw in Chapter 2, was medieval Mediterranean trade between the tenth century and fourteenth centuries, including the militant religious movements known as the Crusades. The Mediterranean, a major sea touching three continents, was an important conduit of technology and culture. From the eastern regions came a history of Judeo-Christian values as well as the material, artistic, and intellectual civilizations of Byzantium and Islam. The former was an important source for the classics, for the Byzantine style in painting, for sculpture and architecture, and for natural philosophy; the latter availed of rich textual repositories on Greek science and medicine, on the systems of counting in India, on Chinese papermaking and astronomical data, and on Jewish medical practice, while making its own important advancements in those fields. The early Renaissance in Italy most certainly developed its own indigenous forms of culture, but it also owed a debt to Constantinople, Alexandria, Cairo, Damascus, Baghdad, and Tabriz and to Cordoba, Palermo, Salerno, and the Christian, Muslim, and Jewish translators knowledgeable in both Arabic and Latin.

The fifteenth century witnessed other developments shaping high culture on the Italian Peninsula. Among them was the steady influx of Greek scholars to Italy, some of whom attended the Council of Ferrara-Florence (1439–45), a meeting among Greek and Latin prelates exploring ancient literature and philosophy in an attempt to negotiate a degree of concord between the western and eastern Christian churches. The Fall of Constantinople in 1453 continued this trajectory of Greek Byzantine immigration to Italy, where scholars fostered the study of Platonism and Neoplatonism. At the same time, Jewish expulsions from various parts of fifteenth-century Germany and from Spain and Sicily in 1492 contributed to the expansion of humanistic learning in Italy. The city of Florence, for example, became an important receptacle for Greek and Hebrew studies, initiating a critical aspect of humanistic scholarship that quickly spread to Lombardy, the Veneto, and the south. Jews taught Hebrew to major humanists like Manetti, Pico, and Valla. Moreover, their knowledge and interpretation of Platonic and Neoplatonic ideas influenced humanism. But it is also important to remember that these fifteenth-century scholarly movements, based on translations of Greek, Hebrew, and Arabic texts, had medieval precedents, particularly in Muslim

Spain; with translators in Toledo, Spain, and Palermo, Sicily; and with the early physicians in Salerno and Padua, who availed themselves of Muslim pharmacy and medicine. That knowledge, of Byzantine and medieval Islamic origins, had arrived in Italy through the port cities of the south.

From its beginnings, then, humanist scholarship was trans-Mediterranean, as was classical culture and Christianity. Its various forms were then shaped by local circumstances and contexts. Humanists in the Italian cities of the center and the north used their skills to address the pressing concerns of their day, whether that be in fifteenth-century forms of government and politics or interregional rivalries, natural philosophy, the worth and education of women, the importance of marriage and childrearing, or religious reform. They often used the classical past as a guide to inform the present, but as they acquired more and more self-confidence they also reached farther than the ancients in aspiring to fame and immortality and conceiving of a new sense of historical time separate from that of the ancient and medieval world. They gave historicity to their collections of ancient manuscripts, fragments of monuments, statues, relics, and other material objects and prized the ones created in their lifetime.

From the mid-fifteenth century, a number of technological innovations created the conditions for a broader exchange of Renaissance ideas, art, and material culture. Foremost among them was the advent of printing, which offered a means for the wide circulation of ideas and expertise. While a version of movable type had been created in China some time prior to the tenth century CE that continued to be suitable for Chinese characters, Europeans moved beyond Asia's technology during the fifteenth century to develop something more suitable for European alphabetical script with the machine print of Johannes Gutenberg (1397–1468) of Germany. Prior to this time, handwriting was the prevalent way to produce multiple copies of a work. There was also the process of smearing ink on wooden blocks of letters and then pressing them on paper, but this method was extremely slow. Gutenberg, on the other hand, carved and cast letters made of lead and zinc that were situated in slots on a metal rack and that could be arranged and rearranged. Ink was smeared on the letters, a screw press applied pressure, and the words were then stamped on paper. Gutenberg produced the first printed Bible in 1455. This was a revolutionary invention. Printing rapidly became an efficient mass-production process by the end of the fifteenth century.

Europeans also improved another earlier invention known to both Chinese and Muslim papermakers, that is, the diffusion of water-powered mills for pulping rags. Paper originally came from China and then was acquired by the Islamic peoples in the tenth century. Europeans first learned about paper in Constantinople. It was initially manufactured in Islamic Spain, reaching northern Italy during the thirteenth century, where it was further developed. The innovations in papermaking and printing advanced the literary vernacular and allowed for the broad dissemination of knowledge, ranging from the humanities to the arts and sciences. Books and engravings were imported and exported throughout Europe via a diaspora of German printers that had moved to Rome and Venice as well as Paris, Seville, and London, and via Italian merchants and printers who were in the export business. Printers were assisted by a host of other artisans that included paper and ink producers, metalworkers, and bookbinders.

The range of new knowledge that came into print, both as texts and as visuals, was vast and far-reaching. Venice was among the leaders with the print shop of Aldo Manuzio (established 1494), which produced editions of religious and secular classics, initially in their original languages but then in the vernacular. The market for books and images in print included the new biblical scholarship of sixteenth-century northern humanists in England and the Netherlands, who played a key role in the religious reformations, and later, among the Jesuit missionary experiences taking place in Asia and the Americas. At the same time that printing became a common medium of communication, the vernacular languages of Italian, English, French, German, Portuguese, and Spanish became standardized and led to an explosion of new literature for ordinary readers on the market. By the mid-sixteenth century popular romances, drama, travel literature, history, astronomy, anatomy, botany, cartography, ballistics, and other specialized disciplines were coming into print, together with calendars, how-to books, woodcuts, cartoons, and broadsides.

Among the new publications coming from Italy and circulating widely was Baldassare Castiglione's handbook of aristocratic conversation and behavior, which became a model for European court society. Another was Machiavelli's political writings, drawn upon as fundamental advice literature for European rulers who were engaged in ongoing debates about the best forms of government and techniques of statecraft during an age of political instability and warfare. Other influential works put into print included Italian architectural treatises like those of Sebastiano Serlio (1474–c. 1554), which became models for aristocratic residences throughout Europe, including the chateaux of the Loire and the courts of Fontainebleau, Moscow, Kraków, and Prague. Serlio's models even reached the Americas, where some Spaniards were building towns in the classical style of architecture. Another influential designer (see Chapter 9) was Andrea Palladio (1508–1570), whose *Four Books of Architecture* (1570) made him one of the most significant innovators in the history of European and American classical architecture.

The list of influential works in print is too large to cover in any comprehensive way, but a few more examples are in order. In military architecture, the printed editions of Giulio Sangallo (c. 1445–1516) and Francesco di Giorgio Martini (1439–1501), who designed bastions around urban perimeters that could withstand modern artillery, changed the mechanics of warfare. By the 1530s and 1540s Italian engineers, architects, and stone masons were traveling across Europe to build these new structures, equipped with printed manuals of fortification and military engineering. The world of music also benefitted from the printing press; by the late sixteenth century the works of major composers were circulating throughout Europe. Finally, the landed discoveries brought about by oceanic voyages produced a new travel literature from Italian, French, Spanish, and English explorers describing the peoples and environments of places outside Europe. The first historian of the New World, Peter Martyr d' Anghiera (1457–1526), an Italian in the service of Spain, wrote *De orba nova* (*The New World*) between 1511 and 1530. Later, Giovanni Battista Ramusio (1485–1557) published *Navigation and Travels* (1557), a collection of explorers' firsthand experiences with new encounters. Ramusio's work included the first European reference to Chinese tea as well as a translation from the Arabic of Johannes Leo Africanus's (born al-Hasan ibn Muhammad al-Wazzan al-Fasi) detailed description of the Maghreb and Nile Valley. The experience of Africanus (1494–1554), a Muslim diplomat from Andalucia that was kidnapped from Tunisia by Christian pirates, became a ward of the pope, and converted to Christianity, underlines the importance of literate travelers who, thanks to the printing press, contributed to the overall diffusion of knowledge. The landed discoveries also resulted in new descriptions of the Americas as well as innovations in mapmaking. In 1538 the Flemish cartographer Gerardus Mercator (1512–1594) published a map that included both the Western and the Eastern hemispheres. His subsequent map of the world, published in 1569, represented an important advance in the history of cartography since the time of the second-century scientist Ptolemy.

Besides printing and papermaking, yet another set of innovations fostering worldly connections and the diffusion of knowledge were the great strides in fifteenth- and sixteenth-century navigation and technology, which Europeans had adapted from older Chinese and Islamic inventions. From the Islamic world, for example, they learned to use the quadrant, which measured the height of the North Star, and the astrolabe, which measured the latitude of the ship. From the Chinese came the magnetic compass, though Europeans learned to use it through contact with the Islamic peoples, and the use of gunpowder, a primary instrument of conquest. However, another momentous turning point came when the Portuguese constructed full-rigged ships during the 1430s, enabling them to harness the energy of the Atlantic winds.

The assortment of improved navigational tools opened up the world to Europeans. Or rather, it enlarged the world beyond what Europeans, or the ancients for that matter, had known, shaking the very foundations of their knowledge. New encounters with flora, fauna, and microbes illuminated the limits of what ancient texts could impart, discoveries that stimulated new efforts to understand the natural world. The Americas, Africa, India, the East Indies, Japan, China, and the Spice Islands provided new medicines, plants, and minerals that changed and broadened understandings of knowledge. Observation as a method of knowing, introduced by humanist scientists, came in part to modify the textual conclusions of the ancients in a broad range of subjects, including cartography and geography as well as botany, medicine, and pharmacy, even though scholars still continued to process what they saw through their humanist training. Some new encounters were received better than others. The Americas introduced maize, turkey, chocolate, and tomatoes to Europe. Maize was the manna that softened the hardships of famine, particularly in sixteenth-century northern Italy. Turkey and chocolate only reached the tables of the wealthy. Europeans suspected that tomatoes were poisonous, rejecting them until the nineteenth century, but potatoes were another crop that saved them from famine. Syphilis, arguably a New World microbe for which there was no effective cure, became endemic and was a source of anxiety for moralists as well as rulers besieged with afflicted armies and navies. Europeans also failed to understand that their efforts to recreate their own natural world in the Americas by transporting flora and fauna inadvertently destroyed indigenous ecosystems, while the arrival of smallpox all but eradicated native Americans.

Navigation and oceanic discovery provided a further means to spread Renaissance classical culture, namely in education, art, and architecture. These exports, it should be said at the outset, did not remain purely in their classical European forms. Rather, they blended according to local norms and aesthetics in what became hybrid cultures. Moreover, some were absorbed more than others. This is an enormous subject. Here only a few examples will be offered. Europeans introduced classical learning to New Spain, with Latin schools in Mexico City and other towns; humanist academies; and humanist literature. They also exported Italian architectural styles, Vitruvian town grids, and the new designs in military fortifications. In painting and sculpture they brought Christian images both in print and with the work of European artists. Money culture was also exported: banking, lending, maritime insurance, checks, letters of exchange, and family merchant firms—all carryovers from the medieval Italian commercial revolution that were taken to Spain via the Genoese—continued to be practiced in commerce with the new lands, along with sixteenth-century innovations in agriculture. On another less positive level, the Genoese, who had centuries of experience with slavery in their commercial ventures around the Black Sea, continued this practice together with the Spanish in Hispaniola after 1495. Moreover, from papal Rome and Catholic Spain came the imposition of Christian values and moral codes on indigenous peoples, with little regard for their own belief systems and customs. The discoveries made clear that Christianity had not reached all parts of the world, and church leaders responded with a militant conversion program.

While conquerors and missionaries were bringing aspects of Renaissance culture to the Americas, other missionaries and settlers carried them to Asia, perhaps with less success. Some classicizing features reached as far as India, Malaysia, south China, and the Philippines. The Jesuits introduced European humanist education and Catholic Counter-Reformation culture to east Asia. The Italian Jesuit Priest Matteo Ricci (1552–1610) brought Greco-Roman classical learning, including rhetoric, philosophy, astronomy, and geography to the Chinese and Francis Xavier (1506–1552), a Spanish Catholic missionary and cofounder of the Jesuits, exposed the Japanese to Latin learning and Christianity. It is difficult to know, however, the degree to which these European classical and Christian programs were absorbed. That is a question beyond the parameters of this text. The point here is to illuminate the attempt to take Renaissance culture abroad rather than assess its overall reception and impact.

Beyond the impact of technological innovations in printing and navigation discussed earlier were the many ways in which the Italian Wars (1494–1559) created conditions for cultural exchange among a broad swath of Italians, Spaniards, and French as well as mercenary soldiers from other lands. Examples from high culture stand out, but that is not to discount the role of mercenary captains and soldiers or itinerant theater troupes and various travelers in bringing about cultural exchange. Italian learning penetrated Europe through French and Spanish humanists who had studied in Italy and then filled the ranks of the various court bureaucracies and diplomatic corps. But there was also cross-fertilization, particularly between Spain and the Italian Peninsula, where the former had long been associated with the Kingdom of Naples. This intensified with the increasing domination of Italy by sixteenth-century Habsburg powers. The Spanish presence in Italy reinforced the transition from communal and seigneurial regimes to the courtly cultures of Western Europe, where aristocratic-minded lawyers and notaries left little room for merchants or the members of the craft guilds to participate in urban government or to become members of their cultural academies. The marriage patterns of these Italian aristocrats also reinforced cross-cultural fertilization, as they forged ties with the Habsburg nobility in Spain and the Low Countries as well as the French aristocracy. A case in point is Catherine de Medici (1519–1589), the wife of Henry II of France, who as queen regent after her husband's sudden death fostered the dissemination of Italian courtly manners and styles in her new kingdom.

Humanists on the move also fostered a European-wide appreciation of classical languages and literature. As we have seen in Chapter 6, many Italians served as secretaries, diplomats, and university lecturers in royal courts abroad. At the same time several humanists from northwest Europe and Spain first studied in Italian universities before returning to their native lands, where they were active in educational and religious reform. Some secular schools still used medieval texts but others, influenced by these humanist-trained scholars, turned to a curriculum centered on classical languages and literature, a program that was useful in the training of notaries and other government officials. Besides the classics, in Protestant areas students training to become pastors also studied improved translations of the Bible, the Church Fathers, and the catechisms of their denominations, while in Catholic areas Jesuit schools offered boys studies in Christian doctrine and Catholic catechism in addition to the classical canon. Jews established their own schools, where Latin and Hebrew was taught along with arithmetic and religious studies. European universities each had their own specialties, whether in law, theology, or medicine but during the sixteenth century most adopted a humanist approach that emphasized learning from Classical Latin, Greek, and Hebrew texts. Medical students also read the Hippocratic Corpus and Galen, while law students reviewed ancient Roman law. It must be said that education for girls was normally not offered in the large, urban-sponsored secular schools or universities but rather through private tutors, the small coed schools of towns and villages, or in the case of Catholic areas through religious orders such as the Angelicas or Ursulines. Convent education from the late sixteenth century tended to be in cloistered institutions. In contrast, the overall trend, at least among males, was a more European emphasis on the importance of a classical education, not just for merchants, physicians, and lawyers but also for the members of the landed nobility.

Artists and architects on the move also carried their techniques and styles from their places of origins to other lands. The works of the Netherlanders Jan Van Eyck (1390–1441), Rogier Van der Weyden (c. 1399–1464), and Hans Memling (c. 1433–1494), particularly their use of colors and oils, were an important influence on Italian painters, while the German Albrect Dűrer (1471–1528) transported the classical techniques and theories he learned in Venice and other parts of northern Italy to Nuremberg. Dűrer was a brilliant master of perspective, one who exceeded his Italian predecessors in its development. He also made printing and engraving important media of artistic expression, genres in great demand during the religious controversies of the sixteenth century. Another German painter, Hans Holbein the Younger (c. 1497–1543), synthesized German, Flemish, and Italian traditions. Holbein spent part of his career in Basel, where he had humanist patrons. He was also included in Thomas More's circle of humanist thinkers and became the court painter for King Henry VIII. Holbein's realistic portraits of Erasmus, More, and King Henry VIII earned him the reputation of being one of the most innovative portrait painters of the sixteenth century.

The noble courts of Europe from Spain to Bohemia and as far east as the Ottoman Empire, in traditions similar to the academies of the Renaissance Italian city-states, were magnets for artists and architects, as well as humanist scholars, poets, and musicians, that would glorify their dynastic lines and great deeds. In the realm of architecture, the medieval Gothic tradition prevailed in northern Europe well into the sixteenth century. However, the decoration and elaboration of native architecture with the classical motifs coming from Italy began to appear first in fifteenth-century Hungary and Russia and later in sixteenth-century northwest Europe and Spain. Matthias Corvinus (King of Hungary and Croatia 1458–1490; Bohemia 1469–1490) was among the first monarchs to import Renaissance architects to his court, along with sculptors, painters, and goldsmiths. Corvinus and his wife,

Beatrice of Naples (1457–1508), both avid patrons of humanism, took inspiration from Beatrice's native lands, bringing Italian artists to decorate their two palaces at Buda and Visegrád. The monarchs also made space at their castle in Buda for a new library whose size would rival that of the Vatican Library in Rome. Corvinus also established an observatory, complete with astrolabes and celestial globes. The king engaged Italian architects throughout his realm to remodel structures or build new ones with classical elements. Farther east, in Moscow, the Grand Prince Ivan III (1440–1505) also called upon Italian designers to rebuild several structures in the Kremlin (c. 1475–1505), including fortifications that were modeled after the new defensive architecture developing on the Italian Peninsula. To the north, Bona Sforza (1494–1557) the daughter of Milanese and Neapolitan nobility whose marriage to Sigismund I of Lithuania made her queen of Poland and Grand Duchess of Lithuania, brought Italian artists, architects, and thinkers to her court in Vilnius. Both she and Beatrice of Naples are reminders of the role aristocratic women who married outside their native lands played in the exchange of Renaissance culture.

Receptivity to Italian architectural styles grew in varying degrees in France during the sixteenth century. This was due in part to the proliferation of humanist circles in these kingdoms but also because the political chaos of the Italian wars encouraged many Italian architects to seek work elsewhere. The growing body of literature on architectural theory and practice that came into print, complete with detailed illustrations, also contributed to the spread of Italian classical forms. France became fertile ground for classical architecture, particularly in châteaux, palaces, townhouses, and civic buildings. The royal patronage of Francis I (1515–1547) was an important catalyst for the spread of Italian design. The king brought Leonardo da Vinci to Amboise to work, and he commissioned renovations at his chateaux in Chambord and Blois. His largest project was his palace and hunting lodge at Fontainebleau (1528–1540), which he aimed to transform into a new "Rome." There Francis invited the Italians Rosso Fiorentino (1495–1540) and Francesco Primaticcio (1503–1570) to advise his French builders. Fiorentino also decorated the king's chambers to illustrate the monarchy with Greco-Roman fables and myths. Sebastiano Serlio (1474–c. 1554), a native of Bologna who had worked in Rome and Venice, joined the project in 1540, upon Fiorentino's death. He was among the most influential writers of architectural treatises during that time, with printed works translated into French, Dutch, German, Spanish, English, and Latin by 1611. Serlio's illustrated *Seven Books of Architecture* (begun in 1537) helped make the classical orders of architecture part of the standard literature in northwest Europe. The first five books dealt with geometry, perspective, Roman antiquity, and church design. The sixth illustrated domestic dwellings that ranged across the social classes, from farming huts to noble palaces. Other Italian artists associated with the Fontainebleau project included Michelangelo (statue of *Hercules*) and Benvenuto Cellini (*Nymphe* for the Porte Dorée). Italian architectural style was also evident in Pierre Lescot's reconstruction

(1546–51) of the Louvre Palace in Paris, first commissioned by Francis I and then continued under the king's successor, Henry II.

Renaissance classicism spread to Spain as well, although the peninsula was also steeped in Islamic and Gothic traditions. Spanish artists and architects had spent considerable time in Italy learning about the classic principles of architecture before returning to their native lands. As the principal patrons of the new classicism, the Spanish monarchs adhered to a profoundly Catholic political iconography, as exemplified in Charles V's palace in Granada. The impressive structure, a bold statement proclaiming the triumph of the Catholic monarchy over what had been a long period of Muslim rule, was designed by the Spaniard, Pedro Machuca, who had studied in Rome between 1515 and 1520. Machuca, exposed to the classical architectural language of such builders as Donato Bramante (1444–1514), was commissioned to associate Charles's imperial monarchy with that of ancient Rome. Charles's successor, Philip II, continued to welcome the Italian Renaissance architectural tradition. He engaged Juan Bautista Toledo, a Spanish architect who had worked on St. Peter's Basilica in Rome and had served as the king's viceroy in Naples, to design the construction of El Escorial (1563–84), a monument to Hapsburg piety, wealth, and glory. Toledo, however, did not live to see its completion. The complex, intended to be the center of Christendom and rivaling Rome, is the largest Renaissance building in the world. It includes a monastery, basilica, royal palace, pantheon where Spanish royalty are buried, library, museum, university, school, and hospital. Elements of Renaissance classicism, in hybrid form with indigenous styles, also spread through Spain's global empire, in the early cathedrals in Mexico City, Puebla, and Lima.

The German-speaking lands, consisting of some 300 separate political entities, were less influenced by the elements of Italian classical style than were the French and Spanish monarchies. Classicism was most evident in the independent cities of the south where humanist circles had planted roots. The imperial city of Augsburg took the lead, under the patronage of the Fuggers, a wealthy banking family with business contacts throughout Europe. Inspired by the palaces of their close commercial associates in Venice, the Fuggers adopted classical facades for their patrician houses. Prosperous families in several other cities in southern Germany followed the Fuggers' example in the design of their houses and public buildings.

Renaissance architecture flowered later in England than the Continent. Thomas Wolsey (*c.* 1470–1507), the chief minister for King Henry VIII, attempted to create a Renaissance palace in the classical style with Hampton Court in 1514, a monumental complex that he gifted to the king. The palace evolved over the sixteenth century, blending Italian workmanship with Gothic-inspired Tudor style. The principles of Italian classicism appeared in other buildings during the seventeenth and eighteenth centuries. The architects that stand out in this regard are Inigo Jones (1573–1652), who designed the Banqueting Hall in 1619 and the Queen's House in Greenwich

(c. 1616–35), and Christopher Wren (1632–1723). Wren revived the architectural models of Andrea Palladio (1508–1570) in his "Georgian" style, which was widely popular in British colonial architecture in the Americas. Palladio's *Four Books of Architecture* (1570) had made him one of the most significant innovators in the history of European and American classical architecture.

Material objects, carried along trade and banking routes as well as missionary travels, were also prime disseminators of culture, whether through painting or textiles, manuscripts or books, or canvas or engravings that circulated throughout Europe and at times as far as Greater Asia or the Americas. Connected to material objects were the women and men who made them, carrying abroad their expertise: artisans who made printing presses, paper, and ink; who bound pages and books; who ground lenses, designed and built ships, laid palace masonry, decorated, wove, embroidered, and mixed colors. They contributed to the collective pool of knowledge and culture through their skills and practices, their experiments, and their observations.

How Did the Preeminence of Renaissance Culture End?

All cultural movements in history are constructed by the historians who write about them. As we have stated time and again, there are no definite beginnings and endings to such phenomena. Rather, one cultural movement morphs into another, again through scholarly interpretation and construction. This text is no different. The beginnings of Renaissance culture were rooted in medieval classical and Judeo-Christian traditions. That in of itself was not new. What was new was the urban, Italian context, in both the public and domestic spheres, in which the patrons of that culture pursued these traditions. A commercial revolution during the twelfth and thirteenth centuries funded the revitalization of Italian cities by peoples who engaged in and prospered from their economic endeavors. It also provided conditions for the broad exchange of ideas and technology. The Italian social and political context differed at this point in time from that of its European neighbors, which was still with few exceptions rural and dominated by a hierarchical, landed nobility headed by a monarch. The public sphere in fourteenth- and fifteenth-century Italian cities, largely the realm of men with the exception of intermittent women rulers, was characterized by civic activism, at least until the sixteenth century when a more passive and philosophical ethos prevailed. In either case, they sponsored new ways of knowing, seeing, and representing the world. The domestic sphere was also a part of those arenas. It included not only the largely male space where business was conducted and politicians and diplomats were received but also chambers designed by wives and husbands that were filled with enduring memories of the family. The domestic sphere also reflected the special interests and activities of women, who often managed property, served as regents, held intellectual gatherings, and proudly displayed their reproductive roles through material culture in advancing the continuity of the lineage. Finally, the domestic sphere was also the realm of the artisan workshop, where ways of knowing were developing out of experience and practice.

From the third decade of the sixteenth century the social context of Renaissance culture in Italy changed. Wealthy merchants and bankers wanted to be aristocrats, leaving civic activism to live in country villas and to supervise and improve, through scientific academies, the cultivation of the land. A more courtly culture prevailed, one that once again drew upon the patrician lifestyles prevalent in the ancient Roman world, but that also emulated the aristocratic behavior of sixteenth-century elites in the rest of Europe. At the same time, Italian court culture was also admired and emulated abroad, with Castiglione as its model. It was also a period when classical studies and artistic styles spread to the cities and courts of Europe, in tandem with the respective social and political agendas of its ruling classes. Further, it was a period when the global empires of northwest Europe were growing, and efforts to increase the profits of these Atlantic powers drove scientific inquiry. Italy was not a major protagonist in the Atlantic story that gradually diminished Mediterranean hegemony from the first two decades of the seventeenth century. By the late sixteenth century Italian elites spent more time at their country villas investing in agriculture rather than the risky business of commerce or conquest. They ossified, setting strict boundaries that excluded those below them. The professional colleges of judges, notaries, and physicians closed the ranks of their associations and dominated civic councils, excluding men associated with the mechanical arts. They gradually excluded families who were not members of their social circles from their aristocratic academies. During this time the marriage market became more restricted, with more sons and daughters entering religious houses in order to preserve the wealth of the dominant lineages over the long term. Women among the more prosperous families that could afford spiritual dowries were increasingly enclosed in convents, a movement that curtailed their public activism in social and religious life.

Humanist study also underwent transformations during the sixteenth century that in some ways were a rejection of ancient wisdom. The biblical criticism of humanist scholars in northern Europe encouraged a Protestant Reformation where the literate could read and interpret the scriptures without clerical participation. Further, scholars engaged in scientific inquiry emphasized the observation of a mechanistic and geographical world, independently of divine causation and not strictly aligned with ancient knowledge. At times although they wanted to correct and improve ancient astronomical or medical knowledge, remaining grounded in precedent, they came in direct opposition to the ancient canon. Italians, and Europeans as a whole, began to define themselves in geographical rather than Christian terms and to physically map their new experiences.

Artistic styles also changed as the High Renaissance of the early sixteenth century ended. Art historians are more comfortable with defining Renaissance periodization, pointing to a new style termed "Mannerism" that emerged in Florence, Rome, and Mantua during the 1520s and 1530s and ended on the Italian Peninsula by 1580. The term itself derives from the Italian word "maniera," meaning style. In painting it was characterized by deliberate artifice over realistic depiction—that is, strange colors, the illogical compression of space, elongated body proportions, and exaggerated anatomy, a bizarreness that had the potential to generate feelings of anxiety. Scholars do not agree on whether Mannerism was a reaction to Renaissance art, or a logical extension of it. An early interpretation attributed the unusual colors and proportions and anti-classicism to the series of upheavals that afflicted early sixteenth-century Italian society, such as the invasions of Italy and the Sack of Rome in 1527, the advent of Protestantism, and Copernicanism. However, this interpretation has fallen out of favor, with some scholars underlining the desire of highly skilled young artists to find new forms, essentially creating an extension to the Renaissance prior to the next artistic movement, termed "Baroque," which began at the start of the seventeenth century. Michelangelo's *Last Judgment* (Figure 8.3) is often viewed as a model for young artists striving to make their mark after most of the technical hurdles of the fifteenth and early sixteenth centuries had been surpassed and even perfected. It was a time when artists like Raphael and Michelangelo had achieved a new status in society: no longer craftspeople, but rather equals in status to scholars and poets. While Mannerism lingered briefly in northern Europe to the end of the sixteenth century, from 1600 Italian and European artistic style changed dramatically. Baroque art and architecture, with its highly ornate colors, textures, and embellishments, adapted more theatrical modes of expression as well as intense, emotional religious feeling.

While one can see definite changes evolving over the sixteenth century on the Italian Peninsula—the installation of foreign regimes, with Spain achieving hegemony; the aristocratization of Italian elites; the shifting economic axes; the advent of Protestantism; and the resurgence of the Catholic Church in society and its increasing influence in both Italian politics and world affairs—one can also make a strong case for Renaissance cultural legacies living on. As outlined earlier, the Renaissance emphasis on humanistic study was only beginning in sixteenth-century Europe, and the importance of the humanities and of receiving a classical education endured at least through the early twenty-first century. Universities on several continents support broad emphasis on language, history, and philosophy even as they prioritize the physical sciences. Machiavelli's *Prince*, Erasmus's *Praise of Folly*, and Thomas More's *Utopia* are among the core canon of works students read. In the realm of higher education, the Italian and European Renaissance are still principal areas of scholarly inquiry, with ongoing research findings continually enriching our field of knowledge. Again in Europe as well as the United States, classical architecture still holds a primary place in public buildings, such as places of government, banks, and museums. Museums—institutions that were begun in Italy during the fifteenth century—hold important collections of Renaissance paintings, sculpture, antiquities, and manuscripts, which people in the millions visit each year. Tourists flock to Rome, Florence, Venice, Paris, London, Madrid, Berlin, Boston, Washington, DC, and New York to view great works in art and architecture. At the same time great art is frequently exported on loan from these venues to other parts of the world for viewing, elevating its visibility and popularity. It is also important to note that mass tourism to Italy, and Europe in general, has popularized the idea of a Renaissance in history. Among its strongest proponents is the film industry, which continues to produce period movies, TV series on such families as the Medici and the Borgia, and to practice camera techniques that were developed out of the Renaissance invention of perspective. If we take into account all the ways that Renaissance culture is still manifested in education, in the fine arts, and in entertainment we can plausibly argue that it continues to live on in the postmodern age.

Think Critically

1. What factors would you include in defining Renaissance culture?
2. What were the principal vehicles for the exchange of ideas and goods?
3. What major changes brought an end to the Renaissance period?

Further Exploration

1. What are the intrinsic problems in defining historical periodization?
2. What is the legacy of the Renaissance?

Further Reading

Burke, Peter. "The Historical Geography of the Renaissance." In *A Companion to the Worlds of the Renaissance*. Edited by Guido Ruggiero, 88–104. Oxford, UK: Blackwell, 2002. An examination of how the Renaissance spread over space and time, changing in the context of how people received and processed it.

Darling, Linda T. "The Renaissance and the Middle East." In *A Companion to the Worlds of the Renaissance*. Edited by Guido Ruggiero, 55–69. Oxford, UK: Blackwell, 2002. A thoughtful essay that presents the Middle East as an active partner in worldwide cultural development from the ninth to the sixteenth centuries.

Davis, Natalie Zemon. *Trickster Travels: A Sixteenth-Century Muslim between Worlds*. New Work: Hills and Wang, 2007. A lively study of the traveler Al-Hasan al-Wazzan's experiences moving amid the cultural worlds of Islam, Christianity, and Judaism.

Fernández-Arnesto, Felipe, and Peter Burke. "The Global Renaissance." In *The Oxford Illustrated History of the Renaissance*. Edited by Gordon Campbell, 426–61. Oxford, UK: Oxford University Press, 2019. A sweeping analysis of cultural encounters and exchanges between the European Renaissance and the cultures of the Byzantine Empire, the Islamic world, Asia, the Americas, and Africa.

Findlen, Paula. "The Renaissance of Science." In *The Oxford Illustrated History of the Renaissance*. Edited by Gordon Campbell, 378–425. Oxford, UK: Oxford University Press, 2019. An important survey of the changing structures of scientific inquiry from the fourteenth to the sixteenth centuries.

Goody, Jack. *Renaissances. The One or the Many?* Cambridge, UK: Cambridge University Press, 2010. A comparative study of the European Renaissance in relation to renaissances that have taken place in Islam and China.

Grafton, Anthony, and April Shelford, Nancy Siraisi. *New Worlds, Ancient Texts: The Power of Tradition and the Shock of Discovery*. Cambridge, MA: Harvard University Press, 1995. A lively study of how mariners, scientists, publishers, and rulers grappled with the evidence of the New World that challenged old world texts and learning.

Long, Pamela O., and Andrew Morrall. "Craft and Technology." In *The Oxford Illustrated History of the Renaissance*. Edited by Gordon Campbell, 338–77. Oxford, UK: Oxford University Press, 2019. An in-depth survey of the European technology and craft development between 1400 and 1600.

Ruggiero, Guido. "Introduction: Renaissance Dreaming: In Search of a Paradigm." In *A Companion to the Worlds of the Renaissance*. Edited by Guido Ruggiero, 1–20. Oxford, UK: Blackwell, 2002. A stimulating essay about the ways in which past and current scholars have imagined the Renaissance as a historical period.

Ruggiero, Guido. "Witchcraft and Magic." In *A Companion to the Worlds of the Renaissance*, Guido Ruggiero, 475–90. Oxford, UK: Blackwell Publishing, 2002. An account of how witchcraft and magic were practiced in everyday culture and used to understand the world.

Smith, Pamela. *The Body of the Artisan. Art and Experience in the Scientific Revolution*. Chicago: University of Chicago Press, 2006. A study that demonstrates the debt early modern science owed to artists and artisans.

GLOSSARY

al-Andalus	The Muslim-ruled area of the Iberian Peninsula beginning in 711 CE and ending with the fall of Granada in 1492.
Annunciation	A moment frequently depicted in art when the Virgin Mary learns from the angel Gabriel that she will give birth to the son of God.
Arian	Proposed by the Alexandrian presbyter Arius in the fourth century CE, the belief that Jesus was created by God and not of substance with the Father. Common in both the eastern and western parts of the Roman Empire it was condemned as heresy at the Council of Nicea in 325 CE.
Augustinians	A Christian religious order founded in 1244 that followed the rule of the fourth-century Church Father Augustine of Hippo.
baptistery	The building adjacent to a Christian church where people were formally admitted to the faith through the symbolic rite of sprinkling water on the forehead, which signified purification.
basilica	The floor plan of a Christian church, adapted from the large, oblong hall of an ancient Roman public building or law court.
Byzantine	Relating to Byzantium (currently Istanbul) or the Eastern Orthodox Church.
Byzantium	Originally the Greek city on the Bosporus named Constantinople in 330; also refers to the continuation of the Roman Empire after its division in 395.

campanile	The Italian term for the church bell tower.
campo	Meaning "field" in Italian, it refers to an open space (that is much smaller than a piazza) within the city walls.
capital (Doric, Ionic, Corinthian)	The decorated top portion of a column or pilaster, named after each of the Greek stylistic "orders," with Doric the most simple and Corinthian the most ornate.
chiaroscuro	Literally "light and dark" in Italian. A technique in painting and drawing that uses shading to render an object three dimensional.
Church Fathers	Theologians who established the intellectual and doctrinal foundations of Christianity, mainly between the fourth and seventh centuries CE. In the western church they included Ambrose, Jerome, Augustine of Hippo, and Pope Gregory I. In the eastern church they included Athanasius of Alexandria, Gregory of Nazianzus, Basil of Caesarea, and John Chrysostrom.
city-state	Includes the city and the surrounding countryside under its jurisdiction.
classical	Making reference to Greek and Roman styles.
clientage	A relationship between patrons and their dependents whereby the latter would give support and services in exchange for protection and various other benefits.
codex (pl. codices)	The ancestor of the modern book. Handwritten manuscript pages made of parchment and bound with wooden panels.
coffered	In architecture, recessed panels, usually in ceilings.
comital	Referring to a count, a rank of the nobility.
commedia dell'arte	A professional theater form developed in sixteenth-century Italy. Improvised comedies with stock characters

	performed in venues ranging from city squares to elite courts.
commenda	A type of stock exchange that permitted anyone with liquid funds to invest in commercial ventures.
commune	A sworn association of citizens that, during the eleventh century in the Italian cities of the center and the north, seized control from the ruling potentates or bishops.
conciliarism	A twelfth- and thirteenth-century discussion over limiting the power of the papacy by overview of a general.
condottiere (pl. condottieri)	A commander of a hired troop of mercenaries.
confraternity	A brotherhood devoted to performing charitable works.
cornice	Decorative molding, generally on the wall just below the ceiling or over a door or window.
corpus juris civilis	The body of civil law, issued under the Byzantine emperor Justinian I between 529 and 534, which became the basis of Roman law in Europe.
courtier	One who attends the court of a lord, prince, or monarch who may advise and flatter in exchange for favors and gifts.
despotism	Rule by one person, called a despot, who holds absolute power.
devotio moderna	A religious movement among the laity between the fourteenth and sixteenth centuries centered in the Low Countries that advocated humility and obedience as well as a simple life.
diocese	In the early Christian churches the administrative unit under a bishop's jurisdiction.
doge	The Venetian word for duke, elected by Venice's citizens in accordance with the city's laws.
Dominican order	A mendicant order founded by Dominic in 1216 devoted to teaching Roman Catholic dogma.
dowry	The cash, goods, land, loans, or other assets the bride's family paid the groom.

endogamy	The custom of marrying within a specific community, in this case among the families of an urban, ruling elite.
episcopal	Of or governed by bishops.
feudal system	A hierarchical system in which large landowners provide land to tenants in exchange for rents, loyalty, and service.
feudatory	A large landowner, generally with noble privileges.
Franciscan order	A mendicant Christian order founded by Francis of Assisi in 1209 devoted to lives of poverty and service to God through preaching and charitable works.
Franks	A tribe that originated in northern France and, adopting Christianity in the sixth century, took the lead in forming the political organization of medieval French territory.
fresco	A method of wall painting where plaster is applied while wet and the drawing and dry powder pigment is placed on top. The painting thus becomes a part of the wall.
Ghibelline	A large faction in medieval politics that supported the Holy Roman Emperor.
Gothic	A style of architecture which began in thirteenth-century France and spread elsewhere in Europe, characterized by pointed arches, rib-vaults, flying buttresses, and large glass windows.
Gratian's *Decretum*	A collection of canon law compiled by the jurist Gratian in the twelfth century. A main source of law for the Latin Church.
Guelphs	A large faction in medieval politics that supported papal power.
guild	An association of merchants or craftspeople that regulated the profession or vocation and provided various social services.
heretic	A person whose practices and beliefs were at odds with the Latin Church.
Holy Roman Empire/Emperor	A political entity in Western, central, and Eastern Europe that developed during the reign of Charlemagne

around 800 CE and lasted to the early nineteenth century. Charlemagne, the first Holy Roman Emperor, claimed to have revived the Roman Empire in the west with Christianity as its main religion.

incarnation — In Christian theology the belief that Jesus, the son of God, was made human by being conceived in the womb of a woman, the Virgin Mary.

Inquisition — An ecclesiastical tribunal that tried criminal cases of heresy, witchcraft, and magic. Spain, Rome, and Venice all had inquisitions.

intarsia — A mosaic composed of shapes of wood.

investiture — The act or ceremony wherein formal office is conferred, such as the pope investing a bishop with office.

Islam — Of the Muslim religion.

Janissary — A member of the Turkish infantry forming the sultan's military support, from the fourteenth to the nineteenth centuries.

Jesuit — A member of the apostolic religious community of the Society of Jesus, founded in 1540.

jurist — A lawyer or a judge.

lance — A long weapon with a wooden shaft and sharp steel head used by horsemen for thrusting.

Levant (adj. Levantine) — A term originating in 1497 that referred to the Mediterranean region of western Asia. From the Italian "levante," or rising, referring to the rising sun east of Italy.

Lombards — Germanic peoples who ruled large parts of the Italian Peninsula between 568 and 774. They were Arian Christians, which put them in opposition to the papacy and the Byzantine Empire.

Magna Graecia — A Latin term used by the Romans to signify "Greater Greece," a group of Greek cities along the southern coasts of the southern Italian Peninsula and Sicily.

magnates	The landed nobility of medieval Italy.
Mamluk Empire	A military-controlled sultanate (1250–1517) that ruled the lands in what are Egypt and Syria in the twenty-first century. The Venetians traded both material objects and goods with the peoples of these regions.
Mannerism	From the Italian word "maniera," meaning style. A form of art that was fashionable in Florence, Mantua, and Rome between 1520 and 1580 and adapted in some parts of northern Europe. Characterized by bizarre colors and disproportionate anatomy and forms.
mendicant	A person who begs for charity in order to subsist; in the Latin Church, a member of an itinerant order, such as the Dominicans, Franciscans, or Augustinians, who renounce their religious orders live by begging, preaching, and assisting the sick.
monastery/monasticism	A building or set of buildings that houses a community of people who have taken religious vows and live in rural seclusion where they devote their days to study, work, and prayer.
Moor (adj. Moorish)	The term Christians used to refer to the Muslim peoples who inhabited medieval Spain.
Muslim	A follower of the religion of Islam.
natural philosopher	A person who studied nature and the workings of the physical universe prior to the nineteenth century CE.
ogive (adj. ogival)	A curved shape, such as a pointed Gothic arch.
Ordinances of Justice	A series of laws enacted in Florence between 1293 and 1295 designed to exclude noble magnates and Ghibelline sympathizers from civic government.
papacy	Referring to the government of the pope, the head of the Latin (or Roman Catholic) Church.
patristics	The study of the Church Fathers.

Persianate	Influenced by Persian art, literature, culture, and/or identity.
perspective	Linear perspective was the artistic technique that converged parallel lines on a flat surface to create the illusion of three dimensions.
piazza (pl. piazze)	The Italian word for a public square.
pilaster	A rectangular column.
podestà	The Italian term for a regional governor.
polyphony	A musical composition wherein a number of parts or voices are sung together in harmony.
Ponent (adj. Ponentine)	To the west, the direction of the setting sun.
popolo	The Italian term for "the people." In medieval and Renaissance Italy the strata of society that included merchants and professionals who set themselves apart from the magnate class of landed nobility.
Quattrocento	Literally the 1400s referring to the fifteenth century.
querelle des femmes	A French term for the "debate about women," a literary discussion carried out in Europe between the fifteenth and eighteenth centuries about women's nature and capacity for learning.
republic/republicanism	Rule by a corporate group, as opposed to one person.
rhetoric	The art of persuasive speaking.
Romanesque	A style of architecture that prevailed in Europe during the eleventh and twelfth centuries CE, characterized by semicircular arches based on ancient Roman forms.
sacrament	In the Christian church, a religious ceremony or ritual that imparted divine grace. Baptism, the Eucharist, and marriage are examples of Christian sacraments.
Sasanian	Related to the Sasanian dynasty that ruled Persia from the early third century CE until the Arab Muslim conquest of 651.

scholasticism	The system of medieval theology and philosophy that prioritized the ancient traditions of Aristotelian logic and the writings of the early church Fathers.
scuola (pl. scuole)	In Venice the term for a charitable association or brotherhood.
signoria (pl. *signorie*)	Deriving from the Italian word *signore*, or lord. Refers to the despotic regimes in central and northern Italy during the thirteenth to fifteenth centuries.
Silk Road	A network of ancient routes linking Europe to the Middle East and Asia originating in the second century BCE and active through the fifteenth century. They were the main arteries of trade as well as political and cultural exchange between Europe and the East.
simony	The buying of ecclesiastical offices, benefices, or privileges.
sonnet	An Italian poetic form, with fourteen lines of five-foot iambics that rhyme according to a formal scheme. Initiated in Italy by Petrarch.
studia humanitatis	The humanistic program of study, which included Latin grammar, rhetoric, poetry, history, and ethics.
studiolo	A small room, or "study" in the private homes of the wealthy, used for reading and scholarly inquiry.
sumptuary laws	Medieval and Renaissance cities imposed restrictions on excessive spending on such items as luxury textiles, banquets, and other purchases that drained funds from the wealthy that could be a source of tax revenues.
tempera	A painting medium that used colored pigments combined with glutinous material such as egg yolk, selected for its fast-drying properties.
three-field system	A system of land cultivation whose purpose was to avoid soil exhaustion. Fields held in common were divided into three parts, and their cultivation was rotated. Two might be planted

with different crops while the third lay fallow.

Timurid–Turcoman A style of Islamic art in Central Asia that originated during the Timurid Empire (1370–1507) and included Persianate, Turco-Mongol, and Chinese elements.

Trecento The Italian word for the 1300s or fourteenth century.

tympanum In architecture, the semicircular wall surface over a door or window. In churches they were generally decorated with sculpture and other ornamentation.

Ursulines A women's religious order founded by Angela Merici (1470–1540) of Brescia in 1535 that was devoted to teaching girls and assisting the sick.

university A corporation for the purpose of higher study.

vanishing point The point on the horizon line in an image or object where parallel lines converge, giving the appearance of depth. This was an essential concept in the technique of linear perspective that artists applied to flat surfaces such as canvas or a stone wall.

vault A roof in the form of an arch or a series of arches.

INDEX

Abbasid Dynasty 18
abbots 28, 117
academies
  agrarian 249, 250
  aristocratic 233, 305
  the Chaff, Florence 175
  cultural 300
  of Design, Florence 175
  of France 175
  the Frozen, Bologna 175
  of Greek philosophy 29
  humanism and 175
  the Impassioned, Naples 175
  Italian 175
  New Spain humanist 299
  private 2
  Renaissance 7
  scientific 305
  the Sleeping, Genoa 175
Acre 48–9, 92
adolescence 104–6, 125
Adrian VI (Pope) 224
Adriatic Sea 24, 44, 46, 87, 144, 192, 197, 230, 231, 251, 284
Aegean Sea 48, 53, 249
Afghanistan 48
Africa 25, 30, 239, 298
  North 8, 10, 18, 20, 22, 28, 29, 30, 34, 37, 48, 50, 59, 60, 61, 73, 77, 84, 214, 215, 217, 228–9, 293
Africanus, Constantinus (Muslim physician, d. 1099?) 29–30, 77
Africanus, Johannes Leo 120, 298
Afro-Eurasia 74
agrarian
  academies 249, 250
  change 41–5
  crisis 97

economies 45, 52, 293
feudal society 4, 8
innovation 233
plains 59
technology 41, 97
workers 100
Agricola, Rudolph
  On Dialectical Invention 170
agriculture/agricultural
  calendar 42
  income 233
  investments 233, 272
  laborers 25, 42, 45, 53
  landscape 29
  production 12
  products 41
  technology 41, 249
  workers 110
al-Andalus 32, 53, 73, 77, 156
Alberti, Leon Battista 162, 181, 182, 186
  On Architecture 181
alchemy 294
Aldine Press 114, 166, 223, 250, 256. *See also* Manutius, Aldus
Aleppo 29, 47, 60, 86, 215, 249
Alexander III (Pope) 32, 56
Alexander IV (Pope) 82
Alexander V (Pope) 129
Alexander VI (Pope) 110–11, 120, 130, 140, 145, 147–8, 217, 223, 228. *See also* Borgia, Rodrigo
Alexandria 29, 49, 53, 84, 92, 249, 293, 295
  Mosque of St. Athanasius 86–7
  trade route to 87
Alfonso I (King of Aragon, Naples, Sicily, Sardinia) 129–30, 136, 141, 143, 159, 201

Alfonso II (King of Naples) 145,
    (husband of Ippolita Sforza and
    Duke of Calabria 161)
Alfonso III (King of Naples) 120
Alfonso VI (King of León and
    Castile) 33
algebra 28, 79
Alighieri, Dante 38
    Divine Comedy 33, 39, 73, 91, 165
    exiled from Florence 71
    Vita Nuova 71
al-kuhl (Arabic for alcohol) 54. *See also*
    distillation
Alps 9, 43, 45, 50, 63, 87, 135,
    147, 293
    humanism across 168–74
al-Qasim, Abu (Abulcasis, Physician
    from al-Andalus) 29
al-Razi (Persian physician) 28
Altino, Italy 24
al-Tusi, Nasir al-Din (astronomer)
    166, 266
Amalfi, Italy 31, 46
    Cloister of Paradise 29
America (North) 4
Anatolia 47, 49, 92, 215
Angelico, Fra 213, 217
    Annunciation 214
    Virgin and Child 214
Angevin dynasty 20, 58, 66, 141, 147
Anglophone audiences 5
Anguissola, Sofonisba 275–7
    Boy Bitten by a Crayfish 275
    The Chess Game 275
    portrait of Margaret of Parma 257
    Self Portrait 276
Annunciation of the Virgin (feast day,
    Venice) 283
antiquarianism 13, 209
antiquity 3, 12, 20–2, 65, 74, 92, 106,
    162, 167, 189, 192, 199, 211,
    217, 234, 272, 291–2, 302
Apennine Mountain Range, Italy 43,
    45, 87, 134, 135
apostles 26, 27, 84, 89, 197
Aquileia, Italy 24
Aquinas, Thomas 80, 269
Arabia 18, 28
Arabic 60, 87, 176

books on humanism 75
classical tradition 13
language 10
literature 33
mathematics 268
numerals 28
script (Kufic) 217
texts 114, 165, 295
verse 91–2
writings 114
Arabs 35 n.1, 150
    Christian 49
architects 119, 159, 182, 210, 213–14,
    278–80, 284, 301–3
architecture
    Baroque 306
    Byzantine 23
    Byzantium and 296
    civic in Italy 85–87
    coffered ceilings 310
    Counter-Reformation and 239
    d' Este, Isabella and 236
    domestic 87
    ecclesiastical 75, 82–85
    Egyptian culture and 217
    England and 303–4
    France and 302
    Gothic 292, 301, 312
    Greco-Roman 2, 3, 10, 28, 73
    Greek 20
    historiography and 5
    Italy, fifteenth century 13, 182–218
    Julius II (Pope) and 272–4
    Medici family and 210
    Mehmed II (Sultan) and 202
    merchant travels and 74
    Michelangelo and 277–9
    military 149, 293, 297, 302
    ordinary people and 294
    Ottoman 202
    Palladio and 280–1
    patronage in Europe 8
    patronage in Italian cities 12
    pious bequests and 100
    political propaganda and 194–209
    Renaissance 1, 279, 291, 299
    Roman inspiration 22, 192, 268, 272
    Romanesque 33, 71, 315
        in France 82

INDEX 321

in Pisa 30, 83
Sangallo, Giulio and 297
Sasanian dynasty 202, 315
science and 166
Serlio, Sebastiano and 297, 302
Sinan and 277–9
Spain and 303
tympanum reliefs 317
USA and 307
Venice and 284–5
Arena (30 ce), Verona, Italy 17
Arena Chapel, Padua, Italy 39, 73, 88
Aretino, Pietro 261
Arianism 22
Ariosto, Ludovico
   Orlando Furioso 256, 261
aristocratization
  of Italian elites 306
  sixteenth-century Italy 233–6
Aristotle 14, 28, 33, 79, 156, 159,
    162–3, 165, 167, 174, 246, 265,
    266–8, 275
Armenia 53, 231
Armenians 49, 215
Arsenal of Venice 46
arsenalotti 46
art(s). *See also* art, fifteenth-century
  antiquities 9
  Byzantine 22
  curriculum 79
  decorative 13, 24, 29, 34, 73, 83,
    122, 214
  fine 3, 5, 260, 307
  healing 115
  High and Late Renaissance
    14, 270–87
  historians of 306
  liberal 4, 79, 157
  magical 115
  martial 122
  material culture and 11
  notarial 75–6, 233
  religious repudiation of 240
  symbolic meaning 13
  traditions 13
  women patrons 11
art, fifteenth-century 181–219
  antiquarianism 209
  artisanal aesthetic 214–17

domestic space 204–8
memory of family 204–8
memory of Renaissance 209
piety and 209–14
politics and 194–204
stylistic and technical
   achievements 182–93
Arte di Calimala, Florence 51
artisans 6, 10, 11, 29
  agents of cultural transfer 29
  aesthetics 214–17
  female and male 13, 73
  imported from Constantinople 22
  luxury trades 122
  masters and 219
  shopkeepers and 250
  skilled 93, 99
artwork 197, 204, 209, 213, 219,
   240, 292
Ascalon (southern Levant) 48
Asia 30, 34, 37, 52, 53, 61, 228–9, 239,
   248, 293, 296, 297, 299, 316
  central 317
  east 86, 300
  Greater 8, 9, 10, 48, 49, 54, 83, 202,
    215, 249, 304
  inner 60
  Levant. *See* Levant
  southeast 268
  southwest 12, 22, 48. *See also* Levant
  western 98, 313
Asia Minor 20, 77
astrology 266, 294
astronomy 14, 76, 79, 166, 171, 265–8,
   297, 300
Atlantic Ocean 7, 8, 14, 47, 49, 230,
   231, 251, 256, 268, 298, 305
Augustine (Bishop of Hippo and Latin
   Father of the Church) 92, 172
Augustinians 60, 85, 238
Augustus (Roman Emperor) 18
Austrian Habsburg territories 231
Averroës' (Ibn Rusud) 28, 77, 79, 114
Avicenna (Ibn Sīnā) 77, 114
   Canon of Medicine 79

Badoer, Girolamo 210
Bagellardo, Paolo 102
Baghdad 29, 49, 53, 295

Balkans 25–6, 33, 120
Bandini, Francesco 164
Barbaro, Ermalao 162
Barbaro, Francesco 102, 162
Barbarossa. *See* Frederick I (Holy Roman Emperor)
Barbary Coast 46
Barcelona, Spain 29, 47, 214
 Museu Nacional d' Art de Catalunya 263
Bari, Italy 29, 46
Baron, Hans 4
Baroque period 252, 306
Bassano, Jacopo 283
Battle of Agnadello 232, 284
Bayezid II (Sultan) 256, 278
Beatrice of Naples 164, 302
Beccadelli, Antonio 158
Becchietti, Oradea 213
Bellano, Bartolomeo 202
Bellini, Gentile 189, 217
 Procession of the True Cross in St. Mark's Square 212
 Saint Mark Preaching in Alexandria 215–16
 Sultan Mehmed II The Conqueror 203
Bellini, Giovanni 189, 211
 Saint Mark Preaching in Alexandria 215–16
Bembo, Pietro 260, 262
Benedictines of Sant' Apollonia 214
Benedict of Nursia 25, 26
 The Rule 18, 25, 26
Benevento, Italy 30, 32
Bentivoglio family of Bologna 131, 139
Berbers 29
Bergamo, Italy 44, 63, 85, 122, 129, 135, 137
 Accademia Carrara 208
Bernardino of Siena (Franciscan friar) 118
Bessarion (Cardinal) 157, 166
Bible 8, 14, 79, 83, 84, 165, 168, 170, 172, 174, 209, 223, 266, 269–70, 296, 300
 Complutensian Polyglot 165, 168, 256, 269
Biondo, Flavio 159

bishops 18, 19, 26–8, 32, 34, 55–6, 59, 117–18, 132, 237, 240, 293
Black Death 97–8, 100. *See also* bubonic plague
black rat *(Rattus rattus)* 99
Black Sea 47–9, 53, 98, 120, 124, 137, 230–1, 292, 299
Boccaccio, Giovanni 33, 39, 92–3
 Concerning Famous Women 162
 The Decameron 73, 92–3, 99, 162, 174, 237
Boethius 22
 The Consolation of Philosophy 18
Bohemia 6, 76, 111, 167, 230, 301
Bologna, Italy 25, 41, 44, 50, 65, 75–6, 91, 114, 119, 129, 131, 134, 138–9, 162, 170, 224, 262, 266, 302
 Canon law 71
 medieval towers in 57
 notarial arts 71
 Roman law 71
Bon, Bartolomeo 198
Books of the Dead, Florence, Italy 101
Bonaventure (1221–1274) 80
Borgia, Cesare (Duke of Valence) 148, 224, 258
Borgia, Jofrè 147
Borgia, Lucrezia 110–11, 206
Borgia, Rodrigo 130, 140, 147, 217, 228. *See also* Alexander VI (Pope)
Borromeo family 135
Botticelli, Sandro 192
 Allegory of Spring 192–3
 The Birth of Venus 182, 192, 194
 The Primavera 192–3
Bracciolini, Poggio 156, 158, 164–5
Brahe, Tycho 266
Bramante, Donato 201, 256, 273–5, 278–9, 303
Brancacci, Felice 210
Brancacci Chapel, Florence, Italy 181, 188
Brescia, Italy 43, 44, 56, 59, 85, 110, 129, 137, 149, 233, 249, 262
Brethren of the Common Life. *See* Brothers of the Common Life
Broletto (town hall, Lombardy) 85

Brothers of the Common Life 166–7, 237
Brunelleschi, Filippo 181, 182, 186, 210, 214, 1995
  Ospedale degli Innocenti 103
Bruni, Leonardo 156, 158, 159, 210
Bruno, Giordano 266
buboes 98
bubonic plague 39, 61, 97, 98, 112, 116. *See also* Black Death
Budé, Guillaume 172, 173
Buonarotti, Michelangelo. *See* Michelangelo
Burckhardt, Jacob 3–5, 7
  The Civilization of the Renaissance in Italy 3
Byzantine Empire 19, 20, 22–5, 31, 47
Byzantines 29, 30, 32, 88
  church 54, 215, 279
  culture 33
  emperors 26
  government 33
  Greek 22
  invasions 41
Byzantium 8, 20, 24, 27, 46, 53, 83–4, 295

caesaropapism 24, 27
Ca' Farsetti, Venice 67, 87
Cairo, Egypt 29, 47, 49, 60, 86, 92, 215, 230, 231, 249, 295
Caldiera, Giovanni 162
Campanella, Tommaso 266
Campo dei Miracoli, Pisa, Italy 84
Campo SS. Giovanni e Paolo, Venice, Italy 135
Canada 4
Cape of Good Hope 223, 228, 249, 268
Carafa, Gian Pietro (Pope) 225, 238, 240. *See also* Paul IV (Pope)
cardinals 114, 117–19, 132, 147, 200, 240, 260, 272, 293
Carmelites 85
Carolingian Renaissance 4
Carpaccio, Vittore 189
  Birth of the Virgin 208
  Cycle of Saint Ursula 211
  The Vision of St. Augustine 155

Carrara, Francesco 157
Carrara, Jacobo I 39, 63
Carrara lords 63, 77, 137, 161
Casa delle Zitelle (refuge for girls, Venice) 246
Cassiodorus 18, 22
Castiglione, Baldassare 297
  Book of the Courtier 172, 224, 256, 260, 262
  portrait of by Raphael 259
Castile 47, 49–50, 223, 228
Catalonia 48, 49
Catelano, Giovanni 116
Catherine of Aragon 169
Catherine of Siena 118
Catholic Reformation 239, 247
Catholics 164, 239
  catechism 301
  Church 106, 174, 229, 238, 243, 252, 285, 306
  clergy 237, 269
  communities 105
  conquest of Muslim territories 32
  doctrine 245
  dogma 112
  and Erasmus 170
  Europe 168
  hierarchy 244
  Inquisitions in Rome and Venice 243
  missionaries 300
  monarchs 228
  political iconography 303
  popes 278
  Protestants and 164, 238, 252, 264
  response to religious change 240
  response to religious schism 238
  resurgence, sixteenth-century Italy 236–9
  sacraments 243
  theology 169, 171, 239
Caucasus 120
Cavalcanti, Guido 91
Cefalù, Sicily 23
Cellini, Benvenuto 302
Celtis, Conrad 170–1
Celts 21, 42
Cereta, Laura 163
Cetto, Sibilia 213
Chalcondylas, Demetrius 172

Champagne region, France 47, 50, 51, 54
Charlemagne 18, 27–8, 32
Charles (Duke of Calabria) 64, 66
Charles I (King of Naples) 39
Charles I of Anjou (King of Southern Italy) 66
Charles of Anjou (King Charles II of Naples) 38–9, 66
Charles V (Holy Roman Emperor) 6, 168, 224, 225, 232, 235, 238, 262, 264, 278, 303
Charles VIII (King of France) 130, 145, 147, 148, 223
Chaucer, Geoffrey
  Canterbury Tales 93, 237
chiaroscuro (light and shade) 186, 310
Chigi, Agostino 261
China 28, 60, 73, 98, 298
  Mongol conquests in 49
  western 48
Christ 28, 83, 88–90, 170, 192, 197, 205, 209, 213–14, 275
Christendom 32, 46, 139, 200–1, 236, 273, 303
Christian Holy League 225
Christianity 23, 168, 296
  conversion into 30
  Latin 22, 27, 74
  split of 27
Christians 2, 12, 123
  Arabs 49
  Bible 269
  bishops 34
  calendar 209
  confraternities 74
  control of the Mediterranean 48
  culture 19, 33, 93
  education of 28
  European 48
  faith 80, 269
  heritage 197
  humanists 239, 264, 269
  international community of 165
  Latin 22, 27, 74
  patrons of the arts and humanities 294
  reform 171
  reformers 237
  revelation 159
  scholars 269
  sermons 237
  theology 159
  writers 172, 174
Chrysoloras, Manuel 156
Chrysostom, John 172
church 28, 213
  Anglican 237
  Byzantine 279
  Christian 238, 270
  cultural sponsor 3
  Greek Orthodox 27
  Latin 22, 26, 27, 75, 82, 106, 237, 264, 270
  mosaics 54
  parish 211
  Roman 209
  Romanesque 82
  secular energies 10
  western Roman Catholic Church 27
Churches
  Basilica of Santa Maria del Carmine, Florence, Italy 188
  Cathedral of San Matteo, Salerno, Italy 29
  Cathedral of Santa Maria Assunta, Pisa, Italy 30
  Holy Apostles in Constantinople 84
  Santa Maria degli Miracoli, Venice, Italy 211
  Santa Maria del Fiore, Florence, Italy 59, 71, 195
  Santa Maria Novella, Florence, Italy 193
  San Vitale, Ravenna 23, 24
  San Zaccaria, Venice 211
  St. Mark's Basilica, Venice 1
  St. Peter's Basilica, Rome 1, 224, 232, 256, 273, 277, 278
Church Fathers 8, 13, 92, 167, 269, 291, 292, 300
Cicero 156, 172, 204, 291
Cimabue 2, 88
Ciompi 133
city-states
  Italian 4, 5, 7, 10, 131, 148, 258, 260–1

politically independent 4
secular 93
cives 56
civic palaces 85–7
clans 56, 65, 136, 161
   Orsini 131–2
Clare of Assisi 71, 80–2, 118
Clement IV (Pope) 38, 58
Clement V (Pope) 91
Clement VII (Pope) 20, 139, 224, 261, 290
clientage 22, 142–3
Cloister of Paradise, Amalfi, Italy 29
Codussi, Mauro
   Ca' Loredan 284
Colet, John 171–2
Colonna, Vittoria 161, 256, 260, 262, 264
Columbus, Christopher 223–4, 229
   fourth voyage 256
   in Hispaniola 256
   second voyage 256
commenda (stock exchange) 48, 311
communal government 12, 19, 37, 85, 137
   eleventh and twelfth centuries 54–60
commune 13, 19, 32, 37–8, 44, 55–6, 58–60, 62, 64, 76, 89, 90, 138, 156
Commune of Rome 19, 37
Como, Italy 85
Company of Divine Love 248
Concordat of Worms 37
condottiere (mercenary captain) 157, 191
confraternities 74, 75, 85, 113–15, 121–3, 209, 211, 213, 233, 238, 248, 251, 285
Conrad IV (King of Sicily) 38
Constantine the Great (Roman Emperor) 27
Constantinople 18, 19, 23, 24, 27, 34, 46, 49, 73, 84, 120, 197
   Fall of 297
Contarini, Gasparo 238, 261
convents 7, 11, 88, 106, 117, 143, 157, 199, 305
   architects and 213
   aristocratic 111

moral behavior in 248
religious orders and 209
women in 117
Copernican theory 267
Copernicus, Nicolas 265, 266, 268, 270
   De Revolutionibus orbium coelestium (*On the Revolutions of the Celestial Spheres*) 257, 266
Cordoba, Spain 29, 295
Corner, Caterina (Queen of Cyprus) 143
Corpus Juris Civilis 22, 76, 79
   and Justinian 76
Corvinus, Matthias (King of Bohemia) 6, 164
Council of Constance 129, 139
Council of Ferrara-Florence 295
Council of Ten, Venice 39, 137
Council of Trent 112, 225, 239, 240
Counter Reformation 238, 240, 247, 284–5, 299
courtiers 142, 260, 261, 277
courts of law
   comital 56
   episcopal 34, 56, 132
crafts 7, 11, 24, 29, 41, 43, 46, 55, 74, 76, 100, 115, 138, 244. *See also* artisans
Crema, Italy 43
Cremona, Italy 32, 63
Crimea 47, 98, 120
Crivelli, Carlo 213
crop rotation 41
Crusades 48, 53, 54, 84, 87, 92
   First 48
   Fourth 84
culture 71–3
   of cities 73–5
   Islamic 33
   Renaissance 25, 34, 295–304
   sixteenth-century 255–87
      High and Late Renaissance in art 270–87
      intellectual response to political change 257–64
      Rome 272–80
      scholarly inquiry 264–70
      Venice 281–7

da Canossa, Ludovico 260
da Castagno, Andrea
  The Last Supper 214
da Fabriano, Gentile 217
  The Adoration of the Magi 210, 218
da Feltre, Vittorino 157
d' Albret, Charlotte 148
Dalmatia 53, 122, 137, 146, 147, 247
Damascus 53, 60
  Great Umayyad Mosque in 84
da Messina, Antonello 189
  Virgin Annunciate 190
da Montefeltro, Battista 161
da Montefeltro, Federico (Duke of Urbino) 130, 132, 181
da Montefeltro, Guidobaldo (Duke of Urbino) 132
da Narni, Erasmo (nicknamed Gattamelata) 191
d' Anghiera, Peter Martyr
  De orba nova (The New World) 298
d'Angoulême, Marguerite
  Heptameron 174
da Pistoia, Cino 91
da Romano, Ezzelino III (feudal lord) 63
d' Ávalos, Fernando Francesco 264
da Vinci, Leonardo 1, 182, 186, 199, 209, 270, 302
  death of 256
  The Last Supper 182, 185, 256, 271
  Mona Lisa 256, 271, 272
  Vitruvian Man 256, 272
death rites 112–13
de' Cerchi, Umiliana 118
de Crenne, Hélisenne 174
de' Crescenzi, Pietro
  Ruralia Commoda 42
de Gama, Vasco 224, 256
de Lovati, Lovato 156
del Buono Giamberti, Marco
  The Story of Esther 206–7. See also di Giovanni, Apollonia
del Piombo, Sebastiano
  Portrait of Vittoria Colonna 263
de' Medici, Catherine 235

de Medici, Cosimo (ruled Florence 1434–64) 129, 139, 144, 166, 181, 192, 223
de' Medici, Cosimo I (Grand Duke of Tuscany 1569–74) 120, 175, 225, 235
de' Medici, Cosimo II (Grand Duke of Tuscany 1609–20) 266
de' Medici, Francesco 235
de' Medici, Giovanni di Bicci 83, 139, 198, 210
de Medici, Giuliano 258
de Medici, Lorenzo (ruled Florence 1469–92) 111, 139, 144, 193, 223, 235, 236, 274, 277, 286
de Medici, Lorenzo II di Piero (ruler of Florence and Duke of Urbino 1516–19) 236
de Medici, Piero di Cosimo (ruled Florence 1464–69) 139, 144
de Medici, Piero II (ruler of Florence 1492–94)130, 258
demographic growth, Italy 41–5
della Francesca, Piero 181, 200
  Federigo da Montefeltro and Battista Sforza, the Duke and Duchess of Urbino 201
  Flagellation of Christ 186, 189
della Mirandola, Giovanni Pico 158, 160, 166, 170, 172, 195
della Rovere, Francesco Maria (Duke of Urbino) 132
  Oration on the Dignity of Man 165
de Montaigne, Michel 174
de Nebrija, Antonio 168
de Pisan, Christine
  Book of the City of Ladies 162
despotisms 12, 62–4, 287
des Prez, Josquin 293
des Roches, Catherine 174
d'Este, Alfonso (Duke of Ferrara) 132, 157, 158, 206
d'Este, Ercole I (Duke of Ferrara) 120, 132, 143, 235
d'Este, Ippolito 261
d'Este, Isabella (Duchess of Mantua) 111, 143, 182, 205–6, 235, 260, 261

d'Este Niccolò II (Lord of Ferrara, Modena, & Parma) 199
d'Este, Niccolò III (Marquis of Ferrara) 157
d'Este, Obizzo (Lord of Ferrara) 38
de Valdés, Juan 168
Dias, Bartolomeu 223, 228
di Banco, Nanni
　Stonemasons at Work 43
di Bondone, Giotto. *See* Giotto
di Buoninsegna, Duccio 90
　Madonna and Child 184
　Maestà 182
Diet of Roncaglia 19, 32, 37, 56
di Giovanni, Apollonia 206. *See also* del Buono Giamberti, Marco
di Michela, Donna Brigida 213
diocese 27–8
Dioscorides 30, 114
　On Materia Medica 166
diplomacy, fifteenth-century politics and 150
distillation 54, 166. *See also* al-kuhl
Doge of Venice 84, 86, 163, 257, 283
Doge's Palace, Venice, Italy 86
Dome of the Rock in Jerusalem 84
domestic palaces 87
domestic settings 11, 209
domestic space 6
　fifteenth-century art 204–8
Dominicans 60, 85
Donatello 181, 211, 214
　David 181
　Equestrian Statue of Gattamelata 191
　Saint Mark 186–7
　St. George 195
dowries 106–7, 112, 136, 139, 246
Ducal Palace, Mantua, Italy 142, 197
Ducal Palace, Urbino, Italy 130
Duchy of Milan 131, 148
Duke of Alba 276
Duke of Ferrara 111, 145, 235
Dürer, Albrect 211, 301

East Indies 298
economic vitality, sixteenth-century Italy 238–51
education 75–82
Edward III (king of England) 50

Egypt 46, 53, 61
Elba Island 45
Eleonora of Aragon 206
Eleonora of Naples 143
Eleonora of Toledo 225, 235
El Escorial, Spain 303
Elizabeth I (Queen of England) 6
Elyot, Thomas 172
Emilia region, Italy 43–4
empirics 114–15
endogamy 111, 123, 136, 142–3
England 6, 50
　humanism in 171–3
Episcopal 34, 56, 132
　officials 55
　orders 118
Erasmus, Desiderius 168, 237
　A Devout Treatise on the Pater Noster 172–3
　Enchiridion (Handbook of a Christian Knight) 256
　On Copia 169–70
　On the Methods of Study 169–70
　New Testament 256
　Novum Instrumentum 170
　The Praise of Folly 170, 224, 256, 306
Etruscans 7, 18, 20, 21
Euclid 77, 166, 265
Euclidian geometry 186, 265, 268, 292
Eugenius IV (Pope) 129, 141, 200
Europe 5, 6, 7, 9, 10, 13, 48, 49, 60, 76
　eastern 26
　in 1500 230
　end of invasions from Asia 37
　monasteries 29
　northern 45, 86
　western 1, 4, 10, 28, 49, 82

Falier–Tiepolo conspiracy, Venice 136
family
　Albizzi 139
　antiquity 65
　aristocratic 144, 210
　behavior 5
　Bellini artists 189
　Borromeo 135
　Carrara 161

chapels 210
Colonna 140, 264
d' Este 111, 120, 132, 143, 157, 158, 182, 205–6, 235, 261
domestic space and the enduring memory of 204–8
dynasties 13, 64–5, 110, 131, 139, 142, 213, 233–4
estate planning 13
Gonzaga 142, 199
Hohenstaufen dynasty 19, 20, 32, 37, 38, 58, 66, 77
marriage alliances 13
memory of in fifteenth-century art 204–8
Medici 65, 111, 144, 206. *See also* individual entries by surname
as a microcosm 162
Ordelaffi of Forli 131
patriarchs 105
politics, fifteenth century 141–5
power and 141–5
princely 130
public life and 13
Roman 80
Sforza of Milan. *See* individual entries by surname
Sforza of Pesaro 131
Trivulzio 135
tombs 210
upper-class 163
Fascism 4
Fedele, Cassandra 163
Ferdinand II of Aragon 147, 148
Ferdinand of Castile 229
Ferrante I (Ferdinand I, King of Naples) 130
Ferrara, Italy 6, 38, 44, 62, 64, 76, 105, 110–11, 120, 131–2, 145, 157, 170, 206, 213
feudatories 32, 62–4
Fibonacci, Leonardo 48, 71, 77
Ficino, Marsilio 115, 172, 192
Dialogues of Plato 159
Platonic Theology 159
Fieschi, Caterina 238
Filarete, Antonio
Treatise on Architecture 181
Filelfo, Francesco 157

Filippo Lippi, Fra 213
Fiorentino, Rosso 302
Florence, Italy 4, 10, 41, 43, 50, 58–9, 61, 62, 64, 102
Arte di Calimala 51
Books of the Dead 101
Baptistery 82, 181, 186, 188
Brancacci Chapel 181, 188
churches. *See* churches
communal government 19, 37
control of Livorno 129
fifteenth-century politics 138–9
Galleria dell' Academia 196
guilds 121
Loggia 194
Misericordia of 113
Ordinances of Justice 20, 39, 59
Orsanmichele Church 187
Palazzi. *See* palazzi
Piazza della Signoria 194
Santa Maria del Fiore Church 195
Santa Maria Novella Church 193
taking control of Pisa, Siena, Perugia, and Bologna 129
Uffizi Gallery 1, 194, 201, 218
Walter of Brienne 39
wool industry 51–2
Florentine Republic 232
folklore 6, 293–4
Fondaco dei Tedeschi, Venice 119
Fondaco dei Turchi, Venice 87
Fondaco of Ca' Farsetti, Venice, Italy 61
Fontainebleau palace, France 302
Fonzio, Bartolomeo 164
food
shortages 60
textiles and 52–4
foreign incursions of Italy 14, 41
Foscarini, Ludovico 163
Fourth Crusade 84
France 6, 8, 29, 50, 100
humanism in 173–4
invasion of Italy 1494 148
monumental history of 3
Franciscans 60, 80, 85, 87–8, 156, 238
Francis I (King of France) 6, 174, 224, 277, 302, 303
Francis of Assisi 71, 79, 80, 88, 312

Franco, Veronica 246–7
Franks 18, 22
Frederick I Barbarossa (Holy Roman Emperor) 19, 32, 37, 56
  death of 38
  defeated by Lombard League of Italian communes 38
  First Lombard League against 37
  jurisdiction of Lombard League 38
Frederick II (Holy Roman Emperor) 19, 20, 32, 57–8, 63, 66, 77, 90–1, 176
  death of 38
fresco painting 39, 40, 74, 81, 88–9, 94, 142, 181, 183, 188, 200, 201, 255
Friuli 54, 129, 134, 137, 247

Gabrieli, Andrea 293
Gabrieli, Giovanni 293
Gaeta, Italy 29
Galen 28, 30, 166
  Conditions of Women, Treatments of Women 77
  Women's Cosmetics 77
Galenic medicine 79
Galilei, Galileo 250, 266
  construction of a telescope 257
  Roman Inquisition and 267
  Starry Messenger 257
Galleria dell' Academia, Florence, Italy 196
Galleria dell' Accademia, Venice, Italy 212
Galleria Nazionale delle Marche, Urbino, Italy 189
Galleria Nazionale della Sicilia, Palermo, Sicily 190
Gambara, Veronica 256, 262, 264
Gattamelata 181. *See* da Narni, Erasmo
gender as a category of analysis 8–9, 11
gendered associations 124
Genoa, Italy 23, 29, 41, 45, 48, 49, 50, 64
  grain import 53
  labor revolts in 100
  luxury cloths in 29
Genoese 19, 20, 37–8, 47–9, 98, 135–6, 228–30, 238, 249, 299

Germanic
  invasions 41
  lands 229, 237
  law 22
  Lombards 24
  Ostrogoths 22
  royal dynasties 28
  tribes 34
Germany 4, 9, 19, 30, 38, 50, 77, 120, 149, 230, 237, 295–6, 303
Ghibellines 32, 56, 58–9
Ghiberti, Lorenzo 181, 186, 214
  Joseph and the Gates of Paradise 188
Ghirlandaio, Domenico 208, 274
Gianni, Lapo 91
Giberti, Gian Matteo 238
Gibraltar 48
Gilbert, Felix 4
Giorgione 189, 270, 281
  The Tempest 256, 281–3
Giotto di Bondone 2, 33, 71, 73, 88–90, 217
  The Arrest of Christ or Kiss of Judas 89
Giustinian, Agnesina Badoer 210
global turn in historiography 8, 10
Golden Bull 19
Gonzaga, Eleonora (Duchess of Urbino) 143
Gonzaga, Federico (Marquise of Mantua) 132
Gonzaga, Francesco 157, 200, 205–6, 235
Gonzaga, Ludovico 39
Gothic 34, 84, 198, 210
  architecture. *See also* architecture
  building 85
  edifices 82
  engineering 83
  European 197
  flamboyant 199
  international 199
  medieval 186
  northern Europe 86
  ornamentation 85, 87
  sculpture 83
  traditions 90, 303
  Tuscan International 186

Goths 18
Gozzoli, Benozzo 186, 209–10, 214
  Journey of the Magi 183, 210
Grand Canal, Venice 87
Great Britain 4, 6, 22
Great Council, Venice 136–7, 211
Great Council Chamber, Venice 197
Greater Asia. *See* Asia
Great Schism 27, 139, 200
Great Umayyad Mosque, Damascus 84
Great Western Schism 129
Greco-Roman 2, 5, 7, 9, 10, 12, 13, 33, 215
  architecture 2, 3, 10, 28, 73
  cultural lexicon 34
  culture 293
  fables and myths 302
  monuments and sculpture 34, 274
Greece 3, 20, 28
Greek
  aesthetics of luxury textiles 54
  antiquity 162
  art 22
  goddess of wisdom 281
  grammar 173
  history 29
  humanist study 156
  literature 73, 157
  manuscripts 159
  mathematics 29
  medicine 29–30, 295
  monuments 217
  natural philosophers 28
  Orthodox religion 22, 26, 27
  philology 170
  philosophy 23, 29, 160, 266
  physicians 77
  poetry 29
  scholars 120
  sculpture 186
  texts 33, 114, 156, 167, 168, 170
  traditions 34
  translations into Latin 33
Greek Islands 137
Gregory I the Great (Pope) 18, 27, 37
Gregory VII (Pope) 19, 32
Gritti, Andrea 257, 283
Grocyn, William 171
Guarini, Guarino 157

Guelfs 58–9, 91
Guicciardini, Francesco
  Dialogue on the Government of Florence 256, 261
  History of Italy, 1494–1534 257, 262
guilds 51, 58, 121–2, 137
  artisan 233
  city's economic life 137
  civic government and 74
  fresco 59
  individual 194
  major 65, 121
  merchant 63
  middle 65
  minor 65, 121, 194
  stone 43
Guiscard, Robert
  In Dante's *Paradiso* 33
Gutenberg, Johannes 233, 296

Hagia Sophia, Constantinople 215, 279
Haifa 48
Hansa (northern) 50
Haskins, Charles Homer 3
Hauteville, Robert 37
Hauteville, Roger 37
health-care 113–16
Hebrew 34, 76, 77, 105, 120, 156, 157, 160, 164–70, 174, 175, 270, 295, 301
Hellenic civilization 20
Hellenistic period 159, 265, 274
Henry II (King of France) 235, 303
Henry III (King of England) 246
Henry IV (Hohenstaufen emperor) 32
Henry VI (Holy Roman Emperor) 19, 38
Henry VIII (King of England) 169, 173, 237, 301, 303
Henry the Navigator 228
heretics 160, 239–48, 252, 258, 294
  sixteenth-century Italy 239–48
Herlihy, David 101–2
Hermitage Museum, St. Petersburg, Russia 286
Hildegard of Bingen 76
Hispaniola 229

historians 2–4, 7–8, 13, 62, 88, 102, 114, 283, 293, 304, 306
historiography 6, 8, 10
Hohenstaufen dynasty 19, 20, 32, 37, 38, 58, 66, 77
Holbein, Hans (the Younger) 301
Holy Land 48
Holy League 224, 232
Holy Roman Emperor 27, 32, 37, 56, 77, 284. *See also specific entries*
Holy Roman Empire 55, 59, 67, 76, 232
Holy Spirit 27
Holy Trinity 159
Homer 157
Horace 157
households 105, 110, 124
humanism 1–4, 6, 8, 10–11, 13, 156–176, 291. *See also* Platonism, Neoplatonism, Neoplatonists
  academies and 175
  across the Alps 168–74
  Arabic 75
  Beatrice of Naples' patronage 302
  Biblical studies and 169, 287
  civic in Florence 138
  England 171–3
  Europe 8, 164–8, 239
  fields of study and 176
  in France 173–4
  in the German Lands 170–1
  Hebrew study 296
  influence 10
  in Italy 13, 106, 156–164
  Kristeller and studies of
  in the Low Countries 169–170
  in medieval Sicily 75
  in Naples 159
  patronage of 176, 306
  science and mathematics 165
  as shared intellectual tradition 164–8
  in Spain 168–9
  twelfth century
  in Venice in 189
  women and 11, 161
humanities 2, 5, 7, 9, 165, 169, 192, 246, 260, 293, 294, 297, 306
Humiliati 85
Huns 18

Iberian Peninsula 8, 20, 34, 66, 77
Ibn al-Jazzar (physician) 30
Ibn Imran (physician) 30
Ibn Suleiman (physician) 30
Ibu al-Shatir (astronomer) 166
Ignatius of Antioch 172
Ignatius of Loyola 169
immigration 23, 60, 120, 192, 295
incarnation 209
Index of Banned Books 168, 225, 240, 266
India 28, 48, 98, 298
Indian Ocean 49, 228
individualism 3
infancy 101–4
  to adolescence 104–6
Inner Asia. *See* Asia
Innocent III (Pope) 19, 38
Innocent VIII (Pope) 210
Inquisition 115, 168, 169, 223, 225, 228, 240, 243–5, 248
intarsia (inlayed mosaics) 83, 200, 215
Investiture Conflict 19, 32, 37, 55, 76
Isabella of Aragon 145, 229
Isabella of Castile 148
Islam 8, 10, 280, 295
  civilizations of 28, 46
Islamic
  artifacts 215
  culture 33
  decorative arts 73
  influence 29
  laws of Muslims 33
  medicine 10
  metalwork 250
  scholarship 10
  societies 12
  trading networks 48
Islamic Spain 215
Istanbul 9, 10, 23
Italian League, collapse of 145–8
Italian Peninsula 3, 7, 8–9, 10, 18, 20, 28, 41, 45, 54, 117, 229, 235, 269, 292–3
Italian Renaissance 5
Italy 1, 2, 4, 5, 6, 7, 8, 9, 10, 12, 23
  in 1494 146
  agrarian change 41–5
  bubonic plague 39

central 19, 23, 30, 38, 50, 60, 85–7, 139, 140, 159
  demographic growth 41–5
  cities destroyed by Huns 18
  communes form in central and northern 37
  decline of kingdom 18
  dominated by Germanic peoples 26
  humanism in 156–64
  invaded by Goths 18
  mariners 48
  migrants to 20
  northern 41–5
  Normans 19, 32, 37
  oligarchies of 65
  Renaissance in 291–4
  ruling elites 13
  southern 66–7
  tower societies 19, 37
  unification in 1861 9
  in the Year 1000 31
Italy, sixteenth-century 223–52
  aristocratization 233–6
  changing regimes 229–32
  economic vitality 238–51
  heretics 239–48
  material consumption 238–51
  oppression 239–48
  political crises 229–32
  resurgence of the church 236–9
  sex workers 239–48
Ivan III (Tsar of Russia) 6, 302

Jacques II (King of Cyprus) 143
Jaffa 48
Janissary 278
Japan 298
Jenson, Nicolas 223
Jerome 172
Jerusalem 19, 60
  Dome of the Rock in 84
Jesuits 169, 225, 237, 239, 297, 299–300
Jewish
  adolescents 105
  communities 33, 120, 244
  culture 79
  expulsion of 295
  law 120
  merchants 46
  migration 120
  oppression of intellectuals 4
  scholars 33
  texts 105
Jewish Ghetto 120
Jews 29, 32, 44, 49, 99, 110, 114, 118, 120, 147, 148, 165, 224, 228, 244, 249, 301
Joanna II of Naples 129, 143
Joanna I of Naples 39, 66
Jones, Inigo 303
Judeo-Christian values 5, 295, 304
Julius II (Pope) 130, 209, 210, 224, 230, 272, 274
Julius III (Pope) 225
Justinian (Byzantine emperor) 18, 22, 23, 24
  Corpus Juris Civilis 76
Juvenal 157

Kepler, Johannes 266
Klapisch-Zuber, Christiane 101–2
Kramer, Heinrich
  Hammer of Witches 115
Kremlin 302
Kristeller, Paul Oskar 4

Labé, Louise 174
laborers 11, 41. *See also* artisans
  agricultural 25, 45
  division of 42
  handicraft 101
  market 133
  movements 6
  opportunities 250
  revolts 100
  rural 52
  seasonal 119
  supply 99
  surplus of 43
  unskilled 6, 55
Ladislao of Naples (King) 139, 141
lance 134, 148
landlords 43, 64, 99, 119, 134
landowners 41, 45, 60, 62, 97–9, 283
Latin Christendom 32
Latin Christianity 22, 27, 74
Latin Curia 236

Latini, Brunetto 91, 156
law
  canon 71, 74–6, 93
  church 28
  civil 22, 33, 135
  enforcement 230
  Germanic 22
  Islamic 33
  Roman 22, 71, 76
Lazio, Italy 20
League of Cambrai 224, 232
League of Cognac 224
Lefèvre d' Etaples, Jacques 173–4
Leo III (Pope) 18
Leonora of Aragon 235
Leopardi, Alessandro 135
Leo X (Pope) 232, 236, 261, 277
Lescot, Pierre 302
Levant (Southwest Asia) 12, 19–20, 33, 37, 46, 48, 53, 60, 77
Levantine community 272
Levita, Elia 269
Lily, William 172
Linacre, Thomas 114, 172
Lippi, Fra Filippo 186
literature 90–1
Lodi, Italy 56
Lombard, Peter
  Sentences 79
Lombard Leagues 19–20, 32, 37–8, 56
Lombards, Italy 18, 22, 24, 28, 29, 32, 50, 63
  defeated by Pepin the Frank 18
  government 33
  Italians 30
  map of 25
London, England
  National Gallery 1, 203
Lorenzetti, Ambrogio 6, 71, 90
  The Effects of Good Government on City Life 40, 68, 90
Lorenzetti, Pietro 71, 90
Loschi, Antonio 158
Louis of Hungary 66
Louis XII (King of France) 130, 148, 224, 235, 274
Louvre Museum, Paris, France 1, 185, 259
Low Countries 50. *See also* Netherlands

humanism in 169–70
Loyola, Ignatius 239
Lucca 29, 62, 64, 139
  labor revolts in 100
  luxury cloths in 29
Lucretius
  On the Nature of Things 165
Luther, Martin 171, 229, 232, 237, 269, 270
  The 95 Theses 256
  New Testament 256
  Ninety-Five Theses 224

Machiavelli, Niccolò 257–8
  The Discourses on Titus Livy 256, 258
  The Prince 172, 224, 256, 258, 306
Machuca, Pedro 303
Macinghi, Alessandra 143
Madelein poets 174
Madrid, Spain
  Prado 1
Maghreb 53
Magistrates of Blasphemy, Venice 248
Magna Graecia 18
magnates 34, 39, 55, 58, 65, 117, 122
Malatesta, Galeazzo (Lord of Pesaro) 161
Malatesta, Sigismondo 204
Malatesta of Rimini 131, 139
malnutrition 101
Mamluk Egypt 49
Mamluk Empire 61
Manetti, Giannozzo 170, 295
Manfredi of Faenza 131
maniera greca 23, 88, 182
Mannerism 280, 306, 314
Mantegna, Andrea
  Camera degli Sposi 200
  Decoration of the Camera degli Sposi 142
Mantua, Italy 6, 43, 56, 63
  Ducal Palace 142
Manutius, Aldus 169, 250, 297. *See also* Aldine Press
Marche, Italy 232
Margaret of Parma 276
Maria of Castile (Queen of Aragon and Naples) 143

Marinella, Lucrezia 163
Marot, Clémont 174
marriage 108–12
　alliances 13, 65, 142, 144
　auspicious 132
　betrothal and 112
　brokers 11
　dispute 107
　dowry and 107
　restricted 143
Marseille, France 48
Marsilio of Padua
　Defensor Pacis 258
Martines, Lauro 5, 62, 191
Martini, Francesco di Giorgio 297
Martini, Simone 90
　Saint Clare 81
Martin V (Pope) 129, 140
Mary of Austria (Queen of Hungary and Bohemia) 6
Masaccio 186
　Tribute Money 188, 197
　Trinity 192, 193
Maser (Treviso), Italy 234
Massachusetts
　Worchester Art Museum 245
Mastino I della Scala 38
material consumption, sixteenth-century Italy 238–51
material culture 8, 11, 13, 73, 102, 204, 215, 251, 258, 296, 305
Maximilian I (Holy Roman Emperor) 148, 171
medicine 29, 77, 79, 93, 114
　civil law and 33
　Greek 3
　Islamic 10
　Muslim pharmacy and 296
　state-sponsored in Milan 116
Mediterranean Sea 2, 8, 10, 12, 14, 20, 22, 29, 34, 48
　Christian dominance of 28
Mehmed II (Sultan); *also* Mehmet 165, 192, 202–4, 217
　conquer of Constantinople 129
Melanchthan, Philip 171
Memling, Hans 301
memory of the Renaissance 209

mendicants 71, 74, 79–80, 82, 84, 87, 117, 293
Menocchio. *See* Scandella, Domenico
Mercator, Gerardus 298
Merici, Angela 238
Messina, Sicily 98
Mesua, John
　Grabadin 76
Metropolitan Museum of Art, New York 207
Michelangelo 1, 2, 210, 240, 264, 270, 273, 277–80
　The David 182, 195, 196, 256
　The Last Judgment 240–1, 257, 280, 306
　Medici tombs 256
　Sistine Ceiling 256
　statue of *Hercules* 302
　statue of *Moses* 256
Michelet, Jules 3, 7
Middle Ages 2, 3, 9, 22–33, 63, 162, 264, 265, 291
migration 25, 33, 76, 120
Milan, Italy 4, 6, 10, 29, 41, 43, 50, 56, 59
　College of Physicians 116
　fifteenth-century politics 134–6
　state-building 116
　textile industries in 51
military hierarchy 24
military skills 75
Miscellanea Medica 78. *See also* Trota of Salerno
Misericordia of Florence 113
modernity 3
monastery/monasticism 25, 28, 56, 74–5, 82, 93, 117, 167, 174, 214, 248, 303
　art 213
　Benedictine Monastery 26
　cathedrals and 105
　dowries 234
　European 29, 165
　manuscripts of antiquity 74
Monreale, Sicily 23
Monte Cassino, Italy 18, 25–6, 30, 75, 77
　Benedictine Monastery 26
Montpellier, France 76, 114

Monza, Italy 85
More, Thomas 169, 172, 301
  Utopia 172, 306
Morocco 29, 48
mosaic art 84. *See also* art(s)
Muir, Edward 4
Museo Dell' Opera Metropolitana (Cathedral Museum), Siena, Italy 184
Muslims 10, 18–19, 29, 32
  colonization 53
  government 33
  Iberian 228
  invasions 41
  Islamic laws of 33
  in Italy 29
  mathematicians 28
  medical practices 30
  medical traditions 30
  physicians 29–30
  in Sicily 28–9
  sultanates of Northern Africa 61
  territories 32
  Timurid-Turcoman culture 202, 317
  traditions 34

Naples, Italy (Kingdom of) 4, 10, 29, 33, 76
  fifteenth-century politics 141
Naples-Apulia, Italy 66
National Gallery, London, UK 1, 203
natural philosophy 3, 5, 10, 76, 79, 166, 267, 270, 295, 296
neighborhoods and parishes 123–4
Neoplatonism 164, 192, 295
Neoplatonists 160
neo-Renaissance 1
Netherlands 6, 10. *See also* Low Countries
New Testament 168, 186, 195
New York
  Metropolitan Museum of Art 207
Nicholas V (Pope) 200
Nicolas of Cusa 265
Nicolas V (Pope) 166
Nogarola, Ginevre 262
Nogarola, Isotta 163, 262

Normans 12, 19, 32–3, 48, 83
North Africa *See* Africa

Oath of Supremacy 173
oceanic trade routes 14
Oderzo, Italy 24
Odoacer (barbarian king of Italy) 18, 22
Old Testament 168, 186, 195, 206
oligarchies 12, 58, 62, 64–5, 138, 150, 233, 234, 257, 287
Order of the Clares 80
Ordinances of Justice, Florence 20, 39, 59
Orsanmichele Church, Florence, Italy 187
Orsini, Alfonsina 236
Orsini, Clarice 144
Oscan tribe 21
Ostrogoths 22, 24
Otto I of Saxony 19
Ottoman Empire 120, 146, 166, 230, 231, 249, 277, 279, 301
Ottomans 9, 23, 120, 149, 150, 165, 197, 217, 225, 228, 277, 284
Ovid 157, 173

Padua, Italy 24, 43, 56, 76–7, 114
  Arena Chapel 39, 73, 88
  Piazza del Santo 191
  Saint Francis the Greater hospital 213
  Scrovegni Chapel 89
Palazzi
  Ca' d' Oro, Venice, Italy 205
  dei Priori (Priors), Perugia, Italy 85
  del Podestà (now the Bargello), Florence, Italy 85
  della Signoria (Vecchio), Florence, Italy 59
  Ducale (Ducal) in Venice 85–7
  Loredan, Venice 87
  Medici Riccardi, Florence, Italy 183
  Pubblico, Siena, Italy 72, 85
  Vecchio in Florence 85, 100
Palermo, Sicily 19, 20, 23, 29, 41
  captured by Muslims 18
  Galleria Nazionale della Sicilia 190
  Norman Kingdom of Sicily 37
Palestine 46, 49

Palio of Siena 123
Palladio, Andrea 234, 280–1, 285
  Four Books of Architecture 281, 297, 304
Pallavicino, Gasparo 260
Palma the Younger 284
Panofksy, Erwin 4
papacy 26, 230, 232, 236, 239, 277
  allies of 66
  corrupt 237
  Great Western Schism 129
  Guelf 91
  Investiture Controversy 32
  militant 252
  in Naples 117
  princely houses 286
  reformed 55
  Renaissance 240
  rivalry with 134
  in Rome 27, 117, 119, 200
Papal Curia 139
papal exile 91
Papal Rome 131
Papal States 4, 12, 19, 228, 233
  fifteenth-century politics and 139–40
Paracelsus 270
Paris, France 10, 114
  Louvre Museum 1, 185, 259
parishes and neighborhoods 123–4
Patriarch of Constantinople 157
patristics 172
patronage 5, 8, 10, 219
  academies and 175
  aristocratic 233
  artistic 5, 13, 75, 120, 181–222, 272, 304
  in Augsburg 303
  in Basel 301
  of Beatrice of Naples 302
  of Borgia, Lucrezia 206
  of Chigi, Agostino 261
  clerical 91, 132
  confraternities 123
  of Corvinus, Matteo 164, 301–2
  of Cosimo I ruler of Florence 181
  of Cosimo I, Grand Duke of Tuscany 175
  of Cosimo II Grand Duke of Tuscany 266
  cultural 12, 33
  of da Montefeltro, Federico 181
  of d' Este, Isabella 182, 235–6, 262
  England 303
  of the Este of Ferrara 261
  in Europe 8
  in Florence 147
  of Francis I (king of France) 302
  of the Fuggers 303
  Galileo and 266
  guilds and 75
  of Henry the Navigator 228
  humanism and 176
  Italian 202
  in Italy (northern) 10, 20 *See also* Renaissance
  in Italy (southern) 12, 33, 66, 292–94
  of Ivan III 302 (Tsar of Russia) 302
  of Julius II (Pope) 272–6
  of Leo X (Pope) 277
  literary 261
  in the Mediterranean 166
  of Mehmed II 202
  Michelangelo and Sinan and 278
  Palladio and 281
  piety and 209–214
  religious censorship and 240
  Renaissance 22
  in Rome, sixteenth century 272–281, 288
  of Sforza, Bona 302
  in Spain 303
  in Venice, sixteenth century 281–7, 288
  of women 11
Paul II (Pope) 200
Paul III (Pope) 240
Paul IV (Pope) 225, 238, 240. *See also* Carafa, Gian Pietro
Pavia, Italy 32, 43, 63
Peace of Cambrai 225
Peace of Constance 19, 56–7
Peace of Lodi 136, 150, 223
Pedro III of Aragon 39, 66
Pepin the Frank 18
periodization, historical 2, 306
Persia 28, 48 53, 87
Persianate 202
Persian Gulf 49, 54

perspective in art 2, 11
  atmospheric 186
  linear 181, 182, 195, 217, 268, 270
  mathematical 88, 192, 271
Perugia
  labor revolts in 100
  Palazzo dei Priori (Priors) in 85
Perugino
  Christ Giving Keys to St. Peter 201–2
Petrarca, Francesco (1304–1374) 1, 33, 73, 91–2, 156, 165
  Ascent of Mont Ventoux 92
Petrarch. *See* Petrarca, Francesco
Philip II (Philip the Prudent) 276–7, 303
Pia, Emilia 262
Piacenza, Italy 43, 50, 63
Piazza della Signoria, Florence, Italy 194
Piazza del Santo, Padua, Italy 191
Piazza San Marco, Venice, Italy 197
Piccolomini, Eneas Silvio 164
Pickel, Konrad 170
Piedmont, Italy 32, 54, 63
piety, fifteenth-century art and 209–14
Pinturicchio 217
Pisa, Italy 23, 29, 33, 45, 48, 59, 83
  Campo dei Miracoli 84
  Cathedral of Santa Maria Assunta 30
  Duomo 29
Pisanello 199, 200
Pisano, Giovanni 71, 90
Pisano, Nicola 71, 83
Pius II (Pope) 164, 200
Pius IV (Pope) 225, 276
Plato 28, 33, 159, 162, 164, 176, 260, 265, 268
Platonic Academy 159, 223
Platonism 295
Plautus 173
podestà (a commander in chief or provincial governor) 58, 135, 137–8
Poland 6
Polesine di Rovigo, Italy 145
political crises, sixteenth-century Italy 229–32

political divisions in 1600 231
politics
  art and 194–204
  consolidation 133–4
  diplomacy 150
  family 141–5
  fifteenth-century 129–151
  Florence 138–9
  intellectual responses 257–64
  Italian League, collapse of 145–8
  Milan 134–6
  Naples 141
  Papal States 139–40
  regional rivalries in Italy 133–4
  principalities 131–3
  republics 131–3
  Rialto 87
  Rome 139–40
  Scuola del Rosario 211
  Scuola di San Giorgio degli Schiavoni 155
  statecraft 150
  thirteenth and fourteenth centuries 60–2
  Venice 136–8
  warfare and 148–50
Poliziano, Angelo 163, 172
Pollaiuolo 210
Polo, Marco 49–50
Polo, Matteo 49
Polo, Niccolò 49
Polyphonic music 286
Ponentine community 272
Pontano, Giovanni 159
Poor Clares 118
popolo in medieval Italy 62, 315
Portugal, colonial claims of 227
Po Valley, Italy 45
Prado Museum, Madrid 1
pregnancy 103
Primaticcio, Francesco 302
princes, expenditures of 132
printing
  industry 8
  press 2, 13
Protestantism 14, 239
Protestant Reformation 167, 170, 277, 305
Protestants 164, 238–40

Ptolemy 28, 33, 166, 268
  Almagest 79, 265–6
  Geography 265–6
Pythagoras 275

Queen Elisabeth of Valois 276
querelle des femmes 162
Quirini, Lauro 283
Qur'an 28, 240, 243
Qushji, Ali 166

Rabelais, François 174
  Gargantua 174
  Pantagruel 174
Ramusio, Giovanni Battista
  Navigation and Travels 298
Ranzano, Pietro 164
Raphael Sanzio 255, 256, 259, 270, 272, 274, 275, 277, 281
  death in 1520 281
  Portrait of Baldassare Castiglione (Sanzio) 259
  The School of Athens 255, 256
Ravenna, Italy 22
  Apse Mosaic 23
  captured by Lombards 18
  Church of San Vitale 23, 24
  Church of St. Apollinare 23
  Mosaic of Empress Theodora 24
Raymond of Capua (Dominican friar) 118
Razes (Persian physician) 30
Red Sea 49
Renaissance 1, 2, 5
  cities 120
  culture 25, 34, 295–304
  historiography 6
  Italy 4, 20
  in Italy 291–4
  music 286–7
  paintings 29
  period 8
  pre-eminence of 304–7
  for women 7
René of Anjou 129
republic/republicanism 2, 129, 133, 197, 262
  freedom against despotism 195
  government 3, 141, 147

Italy 7, 13, 64, 65, 111
  liberty 284
  maritime 84, 137
  oligarchic 160
  principalities and 14, 131–3
  ruled by standing councils 131
Reuchlin, Johann 170
rhetoric 2, 4, 13, 62, 76
  art of 170
  of civic humanism 138
  Greco-Roman 300
  skills 75, 159, 237
  trained orators 157
Rhineland 50
Rialto, Venice, Italy 87
Riario, Girolamo (Lord of Imola) 111
Ricci, Matteo 300
Richard III (King of England) 172
Rienzo, Cola di (tribune of Rome) 129, 140
rinascita 2, 6
Robert of Anjou at Naples 64, 90
Robert the Wise 39, 66, 176
Robusti, Jacobo. *See* Tintoretto
Robusti, Marietta 277
Roger II (Norman king)) 19, 37
Romagna, Italy 28, 62, 65, 134, 232, 262
Roman 22
  academy 171
  antiquity 162
  architecture 192
  Catholic 26, 27
  Catholic Church 229
  Catholicism 171
  citizenship 115
  coins 199
  conquest of Italy 21
  conquests 42
  disintegration of 34
  engineering 22
  Inquisitions 115
  law 76
  models 5
  nobility 147
  roads 43
Roman Empire 2, 22, 26
  legalization of Christianity in 27
Romanesque architecture. *See listings under architecture*

Roman Republic 18, 21, 76, 158
Rome, Italy 3, 6, 10, 24, 25, 28, 76
   Commune of 19
   communities of people 119
   conquest of Italy 21–2
   Etruscan rule in 18
   fifteenth-century politics 139–40
   Otto I of Saxony 19
   papacy in 27
   papal leadership in 27
   popes of 26
   Sistine Chapel 1
   sixteenth-century culture 272–80
   Sistine Chapel, Vatican Museums 1, 181, 241
   St. Peter's Basilica, Rome 1, 224, 232, 256, 273, 277, 278
   Vatican Museums 1, 202, 241, 255
Roper, Margaret More 172
Ruggiero, Guido 6
Russia 6, 26

Sack of Rome in 1527 232, 280, 306
sacraments 118, 171, 239, 243, 294, 315
Saint Francis of Assisi. *See* Francis of Assisi
Saint Francis the Greater Hospital, Padua, Italy 213
Saint John the Baptist 211
Salamanca, Spain 76
Salerno, Italy
   Cathedral of San Matteo 29
   eleventh-century texts 30
Salonica, Greece 53
Salutati, Coluccio 129, 138, 156, 157, 158
Samnite tribe 21
Sangallo, Giulio 297
Sanmichele, Michele 284
Sansovino, Jacopo 280, 284–5
   Ca'Corner della Ca'Grande 257, 284
Sanzio, Raphael. *See* Raphael
Sardinia 45
Sasanian dynasty 202, 315
Savonarola, Girolamo 118, 147, 172
Scandella, Domenico (Menocchio) 243–4
schism
   religious 229, 237–8

scholarly inquiry, sixteenth-century 264–70
scholasticism 79, 292
School of Tintoretto
   Veronica Franco 245
Scrovegni, Maddalena 161
Scrovegni Chapel, Padua, Italy 88–9
Scrovegno, Enrico of Padua 88
sculpture
   architecture and 295
   Gothic 83
   Greek 186
   marble 187, 196
   painting and 87–90
   tympanum reliefs 205, 219
   wet drapery 186
Scuola del Rosario, Venice, Italy 211
Scuola di San Giorgio degli Schiavoni, Venice, Italy 155
Sea Routes, European 227
Second World War 4, 6
secularism 3, 82, 237, 292
Seljuq Turks 19
Seneca 157, 291
serfs 43, 55
Serlio, Sebastiano 284, 297
   Seven Books of Architecture 302
Servites 85
Seville, Spain 49, 229, 297
sexuality 106–8
sex workers, sixteenth-century Italy 239–48
Sforza, Alessandro (lord of Pesaro) 161
Sforza, Battista 161, 181
Sforza, Bona (Queen of Poland) 6, 302
Sforza, Caterina (countess of Forlì) 130, 143
Sforza, Caterina Riario 111
Sforza, Francesco (Duke of Milan) 116, 136, 157, 161, 199
Sforza, Galeazzo Maria (Duke of Milan) 111, 200
Sforza, Giangaleazzo Maria 145
Sforza, Ippolita Maria 136, 161
Sforza, Ludovico (Duke of Milan) 130, 145, 147, 149, 182, 199
Sforza of Pesaro 131
Shakespeare, William 173
   Antony and Cleopatra 173

Comedy of Errors 173
Julius Caesar 173
Titus Andronicus 173
Troilus and Cressida 173
sharecropping 119
Shiraz 29
Sicilian Poetic School 91
Sicilian Vespers 20, 39, 66
Sicily, Italy 10, 19, 20
   Angevins expelled from 39. *See also* Sicilian Vespers
   cross-cultural fertilization 29
   Hohenstaufen dynasty in 20
   Muslims in 28, 29
   Norman 19, 32, 37, 48
Siena, Italy 62, 64, 76
   labor revolts in 100
   Museo Dell' Opera Metropolitana (Cathedral Museum) 184
   Palazzo Pubblico (Public) 72, 85
   Palio 123
Sigismund I (Holy Roman Emperor and Bohemian King) 161
Sigismund I (King of Poland and Grand Duke of Lithuania) 302
signoria 62–3, 138, 149, 316
Silk Road (and Routes) 20, 34, 52–3, 73, 87
silk weaving 29
Sinan, Mimar (architect) 227–80
Sistine Chapel, Vatican Museums, Rome, Italy 1, 181, 241
Sixtus IV (Pope) 111, 145, 181, 201, 209, 210, 223, 228, 273
slave trade 120
socialization 97–125
  confraternities 123
  death 112–13
  gendered associations 124
  guilds 121–2
  health-care 113–16
  households 124
  infancy 101–4
  infancy to adolescence 104–6
  marriage 108–12
  modes of 116–21
  neighborhoods and parishes 123–4
  sexuality 106–8
  standard of living 100–1

  widowhood 112
Society of Jesus 169
Soderini, Piero 258
sonnet 91, 165, 173–4, 262–4
sovereignty 28, 32, 131, 139, 260
Spain 6, 8, 10, 22, 28, 29, 46, 48, 50
   colonial claims of 227
   humanism in 168–9
Spanish Hapsburgs 231, 284
Spanish rule of Italy 14, 251
Spenser, Edmund
   The Faire Queene 173
Spice Islands 298
spices 54
Sprenger, Jakob
   Hammer of Witches 115
standard of living 100–1
state-building, Milan, Italy 116
statecraft, fifteenth-century politics and 150
Stephen III (Pope) 18
Strozzi, Alessandra Macinghi 143
Strozzi, Filippo 144
Strozzi, Lorenzo 144
Strozzi, Matteo 143–4
Strozzi, Palla 210
studia humanitatis 13
studiolo 200
Suleiman the Magnificent 224
Süleymaniye Mosque, Istanbul, Turkey 279
sumptuary laws 250
Switzerland 149
Syracuse, Sicily 29
Syria 46, 54, 61

Tarabotti, Arcangela 163–4
technology 3, 5, 10, 14, 20
  agrarian 41, 97
  agricultural 41, 249
  military 148
  naval 149
  navigation and 298
Terrence 157, 173
textiles
  aesthetics of luxury 54
  designs 34
  foods and 52–4
  handicrafts 21

industry 45, 50–1, 234
manufactures 41, 139
production 61, 100, 133
trades 120
workers 122, 133
Theodora (Byzantine Empress) 23, 24
  mosaic of 24
Theodoric (Ostrogothic king of
    Italy) 18, 22
Theodosius (Emperor) 26
  making Christianity as state
    religion 27
Theophrastus 114
Third Orders 118
three-field system 41
Timurid–Turcoman 202, 217. *See also*
    Muslims
Tintoretto, Jacobo 277, 284
  Adoration of the Cross 285
  Baptism of Christ 285
  *The Birth of St. John the
    Baptist* 285–6
  ceiling of the Sala delle Quattro Porte
    257, 284
  painting for Venice's artisans 257
  *Presentation of Christ at the
    Temple* 285
  Saint Barbara 285
Titian (Tiziano Vecelio or Vecelio) 189,
    210, 257, 270, 283
  Portrait of the Doge of Venice 257
  Presentation of the Virgin 257, 285
Toledo, Juan Bautista 283, 303
Toledo, Spain 19, 33, 35, 77, 165, 296
Torino, Italy 43
Tornabuoni, Lucrezia 143–4, 147
tower societies, Italy 19, 37
Treaty of Constance 32
Treaty of Granada 148
Treaty of Tordesillas 223, 268
Treviso, Italy 24, 43
Trota of Salerno 77–8. *See also
    Miscellanea Medica*
Trotula on women's medicine 77
Turkic Mamluk Empire 61
Tuscans 50
Tuscany 1, 2, 5, 20, 28, 43–4, 58, 65,
    72, 110, 138, 182
  grain import 53

serfs 43
tympanum reliefs 205, 219. *See also*
    architecture, sculpture
Tyndale, William 170
Tyre 48
Tyrol 54

Uccello, Paolo 181, 186
Uffizi Gallery, Florence, Italy 1, 194,
    201, 218
Umbria, Italy 21, 43–4
United States 4, 6, 280, 281, 307
Universities
  Leuven 169
  Oxford 76, 172
  Padua 71
  Paris 169
  Pavia 116
  Turin 169
  Valencia 169
  Wittenberg 171
urban economies 45–52
Urban II (Pope) 19, 37
Urban IV (Pope) 82
urbanization 5, 10, 41, 50, 52, 67,
    106, 292
urban revitalization 37–67
Urban VI (Pope) 139
Urbino, Italy 6
  Ducal Palace 130
  Galleria Nazionale delle Marche 189
Ursulines 225, 237–9, 301

Valla, Lorenzo 157, 159, 168, 295
  The Donation of Constantine 159
Van der Weyden, Rogier 301
Van Eyck, Jan 186, 301
  The Arnolfini Portrait 109
vanishing point 182
Varano of Camerino 131, 161
Vasari, Giorgio 2, 3, 7, 88, 186
  rinascita 2, 6
Vatican Museums, Rome, Italy 1, 202,
    241, 255
Venetians 19
  Inquisition and 115, 243–5
  trade routes 47
  watercraft 46
Veneto 62, 63

Venice, Italy 4, 5, 10, 12, 18, 19, 24, 28, 41, 45, 48–9, 50, 54, 56, 59, 62, 64
  annexation of Bergamo and Brescia 129
  annexation of Padua and Verona 129
  Arsenal 46
  Book of Gold 39
  Ca' Farsetti 67, 87
  Campo SS. Giovanni e Paolo 135
  Casa delle Zitelle (refuge for girls) 246
  Churches. *See* churches
  churches of seventh-century 23
  control of Friuli 129
  Council of Ten 39, 137
  Doge's Palace 86
  fifteenth-century politics 136–8
  Fondaco of Ca' Farsetti 61
  Fondaco dei Tedeschi, Venice 119
  Fondaco dei Turchi, Venice 87
  Galleria dell' Accademia 196, 212
  grain import 53
  Grand Canal 87
  Great Council 39, 136–7, 211
  luxury cloths in 29
  Magistrates of Blasphemy 248
  Palace of Ca' D' Oro 205
  Palazzi. *See* palazzi
  Piazza San Marco 197
  patriarchy of 27
  Queen of Virginity 197
  raided by Constantinople 38
  Rialto 87
  Scuola del Rosario 211
  Scuola di San Giorgio degli Schiavoni 155
  secular architecture 85
  sixteenth-century culture 281–7
  St. Mark's Basilica 1
  textile industries in 51
  trade privileges with Constantinople 37
  watercraft 56
Vercelli, Italy 63
Vergeri, Caterina 213
Vergerio, Piero Paolo (statesman and canon lawyer) 156–7
Verona, Italy 43, 63
  Arena (30 ce) 17
  labor revolts in 100
  Palazzo della Ragione (Justice) in 85
  Palazzo Pubblico (Public) in 85
Veronese, Paolo 240, 283, 284
  Feast in the House of Levi 240, 242
Verrazzano, Giovanni 256
Verrocchio, Andrea del
  Monument to Bartolomeo Colleoni 135
Vesalius, Andreas 267–8
  On the Structure of the Human Body 257
Vespucci, Amerigo 224, 229, 256
Vicenza, Italy 43, 63
Victims of the Black Death Being Buried at Tournai 98
Villa Barbaro, Maser (Treviso, Italy) 234
villa culture 14, 272, 280, 281, 283, 287, 305
Virgil 156, 157, 173
Virgin Mary 88, 209, 210, 211, 248
virtue as a concept 117, 157, 160, 163, 195, 206
Visconti, Bianca Maria (Duchess of Milan) 136, 161
Visconti, Filippo Maria (Duke of Milan) 63, 136, 199
Visconti, Giangaleazzo (Duke of Milan) 63, 129, 134, 158, 199
Visconti, Matteo I (Lombard lord) 63
Visconti, Ottone 38, 39, 63
Visconti, Valentina 148
Vitruvius 159, 192
  On Architecture 181–2
Vives, Juan Luis 168–9
Volsci tribe 21
Volterra, Italy
  Palazzo dei Priori (Priors) in 85
von Andernach, Johann Guinther 114
Vulgate of Jerome 174

Waldseemüller, Martin
  Cosmographiae introduction 256
  Map of the World 226
Walter of Brienne 39, 64
War of the fists, Venice 122–3

warfare, fifteenth-century politics
    and 148–50
War of Ferrara 145
watercraft in Venice 46
widowhood 112
Wolsey, Thomas 303
women
    aristocratic 11, 106, 235, 302
    as a category of analysis 8–9
    Circassian 124
    educational experience 160
    equality of 162
    excluded from schools 75
    in failed marriages 248
    medicine 77
    Middle Eastern 217
    Mongolian 124
    natal families 106
    physicians 114
    patrons 11
    religious orders 118
    Russian 124
    scholarly productivity of married 163
    Tatar 124
    Trotula on women's medicine 77
    unmarried 7
    upper-class 82
    worth and education of 296
    writings/writers 80, 163
Women's Cosmetics (Galen) 77
Wood Masters 43
wool industry 51–2
Worchester Art Museum,
    Massachusetts 245
Wren, Christopher 304
Wyatt, Thomas 173

Xavier, Francis 300
Xenopsylla cheopis 99

Yersinia pestis 98

Zitelle Periclitanti 248